Big Data in Small Business

To Sophia and Seham, with all my love—Carsten

For my daughters Victoria and Elizabeth, with all my love—Adam

To all the great executives who shared their experiences from their data utilization journeys—Thomas

For the authors of the chapters in this book—Torsten

Big Data in Small Business

Data-Driven Growth in Small and Medium-Sized Enterprises

Edited by

Carsten Lund Pedersen

Assistant Professor, Copenhagen Business School, Denmark

Adam Lindgreen

Professor, Copenhagen Business School, Denmark and Extraordinary Professor, Gordon Institute of Business Science, University of Pretoria, South Africa

Thomas Ritter

Professor, Copenhagen Business School, Denmark

Torsten Ringberg

Professor, Copenhagen Business School, Denmark

Edward Elgar
PUBLISHING

Cheltenham, UK • Northampton, MA, USA

Published by
Edward Elgar Publishing Limited
The Lypiatts
15 Lansdown Road
Cheltenham
Glos GL50 2JA
UK

Edward Elgar Publishing, Inc.
William Pratt House
9 Dewey Court
Northampton
Massachusetts 01060
USA

Paperback edition 2022

A catalogue record for this book
is available from the British Library

Library of Congress Control Number: 2021943523

This book is available electronically in the **Elgar**online
Business subject collection
http://dx.doi.org/10.4337/9781839100161

ISBN 978 1 83910 015 4 (cased)
ISBN 978 1 83910 016 1 (eBook)
ISBN 978 1 0353 0678 7 (paperback)

Printed and bound by CPI Group (UK) Ltd, Croydon, CR0 4YY

Contents

Figures

Tables

About the editors and authors

EDITORS

Carsten Lund Pedersen is Assistant Professor in the Department of Marketing at Copenhagen Business School. His research interests include business-to-business (B2B) digitization processes (i.e., how do B2B firms become digital, and how do they commercialize data?), the autonomy of frontline employees (i.e., how do frontline employees make decisions on their own, without asking for permission from immediate managers?), and empathy-based marketing (i.e., can marketing be interpreted as an empathetic process?). His work has been published in *Industrial Marketing Management*, *Psychology & Marketing*, and *MIT Sloan Management Review*, as well as in digital articles available through HBR.org, SMR, CMR Insights, Nature, and NatureIndex, among others. Carsten earned his doctoral degree (industrial Ph.D. in collaboration with TDC A/S) with a thesis on the collective wisdom of frontline employees, in 2016. As a part of his degree program, he was a visiting fellow at the MIT Sloan School of Management. Carsten received the EliteForsk Travel Grant in 2015 and the DSEB Dissemination Prize in 2017, and he was nominated for a DSEB teaching prize in 2018. Prior to joining academia, Carsten was employed by Telenor and Cybercity, where he gained practical experience with marketing, customer relationship management, and digitization.

Adam Lindgreen studied engineering, chemistry, food science & technology, and physics in Denmark and abroad prior to earning his doctoral degree in Marketing at Cranfield University. He has held academic positions with top universities in Belgium, New Zealand, the Netherlands, and the United Kingdom. He is Professor of Marketing and Head of the Department of Marketing at Copenhagen Business School.

In addition to his articles in leading academic journals, he has published 29 practitioner-relevant books. He has taught marketing-related courses (undergraduate, graduate, Ph.D., and executive levels), and he has been awarded the Dean's Award for Excellence in Executive Teaching.

Adam's interdisciplinary research interests include business and industrial marketing, consumer marketing, corporate social responsibility, sustainability, and evolutionary psychology. In his spare time, he is an avid genealogist and has published widely in leading academic journals on this topic. His research has been funded by the Danish Research Academy, the (UK) Higher Education Innovation Fund, the (US) Marketing Science Institute, and the National Fund for Scientific Research (Belgium). His research has won several awards. Much of Adam's research is done in collaboration with companies.

Adam is a member of the International Scientific Advisory Panel of the New Zealand Food Safety Science and Research Centre (a partnership among government, industry organizations, and research institutions). He also is a member of the Chartered Association of Business

Schools' Academic Journal Guide (AJG) Scientific Committee in the field of marketing, as well as the Det videnskabelige Råd for Lex.dk.

Thomas Ritter holds a Master of Business Engineering and a doctoral degree (Dr.rer.pol.) from the University of Karlsruhe. After a position at the University of Bath, he joined Copenhagen Business School where he is Professor of Market Strategy and Business Development in the Department of Strategy and Innovation. At Copenhagen Business School, he served as Associate Dean for the Bachelor of International Business program and the full-time MBA program, and he was Academic Director of the CBS Competitiveness Platform.

Thomas's research focuses on business relationship management, data-driven business development, business model innovation, and strategy. He has published numerous articles in leading outlets, including *Journal of Service Research*, *Journal of Product Innovation Management*, *Industrial Marketing Management*, and *Harvard Business Review*, amongst others. He is mentioned on the Stanford Top 2% Scientist list in 2020 and is the only author with three papers on the *IMM* Classics list. His work has been intensively downloaded and cited. Currently, he is heading two research projects funded by the Danish Industry Foundation that investigate the integration of products, services, and data, as well as the use of customer data for growth.

Thomas is a highly regarded educator. He teaches mainly on the MBA and executive level, and he contributes to executive and non-executive board programs. He has more than 20 years' experience working with consulting firms of all sizes and from many industries.

Torsten Ringberg is Professor of Marketing at Copenhagen Business School. He has an MBA, M.A. (Psychological Anthropology), and Ph.D. in Marketing (Penn State University). His work has appeared in top-tier international academic business journals, such as *Journal of Marketing*, *Journal of Consumer Research*, *Journal of Consumer Psychology*, *Management Studies*, and *Annals of Tourist Research*. He regularly reviews for leading journals and presents at leading international consumer behavior conferences. He has won two Best in Practice Awards from the American Marketing Association/Milwaukee, based on two strategic consulting projects for large US corporations that uncovered managers' and consumers' subconscious mindsets. He publishes on topics such as embodied cognition, mental mindsets, the use of big data, and how managerial mindsets affect the successful adoption of digital technologies. Torsten has received funding from the Danish Research Council and the Danish Industrial Foundation.

Torsten is actively engaged in helping mid- to large-size organizations optimize their managers' strategic mindsets relative to customer preferences. He is member of the Danish Competition Council, which ensures fair competitive market conditions for both online and physical businesses. Torsten has served as an expert witness in important court cases, regularly evaluates large funding applications for researchers involved with small and medium-sized enterprise projects, and heads the Torben and Alice Frimodt Fund (supporting projects in sciences, environmental non-governmental organization, and humanitarian causes).

AUTHORS

Henrik Andersen has 35 years' experience in global consultancy, where he has advised firms from a broad range of industries. In 2002, he founded Andersen&Partners Management

Consulting, prior to which he was a partner at PricewaterhouseCoopers Management Consulting for the EMEA region. Henrik's focus is on strategic planning, organizational and cultural change, customer relationship management, and customer segmentation. His work in these areas has been published in books and numerous articles.

Poul Houman Andersen is Professor of Marketing at Aalborg University Business School and head of the marketing and sales group. He is also part-time Professor of Supply Chain Management at the Norwegian University of Science and Technology. Poul received his degree from Aarhus University. He has published across several disciplines, including marketing, strategy, purchasing and supply management, and research methodology.

Shirley Y. Coleman is Technical Director of the Industrial Statistics Research Unit, School of Mathematics, Statistics and Physics, Newcastle University, where she works on data analytics in small and medium-sized enterprises and specializes in statistical and machine learning techniques applied to company data. Shirley publishes in trade and academic journals and is co-editor of several books. She is a chartered statistician and actively mentors early career statisticians while also developing relationships with business and industry.

Annie V. Dang is a law student at Georgetown University Law Center. She was previously a research associate at Harvard Business School, focusing on entrepreneurship, innovation, and small business, as well as an investigative analyst in the Major Economic Crimes Bureau of the Manhattan District Attorney's Office. Annie received her Bachelor of Arts from Harvard University and has published with the National Bureau of Economic Research.

Heikki Karjaluoto is a Professor in the University of Jyväskylä School of Business and Economics, where he heads the Department of Marketing. Heikki received his D.Sc. degree from the University of Jyväskylä. He has published in *Business Strategy and the Environment*, *Computers in Human Behavior*, *European Journal of Marketing*, *Industrial Marketing Management*, and *Internet Research*, among others.

Christian Kowalkowski is Professor of Industrial Marketing at Linköping University and is affiliated with the Centre for Relationship Marketing and Service Management at Hanken School of Economics in Helsinki. Christian's research interests include service growth strategies, service innovation, and business-to-business (B2B) subscription business models. His work has been published in journals such as *Industrial Marketing Management*, *Journal of Business Research*, and *Journal of Service Research*. He is the servitization editor for the *Journal of Service Management*, associate editor of the *Journal of Services Marketing*, and advisory board member of *Industrial Marketing Management*. He is the co-author of *Service Strategy in Action: A Practical Guide for Growing Your B2B Service and Solution Business* (www.ServiceStrategyInAction.com, Service Strategy Press, 2017), the leading book for industry executives on how to navigate the transition from a goods-centric to a service-savvy business model.

Paul Matthyssens is Professor of Strategic Management at the University of Milano-Bicocca, DEMS. He received his doctorate in Applied Economics from the University of Antwerp in 1986. Known for his work on service-oriented strategy, his research interests also include business and industrial marketing, value innovation, global strategy, and purchasing strategy. From 2013 to 2018, Paul was Dean of AMS. He received the Full-Time Master Teacher Award in 2014. As an avid visiting professor, Paul has taught at several universities internationally, including Copenhagen Business School, Stockholm School of Economics, and Fordham University. He has also published around 100 articles in top academic journals, such as *Journal of Management Studies, Strategic Organization, Industrial Marketing Management, Long Range Planning, Technovation, Journal of Business & Industrial Marketing, Psychology & Marketing, International Marketing Review*, and *Journal of Purchasing & Supply Management*. He also serves on the editorial boards of different international magazines.

Joel Mero is Assistant Professor of Marketing at the University of Jyväskylä School of Business and Economics. Joel received his D.Sc. degree from the University of Jyväskylä. He has published in *Industrial Marketing Management, Electronic Markets*, and *Marketing Management Journal*, among others. Some of the research conducted for the chapter he contributed to this volume was performed before August 2020, when he acted as Assistant Professor in LUT University School of Business and Management.

Karen G. Mills is a Senior Fellow at the Harvard Business School, where she is part of the entrepreneurship faculty. She served in President Barack Obama's Cabinet as the Administrator of the US Small Business Administration from 2009 to 2013 and was a member of the President's National Economic Council. Karen is the President of MMP Group and a longtime venture capitalist and private equity investor. Her current research focuses on small businesses, US competitiveness, and innovation. Karen is the author of the book *Fintech, Small Business & the American Dream*, as well as several papers on small business lending and supply chains.

Dana Minbaeva is Professor of Strategic and Global Human Resource Management in the Department of Strategy and Innovation, and Vice-President for International Affairs, at Copenhagen Business School. Her research on strategic international human resources management has appeared in top international journals, numerous book chapters, and reports. Dana is a co-founder of Nordic Human Capital Analytics (www.nhca.dk).

Camilla Nellemann works for the Manufacturing Academy of Denmark (MADE), where she manages a research project on digital learning factories. She was previously a postdoctoral researcher at Copenhagen Business School, funded by MADE. Camilla holds a doctorate in International Management from Rikkyo University, and advises businesses and private individuals on Japanese culture.

Frederikke Amalie la Cour Nygaard has a Master's degree in Business Administration and Economics, with a specialization in human resources management, from Copenhagen Business School. Throughout her career, she has worked with data and personnel processes in various organizations. Frederikke is currently the human resources analyst at the Danish Ministry of Climate, Energies and Utilities.

Sena Ozdemir is Senior Lecturer in Marketing at Lancaster University Management School. Her research spans a range of subjects, including strategic alliances in new product development (NPD), interfirm cross-functional NPD team integration, global NPD, the use of big data analytics (including customer and marketing analytics) and other digital technologies for innovation, and social and sustainable innovation. Sena's cross-disciplinary research areas include marketing and business-to-business marketing, strategy, operations, and innovation, designed to advance scholarship on NPD practices and performance. Her research informs scholars of marketing and innovation, practitioners such as marketing and product development managers, and innovation policy makers. She currently serves as an editorial board member for the *Journal of Business-to-Business Marketing*. Her publications have appeared in journals such as *Industrial Marketing Management, Journal of Business Research, British Journal of Management, International Marketing Review, Journal of Business-to-Business Marketing, Qualitative Market Research: An International Journal*, and *Innovation: Organization & Management*.

Torben Pedersen is Professor of International Business at Bocconi University, Milan. His research interests focus on the interface between strategy and international management, and he has published more than 100 articles and books related to the managerial and strategic aspects of globalization. His research has appeared in prominent journals such as *Academy of Management Journal, Strategic Management Journal, Journal of Management, Journal of International Business Studies, Journal of Management Studies,* and *Organization Science.* In addition, Torben has written more than 25 teaching cases, published by case clearing houses or in teaching-oriented books. He is a Fellow of the Academy of International Business, European International Business Academy, and Strategic Management Society.

Helle Rootzén is the CEO and founder of andhero, which she started in 2020. Until 2020, she was Professor of Learning Technology and Digitalization at the Technical University of Denmark (DTU), leader and founder of the Center for Digital Learning Technology, and director of DTU Compute. Helle received her doctoral degree from DTU. She is one of the Danish Academy of Technical Sciences' "Digital wise men" and a member of several boards. She has published in *Statistics in Medicine, International Conference on Computer Supported Education, European Conference on e-Learning, Acta Oncologica*, and the *European Consortium for Mathematics in Industry*, among others.

Pernille Rydén is Dean of Education at the IT University of Copenhagen. She received her doctoral degree from CBS in research strategic cognition, with a particular focus on the human and organizational conditions for success with digital technologies in private and public organizations. Pernille has published in outlets such as *California Management Review, Industrial Marketing Management*, and *Journal of Interactive Marketing* and is also the lead author of the book *Disrupt Your Mindset to Transform Your Business with Big Data*.

Vania Sena is the Chair of Enterprise and Entrepreneurship and Director of the Centre for Regional Economic and Enterprise Development (CREED) at the University of Sheffield. She established the ESRC Business and Local Government DRC (based at the University of Essex) in 2013, and she is a co-investigator in the ESRC Productivity Insights Network (PIN). Her first degree was awarded *cum laude* by the University of Naples, Federico II; her postgraduate studies in Economics were carried out at the University of York, where she was awarded both an M.Sc. and the D.Phil. Vania's research focuses mainly on econometric analyses of the determinants of productivity growth, at both micro and macro levels, with an emphasis on innovation, human capital, and intellectual property. She also has an interest in the use of alternative methods (e.g., linear programming analysis) for measuring productivity. Her most recent research addresses the relationship among innovation activities, trade secrets, and total factor productivity. Her work has been published in *Journal of Economic Literature, Journal* *of Corporate Finance*, *Journal of Banking and Finance*, *Small Business Economics*, *Journal of Comparative Economics*, *The Economic Journal*, *Scandinavian Journal of Economics*, *European Journal of Operational Research*, and *Oxford Bulletin of Economics and Statistics and Regional Studies*, among others. Vania has received funding from several bodies, including ESRC, Nuffield, NESTA, Leverhulme Trust, IPO, UKTI, and the British Academy. She is a member of the Operational Society General Council and the OR Analytics Development Group. She has been a visiting fellow at Harvard University and Rutgers University.

David Sörhammar is Associate Professor of Marketing at Stockholm Business School, Stockholm University. His research interests include service growth strategies, cocreation, and innovations. David's research has been published in journals such as *Industrial Marketing Management*, *Journal of Business Research*, and *Marketing Theory*.

Bieke Struyf is a doctoral candidate at the University of Antwerp and researcher at the Antwerp Management School. She focuses on identifying value-creating strategies, barriers, and critical success factors that contribute to effective digital transformation in the Flemish manufacturing industry. With her multilevel, multidisciplinary research, under the supervision of Paul Matthyssens and Wouter Van Bockhaven, Bieke investigates the impact on and mobilization of individual employees, the organization, and its surrounding ecosystem.

Tanja Tammisalo is a graduate researcher from LUT University who currently works as a digital marketing specialist at iProspect.

Bård Tronvoll is Professor of Marketing at Inland Norway University of Applied Sciences and at CTF-Service Research Center at Karlstad University. He is a member of the editorial advisory board for *Journal of Service Management*, and his work has been published in *Journal of the Academy of Marketing Science*, *Journal of Service Research*, *Journal of Business Research*, *European Journal of Marketing*, *Journal of Service Management*, and *Marketing Theory*. Bård's research interests include marketing theory, service innovation, customer complaining behavior/service recovery, and digitalization.

Jan Trzaskowski is Law Professor at Copenhagen Business School. For more than two decades, he has dealt with legal and regulatory aspects of information technology, with a particular focus on data and consumer protection law. Jan has a keen interest in human decision-making, persuasive technology, and the societal implications of information technology.

Wouter Van Bockhaven is a researcher, Lecturer, and Assistant Professor at the Antwerp Management School. He received his doctoral degree in Applied Economics from the University of Antwerp in 2014. His research focuses on how firms can develop innovation networks to tackle institutional and social barriers that prevent the creation of shared value. Combining qualitative and quantitative approaches, Wouter aims to address the real-life challenges experienced by managers in pharmaceutical, medical devices, machine building, and steel industries. His work has been published in *Industrial Marketing Management* and *Journal of Business and Industrial Marketing*.

'This is a very timely book. SMEs with limited resources have to understand the power of big data and ensure that they are not left behind by the large platforms. This book is insightful and rigorous. It features multiple perspectives and guidelines provided by a group of excellent experts. It's a very valuable guide for practitioners and a great teaching resource for faculty and students.'
Markus Reihlen, Former Vice President, Professor of Strategic Management, and Principle Investigator of the Digital Entrepreneurship Project, Leuphana University of Lüneburg, Germany

'Creating actual digital innovation roadmaps for SMEs based on big data beyond the hype of the words is of great value. I welcome this contribution to increasing competitiveness for SMEs through data, digital competencies, and innovative solutions that increase companies' insight into customers' needs and challenges.'
Per B. Brockhoff, Professor, Head of Department, M.Sc., Ph.D., R, Technical University of Denmark

'I have often seen how data is given too little attention when companies undertake digitalization efforts. That is a shame, since access to high quality data is like having a superpower, and this superpower is accessible to any business that is willing to do the work. Good to see a book that focuses on the opportunities for small and medium-sized businesses!'
Pernille Erenbjerg, Board Member at Genmab, Nordea, Nordic Entertainment Group and Millicom, Denmark

'The importance of big data competence cannot be overstated, and should not be out of the reach of smaller firms. Small and medium-sized enterprises should be able to increase their success by building big data capabilities and creating data-driven growth. This book shows how smaller firms have developed big data competence and digitization capability, implemented artificial intelligence techniques, and identified customer growth potential through customer insight analysis. The authors provide realistic guidance for implementation using real-life successful examples. In sum, this book provides a roadmap to small and medium-size enterprises that wish to facilitate their adoption of big data capabilities and become fully digitally enabled.'
C. Anthony Di Benedetto, Fox School of Business, Temple University, USA

'I congratulate the authors for focusing on how small and medium-sized businesses can make the most of big data based small investments and fast experimentation for quick wins. Agility is key, and this excellent book exactly shows how SMEs can move fast – to win fast – in the data space.'
Wolfgang Ulaga, Senior Affiliate Professor of Marketing at INSEAD & Director of the Marketing & Sales Excellence Initiative (MSEI), France

'Through my active involvement in SMEs, I see the struggles and the successes of SMEs' data utilization journeys. I very much hope that this book will inspire many executives on how to successfully engage in data-driven business development.'
Jan Damsgaard, Professor of Digitalization, Copenhagen Business School and Board member at SME Denmark & National Digital Expert Advisor, Denmark

Introduction to *Big Data in Small Business*

Carsten Lund Pedersen, Adam Lindgreen, Thomas Ritter and Torsten Ringberg

This is a book about big data in small businesses. How do small and medium-sized enterprises (SMEs), with limited resources, thrive in a context abundant with data? To address this central question from multiple viewpoints, we introduce a collection of experiences, insights, and guidelines from a variety of researchers, each of whom provides a piece to solve this puzzle.

Today, data often are described as "big," and they also are increasing in size with each day that passes. Accordingly, the promise of success linked to using these data is presumed to be similarly big, and expectations are still rising. Yet for many firms, especially SMEs, each of the steps they take is quite small. Even if firms can only take small steps, designing a pathway that comprises many, well-placed small steps can create movement and progression. Thus, there is no contradiction between small steps and big data success. It "merely" requires patience, cadence, and an ability to maintain a balance.

In our ongoing research on data commercialization, we often encounter firms that profess to feeling overwhelmed by the amount of data available and the expectations set, both by themselves and partners in their business ecosystem. The feeling of being overwhelmed is intensified by the lack of resources, which is especially pressing for SMEs. Despite these challenges, we also have often encountered intriguing business development initiatives by SMEs that circumvented the obstacles.

These experiences triggered our interest in crafting a book that would be full of ideas to inspire big data-driven success by SMEs that make smaller investments. We are not talking about million-dollar bets and unicorns; rather, our focus is on solid work and experiments that guide the data utilization journey for SMEs. It is not that we are against million-dollar projects and moon-is-the-limit ambitions, but there must be a place for "ordinary" data-driven journeys that firms of any size can take. Before we introduce the chapters of the book, we thus present some general issues and challenges for SMEs seeking to leverage big data today.

BIG DATA

There are more and more digital data, pertaining to basically everything. Digitization is "the technical process of converting streams of analog information into digital bits of 1s and 0s with discrete and discontinuous values" (Brennen & Kreiss, 2016, p. 1), which leads to the "increased availability of digital data enabled by advances in creating, transferring, storing, and analyzing digital data" (Ritter & Pedersen, 2020, p. 181). This staggering development has been well documented. For example, Internet users generate approximately 2.5 quintillion bytes of data each day, and every person is estimated to generate about 1.7 megabytes of data each second.[1] In the third century BCE, the sum of human knowledge was believed to be housed in the Library of Alexandria; today, every person alive could obtain 320 times as much information as historians estimate was stored there (Mayer-Schönberger & Cukier, 2013).[2]

Beyond statistics though, just consider what you likely have done today. In your pocket, you have a smartphone that tracked your geolocation on your way to work. The smartphone also gathered meta-data about the people you called or texted and the apps you checked, logging for all of these interactions how long you spent. When you bought this book, information about where you bought the book became available to your credit card company; if you purchased it online, the retailer also collected information about your purchase (e.g., how long you browsed, what other books you clicked on), which it will use to suggest other books of potential interest to you. Everything that we do leaves digital breadcrumbs.

To deal with this wealth of information, data have been described and classified in a multitude of ways. We suggest their massiveness should be framed along three dimensions (similar to the 3Vs of data;[3] see Chapter 13 for a related discussion). First, diversity (partially related to *variety*) refers to the many different digital data points pertaining to a subject or object. For every person with a device in her or his pocket, data about location position and speed of movement are available, which then can be combined with data about weather conditions and traffic. In homes, various devices register water, heat, and energy consumption, as well as music, radio, and television usage. Each piece of industrial equipment also produces data about sound, vibration, temperature, production efficiency, and so forth. This massive diversity of data is only likely to continue increasing as digitization continues to spread.

Second, comparability (partially related to *volume*) relates to the data being collected about specific subjects and objects. Knowing the condition of one industrial machine is helpful; being able to compare these data with data gathered from other machines likely offers even more insights. Accordingly, industrial maintenance programs are built on data gathered from many machines that get compared to eliminate potential error sources. As consumers, we are accustomed to such comparisons: Amazon, Spotify, and other platforms suggest what other users, seemingly similar to us, have chosen.

Third, alteration (partially related to *velocity*) reflects changes in individual measures, including how often and how quickly data points are updated. We have experienced huge shifts toward the real-time, so currently updated data are often available. Mobile devices provide an exact current location, banking apps provide a precise balance in that moment, and the oil temperature gauged by a control center reflects the machine's condition just seconds ago. Driven by always-on measurement devices and high-speed connectivity (e.g., fiber cable networks, 5G mobile networks), data are produced infinitely; that is, data are available about many aspects pertaining to many objects, and those data also are available many times.

Figure I.1 illustrates this explosion of data, which we attribute to developments in three dimensions: more aspects, more objects, and more often. For a firm, a good exercise is to visualize its own data situation along these three dimensions, relative to its competitors:

- How many different data points do we have access to? How many do our competitors access?
- How many different objects do we have data about? How many do our competitors have?
- How often do our data get updated? How often do our competitors update their data?

The larger the square in Figure I.1, the more extensive are the data available to the organization. The size of the quadrant along these three dimensions illustrates how much data are available for the organization—stated differently, the size of the quadrant indicates just how big the data are. This assessment thus can reveal the competitive situation of an organization in terms of its digital data development. This is not to say that a firm must lead on all three dimensions simultaneously to be successful; as Chapter 5 argues, there is beauty in smallness and appropriate winning strategies. But the mapping helps illustrate where an organization stands and which strategic options are available to it.

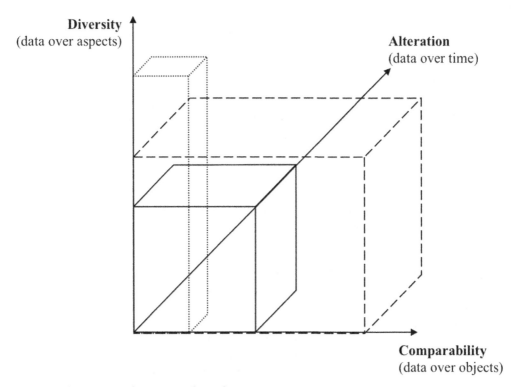

Figure I.1   Data bigness on three dimensions

BIG SUCCESS

Data alone do not equate to business success, despite a general assumption that they do, as manifested in claims like "data is the new oil" that can do virtually anything for a business.[4] But data must be used before they can contribute to firm performance or market success.

In the meantime, digitization continues to change business practices, business models, and marketplaces (Ritter & Pedersen, 2020), and not all of these changes are value-creating, nor is their potential being fully exploited. Rather, businesses' vast opportunities are wide, unpredictable, and ever-changing, without any visible horizon. Consider several stylized facts that support this claim:

- 95 percent of businesses identify the need to manage unstructured data as a problem for their operations; some estimates posit that only 0.5 percent of all data are actually analyzed.[5]
- Predictions describe the "datafication" of all aspects of life and its commercialization, yet few of these predictions come to being. Google Glass may have datafied the gaze (Mayer-Schönberger & Cukier, 2013), but little commercial value has originated from these data.[6]

As the chapters in this book argue, there are many different business areas that can use data to realize opportunities: human capital (Chapter 8), learning and training (Chapter 9), sales (Chapter 11), and business development (Chapter 12), to name just a few. A common denominator is that firms need to specify concrete projects based on these data, whether it is a marketing project, a sales project, or an operations project. With such a project in place, firms can describe the aim (e.g., cost efficiency, revenue, both). In turn, the measure of success, achieved with data, becomes more tangible for companies.

BIG LIMITATIONS

Most companies facing the contemporary challenge of preempting threats and pursuing opportunities through digitization are SMEs with limited budgets and resource constraints, yet most practitioner-oriented research and advice focuses on Silicon Valley mega-companies that were born digital (e.g., Google, Facebook, Uber) or iconic behemoths undergoing a digital transformation (e.g., Maersk, Siemens, GE). Unfortunately, SMEs get overlooked in research into business applications of digital data, so the guidelines available are either unrealistic (e.g., require more resources than SMEs have available) or not relevant (e.g., they are already agile).

Being small thus can be a limitation; to deal with big data, firms may require substantial resource investments and time, two dimensions that SMEs rarely have in abundance. But even if SMEs face big limitations in their work in the data-related domain, they can overcome them by being aware of the limitations, working within them, and using the related restrictions to think creatively. When SMEs find their own way, it can lead to novel, alternative solutions to pressing challenges.

BIG PARADOXES

Finally, like any organization, SMEs confront paradoxes that hinder easy solutions but also enable unique successes when effectively solved.

Paradox 1: Lack of Data about Data

Along with the massive increase in data, we also acknowledge the lack of realization of business opportunities, particularly by SMEs. This problem can be attributed, at least partially, to the counterintuitive situation in which data exist about nearly everything, but not enough data reveal the success of data-driven initiatives. That is, decision makers often lack specific data to support valid assessments of business cases related to big data. Choosing the right initiative then becomes a gamble, without input for making a reliable business case. This situation is particularly challenging for firms with small budgets that cannot initiate a large portfolio of projects and hope that some succeed, while funding a plethora of unsuccessful ones.

Paradox 2: Voices from the Top vs. Solutions from the Bottom

Digitization and data-driven business development are discussed everywhere; virtually every top management team has added some digital component to their strategy. Every day, we read about a CEO or politician who argues for the importance of increased levels and paces of digitization and digitalization, and those calls grew even louder in response to the social distancing measures imposed by the coronavirus crisis. However, these discussions are solely agendas. The true development of data-driven business comes from the frontline: engineers with insights into machines and operations, IT experts with capabilities in data and analytics, customer-facing employees who can account for customer needs and value creation—and sometimes, teams of representatives from all these groups who come together around a data project.[7] A stealth innovation can be blocked by an organization that is not ready to promote autonomous projects to official strategy status. So data-driven success requires resolving this issue, and SMEs might stand a better chance, due to the shorter distance between top and bottom, stronger cross-functional insights, and cooperation that tend to appear in their organizations.

Paradox 3: The More Personal Data about the Customer, the Farther Away the Customer Wants to Be

Firms know a lot about their customers, reflecting the diverse data they collect. Applying such data brings firms closer to their customers, which allows for a better understanding of their needs and more appropriate value propositions. But the use of data also reveals just how up-close-and-personal suppliers can get, which may alienate customers and cause them to limit further access to their data. Some data utilization clearly appears creepy at times, like big brother or surveillance capitalism (Zuboff & Schwandt, 2019), and it evokes the so-called personalization paradox (Aguirre et al., 2015). There is a fine balance between establishing close, supportive links with customers and respecting their privacy. Similar arguments hold for employees, suppliers, and nearly every other actor in a firm's business ecosystem.

No solutions to these paradoxes are easily available or obvious; decision makers also must actively address them on an ongoing basis. In doing so, they can make better informed decisions for how to deal with the intricate dilemmas encountered with big data.

REMAINDER OF THE BOOK

This book is about the lessons, successes, and failures that SMEs encounter on their quest to obtain data-driven growth. These firms must take small steps toward their goals, because of their limited resources to invest and need to realize immediate success. In describing the journey that SMEs take, one step at a time, we have tried to produce a text that addresses the concerns and challenges faced by practitioners. Accordingly, it consists of four general parts, each comprised of related chapters:

- Part I: Foundations: Getting the Basics Right
- Part II: Capabilities: Getting Digitization Right
- Part III: Functions: Getting All Business Areas into Big Data Mode
- Part IV: Transformations: Getting There the Right Way.

Part I: Foundations: Getting the Basics Right

The first part of the book consists of three chapters. Starting us off, Karen Mills and Annie V. Dang propose that the world of small business can be transformed by "Building Small Business Utopia: How Artificial Intelligence and Big Data Can Increase Small Business Success." They note the frictions, barriers, and stagnation that small businesses confront when seeking access to capital from conventional lenders but also the great promise of financial technology, or "fintech." Emerging fintech firms leverage big data and artificial intelligence, then build automated underwriting processes and dashboards that streamline the customer experience, make lending applications more efficient, and even help small firms track their cash flows. The success of this market prompted conventional banks and big tech platforms to develop new products and services to appeal to small business customers, expanding their financial access even further. The authors make a convincing case that the resulting product–service ecosystem, or small business utopia, by providing both capital and insights to small businesses, will enable them to prosper, innovate, and grow.

Rather than embracing a utopian ideal, Jan Trzaskowski establishes some practical recommendations for how small businesses should be using big data today, so that they can comply with existing regulations. In "GDPR Compliant Processing of Big Data in Small Business," he proposes six principles that summarize the 99 articles and 173 recitals of the European Union's General Data Protection Regulation, which SMEs then can integrate into their operations.

In addition to ensuring compliance, SMEs must address other demands, such as overcoming their size liabilities, so in "Big Data and SMEs," Vania Sena and Sena Ozdemir propose practical ways they can leverage big data to reduce coordination costs and enhance team-level collaboration. With an organizational perspective, this chapter outlines how business performance can depend on big data investments, with both theoretical and empirical insights for how SMEs can exploit the big data they gather.

Part II: Capabilities: Getting Digitization Right

The second part of the book consists of four chapters, each of which covers a distinct practice or strategy related to effective digitization. For example, in their effort to define data-enabled value-creation strategies that SMEs can use, Bieke Struyf, Wouter van Bockhaven, and Paul Matthyssens detail effective resource configurations. Their in-depth case study, as reported in "Value-Creation for Industry 4.0 and SMEs' Data-Driven Growth: Strategies and Resource Alignment," illustrates how an SME can evolve to a digital platform instigator—and create radically new value-creation opportunities—by overcoming challenges, designing effective organizational processes, and ultimately adopting Industry 4.0 technology. In particular, the case firm's network capabilities, innovative nature, and incremental digital capability development efforts supported its shift away from digital servitization and toward digital platform strategies. The authors use these insights to propose a framework of data-enabled value-creating strategies, detailing the capabilities that underlie successful versions, along with a self-evaluation tool that SME managers can use to develop their own digital transformations.

Capabilities also are front and center, along with a project view, in the framework proposed by Carsten Lund Pedersen and Thomas Ritter in the next chapter. To inform data-driven growth in SMEs, they argue that a digitization capability consists of three dimensions (data, analytics, and permission), and data-driven projects involve seven key scenarios. By "Analyzing and Developing Digitization Capabilities for Data-driven Projects in SMEs," they detail both the steps involved in firms' data-utilization journeys and the ways firms could apply their framework to develop a digitization capability.

Another case study, describing "How a Glass-Processing SME Developed Its Big Data Competence," proposes that an SME called Glaston actually used three dynamic capabilities to overcome its limited funds and technical know-how. In defining the firm's big data competence, Joel Mero, Heikki Karjaluoto, and Tanja Tammisalo describe how Glaston combined its market listening and business imagination skills to monitor industry-level technological developments, then apply them in big data use cases relevant for its operations. With open innovation, Glaston also was able to complement its internal resources and partner with external actors, and then its culture of experimentation enabled it to develop a portfolio of big data initiatives, which it pilot tests carefully before undertaking any full-scale implementation.

Shirley Y. Coleman agrees with the benefits of partnering; she proposes the promise of "Data Excellence in SMEs through Engagement in University Partnerships." If SMEs work with universities to expand their data capabilities, they might overcome their relatively small pools of in-house expertise, while still leveraging their flexibility and agility, to take advantage of the proliferation of data and digital communication associated with Industry 4.0. The author uses her experience of working with SMEs and developing university partnerships to outline both benefits and risks, as well as to summarize some key lessons learned, to inform other SMEs as they develop plans for their own partnerships.

Part III: Functions: Getting All Business Areas Into Big Data Mode

The four chapters in this third part acknowledge the need to get all departments and operations to embrace big data, even in SMEs. For example, SMEs might ignore the benefits of human capital analytics (HCA), according to Frederikke Amalie la Cour Nygaard and Dana Minbaeva, because most studies of HCA address large, complex organization. But in "Capitalizing on Human Capital Analytics in Small and Medium-Sized Enterprises," they challenge this misconception by detailing how and why HCA is highly relevant for SMEs, and then offer examples of how they can capitalize on HCA to ensure value creation and competitive advantages.

Next, Camilla Nellemann and Torben Pedersen consider "How Experimental Data Can Optimize E-Learning," offering the novel prediction that big data can help clarify user behaviors in not just e-learning but also other consumption contexts. When firms can identify behavioral patterns exhibited by their customers, then adapt their offerings to them, using both experimentation and data analytics, they can perform better. To provide evidence for their argument, the authors describe how a software company experimented with ways to teach customers how to use their products efficiently and thereby discovered that moving physical teaching into a virtual space provided notable benefits, for both e-learners and the firm.

Beyond just efficiency though, SMEs often rely on informal, personal relationships to establish and maintain their competitive advantage. Thus, Poul Houman Andersen wonders and investigates "How Do Big Data Impact Business Market Relationships?" The impact of big data on this competitive advantage appears to reflect the specific interaction patterns between buyers and sellers, which themselves emerge in continuous, interactive market processes. Accordingly, big data constitute meaningful resources that offer potential opportunities, because small businesses can develop data-supported market relationships. The challenges, tasks, and issues facing small business owners even align notably with the services that can be rendered by big data.

Henrik Andersen and Thomas Ritter also consider business relationships, namely, the links of suppliers with their various customers, which differ according to the extent to which suppliers can provide market offerings that match the customers' demands, sizes, and procurement policies. In "Revenue Blueprinting: Identifying Growth Potential Using Customer Data and Customer Insights," they propose that suppliers can achieve revenue growth potential if they leverage their best implemented practices, using carefully calculated and verified revenue blueprints that reflect the revenues achieved through each practice. These revenue blueprints highlight the firm's own best implemented practice, while also accounting for current market offerings and customers. In turn, SMEs can seek revenue growth without having to make expensive new investments or undertake substantial training.

Part IV: Transformations: Getting There the Right Way

This fourth and final part of the book includes two chapters. First, in "Transforming Small and Medium-Sized Enterprises (SMEs) to Digitally Enabled Landscapes," Bård Tronvoll, Christian Kowalkowski, and David Sörhammar detail the challenges of digital servitization for SMEs, then propose three transformational shifts (dematerialization, identity, and collaboration) that can help them overcome and even embrace these challenges. Such shifts require SMEs to be close to customers, with a strong understanding of their needs. In particular, the collaboration shift should be relatively easier for SMEs, because these small firms already likely coordinate their activities with other actors. But the dematerialization shift (i.e., separate information from the physical world) may be more difficult, because it requires sophisticated technical competencies and financing strength. Finally, the identity shift might be hard too, if the SMEs' culture remains resistant to change.

Second, Pernille Rydén and Helle Rootzén present the real-world experience of 12 Danish SMEs that have engaged in digital transformation learning processes as the first steps in their big data journeys. Specifically, with their chapter, "Facilitating Big Data Transformation in Danish SMEs: Insights for Managers," these authors detail the purpose, principles, processes, potential, barriers, and methods that emerged from "KomDigital," a digital learning concept for SMEs develop by the Technical University of Denmark (DTU). The authors thus suggest practical steps for other SMEs, describing not just managerial concerns but also key drivers of digital learning and transformation. In particular, if they can increase their big data technology competence, SMEs can better exploit both data and analytics to identify consumer insights, expand their business intelligence, enhance their decision-making power, and evoke new ways of thinking and interacting with their markets.

CLOSING REMARKS

We extend a special thanks to Edward Elgar and its staff, who have been most helpful throughout this entire process. Equally, we warmly thank our contributors, who exhibited a desire to share their knowledge and experience with the book's readers—and a willingness to put forward their views for possible challenge by their peers. We hope that this compendium of chapters and themes contributes to our colleagues' and practitioners' own research and practice. The chapters in this book can help fill some knowledge gaps related to important aspects of capabilities, functions, and transformations of big data that drive business growth; we hope they also stimulate further thought and action pertaining to these topics.

NOTES

1. https://techjury.net/blog/big-data-statistics/#gref (accessed February 25, 2021).
2. https://www.foreignaffairs.com/articles/2013-04-03/rise-big-data (accessed February 25, 2021).
3. https://www.forbes.com/sites/oreillymedia/2012/01/19/volume-velocity-variety-what-you-need-to -know-about-big-data/ (accessed February 25, 2021).
4. https://www.economist.com/leaders/2017/05/06/the-worlds-most-valuable-resource-is-no-longer -oil-but-data (accessed February 25, 2021).
5. https://techjury.net/blog/big-data-statistics/#gref (accessed February 25, 2021).
6. https://www.forbes.com/sites/siimonreynolds/2015/02/05/why-google-glass-failed/ (accessed February 25, 2021).
7. https://sloanreview.mit.edu/article/let-your-digital-strategy-emerge/ (accessed February 25, 2021).

REFERENCES

Aguirre, A., Mahr, D., Grewal, D., de Ruyter, K., and Wetzels, M. (2015). Unraveling the Personalization Paradox: The Effect of Information Collection and Trust-Building Strategies on Online Advertisement Effectiveness. *Journal of Retailing*, 91(1), 34–49.

Brennen, S.J., and Kreiss, D. (2016). Digitalization. In K.B. Jensen, R.T. Craig, J.D. Pooley, and E.W. Rothenbuhler (eds), *The International Encyclopedia of Communication Theory and Philosophy*, Hoboken, NJ: John Wiley & Sons, pp. 1–11.

Mayer-Schönberger, V., and Cukier, K. (2013). *Big Data: A Revolution That Will Transform How We Live, Work and Think*, London: John Murray.

Ritter, T., and Pedersen, C.L. (2020). Digitization Capability and the Digitalization of Business Models in Business-to-Business Firms: Past, Present, and Future. *Industrial Marketing Management*, 86(4), 180–90.

Zuboff, S., and Schwandt, K. (2019). *The Age of Surveillance Capitalism: The Fight for a Human Future at the New Frontier of Power*, London: Profile Books.

PART I

Foundations: getting the basics right

1. Building small business utopia: how artificial intelligence and Big Data can increase small business success

Karen G. Mills and Annie V. Dang

1.1 INTRODUCTION

Alex hears a chime, looks up from her espresso machine, and glances at the clock. Her coffee shop opens for the day in half an hour. As she finishes steaming her milk, she leans over to check her phone and investigate the source of the sound. It's a notification from her Small Business Insights dashboard: "Alex, it's time to order new water filters, descaling powder, and cleaning tablets for your annual spring cleaning." Alex walks over to the café's counter and consults her dashboard. She clicks the reminder on the home screen and takes a sip of her coffee as the machine quickly analyzes her past buying behavior and scans for the best deals online. She then reviews the bot's suggestions for purchases. Seeing that she is getting a great price and the fastest shipping available, Alex happily taps the "buy" button. In a split second, her order is placed, and the real-time cash flow projections on the right side of her screen update to reflect the latest expense.

With 15 minutes to go before the shop opens, Alex takes a moment to review the messages in the "employee" tab of her dashboard. There are two alerts that require her attention. It looks like Sean, a barista, cannot make his shifts this weekend. The platform received his request for a shift trade last night, pinged available employees based on their schedules, and found a replacement who could handle the busy weekend hours. All Alex has to do is approve the switch. Alex then asks her dashboard to estimate what her cash will look like after she pays her employees this week. The projections look positive, so she authorizes the machine to send out paychecks tomorrow morning.

The second alert informs Alex that she may need a loan at the end of the month. The town is holding a summer fair and her business will be featured with its own booth. She will need to pay for extra employees that weekend to staff both the café and the booth, and she will need to make additional inventory purchases of ice and coffee beans for cold brew, as the weather is sure to be warm. "Don't worry!" Alex's bot chirps. "It looks like you'll need about $4000 to prep for the fair, but you are preapproved for several loans and the terms are good. We can touch base again in a week."

Alex returns to the "home" screen and scans the various graphs predicting cash flow and highlighting future spikes in spending. Her dashboard bot, an animated coffee mug, pops up on the screen to give her a weekly industry update: "Alex, as I mentioned to you last month, cafés in your area are increasingly stocking alternative milk options. The number of local coffee shops offering oat milk has increased by 35 percent in the last two weeks. Do you want to start stocking oat milk as well?" Alex and her baristas have noticed more customers requesting this option. She tells the bot to go ahead and order enough for the next two weeks based on other cafés' usage levels, and to track the customer uptake. "Fantastic!" the bot responds. "I will order enough for two weeks and show you how well it sells. If it is popular, I will find you a permanent oat milk supplier." Alex takes another sip of her cappuccino and releases a contented sigh, ready to start the morning shift. She taps the "open" button on her dashboard and smiles as the LED sign at the front of the shop comes to life.

This is a normal day in the life of Alex, our coffee shop owner. In many respects, she begins her day in the same way as generations of small business owners before her, with an eye to her customers, her employees, and her cash reserves. Yet, something has changed. In an era marked by advanced technologies like artificial intelligence (AI) and machine learning,[1] Alex possesses data-driven tools and insights into her small business that have previously only been available to larger firms. Her dashboard instantaneously collects and analyzes information about her café, and integrates it with e-commerce platforms, her payroll provider, her point-of-sale system, and the best practices of similar businesses in her region. It not only aggregates existing data on her business, but also offers real-time insights and automated decisions that can increase sales and help Alex access credit to avoid a cash crisis.

In this chapter, we explore how technology can change the game for small business owners in two important and related ways: by giving them information on how to run their business, and by providing them with access to the capital they need to grow and prosper. Both developments are rooted in the ability to seamlessly gather relevant digital information about a small business from multiple avenues and to translate that data into useful insights about the business's prospects, benefitting borrowers and lenders alike. By constructing an integrated, intelligent financial ecosystem—which we call "Small Business Utopia"—these technological breakthroughs have the potential to transform businesses like Alex's café and the entire small business world.

Small businesses play a critical but often overlooked role in nearly every economy. They have been plagued by difficulties in obtaining capital due, in part, to cumbersome banking systems that tend to favor larger clients and are slow to innovate when it comes to small business products. In recent years, however, new technologies have begun to revolutionize the financial services sector and small business lending, in particular, has proven ripe for change. Financial technology firms, or "fintechs," have entered the small business lending market in droves, where they compete with traditional banks and spur them to rethink their long-standing approaches to small business. The innovations generated in this dynamic environment are creating more opportunities for creditworthy small businesses to access capital and complementary tools like Alex's dashboard, leading to greater small business longevity and success.

Although this is an exciting and positive set of developments, the use of Big Data, AI, and machine learning is not without risk. Inherent in the automation of tasks and processes is the decline or removal of human oversight with potentially negative, albeit unintended, consequences. These risks present a challenge for regulators and policymakers around the world, as they must rethink outdated principles and create "smart" regulation to address inevitable questions of data access and ownership, data transparency, and data security. The issues associated with technology are not insignificant and the stakes are particularly high when it comes to financial data. However, if the evolution of policy and regulation can responsibly meet the pace of technological change, the rewards for small businesses and for overall economic prosperity could be transformative.

1.2 SMALL BUSINESS IS IMPORTANT TO THE ECONOMY

Small businesses form the lifeblood of many economies. Half of the people who work in the United States (US) own or work for a small business.[2] Notably, however, the proportion of people employed by small businesses in the US is near the lower end for developed economies. In the European Union (EU), micro, small, and medium-sized businesses make up two-thirds of employment (e.g., 72 percent in Spain, 64 percent in Denmark, and 54 percent in the United Kingdom).[3] The sheer number of small firms and their workforces in the US and in Europe underscores their significance to their respective economies.

Despite these substantial employment numbers, small businesses are often excluded from policy conversations and economic models, which tend to focus elsewhere: on consumers, on investments made by bigger businesses, and on government spending. It is therefore not surprising that relatively few measurements and tools exist in either the public or private spheres to track the impacts of technology on the critical small business sector. However, a growing body of research powerfully demonstrates that small businesses, especially new and young firms, are vital for employment growth, productivity, and innovation.[4]

In many respects, the world of the small business owner has exhibited minimal change over the last 50 to 100 years. Small businesses focus on their products and services, and they devote much of their energy to customers and employees. They often use cash for transactions and keep paper records. This leaves these business owners with little capacity to gather analytical information and glean business insights beyond their personal experiences and wisdom gained from years of operation. Combined with the reality that many small businesses operate with thin margins and low cash buffers, this helps explain why small business failure rates are so high—less than half of US small businesses survive beyond five years.[5] In fact, a study by U.S. Bank found that 82 percent of small businesses in the US fail due to cash flow problems.[6] With access to relevant data and the ability to translate that information into meaningful insights, all of this could change.

Twenty-first century technologies have dramatically disrupted and revolutionized the ways in which we live and work—from how we communicate to how we shop and seek entertainment. They have allowed small businesses to diversify their sales channels beyond brick-and-mortar stores in a shift towards advertising and selling online and over social media. Technological advancements have also occurred in the financial services sector in the form of digital currencies, real-time payments, and mobile bank applications. Moreover, there are no signs that the pace of change is slowing, as the coronavirus pandemic has led customers to seek out contactless digital banking experiences as opposed to physical branch interactions.

One particular innovation has proven pivotal in transforming the financial services sector: the development of application programming interfaces (APIs)[7] by banks, accounting platforms, and infrastructure software companies. APIs allow multiple streams of data to be accessed and integrated into innovative products and services. Financial institutions then use AI and machine learning to transform this newly available data into actionable insights that inform credit underwriting models and reduce operating costs by increasing the speed and accuracy of predictions. As they gain traction, APIs and the applications they enable can benefit both lenders and their small business customers by improving an area of historical difficulty: access to capital.

1.3   ACCESS TO CAPITAL

In 2009, the world found itself in the midst of a monumental financial crisis, one that would have lasting ramifications for the banking system and alter our understanding of the economic role of small businesses. The global financial crisis hit small enterprises disproportionately hard. Why? At its core, the 2009 financial crisis was a credit crisis. Banks had become over-extended on mortgages and effectively curtailed lending to small firms, which were deemed riskier and less profitable to serve. This signified a devastating turn for small businesses, which are particularly dependent on credit to survive. When the lending dried up, millions of small businesses throughout the world failed, leading to a massive decline in small business employment. In the first quarter of 2009 alone, the US lost 1.8 million small business jobs.[8] The crisis taught a painful but valuable lesson: small businesses are important to the economy and access to capital is critical for small businesses.

Since the financial crisis, researchers have sought to better understand why small businesses were so sensitive to the economic downturn. They identified a number of reasons, the most striking of which is the fact that small businesses have extremely low cash buffers, with the median US small business holding only 27 days of cash. This means that at any point in time, the typical small business only has enough cash for less than a month of expenses and other outflows. If a customer were to pay late or if the business were to experience a disruptive event, such as an external economic or health crisis, the delay or loss of revenue could be life-threatening. Businesses in certain industry verticals are even more vulnerable—retail stores only have 19 days of cash on hand and restaurants have only 16 days.[9] These low cash reserves highlight the importance of seamless access to credit and real-time cash management for the health and survival of small businesses.

1.4   BARRIERS AND FRICTIONS IN SMALL BUSINESS ACCESS TO CAPITAL

For generations, the process of small business lending has remained fairly static despite technological advancements and widespread gravitation towards digital interfaces and experiences. A small business owner seeking a loan typically photocopies a pile of paperwork, walks down the street to their banker, hands over the documents, and then waits weeks or even months to receive a decision. Often, the banker makes several requests for additional information or asks the business owner for a personal guarantee or some form of collateral. Even after such a comprehensive review and agonizing wait, the banker might still say "no," leaving the business to begin again with yet another lender. This slow process presents a major problem for small businesses, which depend on timely access to capital to offset their slim cash buffers. On the other side, lenders are focused on minimizing losses, which has traditionally required a meticulous, time-intensive assessment of the business to ensure it is a risk they are willing to assume. Two distinct structural frictions make the small business lending process especially challenging for banks: *information opacity* and *heterogeneity*.

1.4.1 Information Opacity

Information opacity refers to the fact that it is incredibly difficult to look inside a small business and conclude whether it is creditworthy. It is relatively easy, for instance, to gather ten data points about a single consumer and decide whether that person should get a mortgage. The same amount of data on a small business, however, fails to provide a similar level of clarity. Information about a business is buried in tax filings, bank statements, sales records, and other financial data, making it difficult for lenders to determine how much money the business is actually making. Often, the small business itself does not even know if it is profitable. However, as large quantities of small business data are digitized and made available, technologies like AI, machine learning, and predictive modeling can make it easier to gather and analyze actual business activity, creating a smoother, better-informed underwriting process.

1.4.2 Heterogeneity

The second friction inhibiting small business lending is heterogeneity. All small businesses are different, not only in terms of the kind of business and the customers served but also in terms of their financial profiles. A recent categorization of small businesses in the US highlights the heterogeneity inherent in small firms (Figure 1.1).[10] Of the 30 million US small businesses, 24 million do not have employees. These are the sole proprietors, freelancers, and members of the gig economy—a growing segment in the US and other parts of the world. Another four million small businesses are characterized as "Main Street" businesses. These are the car repair operations, restaurants, and cafés that embody the spirit of the community while also creating a significant number of jobs and providing a path to economic mobility. More than one million US small businesses operate in supply chains, selling their products and services to other businesses or the government. Only a tiny proportion of the 30 million small businesses in America—around 200,000—are high-growth startup firms on track to become the next Google or Amazon. In this chapter, we do not address the last category, as high-growth firms access a separate capital market (e.g., venture capital) from the vast majority of other small businesses, which borrow from banks and similar financial services providers.

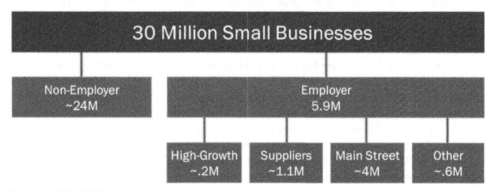

Source: Mills (2019).

Figure 1.1   Categorization of small businesses in the United States

The diversity of small businesses has long been a source of friction preventing banks from establishing effective credit models. One day, the client is a retail shop on Main Street, while the next day it may be a dentist or a packaging supplier. For each type of business, the credit file looks quite different, making it challenging for a loan officer to develop widely applicable expertise. New technologies can significantly reduce this barrier. Imagine a lender that has the ability to access and interpret the financial profiles of 1000 dry cleaners. This lender will find it easier to assess whether the 1001st dry cleaner being considered for credit can operate profitably and ultimately repay a loan. In the US, Live Oak Bank is one financial institution that has successfully used industry data to build underwriting expertise in specific sectors. The bank gained traction by focusing on distinct verticals—first, veterinarians, then poultry farmers, and eventually funeral homes and other kinds of businesses—developing algorithms attuned to the credit characteristics of each segment.

1.5   A CASE STUDY IN INNOVATION: FINTECH

The period from 2010 to 2015 saw a burst in innovation and the rise of a new breed of digital lender: financial technology firms, or "fintechs," which leverage AI and machine learning to accelerate underwriting. Early entrants, like Lending Club, started with consumer lending. They mounted a formidable challenge to traditional banks with streamlined online applications and quick response times. Small business lenders like Kabbage and OnDeck followed, using alternative cash flow data from borrowers' bank accounts to conduct credit assessments. Their automated processes cut loan decision times from weeks to minutes, with funds entering a small business's bank account in a matter of days. Despite the high interest rates charged on these loans, the ease of the application process and the rapid turnaround held massive market appeal.

The fintech entrants delivered a better customer experience by automating previously manual processes, including data collection, risk modeling, and credit decisions. This proved beneficial in tackling a critical gap in the small business lending market: small-dollar loans. More than 78 percent of US small businesses seek loans of less than USD 250,000 and nearly 40 percent want loans of less than USD 50,000.[11] For banks using a traditional underwriting process, these loans are simply not profitable, leading to a high level of unfulfilled credit needs, especially among the smallest businesses.[12] Fintechs and other tech platforms took note, targeting the small-dollar loans that banks refused to make. Lenders like Square, PayPal, and Intuit QuickBooks went on to deliver billions of dollars in credit to hundreds of thousands of small businesses. To date, Square has originated USD 6.3 billion in loans with an average loan size of less than USD 6000.[13]

As additional fintech challengers entered the field, market commentators boldly predicted that David (the fintechs) would kill Goliath—that the traditional banks had had their day. However, the financial services landscape that emerged from the period of heightened activity in the early 2010s proved more complex than initially anticipated. Fintechs faced several key disadvantages. Without established brands and trusted reputations, they found it difficult to locate customers. It is hard to reach small businesses at the precise moment when they need a loan. Their heterogeneity means they do not all engage with the same types of media or congregate naturally in one place, such as an industry convention. Small business owners do not have time to search for and compare lending options, as they are busy actually running their businesses. Therefore, the fintechs' marketing costs were exceptionally high, reaching more than 40 percent of revenue at times.[14]

On the other hand, traditional banks, especially local community banks, tend to hold long-standing, trusted relationships with their small business clients. They have natural avenues to interact with and cross-sell different services to their customers. Banks also possess a second major advantage in the form of access to low-cost deposits to fund their loans. New entrants relied on expensive funding sources, often from risk-capital providers like hedge funds. This significantly increased the costs of their loans and made some of their offerings dangerously high-priced for small business owners.

1.6 THE SMALL BUSINESS LENDING LANDSCAPE

After a few fast-paced years of fintech growth, the banks woke up and decided that they would not cede the small business market to the new competitors. Large banks in particular had the resources to invest in technology and construct their own data-driven tools.[15] The fintechs had largely improved the front-end customer experience—an innovation that banks and tech companies discovered they could replicate.

The small business lending landscape evolved into a competitive arena with four primary sets of players: traditional banks, fintech challenger banks, Big Tech platforms, and fintech infrastructure companies. Large and small banks recommitted to small business loans and services, increasingly pursuing a digital-first strategy. They invested heavily in automated products, like Bank of America's mobile chatbot "Erica" and HSBC's branch banking bot "Pepper." Challenger banks based on purely digital experiences, as opposed to physical branches, continued to enter in droves—including Radius Bank and Chime in the US; NorthOne in Canada; Nubank in Brazil; Revolut, Starling, OakNorth, and Monzo in the UK; N26 in Germany; and Judo in Australia. The third category of competitors, large technology players including Amazon, PayPal, Square, Stripe, and Intuit QuickBooks, all developed successful small business lending arms thanks to their customer reach, strong technical expertise, and superior user experience. The fourth group, fintech infrastructure players, catered to the emerging technology needs of the other three segments, building API pipelines to feed the data in a standardized format into lending algorithms and business analysis tools. They included data aggregators like Plaid and Yodlee in the US, and TrueLayer and Bud in the UK.

With a crowded field of players all vying for a piece of the market, the scene has been set for a real transformation in small business lending. Banks and fintechs, armed with new data on small businesses funneled through APIs, are focused on turning the information streams into actionable insights using AI and machine learning. These insights offer immense value for lenders—they can lower the cost of traditional underwriting and make the process more efficient overall, while also opening the door to a new suite of innovative products and services aimed at helping small businesses access capital (Figure 1.2).

Even more revolutionary has been the growing realization that these same information streams and credit algorithms could change the game in a separate but related way—the insights could be made directly available to small business owners in the form of a dashboard or some other tool that provides information on both current and forecast cash flows, thereby equipping small businesses with a clearer view of their finances.

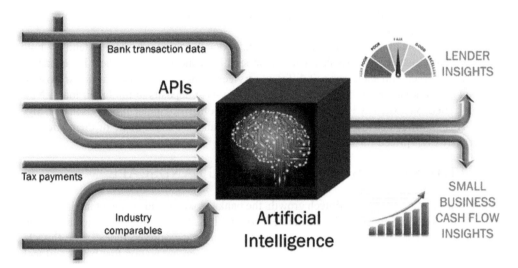

Bank transaction data

APIs

Tax payments

Industry comparables

Artificial Intelligence

LENDER INSIGHTS

SMALL BUSINESS CASH FLOW INSIGHTS

Figure 1.2   The use of AI and machine learning in financial services

1.7   SMALL BUSINESS UTOPIA

On the main street in Brunswick, Maine—aptly named "Maine Street"—sits a string of reddish-brown brick buildings housing local small businesses, from restaurants to boutiques to running apparel shops. At the end of one block, with a conspicuous white clapboard storefront, lies a charming taproom called Moderation Brewing Company. The business's owner, Mattie, recently offered some insight into the difficulties she experiences when trying to sort out her pub's finances. At the end of a long shift, she goes home, sits on her bed, and evaluates her business's financial health. On her laptop, she loads her accounting software. On her tablet, she logs into all of her business's bank accounts. On her phone, she pulls up her credit card statements. Then she brings out her paper spreadsheets and tax documents. By the time she is finished, she has six or seven screens open and loose-leaf sheets sprinkled across the bed.

Many business owners like Mattie struggle to manage their finances and understand their cash flows while simultaneously running their business. How revolutionary would it be if these time-intensive tasks were automated and combined into a single, user-friendly dashboard? Today, APIs can power the kind of integrated tool that Alex seamlessly navigated at the start of this chapter. Previously disparate sources of data can be gathered into a central place for analysis and help small business owners make informed decisions. This data-driven ecosystem has the potential to be so transformative that we have named it "Small Business Utopia."

In this "Small Business Utopia," information from the point-of-sale system, the payroll portal, the accounting platform, tax preparation software, and bank accounts would all be integrated. In addition, staffing and recruiting tools could be linked to the dashboard and thereby automate personnel management, including shift-assignment changes, job postings, and even employee healthcare benefits. A key functionality of this hypothetical dashboard would be the cash flow predictor, which would use historical sales and expense data as well as owner input to forecast cash usage and predict potential shortfalls.[16]

This real-time intelligence could also be used by banks or other lenders to underwrite more quickly or even proactively. Imagine a small business with a cloud of preapproved credit floating over its head. The Small Business Insights platform might tell Alex, "I see that you will need USD 4000 in two weeks to pay for seasonal supplies. Don't worry—you are preapproved for a loan of that amount. Press here and it will be available in your account today." This deep and shared understanding of cash flows between lenders and borrowers would help small businesses avoid life-threatening liquidity crises and ensure that they obtain the right kind of loan—one that fits their business in terms of amount, duration, and cost—at the precise moment they need it.

Lenders also stand to benefit greatly from this new technology ecosystem. If small business owners can access capital and insights that enable them to run their businesses more successfully, they will be less likely to fail. This would reduce the risks that bankers face in small business lending by minimizing defaults and allowing banks to decrease their costs for loan reserves. In turn, they could pass these savings on to customers in the form of lower interest rates, creating a virtuous cycle in small business banking.

Moreover, the lender could return to the role of relationship banker. Instead of spending hours with a client asking for information and analyzing financial records in a manual underwriting process, lenders could utilize real-time data to better understand loan needs and ability to repay. The time savings would allow the lender to sit down with small business owners and engage in substantive conversations regarding their businesses, including the need for expansion capital and other long-term goals. In a world where many fear that automated machines will ultimately replace certain jobs, the concept of "Small Business Utopia" could mark a return to human interaction and the lasting importance of relationship banking.

"Small Business Utopia" may be closer than we think. Companies like Intuit QuickBooks are already using AI to drive a suite of interactive products and tools, like the Cash Flow planner, which forecasts a small business's future income and expenses, while also tracking other aspects of operations, such as invoice and payroll activity.[17] The insights generated by tools like the Cash Flow planner could allow for more accurate evaluations of a business's creditworthiness. However, despite the potential for these innovations to bring positive change to the world of small business lending, we must resist the appeal of rose-colored glasses. The proliferation of such technologies must be accompanied by an in-depth public discussion of how the data that power them is gathered, used, and regulated.

1.8   THE DARK SIDE OF THE BLACK BOX

Research has shown that gaps exist in traditional lending markets due to a lack of banking services in certain regions or systemic barriers that prevent particular populations from accessing credit.[18] One estimate of the size of the gap in the US can be explored by examining the portfolio of the US Small Business Administration (SBA). This government agency provides credit assistance to the nation's small businesses by guaranteeing approximately 75 percent of each loan in situations where banks need additional credit support to grant loan approval. The SBA's portfolio is large—more than USD 100 billion—and over-indexes in women- and minority-owned businesses, which provides an indication of where market imperfections occur. Given that the loss rate on the portfolio is less than 5 percent (i.e., 95 percent of

SBA-guaranteed loans are paid back), it is clear that the vast majority of these small businesses are creditworthy. Nevertheless, they are overlooked in the current banking environment.

Of course, it is not the case that every small business should get a loan. Some businesses seeking funds are struggling because they do not possess a good business model or their product fails to fulfill a market demand. These firms should not receive loans, because when they do go out of business, the debt becomes an additional obligation that must be repaid. The ultimate goal is for all *creditworthy* businesses to obtain the capital they need to operate and succeed. Technology has the power to fill some of the existing market gaps by better identifying and funding these creditworthy businesses.

However, the rewards promised by the use of innovative technologies in financial services inevitably come with significant risks. This is the "dark side of the black box." Even as improved lending algorithms provide access to capital to more deserving businesses, no formula is infallible. In AI and machine learning circles, the mantra "garbage in, garbage out" expresses the reality that outcomes from predictive models are highly dependent on the inputs. Algorithms often learn from past behavior and data, so what happens when the data itself is biased? What if the machine takes in previous loan records and decides that it should not lend to small businesses operating in certain geographies? This could lead to a shortage of investments and opportunities in traditionally underserved areas and exacerbate market inequities. Currently, women- and minority-owned businesses tend to receive fewer loan approvals relative to their proportion of business ownership.[19] An automated decisioning system biased by historical information could miss opportunities to lend to these creditworthy borrowers.

Another set of issues revolves around data transparency. What if a business owner who believes they are a good risk is rejected for a loan? Are they able to look inside the algorithm to understand what portions of the application raised red flags? What if a business owner's credit history has an error in it? Does the applicant get to correct that mistake? As the model learns from the data it is fed and continually updates itself, is it even possible to isolate and identify the determinants of the outcome? How do we ensure that the relevant regulatory parties develop the expertise needed to accurately and effectively analyze algorithms for just outcomes? Moreover, who ultimately owns the data?

1.9   REGULATION

Responsibility for addressing these questions lies with financial regulators. In the wake of the 2009 global financial crisis, regulation was enacted in direct response to the overextension of banks' balance sheets. Financial institutions bemoaned the resulting compliance burdens and lobbied fiercely for their relaxation. As the regulatory conversation moves to address the new technological advancements in financial services, this outdated binary view of "less versus more" regulation is counterproductive. An increasingly connected digital world calls for "smart," forward-looking financial services regulation, where the focus shifts to the real and pressing issues concerning data access and ownership, data transparency, and data security.

1.9.1   Data Access and Ownership

To build a "Small Business Utopia," financial services firms need access to a great deal of data. Therefore, a regulatory environment conducive to innovation must promote, rather than restrict, data access, while keeping small business protections front of mind. The extensive use of data aggregation in financial services, especially in underwriting, raises a crucial question: Who owns the data? Regulators in the EU answered that question in 2015 with the passage of the Revised Payment Services Directive (PSD2), which clearly states that customers own their data.[20] PSD2 requires incumbent banks to share financial information with third parties, such as fintechs, when requested to do so by their clients.

The UK took these regulations a step further in January 2018 by launching the Open Banking Standard, which mandated that Britain's major banks share their data with permitted third parties in a standardized and secure API format.[21] These explicit regulations around data ownership and data access may be one reason why the UK is home to so many innovative fintech startups. More recently, the Financial Conduct Authority (FCA), a UK regulatory body, solicited input on the concept of Open Finance, an extension of Open Banking principles beyond banking to other financial services, such as insurance, mortgages, and investments.[22]

The UK standard has served as an important model for the rest of the world. In the last few years, several countries have begun to implement their own Open Banking regulations, including Japan, Singapore, Australia, and Mexico. The adoption of Open Banking regulations in the US and across the globe is essential for ensuring the development of the kinds of products and services described in this chapter. When consumers and small businesses have more control over their financial data and can permit creative new firms to securely access that information, more innovation will result.

1.9.2 Data Transparency

The shift towards greater use of data in financial services raises issues around visibility into the data itself and the way it is used to make decisions. If a business owner's loan application is rejected, there should be full transparency as to why, so the borrower can understand the shortfalls in their business, correct any errors in their credit file, and take steps to improve. The fintech firms that emerged from the financial crisis distinguished themselves from traditional players through the sheer volume of data gathered and their ability to interpret it for use in underwriting and fraud detection. These data sources, which are often nontraditional, range from the amount of time spent filling out the loan application to the small business owner's social media activity. While many firms have taken care to eliminate markers like race, gender, and other protected categories from their inputs, the US and many other jurisdictions lack clear and enforceable regulations governing the use of algorithms and defining the degree to which regulators can oversee and monitor their inputs and outputs. This has led to significant anxiety regarding the potential for these credit models to have unintended disparate impact, especially for women- and minority-owned businesses. Therefore, concretely defining the role of financial regulators in ensuring that these new technologies neither replicate nor exacerbate current biases in small business lending—even as they widen access to credit—is of the utmost importance.

As these technologies become more widely used, financial regulators will face thorny questions regarding their right to access and evaluate private companies' predictive models, especially when their outcomes may be discriminatory. What is the legal basis for a regulator to look inside the black box? What parts of a lender's underwriting code are proprietary? Can the regulator determine whether the discriminatory result was due to the algorithmic model, the data itself, or some combination of both? What level of responsibility should the lender bear? Regulators continue to grapple with these questions, but there is agreement on several foundational principles: (1) Regulatory agencies need to develop additional expertise to monitor AI and machine learning activity in financial services; (2) The algorithms should be explainable and transparent; and (3) Better measurement of small business lending outcomes will help identify market gaps and potentially discriminatory activities.

1.9.3   Data Security

Regulatory discussions concerning data ownership and transparency must also consider the related issue of data security. It is essential to protect a small business owner's sensitive financial information. If the data are misused or breached, where does the liability fall? In the UK, Open Banking determined that the banks' responsibility ends with the transfer of the data to a third party. The FCA only authorizes firms to receive the data if they can demonstrate that they have the requisite protocols in place to prevent data leakages. Other countries without Open Banking standards, such as the US, lack clarity regarding liability in data transfer.

Regulators face an enormous challenge as they attempt to balance both the benefits and risks of new financial technologies. They must proactively foresee issues and put preemptive backstops in place, keeping in mind that while small businesses stand to gain greatly from innovations in financial services, they must also be protected from bad actors and hidden biases.

1.10   PREDICTIONS FOR THE FUTURE

The story of David and Goliath is still running its course. Only time will tell who among the traditional banks, fintechs, and tech platforms will emerge victorious in the realm of small business lending. As we look towards the future, three primary questions will determine the winners and losers: (1) Who has the customers and the recognized brands; (2) Who has access to low-cost capital; and (3) Who has the best technology and talent?

Banks and Big Tech companies have a natural advantage in the future of small business lending due to their trusted name recognition. Banks, in particular, have the added benefit of access to low-cost capital from deposits. As consumer margins continue to be squeezed, banks will increasingly view small business lending as an important market and take the necessary steps to stay competitive. Although fintech challenger banks are equipped with innovative technologies, they depend on expensive capital from investors, which often translates into exorbitantly high interest rates on small business loans. As they lack well-known brands, they are forced to spend much of their money on customer acquisition. Recognizing that such business models may be unsustainable, many fintechs are actively pursuing partnerships with banks to gain access to their balance sheets and customers. Their partner banks, meanwhile, benefit from insights into the fintechs' groundbreaking technologies.

One thing is certain: the ultimate winners in this shifting environment will be the world's small businesses. By harnessing the power of new technologies, financial services providers can fundamentally reinvent how small businesses access the capital they need to start, scale, and succeed. In the optimal future state, all creditworthy small business owners will be able to obtain a loan that meets their specific needs. There will be less disparity in which businesses obtain capital, and fewer small businesses will fail because they will possess the tools needed to anticipate and withstand cash crises. Small businesses seeking credit will enjoy a better customer experience and loan costs that are commensurate with their risk. They will spend less time filling out and worrying about loan applications, and get back to doing what they do best—running their small businesses and contributing to national growth and productivity.

1.11 CONCLUSIONS

Small business lending has a long history. The concepts of credit, lending, and borrowing can be traced back more than three thousand years to the Third Dynasty of Ur in Mesopotamia. Cuneiform clay tablets unearthed from that time tell the story of a rich economic society highly versed in the extension of capital to bakers, builders, farmers, fishermen, scribes, and shepherds to fund their business operations—from acquiring land to purchasing inventory.[23, 24, 25]

A 59-tablet archive illuminates the financial dealings of Turam-ili, a head merchant in the Ur III period. Turam-ili took on the role of a banker, overseeing other merchants and the "bala," which was a central account to which merchants made deposits of silver, grains, building materials, and other goods that could then be lent out to surrounding businesses and used for various financial transactions.[26] In one text, Turam-ili provided a loan of silver to Nur-Adad, another merchant, with interest set at 20 percent. A beer brewer, on the other hand, received a loan of barley at an interest rate of more than 33 percent.[27]

Small business owners today would find many of Turam-ili's activities familiar despite the vast stretch of time between them. The dynamics of small business lending have remained so consistent over the centuries precisely because the operations of small businesses, at their core, have not changed. Like entrepreneurs today, the small business owners of 3000 years ago needed capital to operate and grow their ventures. Their profit margins were not large enough to fund big purchases, making lending and borrowing a necessary aspect of the financial ecosystem. Just like contemporary small businesses, they experienced inherent frictions and barriers in obtaining loans.

But now, millennia after the first small business loans were recorded, it is possible we have arrived at a transformative moment for small businesses and the way they access capital. In the past, the macroeconomic misconception that small businesses do not contribute substantially to the economy has led to policy missteps and the perpetuation of a "small business paradox"—politicians and government officials frequently proclaim the importance of small businesses in campaign agendas and soundbites, but often fail to implement meaningful policies to help them grow and prosper. However, two major crises in the twenty-first century—the 2009 credit crisis and 2020 global coronavirus pandemic—have underscored the economic significance of small businesses and revealed the fundamental need to serve them better.

The COVID-19 crisis thrust small business cash flows into the spotlight, demonstrating how devastating forced closures could be for businesses dependent on foot traffic and social interaction. Governments across the globe responded quickly, pouring hundreds of billions of dollars into small businesses. Several European nations opted to provide aid through direct government payments. Elsewhere, relief funding was predominantly distributed by banks, such as the US Paycheck Protection Program (PPP) and the UK Coronavirus Business Interruption Loan Scheme (CBILS).

These efforts have signaled an increased understanding of the small business sector and its distinct needs. But there is more work to be done. Small businesses are the backbone of the global economy and they form the fabric of our communities. Novel innovations in technology built on the availability of data and AI can address the underlying issues that have historically hampered lenders and ensure that creditworthy borrowers can access the capital they need to succeed. The resulting "Small Business Utopia" ecosystem will empower small businesses to make better financial decisions as tools like Alex's dashboard become a reality. With decisive actions by policymakers and regulators, the next phase of change can mean that fewer small businesses fail and more entrepreneurs can pursue their dreams.

NOTES

1. Artificial intelligence, or AI, is the ability of machines to work intelligently—to analyze data and make decisions based on their analysis. Machine learning is the process by which computers, after initial programming or the introduction of a certain algorithm, continue to learn based on newly introduced data sets. AI systems often use machine learning to suggest solutions to defined problems. For example, many small business lenders use AI in their underwriting processes, where they test and iterate on their algorithms to predict the risk and creditworthiness of potential small business borrowers. These lenders often rely on the data set of previous loans and their outcomes, and use machine learning to adjust the algorithm (e.g., reassigning weights to certain factors) as more data becomes available.
2. US Small Business Administration Office of Advocacy (2019), "Frequently Asked Questions," accessed June 1, 2020, at https://cdn.advocacy.sba.gov/wp-content/uploads/2019/09/24153946/Frequently-Asked-Questions-Small-Business-2019-1.pdf. The US Small Business Administration defines a small business as any independent business with fewer than 500 employees.
3. European Commission (2019), "2019 SBA Fact Sheet & Scoreboard," accessed June 1, 2020, at https://ec.europa.eu/docsroom/documents/38662/attachments/1/translations/en/renditions/native; "2019 SBA Fact Sheet: Spain," accessed June 1, 2020, at https://ec.europa.eu/docsroom/documents/38662/attachments/27/translations/en/renditions/native; "2019 SBA Fact Sheet: Denmark," accessed June 1, 2020, at https://ec.europa.eu/docsroom/documents/38662/attachments/8/translations/en/renditions/native; "2019 SBA Fact Sheet: United Kingdom," accessed June 1, 2020, at https://ec.europa.eu/docsroom/documents/38662/attachments/29/translations/en/renditions/native. In the European Union, "micro" firms are defined as those with 0 to 9 employees, "small" firms have 10 to 49 employees, and "medium" firms have 50 to 249 employees.
4. See Decker et al. (2014); Kerr et al. (2014); Acemoglu et al. (2013); Haltiwanger et al. (2013); Van Praag and Versloot (2007).
5. US Small Business Administration Office of Advocacy (2016).
6. Desjardins (2017).
7. Application programming interfaces, or APIs, is a general term used to describe the software protocols that allow third-party developers or firms to gain access to shared data and build tools and integrations on top of that data.
8. Authors' analysis of data from the US Bureau of Labor Statistics, "Table E. Quarterly net change by firm size class, seasonally adjusted."
9. Farrell and Wheat (2016).
10. See Mills (2019); Delgado and Mills (2020).
11. Federal Reserve (2020).
12. See Mills (2019).
13. US Securities and Exchange Commission (2020).
14. In 2015, Lending Club's sales and marketing costs totaled 40 percent of revenue. OnDeck's costs reached 24 percent of revenue. See Lending Club (2016); Securities and Exchange Commission (2015).
15. In 2019, JPMorgan Chase spent the most money on technology out of all US banks, setting aside USD 11.4 billion for its tech budget. Bank of America was second at USD 10 billion and Wells Fargo was third at USD 9 billion. From DeFrancesco (2019).

16. Numerous technology companies are already developing or offering these kinds of "Small Business Utopia" tools. For example, Bank of America released its Business Advantage 360 small business cash flow predictor in February 2019, and payroll provider Gusto has recently expanded into health-care and other human resource integrations.
17. QuickBooks (2020).
18. See Stein et al. (2010); Robb and Morelix (2016); Fairlie and Robb (2010).
19. See Barr (2015); Robb (2013).
20. European Commission (2015).
21. Open Banking Implementation Entity, "What is Open Banking?"
22. Financial Conduct Authority (2019).
23. Garfinkle (2004).
24. Goetzmann (2016).
25. Powell (1996).
26. Van De Mieroop (1986).
27. Garfinkle (2002).

REFERENCES

Acemoglu, D., U. Akcigit, H. Alp, N. Bloom, and W. Kerr (2013), "Innovation, Reallocation and Growth," *National Bureau of Economic Research* Working Paper No. 18993 (Revised November 2017).

Barr, M.S. (2015), "Minority and Women Entrepreneurs: Building Capital, Networks, and Skills," *Brookings Institution, The Hamilton Project*, accessed June 9, 2020 at https://www.brookings.edu/wp-content/uploads/2016/07/minority_women_entrepreneurs_building_skills_barr.pdf.

Decker, R., J. Haltiwanger, R. Jarmin, and J. Miranda (2014), "The Role of Entrepreneurship in U.S. Job Creation and Economic Dynamism," *Journal of Economic Perspectives*, 28 (3), 3–24.

DeFrancesco, D. (2019), "Here's a Breakdown of How Much U.S. Banks Are Spending on Technology," *Business Insider*, accessed 3 June 2020 at https://www.businessinsider.com/heres-a-breakdown-of-how-much-us-banks-are-spending-on-technology-2019-3?r=U.S.&IR=T.

Delgado, M. and K. Mills (2020), "The Supply Chain Economy: A New Industry Categorization for Understanding Innovation in Services," *Research Policy*, 49 (8), accessed February 25, 2021. https://www.sciencedirect.com/science/article/abs/pii/S0048733320301177.

Desjardins, J. (2017), "Here's Why Small Businesses Fail," *Business Insider*, accessed June 6, 2020 at https://www.businessinsider.com/why-small-businesses-fail-infographic-2017-8?r=U.S.&IR=T.

European Commission (2015), "Payment services (PSD 2)—Directive (EU) 2015/2366," accessed June 22, 2020 at https://ec.europa.eu/info/law/payment-services-psd-2-directive-eu-2015-2366_en/.

European Commission (2019a), "2019 SBA Fact Sheet & Scoreboard," accessed June 1, 2020 at https://ec.europa.eu/docsroom/documents/38662/attachments/1/translations/en/renditions/native.

European Commission (2019b), "2019 SBA Fact Sheet: Denmark," accessed June 1, 2020 at https://ec.europa.eu/docsroom/documents/38662/attachments/8/translations/en/renditions/native.

European Commission (2019c), "2019 SBA Fact Sheet: Spain," accessed June 1, 2020 at https://ec.europa.eu/docsroom/documents/38662/attachments/27/translations/en/renditions/native.

European Commission (2019d), "2019 SBA Fact Sheet: United Kingdom," accessed June 1, 2020 at https://ec.europa.eu/docsroom/documents/38662/attachments/29/translations/en/renditions/native.

Fairlie, R.W. and A. Robb (2010), "Disparities in Capital Access between Minority and Non-Minority-Owned Businesses: The Troubling Reality of Capital Limitations Faced by MBEs," *U.S. Department of Commerce, Minority Business Development Agency*, accessed June 9, 2020 at https://www.mbda.gov/sites/mbda.gov/files/migrated/files-attachments/DisparitiesinCapitalAccessReport.pdf.

Farrell, D. and C. Wheat (2016), "Cash Is King: Flows, Balances, and Buffer Days," *JPMorgan Chase Institute*, accessed June 3, 2020 at https://www.jpmorganchase.com/corporate/institute/document/jpmc-institute-small-business-report.pdf.

Federal Reserve (2020), "Small Business Credit Survey: Report on Employer Firms," accessed June 6, 2020 at https://www.fedsmallbusiness.org/survey/2020/report-on-employer-firms.

Financial Conduct Authority (2019), "Call for Input: Open Finance," accessed June 5, 2020 at https://www.fca.org.uk/publications/calls-input/call-input-open-finance.

Garfinkle, S.J. (2002), "Turam-ili and the Community of Merchants in the Ur III Period," *Journal of Cuneiform Studies*, 54, 29–48.

Garfinkle, S.J. (2004), "Shepherds, Merchants, and Credit: Some Observations on Lending Practices in Ur III Mesopotamia," *Journal of the Economic and Social History of the Orient*, 47 (1), 1–30.

Goetzmann, W. (2016), *Money Changes Everything: How Finance Made Civilization Possible*, Princeton, NJ: Princeton University Press.

Haltiwanger, J., R.S. Jarmin, and J. Miranda (2013), "Who Creates Jobs? Small Versus Large Versus Young," *The Review of Economics and Statistics*, 95 (2), 347–61.

Kerr, W.R., R. Nanda, and M. Rhodes-Kropf (2014), "Entrepreneurship as Experimentation," *Journal of Economic Perspectives*, 28 (3), 25–48, https://pubs.aeaweb.org/doi/pdfplus/10.1257/jep.28.3.25.

Lending Club (2016), "Lending Club Reports Fourth Quarter and Full Year 2015 Results and Announces $150 Million Share Buyback," *PRNewswire*, accessed June 16, 2020 at https://www.prnewswire.com/news-releases/lending-club-reports-fourth-quarter-and-full-year-2015-results-and-announces-150-million-share-buyback-300218747.html.

Mills, K.G. (2019), *Fintech, Small Business & the American Dream*, Cham, Switzerland: Palgrave Macmillan, an imprint of Springer Nature.

Open Banking Implementation Entity, "What is Open Banking?" accessed June 20, 2020 at https://www.openbanking.org.uk/customers/what-is-open-banking/.

Powell, M.A. (1996), "Money in Mesopotamia," *Journal of the Economic and Social History of the Orient*, 39 (3), 224–42.

QuickBooks (2020), "Use the Cash Flow Planner to Predict Future Income and Expenses," accessed July 17, 2020 at https://quickbooks.intuit.com/learn-support/en-us/payments-account/use-the-cash-flow-planner-to-predict-future-income-and-expenses/00/470980.

Robb, A. (2013), "Access to Capital among Young Firms, Minority-owned Firms, Women-owned Firms, and High-tech Firms," *SBA Office of Advocacy*, accessed June 9, 2020 at https://www.sba.gov/sites/default/files/files/rs403tot(2).pdf.

Robb, A. and A. Morelix (2016), "Startup Financing Trends by Race: How Access to Capital Impacts Profitability," *Kauffman Foundation*, accessed June 18, 2020 at https://www.kauffman.org/entrepreneurship/reports/startup-financing-trends-by-race-how-access-to-capital-impacts-profitability/.

Stein, P., T. Goland, and R. Schiff (2010), "Two Trillion and Counting: Assessing the Credit Gap for Micro, Small, and Medium-size Enterprises in the Developing World," *International Finance Corporation*, accessed 12, June 2020 at https://www.ifc.org/wps/wcm/connect/industry_ext_content/ifc_external_corporate_site/financial+institutions/resources/two+trillion+and+counting.

US Bureau of Labor Statistics, "Table E. Quarterly net change by firm size class, seasonally adjusted," Business Employment Dynamics, accessed June 16, 2020 at https://www.bls.gov/bdm/bdmfirmsize.htm.

US Securities and Exchange Commission (2015), "On Deck Capital Inc. Form 10-K," accessed June 16, 2020 at http://d1lge852tjjqow.cloudfront.net/CIK-0001420811/2e36150d-a925-4b94-ad17-1d111b90ba94.pdf.

US Securities and Exchange Commission (2020), "Square, Inc. Form 10-K," accessed June 7, 2020 at https://www.sec.gov/ix?doc=/Archives/edgar/data/1512673/000162828020002303/sq-20191231.htm.

US Small Business Administration Office of Advocacy (2016), "Survival Rates and Firm Age," accessed June 1, 2020 at https://www.sba.gov/sites/default/files/SurvivalRatesAndFirmAge_ADA_0.pdf.

US Small Business Administration Office of Advocacy (2019), "Frequently Asked Questions," accessed June 1, 2020 at https://cdn.advocacy.sba.gov/wp-content/uploads/2019/09/24153946/Frequently-Asked-Questions-Small-Business-2019-1.pdf.

Van De Mieroop, M. (1986), "Turam-ili: An Ur III Merchant," *Journal of Cuneiform Studies*, 38 (1), 1–80.

Van Praag, M. and P.H. Versloot (2007), "What Is the Value of Entrepreneurship? A Review of Recent Research," *Small Business Economics*, 29, 351–82.

2. GDPR compliant processing of big data in small business

Jan Trzaskowski

The processing of personal data has received significant attention in the wake of the adoption of the General Data Protection Regulation (GDPR).[1] Few European Union (EU) laws have attracted similar popular and global attention.

While the GDPR has directed much-needed attention to the importance of privacy—which includes the protection of personal data—it has at the same time instilled an unhealthy fear in organisations and individuals. As a result, some businesses fail to realise the full potential of big data.

The aim of this chapter is to distil the 99 articles and 173 recitals of the GDPR into six overarching principles—of more or less equal importance—that are easy to understand and integrate into the operation of small business.[2]

The six principles (*Legitimacy*, *Proportionality*, *Empowerment*, *Transparency*, *Accountability* and *Security*) overlap, and may, ultimately, be reduced to a mere matter of 'due diligence'.

For compliance purposes, the principles can roughly be grouped into three pairs: (1) lawful processing (*Legitimacy*, including *Proportionality*), (2) data subject's rights (*Empowerment*, including *Transparency*) and (3) data controller's obligations (*Accountability*, including *Security*).

2.1 INTRODUCTION

We assume that the reader is or represents a 'data controller', i.e. the natural or legal person who—alone or jointly—determines the purposes and means of the processing of personal data. Here, the term 'data controller' is used to denote the small business that processes big data.

We will not cover the use of (external) data processors or transfers of personal data to countries outside the European Union and the European Economic Area; in these situations, smaller businesses should team up with organisations that take responsibility for GDPR compliance.

In the context of using personal data for marketing purposes, data protection law also constitutes a cornerstone of modern consumer protection law.[3] In that vein, GDPR compliance can play a part in the business's commercial positioning, including corporate social responsibility.

2.1.1 Interpretation and Scope of Application

Despite the importance of privacy and the processing of personal data, there is still only a limited amount of case law from the Court of Justice of the European Union (CJEU) on this subject. Given the continuity of principles, case law concerning the 1995 Data Protection Directive remains relevant for the GDPR.

In the absence of case law, inspiration can be drawn from guidelines, recommendations and so on from the European Data Protection Board, whose interpretations are not authoritative (binding), but may serve as valuable guidelines.[4]

The GDPR applies to 'processing' of personal data, which is information relating to an identified or identifiable natural person (the 'data subject'). Thus, anonymisation is a powerful tool to keep activities outside the GDPR. Processing covers 'any operation' performed on personal data, including collection, use, disclosure and deletion.

The territorial scope of the GDPR includes (1) data controllers established in the European Union and (2) the processing of data concerning data subjects in the European Union with a view to offering products or monitoring behaviour within the Union, even when the data controller is not established within the Union.

2.1.2   Big Data

Big data is not easily defined, but the term usually denotes large sets of data with high variety and variability. The GDPR applies equally to big and small data (sets).

What is particularly relevant for big data is that the processing reveals patterns beyond the individual data points. Such analyses may reveal correlations and predictions that are not likely to be discovered through mere (human) logic.

The 'bigness' adds a layer of abstraction that provides traders, politicians, authorities and so on with more precise information regarding such things as certain aspects of individual preferences and expected behaviour. This predictiveness is of a probabilistic nature, which often is significantly better than no knowledge at all.

Old, supposedly worthless personal data may at some point in time become valuable, for instance when used together with additional information in big data analyses or with new technology such as face and emotion recognition.[5]

Alan F. Westin demonstrated interesting foresight by stating (in 1967) that 'the most significant fact for the subject of privacy is that once an organization purchases a giant computer, it inevitably begins to collect more information about its employees, clients, members, taxpayers, or other persons in the interest of the organization'.[6]

2.1.3   Small Business

As the aim of the GDPR is to protect the fundamental rights and freedoms of natural persons, the rules do not provide lower requirements for smaller businesses: Data subjects enjoy the same protection regardless of the size of the data controller. However, smaller businesses' processing often has less impact on the rights and freedoms of the data subject.

One exception is found in Article 30(5) concerning 'records of processing activities', discussed below under *Accountability*, where obligations do not apply to organisations employing fewer than 250 persons, unless (!) the processing (a) is likely to result in a risk to the rights and freedoms of data subjects, (b) the processing is not occasional or (c) the processing includes sensitive data.

With respect to drawing up codes of conduct (Article 40) and certification (Article 42), it is mentioned that 'the specific needs of micro, small and medium-sized enterprises' must be taken into account. It also follows from Recital 13 that 'the Union institutions and bodies, and Member States and their supervisory authorities, are encouraged to take account of the specific needs of micro, small and medium-sized enterprises in the application of this Regulation'. The legal implications of this account-taking and encouragement are neither clear nor likely to be significant.

For smaller businesses, it is in itself a benefit that there is one single framework for processing personal data in a market of roughly half a billion people.

2.2   SIX PRINCIPLES

2.2.1   ONE: Legitimacy

Discussions about privacy are far from new,[7] and privacy plays an important role in both democracy and individual autonomy, where a balance must be struck between solitude and companionship; both are necessary for developing democracy and individual agency.

Privacy may be explained and discussed from a socio-political, psychological, historical and even evolutionary perspective, and it is important to bear in mind that law cannot explain privacy as it (only) reflects the political choices made. This fact by no means makes the law superfluous or unimportant, especially when one takes into account the risk of fines up to EUR 20,000,000 or 4 per cent of the total worldwide annual turnover (whichever is higher).

The right to privacy, including the protection of personal data, is enshrined as a 'fundamental right' in EU law—i.e. law on a treaty level[8]—together with other democratic freedoms such as freedom of thought and expression. It follows from Recital 4 of the GDPR that 'the processing of personal data should be designed to serve mankind'.

Data protection law is a complex subject, not so much due to lack of clarity in the applicable provisions, but more because a complex weighing-up of interest is necessary. As it further follows from Recital 4:

> the right to the protection of personal data is not an absolute right; it must be considered in relation to its function in society and be balanced against other fundamental rights, in accordance with the principle of proportionality.[9]

Thus, privacy is a matter of balancing legitimate interests, including other fundamental rights—such as the freedom of expression and the right to information—that are also necessary in a democracy.

Personal data may be processed for legitimate purposes that are specified and explicit. The collected data may not be further processed in a manner that is incompatible with the purposes for which the data was collected (Article 5(1)(b)). Marketing is a legitimate purpose!

Legitimacy may be perceived as the overarching principle that includes the general requirement of fair and lawful processing (Article 5(1)(a)). When businesses use personal data that are protected as a fundamental right, they are the ones who should ensure that the processing is legitimate. The protection of privacy requires that derogations and limitations must apply only in so far as is strictly necessary[10] and exception must be narrowly construed.[11]

The businesses do not 'own' the personal data, nor are they otherwise entitled per se to process personal data.[12] They are, however, allowed—with limitations and requirements laid out in the GDPR—to infringe on the citizen's right to privacy.

One of the defining characteristics of big data analysis is that it relies on probabilities and as such is imprecise. The principle of 'accuracy' (Article 5(1)(d)) may be important, as it requires personal data to be 'accurate and, where necessary, kept up to date'. The data controller must take 'every reasonable step' to erase or rectify inaccurate personal data. In that vein, consideration must be given to the purposes for which the data are processed. The extent to which the use of probabilistic data is in conformity with the accuracy principle is not settled in case law

In addition to serving a legitimate purpose, personal data must be processed fairly and be based on a 'legitimate basis', as dealt with immediately below under *Proportionality*.

2.2.2   TWO: Proportionality

Due to the myriad guises that data processing may take, the principle of *Legitimacy* is coupled with a *Proportionality* principle that permeates the GDPR. The principle is visible in frequent references to what is 'necessary', 'adequate', 'appropriate', 'compatible', 'reasonable' and so on.[13]

The *Legitimacy* of processing depends on the nature, scope, context and purposes of processing as well as the risks of varying likelihood and severity for the rights and freedoms of natural persons. The rules aim to strike the appropriate balance between the protection of the data subject's rights and the legitimate interests of data controllers, third parties and the interest of the public. For example, the same video surveillance may be lawful for security reasons, but unlawful for marketing purposes.

According to the general principles laid out in Article 5, personal data should be limited to what is necessary ('data minimisation') and not kept longer than necessary ('storage limitation'). In this context, necessity is relative to 'the purposes for which the personal data are processed', as discussed above under *Legitimacy*.

The principle of 'purpose limitation', introduced above, provides that personal data may not be further processed 'in a manner that is incompatible with' the purposes for which they are collected,[14] which also reflects a *Proportionality* test.

The processing of personal data must be based on the data subject's consent or (!) some other legitimate basis laid down by law.[15] There must be a legitimate basis for each purpose for which personal data are processed.

Consent requires a 'freely given, specific, informed and unambiguous indication of the data subject's wishes' which 'signifies agreement to the processing'.[16] The request for consent must be 'presented in a manner which is clearly distinguishable from ... other matters' and consent may be withdrawn 'at any time' (Article 7).

Despite consent, the processing of personal data is still restricted by the principles for lawful processing (Article 5), including Legitimacy and *Proportionality*.

Personal data can be processed (without consent) if this is necessary for, inter alia, the performance of a contract or compliance with a legal obligation. Together, these legitimate bases justify processing that is necessary for delivering products and complying with tax and accounting obligations.

Processing is also lawful (without consent), if it passes the balancing test, which—to some extent—can be used to justify processing for marketing purposes. The balancing test (Article 6(1)(f)) allows the data controller to process personal data when the processing is necessary for (legitimate) purposes, unless these interests are overridden by the interests or fundamental rights and freedoms of the data subject.

The term 'necessity' has it own independent meaning in EU law and must be interpreted in a manner that reflects the objectives of data protection law.[17]

As discussed below under *Empowerment*, consent and the balancing test share the 'disadvantage' that the data subject may object to the processing, in the former case by means of withdrawing consent. The data subject cannot object if the processing is (genuinely) necessary for the performance of a contract.

Data-driven business models often rely on the delivery of an ancillary product such as a social media service or a loyalty programme as a means of justifying data processing. The ancillary product is usually offered free of charge and often entails infringements on privacy and agency that are not clearly understood by the data subject,[18] cf. the principle of *Transparency*.

The data controller may rely on contractual necessity in the context of the ancillary product, but it is not settled case law as to what extent the data controller can claim contractual necessity as a basis for using the same data for marketing purposes.[19] Nevertheless, it seems peculiar when Facebook insists that its extensive data processing for delivering its social media service is also 'necessary' for marketing purposes.[20]

Freedom of contract is an important legal concept, but if the data controller has unrestricted power to determine what is necessary, the data subject is deprived of his right to object, as discussed below under *Empowerment*.

One could claim that it is not a necessity that a product be offered free of charge or that a company maintain certain profit margins. Eventually, the courts must strike a balance between the freedom of contract and the protection of privacy, the latter being a fundamental right as discussed above.[21]

Unless the processing is genuinely necessary for the performance of a contract with the data subject or the impact on the data subject's privacy is limited, the safe bet is to obtain consent. When the processing is in fact necessary for the performance of a contract, however, consent is not the appropriate legitimate basis.[22]

When processing sensitive personal data,[23] consent must always be obtained. This includes, e.g. big data analyses intended to extract 'sensitive data' from 'normal data'.

Proportionality also plays a role in connection to the data controller's general obligations (Chapter IV) that are dealt with below under *Accountability*. When determining the responsibility of the data controller (Articles 24 and 25), account must be taken of 'the nature, scope, context and purposes of processing as well as the risks of varying likelihood and severity for the rights and freedoms of natural persons'. For implementing certain measures, additional account must also be taken of 'the state of the art' and 'the cost of implementation' (Articles 25 and 32).

As dealt with below under *Security*, technical and organisational measures must be 'appropriate' (Article 5(1)(f)), and in the context of rectification and erasure (Section 3, dealt with below under *Empowerment*), account must be taken of 'available technology and the cost of implementation' as well as 'disproportionate effort'.

As a general principle, it follows from Article 52(1) of the Charter of Fundamental Rights of the European Union that limitations to the freedoms set out in the Charter must—'subject to the principle of proportionality'—be necessary and must genuinely meet (a) objectives of general interest recognised by the Union or (b) the need to protect the rights and freedoms of others.

Borrowing freely from Article 5(1) of the Treaty on European Union, the proportionality principle would entail that the processing of personal data must not exceed what is necessary to achieve the (legitimate) objectives. In that vein, the availability of less intrusive means should also be considered.[24] This is e.g. clear in the GDPR when it requires 'appropriate safeguards', which may include pseudonymisation (separation between identity and the data being processed).

2.2.3   THREE: Empowerment

Human agency and the right to self-determination are central concepts in legal theory as well as in consumer protection law, where the regulatory framework is aimed at empowering the consumer to act in accordance with his or her preferences.[25]

Despite *Empowerment*, the data subject does not have absolute control over what data are being processed about them and by whom. Here, we primarily focus on the data subject's rights, which are closely coupled with *Transparency*, dealt with below.

It is a popular mistake to assume that the data subject 'owns' their personal data and that the data amounts to a currency, which can be used as payment. The Charter provides for 'respect of privacy' and 'protection of personal data', which does not amount to ownership (in a legal sense) where title can be transferred.[26]

Personal data as payment may, however, be a helpful metaphor in the context of weighing up of interest as discussed above under *Proportionality*. Often, attention is the real means of 'payment', which becomes even more valuable when coupled with personal data.[27]

Consent is one of the clearest examples of *Empowerment*.[28] In addition to being specific and informed, consent must be freely given and constitute an 'unambiguous indication of the data subject's wishes' that 'signifies agreement to the processing of personal data' (Article 4(1)(11)). Consent requires both *Transparency* and a clear affirmative action which precludes 'silence, pre-ticked boxes or inactivity' from constituting consent.[29]

'Freely given' in the context of consent requires a genuinely free choice, which is not the case if the data subject is 'unable to refuse or withdraw consent without detriment' (Recital 42). Similarly, it is provided in Article 7(4) that 'utmost account' must be taken of whether, inter alia, the performance of a contract is conditional on consent that goes beyond what is 'necessary for the performance of that contract'.

In addition to situations where consent is required, the data subject is empowered through rights concerning access, rectification, erasure and objection. The first two rights are enshrined in the Charter (Article 8(2)).

The data subject has the right to obtain confirmation as to whether or not personal data concerning him or her are being processed. If personal data about the data subject are being processed, the data subject has a right of access to the personal data as well as information about the purposes, categories, envisaged storage period and other information detailed in Article 15.

The right to obtain rectification of inaccurate personal data (without undue delay) is found in Article 16 and is well aligned with the accuracy principle, mentioned above under *Legitimacy*.

The so-called 'right to be forgotten' in Article 17 entails that the data subject can request the deletion of even accurate data (without undue delay). The right is, however, limited to certain grounds, including that the data are no longer necessary for the purpose or consent is withdrawn (and there is no other legal ground for the processing). The data controller may anonymise the data to honour the request.

As mentioned above under *Proportionality*, the data subject may withdraw his consent at any time (Article 7(3)).

When the balancing test provides the legitimate basis for processing, the data subject has the right to object to the processing (Article 21(1)). The data controller must comply, unless (!) he or she 'demonstrates compelling legitimate grounds for the processing which override the interests, rights and freedoms of the data subject'.

Where personal data are processed for direct marketing purposes, the data subject may object at any time to such marketing, which includes related profiling. The use of cookies and e-mail for marketing purposes is regulated in the ePrivacy Directive[30] (Articles 5 and 13, respectively) and consent is usually required. Cookies may be stored and accessed without consent 'where the technical storage or access is strictly necessary [to enable] the use of a specific service explicitly requested by the subscriber or user'.[31]

Other rights include a right to data portability (Article 20) and not being subject to automated individual decision-making, including profiling (Article 22).

It is not clear from case law to what extent Article 22 on 'automated individual decision-making, including profiling,' affects big data analyses for marketing purposes. In order to fall under Article 22, the decision must produce a legal effect concerning the data subject or significantly affect him or her in a similar way.[32] The user's right not to be subject to automated decisions does not apply in case of consent or contractual necessity.

2.2.4   FOUR: Transparency

Transparency is an important, general feature of EU law, and transparent processing of personal data is a prerequisite for *Accountability* towards authorities as well as *Empowerment* of the data subject.[33] The principle is closely linked to both *Legitimacy* and *Proportionality*.

Transparency is also an important part of consent that must be both specific and informed. In addition, the request for consent must be presented in a manner which is clearly distinguishable from other matters, such as contractual terms (Article 7(2)).

Articles 13 and 14 contain comprehensive information requirements to inform the data subject about the data controller's identity and contact details, purposes for and categories of personal data processed, and the data subject's rights, as well as other information 'necessary to ensure fair and transparent processing in respect of the data subject'.

When the data controller relies on the balancing test as legitimate basis, the data subject must be informed about the legitimate interests pursued.

In the context of 'automated decision-making, including profiling' (Article 22), *Transparency* entails providing 'meaningful information about the logic involved', as well as 'the significance and the envisaged consequences of such processing for the data subject'.

This obligation could serve as inspiration for ensuring overall transparency in the context of data-driven business models.[34]

The data subject's right to object to the processing of personal data for direct marketing purposes and/or based on the balancing test must explicitly be brought to attention at the time of the first communication with the data subject at the latest (Article 21(4)). Similarly, the data subject must—prior to giving consent—be informed about his right to withdraw consent (at any time)(Article 7(3)).

Information provided to the data subject must be in writing (including by electronic means) and must be provided in a 'concise, transparent, intelligible and easily accessible form, using clear and plain language' (Article 12(1)).

The GDPR does not require the data controller to post a privacy policy on their website, but it is often an efficient way of informing the data subject—for instance, by means of a hyperlink—and also of organising the record of processing activities discussed below under *Accountability*.

2.2.5   FIVE: Accountability

A significant part of the GDPR's substantive rules stems from the 1995 data protection directive[35] replaced by the GDPR. One significant change, however, is made clear in Article 5(2), which provides that the data controller is not only responsible for compliance, but must also be able to demonstrate compliance.

This principle is substantiated in Article 24, according to which, the data controller must implement 'appropriate technical and organisational measures' to (a) ensure and (b) be able to demonstrate that processing is performed in accordance with the GDPR.

These measures must be kept up to date and, as discussed above under *Proportionality*, must take into account the nature, scope, context and purposes of processing. The risks of varying likelihood and severity for the rights and freedoms of natural persons must also be considered. The implementation of these measures must—'when proportionate'—include 'appropriate data protection policies'.

In connection with consent, it is required that the data controller be 'able to demonstrate' that the data subject has consented to processing (Article 7(1)).

One of the most concrete measures of *Accountability* is found in the requirement of maintaining a 'record of processing activities' (Article 30). The record must be in writing, including in electronic form, and must contain (a) the name and contact details of the data controller, (b) the purposes (note that this is in plural) of the processing, (c) a description of the categories of data subjects and of the categories of personal data, (d) categories of recipients to whom the personal data may be disclosed and (e) possible transfers of personal data to third countries (i.e. outside the European Union and the European Economic Area). 'Where possible', the record must also include (f) the envisaged time limits for erasure of the different categories of data and (g) a general description of the technical and organisational security measures.[36]

The record of processing activities must be available to the supervisory authority (on request), but there is no obligation to publish it, for instance in the guise of a privacy policy, as suggested above under *Transparency*.

Prior to the processing of personal data that is 'likely to result in a high risk to the rights and freedoms of natural persons', the data processor must carry out a 'data protection impact assessment' (DPIA) of the envisaged processing (Article 35). This is, inter alia, required in the case of 'a systematic and extensive evaluation of personal aspects relating to natural persons which is based on automated processing, including profiling, and on which decisions are based that produce legal effects'.

If the assessment indicates that the processing would result in a high risk in the absence of measures taken by the data controller to mitigate the risk, the data controller must consult the supervisory authority prior to processing (Article 36).

In certain situations, the data controller is obliged to designate a 'data protection officer', including in cases where 'the core activities ... consist of processing operations which, by virtue of their nature, their scope and/or their purposes, require regular and systematic monitoring of data subjects on a large scale' (Article 37).

These requirements can also be viewed as examples of *Proportionality* as discussed above.

Compliance is further supported by the requirement of data protection by design and by default (Article 25).[37] The data controller must implement 'appropriate technical and organisational measures' to (1) ensure compliance, (2) integrate necessary safeguards and (3) ensure that only necessary personal data are processed by default (settings). This provision is new to the GDPR and corroborates all principles discussed in this chapter; just add 'by design' after each of the six principles.

2.2.6   SIX: Security

Securing personal data is of paramount importance in order to avoid the risk of e.g. accidental/unlawful destruction, loss, alteration, unauthorised disclosure of, or access to personal data transmitted, stored or otherwise processed.

In many cases, the real threat in the context of personal data is not the data controller's exploitation, but rather lack of security measures resulting in data breaches and subsequent exploitation by third parties, including e.g. employees and subcontractors. Thus, 'data minimisation' and 'storage limitation', discussed above under *Proportionality*, as well as anonymisation and pseudonymisation, may be perceived as means to comply with the *Security* principle.

Edward Snowden's surveillance revelations[38] have shown that personal data collected by businesses may also be accessed by governments—with or without the cooperation of the business.

The data controller must implement 'appropriate technical and organisational measures to ensure a level of security *appropriate to the risk*'.[39] Account must be taken of 'the state of the art, the costs of implementation and the nature, scope, context and purposes of processing as well as the risk of varying likelihood and severity for the rights and freedoms of natural persons', as discussed above under *Proportionality*.

Security measures may include (Article 32(1)):

- the pseudonymisation and encryption of personal data;
- the ability to ensure the ongoing confidentiality, integrity, availability and resilience of processing systems and services;
- the ability to restore the availability and access to personal data in a timely manner in the event of a physical or technical incident;
- a process for regularly testing, assessing and evaluating the effectiveness of technical and organisational measures for ensuring the security of the processing.

The data processor must take steps to ensure that any natural person acting under the authority of the data controller or the data processor, who has access to personal data, does not process them except on instructions from the data controller (Article 32(4)).

In case of a 'personal data breach', the data controller must (without undue delay) notify the supervisory authority (Article 33) and data subjects (Article 34). In line with the *Proportionality* principle, the latter must only be informed when the personal data breach is likely to result in 'a high risk to the rights and freedoms of natural persons'.[40]

2.3   CONCLUSIONS

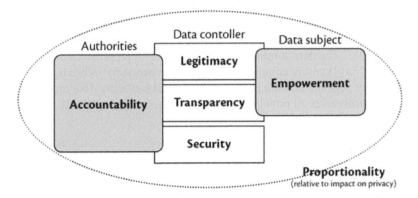

Figure 2.1   *The data controller must—subject to the principle of Proportionality—*
                 ensure Legitimacy, Transparency and Security to demonstrate Accountability
                 and ensure Empowerment of the data subject

By observing the following six principles, small businesses can ensure fair and lawful processing of big data in accordance with the GDPR:

- *Legitimacy*. Privacy is a fundamental democratic right, and in order to lawfully infringe on the data subjects' right to privacy, the data controller must pursue a legitimate purpose—also considering the legitimate interests of data subjects, third parties and the public—in a fair and careful manner.
- *Proportionality*. The protection of personal data—including the data controller's obligations and the need for consent—is relative to the legitimate purpose pursued as well as the impact on the data subject's right to privacy, including the nature, scope, context and purposes of processing.
- *Empowerment*. The data subject is—to a large extent—in control of what data concerning him or her can lawfully be processed, including by means of consent and the rights of access, rectification, erasure and objection.
- *Transparency*. To be empowered, the data subject must have information about the data controller and the processing, and be able to understand his or her rights and the implications of the processing. Note that information does not always entail transparency!

- *Accountability*. The data controller must be able to demonstrate compliance with the GDPR, including by maintaining a record of processing activities, carrying out data protection impact assessments and ensuring data protection by design and default.
- *Security*. When the data controller is entrusted with personal data, appropriate technical and organisational measures must be in place to safeguard against unauthorised or unlawful processing as well as accidental loss, destruction or damage.

The six principles can be illustrated as shown in Figure 2.1.

NOTES

1. Regulation (EU) 2016/679 of the European Parliament and of The Council of 27 April 2016 on the protection of natural persons with regard to the processing of personal data and on the free movement of such data, and repealing Directive 95/46/EC (General Data Protection Regulation). https://eur-lex.europa.eu/eli/reg/2016/679/oj.
2. Article 5 of the GDPR prescribes seven general principles that are incorporated into the text. These principles do not summarise the GDPR or carry equal weight. For this aim, the eight principles of the 1980 OECD Privacy Guidelines (updated in 2013) may be more helpful: 'collection limitation', 'data quality', 'purpose specification', 'use limitation', 'security safeguards', 'openness', 'individual participation' and 'accountability'. For more traditional introductions to the GDPR, see e.g. Jan Trzaskowski and Max Gersvang Sørensen, *GDPR Compliance* (Ex Tuto 2019) and Christopher Kuner, Lee A. Bygrave and Christopher Docksey (eds), *The EU General Data Protection Regulation (GDPR)—A Commentary* (Oxford University Press 2020).
3. See Jan Trzaskowski, *Your Privacy Is Important to Us!* (Ex Tuto 2021, forthcoming).
4. See e.g. opinion of Advocate General Szpunar in Case C-673/17, *Planet49*, ECLI:EU:C:2019:246, paragraph 81, referring to 'the non-binding but nevertheless enlightening work' of the Article 29 Working Party (now replaced by the European Data Protection Board).
5. Peter Lewinski, Jan Trzaskowski and Joasia Luzak, 'Face and Emotion Recognition on Commercial Property under EU Data Protection Law', *Psychology & Marketing*, 2016, Vol. 33, No. 9, pp. 729–46.
6. Alan F. Westin, *Privacy and Freedom* (Atheneum 1967), p. 161.
7. See e.g. Samuel D. Warren amd Louis D. Brandeis, 'The Right to Privacy', *Harvard Law Review*, Vol. 4, No. 5. (15 December 1890), pp. 193–220; Alan F. Westin, *Privacy and Freedom* (Atheneum 1967); and Sarah I. Igo, *The Known Citizen* (Harvard University Press 2018).
8. Articles 7 and 8 of the Charter of Fundamental Rights of the European Union. See also Article 6 of the Treaty on European Union and Article 8 of the European Convention on Human Rights.
9. As general principles for interpretation of EU law, account must be taken of both the wording and the objectives pursued, as well as the legislative context and the provisions of EU law as a whole. See, for instance, Case C-673/17, *Planet49*, ECLI:EU:C:2019:801, paragraph 48 with references.
10. Case C-473/12, *IPI*, paragraph 39 with references.
11. Case C-212/13, *Ryneš*, ECLI:EU:C:2014:2428, paragraph 29 with references.
12. See also Directive (EU) 2019/770 of 20 May 2019 on certain aspects concerning contracts for the supply of digital content and digital services, recital 24: 'personal data cannot be considered as a commodity'.
13. See also European Data Protection Supervisor, 'Guidelines on assessing the proportionality of measures that limit the fundamental rights to privacy and to the protection of personal data', 19 December 2019.
14. Article 5(1)(b). See also Article 6(4).
15. Charter of Fundamental Rights of the European Union, Article 8(2). The GDPR is such a 'law' that lays down legitimate bases for data processing.
16. According to the definition in Article 4(1)(11). See also European Data Protection Board, 'Guidelines 05/2020 on consent under Regulation 2016/679', Version 1.1, 4 May 2020.
17. Case C-524/06, *Huber*, ECLI:EU:C:2008:724, paragraph 52.

18. See Jan Trzaskowski, 'Data-driven business models', in Eleni Kosta and Ronald Leenes (eds), *Research Handbook on EU Data Protection Law* (Edward Elgar 2021, forthcoming).
19. See similarly European Data Protection Board, 'Guidelines 08/2020 on the targeting of social media users', paragraph 43: Consent and the balancing test are—'Generally speaking'—the two 'legal bases which could theoretically justify the processing that supports the targeting of social media users'.
20. See also European Data Protection Board, 'Guidelines 2/2019 on the processing of personal data under Article 6(1)(b) GDPR in the context of the provision of online services to data subjects', Version 2.0, 8 October 2019, paragraph 25: '[Contractual necessity] will not cover processing which is useful but not objectively necessary for performing the contractual service …, even if it is necessary for the controller's other business purposes.'
21. In this context, the Unfair Contract Terms Directive (Directive 93/13/EEC) must be observed, as it addresses 'standard contract terms' that—'contrary to the requirement of good faith'—cause a significant imbalance in the parties' rights and obligations arising under the contract, to the detriment of the consumer (Article 3). See also GDPR Recital 42.
22. European Data Protection Board, 'Guidelines 2/2019 on the processing of personal data under Article 6(1)(b) GDPR in the context of the provision of online services to data subjects', p. 7.
23. Article 9. These 'special categories of personal data' comprise (exhaustively) personal data revealing 'racial or ethnic origin, political opinions, religious or philosophical beliefs, or trade union membership, and the processing of genetic data, biometric data for the purpose of uniquely identifying a natural person, data concerning health or data concerning a natural person's sex life or sexual orientation'.
24. See also Joined Cases C-92/09 and C-93/09 C-92/09, *Volker und Markus Schecke and Eifert*, ECLI:EU:C:2010:662.
25. See e.g. Jan Trzaskowski, 'Lawful Distortion of Consumers' Economic Behaviour—Collateral Damage Under the Unfair Commercial Practices Directive', *European Business Law Review*, 2016, Issue 1, pp. 25–49.
26. Cf. Article 17(1) of the Charter (the right to property) stating that 'everyone has the right to own, use, dispose of and bequeath his or her lawfully acquired possessions'.
27. J. Trzaskowski, Savin, A., Lindskoug, P. and Lundqvist, B., *Introduction to EU Internet Law* (2nd edition, Ex Tuto 2018), chapter 3 (Personal data and privacy).
28. See also European Data Protection Board, 'Guidelines 05/2020 on consent under Regulation 2016/679', Version 1.1, 4 May 2020.
29. Recital 32. See also Case C-673/17, *Planet49*, ECLI:EU:C:2019:801.
30. *Directive* 2002/58/EC as amended by Directive 2009/136/EC. See also proposal for an ePrivacy *Regulation*, COM/2017/010 final, 2017/03 (COD) and Jan Trzaskowski, 'Unsolicited Commercial Communication in Social Media', *European Business Law Review*, 2014, Issue 3, pp. 389–406.
31. Recital 66 of Directive 2009/136/EC amending the ePrivacy Directive.
32. Article 29 Working Party, 'Guidelines on Automated individual decision-making and Profiling for the purposes of Regulation 2016/679', WP251 rev.01 (adopted 3 October 2017, revised 6 February 2018), p. 21.
33. See also Article 29 Working Party 'Guidelines on transparency under Regulation 2016/679', WP260 rev.01, 11 April 2018.
34. See similarly Case C-673/17, *Planet49*, ECLI:EU:C:2019:801, paragraph 74: 'clear and comprehensive information' (in the context of cookies) 'implies that a user is in a position to be able to determine easily the *consequences* of any consent' and that the information must be 'sufficiently detailed so as to enable the user to *comprehend* the functioning of the cookies employed' (emphasis added).
35. Directive 95/46/EC of the European Parliament and of the Council of 24 October 1995 on the protection of individuals with regard to the processing of personal data and on the free movement of such data.
36. Organisations with fewer than 250 employees need only maintain records of processing activities for the types of processing mentioned in items (a)–(c). See e.g. Working Party 29, 'Position paper

on the derogations from the obligation to maintain records of processing activities pursuant to Article 30(5) GDPR' (19 April 2018).

37. See also European Data Protection Board, 'Guidelines 4/2019 on Article 25 Data Protection by Design and by Default', Version 2.0, 20 October 2020.
38. See Glenn Greenwald, *No Place to Hide* (Metropolitan Books 2014), https://www.theguardian.com/us-news/edward-snowden and https://theintercept.com/ (accessed 25 February 2021).
39. Article 32, emphasis added. See similarly Article 5(1)(f).
40. See also Article 29 Working Party, 'Guidelines on Data Protection Impact Assessment (DPIA) and determining whether processing is "likely to result in a high risk" for the purposes of Regulation 2016/679', WP 248 rev.01, 4 October 2017.

3.   Big Data and SMEs

Vania Sena and Sena Ozdemir

3.1   INTRODUCTION

The concept of Big Data emerged around 20 years ago (Laney, 2001; McAfee et al., 2012) and although there was some confusion on what it meant and what was really behind the label (Laney, 2001; Gandomi and Haider, 2015), Big Data quickly became shorthand for large volumes of data – both structured and unstructured – generated by the routine activities of individuals and organisations (Manyika et al., 2011; Davenport et al., 2012). The words "Big Data" by themselves have become more and more popular (Davenport, 2014; Gandomi and Haider, 2015). The reasons why the concept of Big Data became quickly popular are well known: the cost of storing data fell substantially over time while low-cost data capture technologies (i.e. mobile phones, social media, apps) became very popular among consumers and small producers (McAfee et al., 2012; Malomo and Sena, 2017).

Twenty years afterwards and now with the words "Big Data" we tend to refer not only to large volumes of data but also to the set of methodologies that allow us to exploit the data themselves (Chen et al., 2012; Kiron et al., 2014; Stubbs, 2014). While Big Data refers to the characteristics of the data generated through different mechanisms (like sensors, websites), data analytics is commonly used to label methodologies that allow us to make sense of Big Data (Kiron et al., 2012; Stubbs, 2014). Analytics has been defined as "the discovery of meaningful patterns – new and novel information and knowledge – in data" (Delen and Ram, 2018). While for a long time they were the preserve of computer and data scientists, these have become part of the tools organisations used to analyse the large volumes of data they produce internally (Chen et al., 2012; McAfee and Brynjolfsson, 2012; Kubina et al., 2015; Mikalef et al., 2018).

As the techniques to exploit Big Data have become common, researchers have started to analyse where and how the exploitation of Big Data can help businesses to improve their performance (La Valle et al., 2011; Schroeck et al., 2012; Davenport, 2014). Big Data have been studied by several sub-fields of management: marketing, operations, human resources management and finance (Cao et al., 2015; Schoenherr and Speier-Pero, 2015; Dubey et al., 2016; Wedel and Kannan, 2016; Wang et al., 2018). Most studies conclude that exploitation of large volumes of data stored by organisations can improve their performance, suggesting a number of channels through which this may happen. Interestingly, they all share a common denominator, that is, the belief that Big Data can affect performance positively because of the changes in the way decisions are made in each functional area. In other words, thanks to the availability of data, managers can make evidence-based decisions across a number of functions and reduce coordination and transaction costs in different functional processes (Akter et al., 2016; Wamba et al., 2017; Mikalef et al., 2018). Importantly, the availability of Big Data can affect not only the operational or routine decisions but can also influence the quality of strategic decision making (MacAfee and Brynjolfsson, 2012; Provost and Fawcett, 2013; Wills, 2014).

Most of the research on Big Data and performance has focused on large firms by default as they have the financial capability to invest in Big Data technologies and infrastructures (La Valle et al., 2011; Schroeck et al., 2012; Davenport, 2014) to analyse them. How do Big Data enter in a discussion of small and medium enterprises (SMEs)? Research on Big Data and SMEs is not very large, and it lacks a framework providing insights into the implications of Big Data on SMEs' performance. Traditionally, the relationship between the different activities of a firm and performance has been analysed using the concept of Value Chain, whose underpinning assumption is that all the processes within an organisation need to be coordinated in such a way that value can be created. The implication is that the drivers of business performance can be identified by breaking down the business into strategically important activities that contribute to the creation of value. The concept of Value Chain can still be useful when trying to understand how Big Data can help businesses to generate value; therefore, several authors have developed the concept of Data Value Chain that describes how data within a business is exploited to improve performance. Data Value Chains are identified by a set of sequential steps (data generation, data collection, data analysis and exploitation) that simplify the mechanisms through which businesses can extract value from data and improve business performance. The key question in this field is the following: Is the impact of Big Data on SMEs different from what we observe among large firms? No study has proposed a Data Value Chain model for SMEs. Most of the existing models propose a basic model which does not consider important phases such as value creation and impact on performance. Still, this can be an important research area built upon the assumption that SMEs are different types of firms altogether and not smaller version of large firms.

Interestingly, research on SMEs has identified a number of key differences among large firms and SMEs. First, SMEs (in particular the very small ones) may have a short lifespan; we refer here to the "liability of newness" which can be rephrased as the "liability of smallness" and refers to the poor survival rate among very small and young firms. Second, empirical research suggests that among those that survive, growth may be slow or close to zero. In other words, SMEs may experience limited growth over their lifespan and, when this happens, it is similar to "growth spurts" which push SMEs towards a new steady state of close-to-zero growth. Third, the size of SMEs may imply that structures and routines within teams are not fully shaped: this may be particularly true for very small SMEs where a few employees may cover several roles and knowledge is mostly tacit and hardly codified. The result is that business performance may suffer because of the knowledge silos that this type of internal structure creates.

So far, no study has looked into how the exploitation of Big Data may address these issues. Against this background, the purpose of this chapter is multi-fold. First, we offer a short review of the main methodologies to capture, store and exploit Big Data and discuss the opportunities they offer to SMEs. Second, we discuss how Big Data can limit the liability of smallness: while there is not much theory around the topic, we try to identify the key channels through which Big Data can help reduce the liability of smallness. We start from an organisational perspective of the liability of smallness and focus on the fact that in small organisations teams cannot work together properly as routines and roles are not fixed in stone. The resulting coordination costs may make small firms difficult to manage but importantly may hinder the development of new products and eventually the survival chances. We therefore explore how the exploitation of Big Data can reduce the coordination costs and facilitate collaboration among teams which in turn may contribute to the development of new products. Finally, we discuss the relationship between business performance and investment in Big Data, both theoretically and empirically. Theoretically, we explore how Big Data help create a competitive advantage among SMEs; in particular we discuss how Big Data may help SMEs acquire specialised knowledge or intelligence which may translate into increases in performance. We also explore the type of capabilities SMEs need to exploit Big Data and how they can acquire them. Empirically, we try to quantify the impact that investments in Big Data infrastructure have on business performance. We are not planning to test specific channels of transmission but rather search for broad correlations which can give an idea of the magnitude of the impact of the investment on business performance. Eventually we hope the chapter may offer SMEs useful insights on how to exploit the Big Data they produce.

The structure of the chapter is as follows. Section 3.2 introduces the concept of Big Data. Section 3.3 presents a broad overview on the Data Value Chain and its different stages. Section 3.4 analyses how Big Data can help SMEs to overcome the "liability of smallness" starting from the literature on capabilities and Big Data. Section 3.5 presents the results of an empirical study on firms' growth. Section 3.6 focuses on the managerial implications of the research discussed in the previous sections while Section 3.7 offers some concluding remarks.

3.2   DEFINING BIG DATA

As mentioned in the introduction, the volume of data available to businesses has increased exponentially (Laney, 2001; Davenport, 2014). We refer here not only to data generated by businesses themselves but also to data from other sources like government, charities and individuals (Dobre and Xhafa, 2014). What drives this growth? Several researchers and consultancy firms have suggested that this growth rate has mirrored the growth in the number of smartphones available to consumers, the development of the internet of things (IOT) and the development of social media apps (Manyika et al., 2011; Schroek et al., 2012; Hashem et al., 2015). By themselves, social media generate large volumes of data as users act as "Datastreams" contributing to the creation of new data. In a sense, Big Data are simply the by-product of lives becoming increasingly digital. At the core, Big Data is shorthand for data that contain semi-structured, structured or unstructured data, although unstructured data are the most common type of Big Data (Davenport et al., 2012). The main feature of unstructured data is that they lack a data scheme and therefore extracting meaning from them can be more complicated (although not impossible) (Davenport et al., 2012). The relative abundance of unstructured data is mostly linked to the fact that apps, cookies, social activity, NoSQL databases and sensors tend to be the most common technologies for data capture (Hashem et al., 2015).

A number of authors have tried to define Big Data. Chen et al. (2014) define Big Data in terms of volume and the velocity with which it is generated from various sources. Laney (2001) builds upon this definition and characterises Big Data using 3Vs, that is, volume, velocity and variety. Here, volume refers to the size of data; velocity refers to the speed by which data are produced by the different sources, while variety refers to the different formats of data which are not only numeric but also audio, picture files, text and so on. Big Data have also been defined by seven criteria, commonly referred to as 7Vs: Volume, Velocity, Variety, Veracity, Value, Variability and Visualisation. Variability refers to the fact that the time dimension of Big Data may vary. Some data can be quarterly or daily or even hourly. Such variability can create data management challenges which are far more pronounced if trying to merge structured and unstructured data. Veracity refers to the quality of the data and the extent to which they are accurate description of the underlying phenomena. Sivarajah et al. (2017) also highlight that there are three challenges created by Big Data (implying that Big Data can be rather defined by the challenges they pose). The first challenge is related to the fact that some of it lacks a scheme. The second challenge refers to the processing power as volume and complexity create problems when transforming and analysing the data. The third challenge is the governance of data, which include issues around privacy, security, governance and ethics.

3.3   DATA VALUE CHAINS

The nature of Big Data implies that businesses have to change the way they use and exploit their data holdings as traditional tools and conventional techniques that are suitable for structured data could not be used any longer. Business analytics has been developed to examine large volumes of raw data to extract information that can be used by businesses to improve performance. The process that allows us to capture, store and analyse data is labelled as the Data Value Chain. It can be divided into several steps such as Data Generation, Data Acquisition, Data Storage, Data Analysis and finally Data Exposition (which allows us to translate data insights into improvements in performance).

3.3.1   Data Generation and Acquisition

Data can be generated by internal processes (such as data generated by Human Resources, for instance) or acquired by external devices such as sensors or websites. As mentioned above, data can be structured or unstructured and need to be cleaned and validated. Data can be acquired in a batch mode or in stream mode and transferred to a storage infrastructure (i.e. a Data lake or data centre) where it is pre-processed to ensure they are not noisy and redundant. Techniques for data pre-processing vary from standard cleaning to transformation and integration (where different data are merged).

3.3.2   Data Storage and Analysis

Systems that provide storage for Big Data have four components: a storage model (which can be either file-based, object-based or block-based), a data model (using distributed storage and NSQL databases), a storage infrastructure and a distributed processing infrastructure that allow us to share data and tasks over several interconnected nodes. Data analysis is about analysing pre-processed stored data in order to find correlations, identify patterns and create actionable insights. Analytics research spans from developing algorithms to designing methodologies to analyse different data from a number of sources.

Descriptive analytics mostly explores patterns and ultimately attempts to understand what has happened or what is happening right now. At the core, it is a cluster of techniques that can visualise data and is able to summarise data. Visualisation is facilitated by maps, graphs and 3D models which are laid over geographical open data. Descriptive analytics relies on historical data and is traditionally used by business intelligence teams (Kubina et al., 2015). There are various forms of descriptive analytics: these include the use of dashboard applications as another form of descriptive analytics that helps the firm to monitor multiple processes in its division at the same time. Diagnostic analytics explores why some phenomena happened and employs exploratory data analysis in order to identify patterns in the data that may give clues as to why some variables move in a certain direction (Delen and Ram, 2018).

Predictive analytics essentially is about estimating the future value of a variable (like efficiency or productivity) based on current and historical data (Liu, 2014). If the outcome variable is a categorical variable, we use classification models (like random forests etc.) to predict the future values of our dependent variable; if the variable is continuous, regression analysis is a possible model for prediction. If the predicted variable is time-dependent, then we use time-series forecasting. Predictive analytics uses supervised, unsupervised and semi-supervised machine learning techniques, and uses forecasting and statistical modelling techniques to determine future possibilities

Prescriptive analytics uses optimisation, simulation and heuristics-based techniques to identify potential courses of action (Delen and Ram, 2018). Many areas of business-like operations, finance and marketing heavily rely on the use of prescriptive analytics to determine their best possible strategy, which would ultimately maximise revenues. Based on the feedback firms get from models of predictive analytics, firms then make use of prescriptive analytics to optimise their business models. Research that uses analytics as the core methodology typically uses methods such as statistics, econometrics, machine learning and network science. However, management research has not fully recognised its potential (Shmueli and Koppius, 2011) as researchers have placed greater focus on causality and on using the data to confirm theoretical models rather than exploring the data and letting them drive the formulation of theories.

3.3.3   Data Exposition

This last step allows businesses to create value and improve performance on the basis of the data that have been collected and analysed. How can Big Data help businesses to improve their performance? Most of the spending on Big Data technologies is taking place in sectors such as banking and finance, oil and gas, healthcare, mobile telecommunications, insurance, e-commerce, media and investment services. Big Data are particularly helpful to the financial sector that uses Big Data for risk management and to improve customer services. Mobile telecommunications have been using Big Data to acquire a large customer base, study consumer behaviour and foster innovation. Within the media and e-commerce sectors, Big Data have helped firms to understand consumers' spending habits and to tailor their products to their preferences.

Overall, Big Data may offer firms two opportunities: (a) the ability to derive insights on its operations in a very granular way and (b) the possibility of changing strategic decision-making in real-time in order to respond quickly to changes of the environment. The implication is that there are two mechanisms through which data allow us to create value: (a) internal route, that is, data are used to improve internal processes and therefore value is created by reducing inefficiencies; (b) external route, that is, data are used to gather intelligence on customers and therefore value is created by increasing sales.

3.4 BIG DATA, CAPABILITIES AND SMEs

In this section we will start exploring how the relationship between performance and Big Data and its contribution to value creation have been conceptualised by management research. Management research describes Big Data as a critical asset in line with the resource-based view (RBV) which has been the predominant theoretical framework to analyse the relationship between Big Data and performance. While RBV has been the main theoretical framework behind a number of well-known contributions, the RBV has been criticised for two main reasons. First, it describes Big Data as the amount of data stored by businesses, but it pays limited attention to the skills and additional resources that are useful to create value from the data. Importantly, access to Big Data skills is more challenging for SMEs than for larger sized firms, which have greater intra-firm resources as well as financial resources to outsource such skills. Similarly, while RBV suggests that Big Data can create value, it does not make explicit suggestions on the organisational mechanisms that transform Big Data into value. In this sense, it can be argued that the effective utilisation of a resource such as Big Data requires the availability of organisational mechanisms that would enable its coordinated usage within diverse intra-firm cross-functional units. Second, RBV has limited value in explaining how the relationship between data resources and value creation may vary over time. This is quite important as RBV may seem to imply that increasing data resources may have a growing impact on value creation while in reality there may be a case of decreasing returns to scale in the relationship between the two variables. Finally, the RBV does not pay attention to the actual value of the knowledge businesses can extract from Big Data; while it is usually assumed that all knowledge from Big Data can be valuable, in reality this is not the case as its value varies with the level of "specificity" of the knowledge itself. For instance, insights from Big Data that are common knowledge may not be very useful as they may not confer a business a competitive advantage.

Some researchers have suggested that the dynamic capabilities approach may be more useful to understand the relationship between Big Data and performance. In these studies, the emphasis is on processes and strategies that firms put in place to exploit its Big Data holdings. So Big Data can create value as long as there are some capabilities (i.e. skills and strategies) to exploit the data. A number of capabilities have been identified as being relevant to explain how value can be created from Big Data. Mikalef et al. (2016) suggest that Big Data capabilities are learning, coordinating (as Big Data allow us to coordinate activities from different business functions) and reconfiguring capabilities, among others. Other Big Data capabilities are linked to the infrastructure (i.e. the capability of storing the data in such a way they can be exploited for the creation of value), the technical expertise (so that insights can be extracted from Big Data) and organisational learning. The real advantage of this shift of focus from RBV to dynamic capabilities is that we have a better understanding of what drives performance at firm level. In other words, storing data per se is not sufficient to generate value but additional resources need to be put in place to unlock its value. Of course, Big Data capabilities and skills at the individual level are also essential for effective implementation of Big Data.

While this is all well, one interesting question is whether Big Data can help SMEs to catch up with large firms. To be able to do, Big Data should be able to alleviate some of the issues around the "liability of smallness". Like any other company, SMEs need to invest in specific internal capabilities (such as data infrastructure, skills, absorptive capacity) before they can use data to create value. However, to what extent does investing in the development of new capabilities help SMEs reduce the "liability of smallness"? This is a question that has no answer at the moment as there is currently no research on Big Data and "liability of smallness". In the remainder of the section, we will try to address this issue in the hope that a potential research agenda in this area can be formulated.

3.4.1   Liability of Smallness

The concept of "liability of newness" has its origins among organisational theorists who noticed that young firms are more likely to fail than established companies (Aldrich & Auster, 1986; Stinchcombe, 1965). The researcher who first introduced the concept was Stinchcombe (1965) who noticed that mortality rates among young firms are larger than among older firms. We can adapt this concept to the case of SMEs which may suffer from poor survival rates or limited growth even when they are not young. In this case, we prefer to talk about the "liability of smallness" rather than the "liability of newness". There are five reasons why we observe the liability of smallness. First, new ventures are initially characterised by low levels of role formalisation and typically lack functional completeness at inception (Stinchcombe, 1965). Small firms are characterised by a fluid organisational structure as roles have to be defined while on the job and as a result, tasks are not carried out efficiently. Importantly, expectations about the roles may be different from their actual content and it can be difficult to ensure they are consistent among each other as there are no former role-holders. The result is that small firms may have to use resources to specify the roles and relationships of individuals in the organisation. In addition, coordination costs can be substantial and can only be reduced over time when roles are crystallised and formalised.

Second, adjustment of roles to personalities may be the norm among small organisations but these can be costly and may not be easy to manage. In a new company, processes are not very bureaucratic and characterised by hierarchical thinking. In other words, they have to reorganise continuously to be able to survive. Indeed, fluid structures and participative coordination should create an environment where information can be shared quickly but, at the same time, can create uncertainty about direction of travel and roles (Autio et al., 2000; Choi & Shepherd, 2005). Third, some organisations may not be part of social networks and therefore have limited legitimacy in the eyes of potential workers. In fact, it is rare that small firms hire established teams and therefore more often than not, they rely on hiring a workforce who may not be interested in working in new or small firms. Fourth, small organisations face challenges in finding customers as these firms often lack reputation in their markets. The importance of this issue for survival has been highlighted by Aldrich and Fiol (1994). They found that new firms have to build their legitimacy on two fronts: on the one hand, they have to build their reputation with external stakeholders and on the other hand, they have to work to establish legitimacy internally with their own teams. In practice, this implies that senior management firms in these businesses have to justify themselves continuously to build trust among employees and customers (Aldrich & Fiol, 1994). Finally, in small organisations where roles and positions are fluid, individuals may try to increase their sphere of influence by hoarding knowledge. In turn, this may create knowledge silos where teams or individuals are a repository of knowledge which they may not be willing to share with other teams even if this may have a negative impact on business performance.

3.4.2 Big Data and Liability of Smallness

How do Big Data enter into a discussion on the sources of the "liability of smallness"? Generally speaking, the liability of smallness is considered to be the result of the internal workings of the SMEs and therefore it is useful to start from how Big Data can influence the behaviour of teams within an SME. At the moment, there is no framework that allows us to explain how Big Data can have an impact on the way different teams interact among each other in the context of SMEs; still, it is important to develop a framework that allows us to interpret how the availability of Big Data can change the relationship among teams in SMEs. A useful starting point is a discussion of how teams interact in small companies. This may lead to an understanding of the conditions that lead to the emergence of the liability of smallness usually observed empirically. Sometimes, teams do not work together well because their activities are not well coordinated and integrated into each other. Additionally, there may be no clarity about the behaviour of other teams, and this may lead to asymmetric information, agency issues and eventually misalignment of objectives among teams.

As a result, a number of mechanisms have been suggested to address such a misalignment ranging from the introduction of performance-contingent incentive contracts to the development of direct monitoring mechanisms. Still, while these solutions would work very well in theory, the reality of the SMEs makes their implementation complicated. First of all, the modern structure of SMEs (i.e. a flat structure) implies there may be too many principals whose activities need to be coordinated. As a result, incentive contracts for the agents can be difficult to design given the number of objectives the different teams may have. As for monitoring, with such a structure, one principal may have too many teams to monitor. In these cases, agency problems will be exacerbated and the expectation is that these will be particularly pronounced in the case of young SMEs.

This situation implies that coordinating devices are needed so that the actions of the different teams are aligned to overarching survival goals. More importantly, their performance has to be tied to the capability of the managing team to develop credible strategy goals and to monitor the outcome of the teams' actions. Still, SMEs vary in their ability to set up targets that have clear and achievable goals that can be measured. In a sense, the belief that small companies have to be free of routines that are typically associated with large firms is so strong that no manager tends to believe that the relationship among teams has to be managed in ways that are technocratic but still compatible with entrepreneurial objectives. In other words, SMEs could invest in the development of a number of "technocratic" competencies that would allow the management of the teams as well as to insulate them from the risks of the liability of smallness. This way, the senior management team can alleviate simultaneously the agency issues discussed above and the problems created by the liability of smallness. Importantly, the development of technocratic competencies would be a building block of a new internal setting with checks and balances which would allow the internal processes and their outcomes to be monitored. The expectation would be then that the SMEs will become more efficient and grow faster so to reduce the gap with large companies.

This is the area where Big Data can trigger a major step-change. Generally, Big Data and associated methodologies tend to be complementary to existing practices but, in reality, they can trigger major changes in the way companies are run. At the moment, there is agreement they can improve procedures and improve services and procedures, but they can change the way decisions are made and implemented within a company. In some sense, these arguments are not very different from pointing out that new technologies can improve the design and implementation of new products, change the internal organisation of a company and enhance internal accountability. Big Data can be considered as a coordination device that enhances the collection and the exploitation of information that can support coordinated decision making.

In the previous section, we have introduced the concept of capabilities and their relationship with the performance of SMEs. Like large companies that need to develop specific capabilities to exploit their Big Data, SMEs – often constrained by resources and capabilities at the organisational (e.g. Big Data infrastructure) and individual (e.g. Big Data skills) levels – need to develop some specific capabilities to be able to exploit data to support their decision making. At the individual level, the first capability refers to the ability to collect new forms of data (such as unstructured data) and link them to the administrative data (e.g. reports on sales) that are typically produced by businesses. The second capability refers to the ability of analysing both structured and unstructured data and to extract insights in real time. At the organisational level, the first capability refers to the ability to develop and maintain data infrastructures and governance policies for Big Data. The second important organisational capability refers to the company's ability to redesign decision making in such a way that insights from data can be fruitfully shared among teams and used to improve the quality of the decisions. Facilitating data sharing is a prerequisite for a redesign of the decision-making processes. As mentioned above, teams tend to be repositories of knowledge which they may hoard to retain their influence and may decide to share it with other teams only if it can perceive it as beneficial (Huber, 1991; Kogut & Zander, 1996; Tsai, 2001).

To understand how Big Data can support the decision-making process at SME level, we try to identify the different stages of the process. These include a first stage where priorities are decided and where coordination among priorities is needed. After that, priorities need to be translated into actions and targets. Finally, interventions are followed by the evaluation stage where outcomes are evaluated against the initial targets. Big Data can help in every stage of the process. Generally speaking, Big Data generates insights that can underpin the first stage. Indeed, granular information on markets and customers may suggest the need for a specific set of products and help to activate the supply chain. Literature has highlighted the importance of social media in this area as social networks (created by social media) can help identify emerging needs. Analytics can be useful as well: use of Natural Language Processing (NLP) can help SMEs to make use of unstructured data which can enhance the informational content of the administrative data. Budgeting is typically considered a sensitive area in young firms. Evidence in this area suggests that Big Data can increase the efficiency of budgeting as they allow us to develop an outcome-based budget that would allow resources to be redeployed where they are needed in the future and not where they have been needed in the past. Importantly, the budgetary process can by itself produce data that can help to detect patterns and be used to develop better interventions at a later stage. Big Data can help streamline the number of targets associated with the design of the teams' activities; they can support the development of early-warning systems that can inform the decision-making process while sentiment analysis or real-time decision support systems can influence implementation. Some of the information sources can be supplemented by Big Data stored by the SMEs which would allow a more granular view of what happens in each team and among teams. This issue touches upon knowledge sharing and the mechanisms that facilitate such processes. Importantly, simple exposure to knowledge is not sufficient to generate knowledge acquisition (Van Wijk et al., 2008). Knowledge acquisition is supported by "trust" and Granovetter (1985) suggested that teams value a trusted source over a reliable one. Indeed, a substantial body of research has shown that with high levels of trust, parties are more willing to engage in knowledge exchange (Coleman, 1990; Nahapiet & Ghoshal, 1998; Tsai & Ghoshal, 1998; Levin & Cross, 2004, Moran, 2005; Peters & Karren, 2009), irrespective of the type and content of knowledge exchanged (García et al., 2008).

We argue that the use of Big Data can help create this trust. Indeed, Big Data can help develop a common language around processes and targets and facilitate the communication among roles and functions. This can be particularly relevant in the case of complex knowledge, which is difficult to share and hence to acquire (Kogut & Zander, 1992; Szulanski, 1996). Use of Big Data technologies can reduce the complexity of knowledge and can facilitate its sharing among teams even in situations where face-to-face interactions are not allowed. Communicating in a shared language may enhance knowledge acquisition (Tsai, 2001) and reduces misunderstandings (Szulanski, 1996; Nahapiet & Ghoshal, 1998).

Finally, Big Data can play a major role in the evaluation phase. Evaluation plays a key role when planning marketing campaigns whose effectiveness needs to be assessed in a continuous way. Real-time data can be used to assess quickly the impact of the interventions and whether corrective actions are needed. Big Data allow real-time decisions while being transparent. All this opens up the possibility of an evaluation cycle where evaluation is carried out continuously.

3.4.3 Liability of Smallness and Absorptive Capacity: Big Data and Specialised Knowledge

How can SMEs build up their capabilities to store and analyse Big Data? As SMEs may be financially constrained, they may rely on the external providers. Empirical studies suggest that as businesses grow, they start to engage in more in-house exploration activities (Rothaermel & Deeds, 2004). Similarly, SMEs striving to grow are more likely to outsource these services than large firms (Barge-Gil, 2010; Zeng et al., 2010). However, from a transaction cost economics (TCE) perspective, this can be a problematic option particularly in uncertain environments where the quality of the transaction cannot be ascertained (Rindfleisch & Heide, 1997). In such a scenario, small firms can be easily exposed to the opportunistic behaviour of the external providers as SMEs may not have the knowledge and skills to assess the quality of the services received (Anderson, 1985; Nooteboom, 1993; Rindfleisch and Heide 1997; Heide 2003). As a result, it is usually argued that SMEs should try to internalise their data infrastructure where possible (Williamson 1985, 1989).

In this section, we argue that this is not always the best option. In this context, it is essential to think about the value of storing and analysing Big Data internally; in turn, this depends on a variety of factors such as the *value* of the knowledge extracted from Big Data as well as the availability of skills that enable effective exploitation of Big Data (Sena and Ozdemir, 2020). The value of Big Data needs to be considered at the broader level by considering how much value a firm may generate by exploiting Big Data as well as the market orientation[1] of the firm. We refer here to the proactive and responsive market orientation concepts (Narver et al., 2004) which consider the different types of market intelligence that are needed by market-oriented firms. While responsive market orientation is about new knowledge that is related to previous experiences of the firm and customers (e.g. identification of existing needs), proactive market orientation is about the search for radically new information and knowledge (e.g. exploration of latent needs) (Narver et al., 2004; Tsai et al. 2008). This implies that while responsive market-oriented firms engage in adaptive (i.e. exploitative) learning, proactive market-oriented firms engage in explorative learning (Jaworski et al. 2000; Narver et al. 2004; Tsai et al. 2008; Ozdemir et al., 2017).

Proactive market orientation requires an exploratory search for radically new information that is highly specific within an industry. We expect that the acquisition of such information will increase the opportunity costs for outsourcing SMEs since the process of knowledge acquisition will require specific knowledge (i.e. less likely to be held by the outsourcing firm) to effectively filter (or detect) the useful information out of a large amount of outsourced data. In addition, since outsourcing firms will be less likely to own the knowledge base to assess the quality of the new information, the cognitive costs of verifying the performance of the information provider are likely to be high. These potential risks are vital when acquiring new information since they are costly to recover in the latter stages of the information processing. Similarly, there will potentially be a limited number of SMEs with dedicated marketing analytics functions and capabilities to unlearn existing knowledge to think "out of the box" to be able to provide valuable insights on radically new information attained through Big Data.

Responsive market orientation, on the other hand, necessitates exploitative search that enables the acquisition of knowledge which may not be too specific. Outsourcing analytical services with lower degrees of novelty will be more cost efficient than trying to acquire it internally. Since small firms will be more familiar with the new information, the transaction costs will also be lower. This view is further supported by the RBV perspective which states that previous knowledge can help businesses to acquire, assimilate and transform externally generated knowledge which is critical for their operations (Cohen & Levinthal, 1990; Zahra & George, 2002). Since non-specific knowledge is commonly available and easier to imitate and substitute, firms should spend less time and effort to acquire such information and rather focus on acquiring inimitable and radically new information and knowledge. Similarly, Choudhury and Sampler (1997) link one of the key concepts of TCE, that is, asset specificity, with the concept of organisational knowledge specificity: knowledge is specific if it is owned by a single firm or by a limited number of firms. For instance, knowledge on radically new technologies would only be owned by a small number of firms within an industry. Choudhury and Sampler (1997: 37) extended the TCE theory by asserting that "in deciding between outsourcing the task of monitoring an environmental information source and retaining the responsibility internally, an organization will choose the option that minimizes the sum of the surveillance costs, the coordination costs, the behavioural contractual costs, and the cognitive transaction costs". Following this line of thought. SMEs with scarce resources and limited growth opportunities will attempt to outsource the analytical function (in charge of the exploitation and analysis of Big Data) even if it is costly to do so and makes them vulnerable to opportunistic behaviour. This effect will be more pronounced if the knowledge is time specific (i.e. the extent to which knowledge loses value unless used immediately after it becomes available) and the environment is turbulent (i.e. there is high environmental uncertainty and rapid market changes) (Boyd & Fulk, 1996).

3.5   MODELLING GROWTH

In this section, we try to model SMEs' growth and show how access to resources which can help Big Data exploitation can accelerate growth among SMEs. We have previously discussed the concept of Big Data capabilities and highlighted the fact that these can be of several types. However, most capabilities that are useful to exploit Big Data tend to be embodied in human capital, and therefore having to access suitably skilled human capital is a precondition for the development of the internal capabilities necessary to exploit Big Data. For these reasons, in this section, we will focus on access to skilled human capital as a proxy for the access to Big Data capabilities.

Typically, business growth is modelled through the Gibrat's law, a favourite topic among applied industrial economists for a long time. First proposed by Gibrat in 1931, it states that a firm's growth rate is independent of its size and is based on the idea that firms (within an industry) draw growth rates from a distribution that is the same for all firms regardless of their previous size. Several studies have then tested the empirical validity of the Gibrat's law (see Sutton, 1997 for a survey) in an attempt to understand when the Gibrat's law applies and what drives the firms' growth in an industry. The empirical literature on the determinants of firms' growth has a long and illustrious history. Gibrat (1931) was the first to present an empirical model of the dynamics of the firms' size and its growth, which has then become known as the Gibrat's law. According to the Gibrat's law, firms face the same probability distribution of growth rates, with each firm's observed growth determined by a random sampling from that distribution. The main implication from the Gibrat's law is that a firm's growth rate is independent of its size.

A rich body of empirical evidence has been produced that has tested the empirical validity of the Gibrat's law, spanning numerous countries and time periods although mostly focusing on manufacturing. The results of tests based on this kind of model have been mixed. Earlier studies (Hart, 1962) which typically included large manufacturing firms provided compelling evidence supporting the Gibrat's law. Some studies have included small firms in the sample and found a negative relationship between firm growth and firm size, so rejecting the Gibrat's law (Evans, 1987; Hall, 1987; Dunne et al., 1989; Dunne & Hughes, 1994; Mata, 1994; Audretsch, 1995; Hart & Oulton, 1996; Audretsch et al., 1999; Almus & Nerlinger, 2000; Becchetti & Trovato, 2002; Goddard et al., 2002). In an attempt to reconcile the contrasting evidence, some studies have changed the approach to the estimation of the Gibrat's law and therefore have started to test whether the firms' growth follows a random walk. Goddard et al. (2002), Del Monte and Papagni (2003), Urga et al. (2003); Oliveira and Fortunato (2003) and Chen and Lu (2003) carried out panel unit root tests with contradictory results.[2] As Sutton (1997) pointed out, the reason for these contradictory results lies in systematic differences in the samples selected. The Gibrat's law holds when only large firms or firms that have exhausted scale economies are included in the sample. As explained by Audretsch et al.

(2004), the firms' growth rates will be independent of their size as long as their likelihood of survival is independent of their size. However, when the likelihood of survival is positively related to firm size, the observed growth rates are no longer normally distributed for each firm size or firm-size class. If size is a requirement for survival, or at least positively influences the likelihood of survival, the consequences of not growing or even experiencing negative growth has a different impact across size classes. The propensity for small firms experiencing low (or negative) growth to exit compared with low-growth large firms biases the samples of surviving small firms towards higher growth enterprises. By contrast, a sample of surviving large firms consists of both low- and high-growth enterprises; thus, when the consequences of not obtaining a high growth opportunity differ systematically between large and small firms in terms of the likelihood of survival, the resulting distributions of actual observed growth patterns across different firm size classes will also vary systematically between large and small firms. Therefore, the Gibrat's law will tend to hold for larger firms but not for smaller enterprises and therefore growth rates will be negatively related to firm size for samples including a full spectrum of large and small firms.

One remarkable fact about the Gibrat's law is its lack of micro-economic foundations. Some authors have tried to add economics to this model, particularly by exploring why the Gibrat's law does not hold. These models point to a number of socio-economic variables influencing firm performance and, moreover, they provide a theoretical explanation for the relationship between size and growth. Jovanovic (1982) developed a theoretical model that could account for possible departures from the Gibrat's law. The model assumes that firms are heterogeneous and that they learn about their true efficiency as they operate in an industry. Failure and growth rates decrease with size and age. Cabral (1995) suggests that the negative relationship between the growth and size can be explained by the fact that entering in a new market requires a sunk investment in capacity. Since small entrants are more likely to exit than large entrants, it is optimal for small entrants to invest gradually which can explain why they tend to grow faster than large entrants. Cooley and Quadrini (2001) develop a theoretical model that introduces financial market frictions and persistent shocks into a learning framework of firm dynamics and produces results consistent with the empirical regularities of the negative effects of initial firm size and of firm age on firm growth. Other empirical evidence also includes the roles of share of foreign participation (Fotopoulos & Louri, 2002) and financial structure (Becchetti & Trovato, 2002; Fotopoulos & Louri, 2002).

Virtually, no empirical paper has analysed how use of Big Data can affect the relationship between a firm's growth and its size. This is not for lack of theories: there are many channels through which Big Data exploitation can condition the growth-size relationship. Exploitation of Big Data may matter to small firms because it facilitates fast growth and allows them to compete with the large firms, so creating the conditions for the rejection of the Gibrat's law. However, the exploitation of Big Data assumes the firms may have access to a set of capabilities which can help them exploit Big Data. Empirically, proxies for capabilities cannot be identified easily and this explains why empirical work in this field is virtually non-existent.

Another issue to consider is the type of industries that may benefit from the exploitation of Big Data.

Most empirical analysis on the Gibrat's law is carried out on manufacturing[3] and very little attention is given to services. The argument underlying the preference for manufacturing is that services are serving only localised markets; therefore, service firms tend to operate in markets where economies of scale can be exploited at relatively small levels of output and therefore these firms do not have to grow to overcome any problem related to surviving. On the contrary, services are a diverse group of industries. Indeed, some service sectors are dominated by large firms organised in networks (e.g. retail, banking, hospitality) with small firms competing with large firms by specialising in niche markets. Investments to store and eventually exploit Big Data are quite common in services so creating the conditions for the rejection of the Gibrat's law. Equally, single-unit firms (i.e. firms that are not organised in networks), which may operate niche markets, may still experience episodes of high growth if they invest in technologies for the exploitation of Big Data. However, as we have pointed out above, investment in Big Data technologies has to be accompanied by the development of internal capabilities for the exploitation of Big Data and ultimately this requires access to a skilled workforce. Therefore, one implication is that the relationship between growth and size in services may be mediated by the access to a skilled workforce and this needs to be taken into account when testing for the Gibrat's law.

The empirical framework we use for our analysis is rather straightforward. As mentioned above, according to the Gibrat's law, firms face the same probability distribution of growth rates, with each firm's observed growth determined by a random sampling from that distribution. If the law holds, we would expect no differences in the mean and variance of growth rates across size classes of firm. If this is not the case, firm sizes regress towards or away from their mean in the Galtonian sense. The company growth path can be explosive, that is, firms tend to grow faster as they get larger (large firms grow faster than small ones). Alternatively, small firms tend to grow faster than larger firms (mean-reverting argument), which corresponds to the tendency for a variable to return to the mean size. It is often the case that the variance of the growth rates decreases as the size of firm increases. In practice, we should expect the size distribution of firms to be approximately lognormal (Hart & Oulton, 1996). The fact that the firm size distribution is approximately lognormal is consistent with the hypothesis that a firm's size is heavily influenced by multiplicative stochastic shocks. Chesher (1979) has shown that the law will not hold if the error terms are serially correlated. Serial correlation in proportionate growth rates can be ascribed to persistence of chance factors which make a company grow abnormally fast or abnormally slowly. In this case, size encourages (or discourages) growth, and when there is serial correlation in growth rates, that growth encourages (or discourages) growth. Thus, departures from the Gibrat's law arise: if sizes regress towards or away from the mean size, if above average growth in one period persists into the next, or if a period of above average growth is followed by one of below average growth.

To test whether the law continues to hold for firms that have access to the skilled workforce which may help build up Big Data capabilities, we interact the size of the firm in the previous period with the previous period's proxy of such access. In this case, small firms grow faster than large ones and this effect is particularly true for small firms that have access to the skilled workforce. However, as the coefficient associated with an interaction term varies, whether the null hypothesis is rejected or not depends on the firm-specific size of the investment. In terms of estimation, the presence of firm-specific effects in the growth model leads to a correlation between a regressor and the error term, hence OLS is a biased and inconsistent estimator. Therefore, we use an estimator (such as the sys-GMM estimator) that allows us to control simultaneously for the presence of firm-level heterogeneity and autocorrelation in the residuals.

Table 3.1   Sys-GMM estimates for the whole sample

Independent variables		
(log)employment (lagged one period)	−0.102	−0.208
	(−4.29)	(−3.78)
(log) access to Big Data capabilities (lagged one period)	0.1065	0.098
	(3.11)	(2.17)
(log)employment (lagged one period)* (log) access to Big Data capabilities (lagged one period)	−0.011	−0.012
	(−2.59)	(−3.01)
Age	-	−0.291
		(−3.81)
# local units	0.0024	0.0020
	(2.84)	(1.98)
Hansen test (*p*-value)	0.192	0.238
Ar(1) (*p*-value)	0.000	0.000
Ar(2) (*p*-value)	0.411	0.561

Note: Time, sectoral and local authorities' dummies are included in all specifications. T-ratios computed using standard errors clustered around industry and local authority.
Source: ONS.

Our empirical analysis is conducted on a sample of British plants, sourced from the British Annual Business Inquiry (ABI). The dataset covers both the production (including manufacturing) and the non-production sector (services). However, the time-series dimension varies across the two: while for the production sector it is possible to have information available up to 1980 (and the early 1970s for some industries), the data for the services sector are available only after 1997. The size of the plant is measured by its total number of employees while its growth is computed as the annual growth of the number of employees. Information on the plants' age (age) has been sourced from the business registry (BSD). The information on the number of local units pertaining to the same firm allows us to compute the number of plants (or local units) owned by each firm; equally, firms that have only one single unit are considered to be single-unit firms. As for the proxies of Big Data capabilities, we decide to focus on the access to such capabilities and more precisely the density of graduate workforce in the local authorities.

Table 3.1 reports the estimates of the Gibrat's law for all service firms in our sample. Standard errors are clustered around industry and local authority. In terms of our parameters of interest, the results suggest that the key parameter is always smaller than one and significant for the sample that includes all the firms and for any value of the density of human capital. Indeed, we test whether it is different from one for different levels of density of human capital (namely, at the minimum, the mean and its maximum value) and we find that for each value, the coefficient is significantly different from one. In other words, in our sample small firms grow faster than large firms and this explains why the value of the coefficient attached to the lagged size of the firm is negative and significant. The classical explanation for the fact that small firms seem to grow faster is that there is a minimum efficient scale of firm and, until this size is reached, the firm experiences decreasing average costs and can therefore enjoy rapid growth. After this point, its average cost curve flattens out and therefore firms experience constant average and marginal costs. However, this also suggests that services in our sample

Table 3.2   *Sys-GMM estimates for the single and multi-unit firms*

Independent variables	Single-unit firms	Single-unit firms	Multi-unit firms	Multi-unit firms
(log)employment (lagged one period)	−0.42 (−5.06)	−0.49 (−5.12)	−0.25 (−1.19)	−0.29 (−0.16)
(log) Access to Big Data capabilities (lagged one period)	0.07 (1.77)	0.09 (1.87)	0.08 (0.42)	0.10 (0.52)
(log)employment (lagged one period)* (log) Access to Big Data capabilities (lagged one period)	−0.02 (−2.69)	−0.02 (−1.89)	−0.07 (−0.78)	−0.05 (−0.68)
Age		−0.29 (−3.91)		−0.32 (−2.89)
# local units			0.002 (3.17)	
Hansen test (*p*-value)	0.136	0.167	0.234	0.240
Ar(1) (*p*-value)	0.000	0.000	0.000	0.000
Ar(2) (*p*-value)	0.569	0.567	0.446	0.509

Note: See Table 3.1.

behave like manufacturing firms in that small services firms need to grow faster to be able to compete effectively with the large firms (small firms' selection bias). This is different from what Audretsch et al. (2004) find for the Dutch hospitality sector (sector dominated by small firms) but it is consistent with the findings of Hart and Oulton (1996) who found a negative relationship between size and growth for the British "distribution and hotel" sector and with what Petrunia (2008) finds for the Canadian retail trade. Our results show first that the relationship between growth and size is negative in British services and second that this negative relationship is driven by the fact that smaller firms are growing faster as long as they have access to a skilled workforce. Also, the Gibrat's law holds for firms that are organised. One possible explanation for the negative relationship between size and growth found is related to the age of firms. Evans (1987) notes that theories of firm dynamics generate growth patterns that vary with the age of the firm. The growth process of small firms may appear different from the growth process of large firms because of age effects. Younger firms, typically with substantial growth rates and highly volatile growth, tend to make up the majority of small firms and the minority of large firms. The negative relationship between firm age and growth has been discussed by a number of empirical studies and in different countries: Evans (1987) and Dunne et al. (1989) for the US, and Dunne and Hughes (1994) for the UK. We therefore consider the impact of age on growth and, unsurprisingly, we find that age has a negative and highly significant influence on business growth, as younger firms tend to grow faster in our sample.

When estimating separately the same model for single-unit firms and multi-unit firms (Table 3.2), we notice that the growth patterns of multi-unit firms differ. Their growth is not dependent on their size. These results are consistent with the previous evidence that the Gibrat's law holds for larger firms. Finally, we estimate our model only on surviving firms (Table 3.3). The results do not change and this suggests that the negative relationship between

Table 3.3   *Sys-GMM estimates for surviving firms*

Independent variables		
(log)employment (lagged one period)	−0.102	−0.121
	(−4.29)	(−2.56)
(log) Access to Big Data capabilities (lagged one period)	0.1065	0.089
	(3.11)	(2.67)
(log)employment (lagged one period)* (log) Access to Big Data capabilities (lagged one period)	−0.011	−0.009
	(−2.59)	(−2.89)
Age	-	−0.301
		(−3.41)
# local units	0.0024	0.0019
	(2.84)	(2.84)
Hansen test (*p*-value)	0.192	0.591
Ar(1) (*p*-value)	0.000	0.000
Ar(2) (*p*-value)	0.411	0.219

Note: See Table 3.1.

size and growth is not driven by small firms exiting quickly but rather by the fact that surviving small firms tend to grow faster than larger firms.

3.6   MANAGERIAL IMPLICATIONS

The literature on SMEs and Big Data (summarised above) identified a number of drivers of the performance gap between large firms and SMEs and suggests a potential number of mechanisms through which the exploitation of Big Data can reduce the gap. In this section, we plan to draw a number of useful lessons for managers that are planning to deploy and exploit their Big Data to improve their business' performance. We want to arrange our managerial implications using the three steps of the Data Value Chain.

3.6.1   Data Capture

As mentioned at the beginning of the chapter, data capture is typically associated with the investment in the technologies and systems that allow us to retain and store the data that are produced by SMEs during their routing operations. While it can be argued that this is a phase that is generally managed by Chief Technical Officers, in reality it is important to bear in mind that the nature of the investment has to be aligned to the overall needs of the business. In other words, the new systems have to be able to capture data that can be useful to other teams in the business to identify in a clear way how they can create value; therefore, managers in SMEs have to able to articulate in a clear way the actual benefits that investments in a data capture system can deliver to the business and then eventually delegate the management of the investment to the Chief Technical Officer.

Another important lesson is that value from data capture systems cannot be created by one system only; for instance, being able to capture sensor data may not generate value unless there is support data capture investment that allows us to integrate them with other types of unstructured data. Indeed, one IT system alone may not be sufficient to exploit the data businesses produce and additional investments may be required because of the synergies that exist among systems. In other words, managers may find it difficult to translate the investment in data capture systems into improvements in performance if not enough attention is paid to the interdependencies among data and systems. In turn, this requires managers to plan in advance the investments they are planning to make in this area and to develop a strong business case around such investments.

3.6.2   Data Analysis

This is an important stage of the Data Value Chain that value creation from data hinges upon. The role of the firm's internal capabilities is crucial as existing skills and knowledge can define the extent to which data are analysed correctly and in such a way the analysis is aligned and useful to a company's strategic objectives. In this context it is important to highlight that most research has emphasised the need for analytical skills that allow us to analyse and make sense of Big Data; in reality, data analysis requires businesses to acquire "translational" skills which allow us to understand the implications of the analytical findings for the business and its strategic objectives. In large firms, these skills tend to be embedded into middle management sitting between the analytical team and the executive team. In SMEs – where some roles are not well defined and because of financial constraints there may be no dedicated analytical team – the best way forward could be to equip each member of the strategic management team with enough understanding of analytics so that they can use the results of the data analysis to drive their decision making. Crucially, this does not imply that every member of the management team has to be proficient in analytics but simply that they can assess the implications of the results for the performance of the firm.

   Another important lesson for SMEs is related to the type of analytical methodologies that can be used to drive business performance. A lot of emphasis is given to data visualisation as a simple suite of methodologies that allow businesses to immediately identify problems and potential patterns of interest. However, data visualisation requires a trained "eye" to make sense of the results and, in the context of SMEs, these skills may be missing. Alternative methodologies such as scenario planning and predictive analytics may be more insightful when trying to identify the drivers of future business performance as they focus not so much on the evolution of performance over time but rather on the contribution of different factors to future performance. For instance, senior management teams can use predictive analytics to quantify the impact of a new marketing campaign on future performance and whether it should continue in the future.

3.6.3   Data Exploitation

Once the data have been analysed, they need to be exploited and used to drive performance upwardly. One key lesson from the literature reviewed in the chapter is that for this to happen the knowledge generated by the data analysis has to be sufficiently specific that it can be a source of competitive advantage for the business. But how can businesses – in particular SMEs – assess whether the knowledge the data analysis has provided is specific enough to drive performance? This is not an easy question to answer as knowledge specificity has to be assessed in the light of the industry characteristics as well as of the competitors; in reality, each business may have a different answer to this question. Importantly, though, businesses need to put in place a process to be able to assess the quality of the knowledge produced from the analysis of Big Data as well as to be able to act upon it. This process has to be managed at the senior level and allow different functions of the business to input into it. Naturally, the implication is that knowledge has to be able to flow and be shared across different parts of a firm; this may have an implication on the structure of firms itself as it requires a concerted effort to avoid the creation of data silos that stop the circulation of knowledge in the company.

3.7   CONCLUSIONS

This chapter has explored the relationship between Big Data and SMEs. Our starting premise is that Big Data offer a number of opportunities to small firms. Like any other organisation, SMEs produce large volumes of data while undertaking their routine activities, and, as a result, they end up storing data of different types and complexity that can be used by researchers to improve our understanding of the drivers of their performance and by practitioners to improve the SMEs' performance. The expectation is that ultimately the exploitation of Big Data can provide managers with a clearer understanding of the drivers of the "liability of smallness" that allow us to overcome it eventually.

NOTES

1. Traditionally, market orientation has been described in three major ways: as a set of behaviours and activities (Jaworski & Kohli, 1993), part of an organisational culture (Day, 1994; Slater & Narver, 1995) and a resource (Hunt & Morgan, 1995; Dutta et al. 1999; Morgan et al. 2009). The behavioural perspective views market orientation as the organisation-wide generation and dissemination of information and responsiveness to market intelligence on customer needs, competitive actions and strategies, and the wider business environment (Jaworski & Kohli, 1993). The cultural perspective focuses on organisational norms and values that drive behaviours which are consistent with market orientation including customer orientation, competitor orientation and inter-functional coordination (Slater & Narver, 1995; Kirca et al. 2005). The resource-based perspective, on the other hand, perceives market orientation as a valuable, rare, socially complex and causally ambiguous resource which enables a firm to produce an offering that aligns with the specific tastes and preferences of his market segments (Hunt & Morgan, 1995; Kirca et al. 2005).
2. Urga et al. (2003) and Del Monte and Papagni (2003) find that firm growth follows a random walk and therefore the Gibrat's law holds. On the contrary, Goddard et al. (2002) and Oliveira and Fortunato (2003) using a panel data of Japanese and Portuguese manufacturing firms, respectively, provide some support for the firm sizes being mean-reverting.
3. There are some remarkable exceptions such as Audretsch et al. (2004) who analysed the Dutch hospitality sector (restaurants, cafes, hotels and camping sites) which is characterised by small and independent firms serving mostly local markets. Their results showed that the Gibrat's law is accepted in most cases consistently with the traditional view that services firms grow at the same rate independently of size. However, Oliveira and Fortunato (2003) find the opposite when analysing the growth patterns of firms from the Portuguese service sectors. Equally, Petrunia (2007) finds that the Gibrat's law does not hold for Canadian retail trade.

REFERENCES

Akter, S., Wamba, S.F., Gunasekaran, A., Dubey, R., and Childe, S.J. (2016). How to improve firm performance using big data analytics capability and business strategy alignment? *International Journal of Production Economics*, 182, 113–31.

Aldrich, H., and Auster, E. (1986). Even dwarfs started small: liabilities of age and size and their strategic implications. In L. Cummings and B. Staw (eds), *Research in Organizational Behavior* (vol. 8), San Francisco, CA: Jai Press, pp. 165–98.

Aldrich, H.E., and Fiol, C.M. (1994). Fools rush in? The institutional context of industry creation. *Academy of Management Review*, 19, 645–70.

Almus, M., and Nerlinger, E. (2000) Testing Gibrat's law for young firms – empirical results for West Germany. *Small Business Economics*, 15(1), 1–12.

Anderson, E. (1985). The salesperson as outside agent or employee: a transaction cost analysis. *Marketing Science*, 4(summer), 234–54.

Audretsch, D. (1995). *Innovation and Industry Evolution*, Cambridge, MA: MIT Press.

Audretsch, D., Santarelli, E., and Vivarelli, M. (1999) Start-up size and industrial dynamics: some evidence from Italian manufacturing. *International Journal of Industrial Organization*, 17(7), 965–83.

Audretsch, D.B., Klomp, L., Santarelli, E., and Thurik, A.R. (2004). Gibrat's Law: are services different? *Review of Industrial Organisation*, 24, 301–24.

Autio, E., Sapienza, H.J., & Almeida, J.G. (2000). Effects of age at entry, knowledge intensity, and imitability on international growth. *Academy of Management Journal*, 43, 909–24.

Barge-Gil, A. (2010). Cooperation-based innovators and peripheral cooperators: an empirical analysis of their characteristics and behaviour. *Technovation*, 30(3), 195–206.

Becchetti, L., and Trovato, G. (2002). The determinants of growth for small and medium sized firms. *Small Business Economics*, 19(4), 291–306.

Boyd, B.K., and Fulk, J. (1996). Executive scanning and perceived uncertainty: a multidimensional model. *Journal of Management*, 22, 1–21.

Cabral, L. (1995). Sunk costs, firm size and firm growth. *Journal of Industrial Economics*, 43(2), 161–72.

Cao, M., Chychyla, R., and Stewart, T. (2015). Big Data analytics in financial statement audits. *Accounting Horizons*, 29(2), 423–9.

Chen, H., Chiang, R.H., and Storey, V.C. (2012). Business intelligence and analytics: from big data to big impact. *MIS Quarterly*, 36, 1165–88.

Chen, J., and Lu, W. (2003). Panel unit root tests of firm size and its growth. *Applied Economics Letters*, 10(6), 343–5.

Chen, M., Mao, S., Zhang, Y., and Leung, V.C. (2014). *Big Data: Related Technologies, Challenges and Future Prospects*, New York: Springer.

Chesher, A. (1979). Testing the law of proportionate effect. *Journal of Industrial Economics*, 27(4), 403–11.

Choi, Y.R., and Shepherd, D.A. (2005). Stakeholder perceptions of age and other dimensions of newness. *Journal of Management*, 31, 573–96.

Choudhury, V., and Sampler, J. (1997). Information specificity and environmental scanning: an economic perspective. *MIS Quarterly*, 21(1), 25–53.

Cohen, W., and Levinthal, D. (1990). Absorptive capacity: a new perspective on learning and innovation. *Administrative Science Quarterly*, 35, 128–52.

Coleman, J.S. (1990). *Foundations of Social Theory*, Cambridge, MA: Harvard University Press.

Cooley, T., and Quadrini, V. (2001). Financial markets and firm dynamics. *American Economic Review*, 91(5), 1286–310.

Davenport, T. (2014). *Big Data at Work: Dispelling the Myths, Uncovering the Opportunities*, New York: Harvard Business Review Press.

Davenport, T.H., Barth, P., and Bean, R. (2012). How big data is different. *MIT Sloan Manage Review*, 54(1), 43.

Day, G.S. (1994). The capabilities of market-driven organizations. *Journal of Marketing*, 58(4), 37–52.

Del Monte, A., and Papagni, E. (2003). R&D and the growth of firms: an empirical analysis of a panel of Italian firms. *Research Policy*, 32(6), 1003–14.

Delen, D. and Ram, S. (2018). Research challenges and opportunities in business analytics. *Journal of Business Analytics*, 1, 2–12.

Dobre, C., and Xhafa, F. (2014). Intelligent services for Big Data science. *Future Generation Computer Systems*, 37, 267–81.

Dubey, R., Gunasekaran, A., Childe, S.J., Fosso Wamba, S. and Papadopoulos, T. (2016). The impact of big data on world-class sustainable manufacturing. *The International Journal of Advanced Manufacturing Technology*, 84(1–4), 631–45.

Dunne, P., and Hughes, A. (1994). Age, size, growth and survival: UK companies in the late 1980s. *Journal of Industrial Economics*, 42(2), 115–40.

Dunne, T., Roberts, M.J., amd Samuelson, L. (1989). The growth and failure of US manufacturing plants. *The Quarterly Journal of Economics*, 104(4), 671–98.

Dutta, S., Narasimhan, O., and Rajiv, S. (1999). Success in high-technology markets: is marketing capability critical? *Marketing Science*, 18(4), 547–68.

Evans, D. (1987). Tests of alternative theories of firm growth. *Journal of Political Economy*, 95(4), 657–74.

Fotopoulos, G., and Louri, H. (2002). Corporate growth and FDI: are multinationals stimulating local industrial development? Discussion paper no. 3128, Centre for Economic Policy Research.

Gandomi, A., and Haider, M. (2015). Beyond the hype: big data concepts, methods, and analytics. *International Journal of Information Management*, 35(2), 137–44.

García, N., Sanzo, M.J., and Trespalacios, J.A. (2008). New product internal performance and market performance: evidence from Spanish firms regarding the role of trust, interfunctional integration, and innovation type. *Technovation*, 28, 713–25.

Gibrat, R. (1931). *Les inequalites economique*, Paris: Sirey.

Goddard, J., Wilson, J., and Blandon, P. (2002). Panel tests of Gibrat's law for Japanese manufacturing. *International Journal of Industrial Organization*, 20(3), 415–33.

Granovetter, M. (1985). Economic action and social structure: the problem of embeddedness. *American Journal of Sociology*, 91(3), 481–510.

Hall, B. (1987). The relationship between firm size and firm growth in the US manufacturing sector. *Journal of Industrial Economics*, 35(4), 583–606.

Hart, P.E. (1962). Size and growth of firms. *Economica*, 29(1), 29–39.

Hart, P.E., and Oulton, N. (1996). The size and growth of firms. *Economic Journal*, 106(438), 1242–52.

Hashem, I.A.T., Yaqoo, I., Anuar, N.B., Mokhtar, S., Gani, A., and Khan, S.A. (2015). The rise of "big data" on cloud computing: review and open research issues. *Information Systems*, 47, 98–115.

Heide, J.B. (2003). Plural governance in industrial purchasing. *Journal of Marketing*, 67(4), 18.

Huber, G.P. (1991). Organizational learning: the contributing processes and the literatures. *Organization Science*, 2, 88–115.

Hunt, S.D., and Morgan, R.M. (1995). The comparative advantage theory of competition. *Journal of Marketing*, 59(2), 1–15.

Jaworski, B.J., and Kohli, A.K. (1993). Market orientation: antecedents and consequences. *Journal of Marketing*, 57(3), 53–70.

Jaworski, B., Kohli, A.K., and Sahay, A. (2000). Market-driven versus driving markets. *Journal of the Academy of Marketing Science*, 28(1), 45–54.

Jovanovic, B. (1982). Selection and the evolution of industry. *Econometrica*, 50(3), 649–70.

Kirca, A.H., Jayachandran, S., and Bearden, W.O. (2005). Market orientation: a meta-analytic review and assessement of its antecedents and impact on performance. *Journal of Marketing*, 69(2), 24–41.

Kiron, D. Shockley, R., Kruschwitz, N., Finch, G., and Haydock, M. (2012). Analytics: the widening divide. *MIT Sloan Manage Re*view, 53(2), 1.

Kiron, D., Prentice, P.K., and Ferguson, R.B. (2014). The analytics mandate. *MIT Sloan Manage Review*, 55(4), 1.

Kogut, B., and Zander, U. (1992). Knowledge of the firm, combinative capabilities, and the replication of technology. *Organization Science*, 3, 383–97.

Kogut, B. and Zander, U. (1996). What firms do? Coordination, identity, and learning. *Organization Science*, 7(5), 502–18.

Kubina, M., Koman, G., and Kubinova, I. (2015). Possibility of improving efficiency within business intelligence systems in companies. *Procedia Economics and Finance*, 26, 300–5.

Laney, D. (2001). 3D *Data Management: Controlling Data Volume, Velocity and Variety*, Stamford: META Group.

LaValle, S. Lesser, E., Shockley, R., Hopkins, M.S., and Kruschwitz, N. (2011). Big data, analytics and the path from insights to value. *MIT Sloan Manage Review*, 52(2), 21–31.

Levin, D.Z., and Cross, R. (2004). The strength of weak ties you can trust: the mediating role of trust in effective knowledge transfer. *Management Science*, 50, 1477–90.

Liu, Y. (2014). Big data and predictive business analytics. *Journal of Business Forecasting*, 33(4), 40.

Malomo, F., and Sena, V. (2017). Data intelligence for local government? Assessing the benefits and barriers to use of big data in the public sector. *Policy & Internet*, 9, 7–27.

Manyika, J., Chui, M., Brown, B. et al. (2011). *Big Data: The Next Frontier for Innovation, Competition, and Productivity*, Washington, DC: McKinsey Global Institute.

Mata, J. (1994). Firm growth during infancy. *Small Business Economics*, 6(1), 27–39.

McAfee, A., and Brynjolfsson, E. (2012). Big Data: the management revolution: exploiting vast new flows of information can radically improve your company's performance. But first you'll have to change your decision making culture. *Harvard Business Review*, 90, 60–8.

McAfee, A., Brynjolfsson, E., Davenport, T.H., Patil, D.J., and Barton, D. (2012). Big Data: the management revolution. *Harvard Business Review*, 90(10), 60–68.

Mikalef, P., Pappas, I.O., Giannakos, M.N., Krogstie, J., and Lekakos, G. (2016). Big Data and strategy: a research framework, MCIS 2016 proceedings, 50.

Mikalef P. Pappas, I.O., Krogstie, J. & Giannakos, M. (2018). Big data analytics capabilities: a systematic literature review and research agenda. Inf Systems and e-Business Management, 16(3), 547–78.

Moran, P. (2005). Structural vs. relational embeddedness: social capital and managerial performance. *Strategic Management Journal*, 26, 1129–51.

Morgan, N.A., Douglas, W.V., and Mason, C.H. (2009). Market orientation, marketing capabilities, and firm performance. *Strategic Management Journal*, 30(8), 909–20.

Nahapiet, J. and Ghoshal, S. (1998). Social capital, intellectual capital, and the organizational advantage. *Academy of Management Review*, 23, 242–66.

Narver, J.C., Slater, S.F., and MacLachlan, D.L. (2004). Responsive and proactive market orientation and new product success. *Journal of Product Innovation Management*, 21(5), 334–47.

Nooteboom, B. (1993). Firm size effects on transaction costs. *Small Business Economics*, 5(4), 283–95.

Oliveira, B., and Fortunato, A. (2003). Does the firm growth follow a random walk? An application with panel data unit root test. Paper presented to the EUNIP conference, Porto, Portugal.

Ozdemir, S., Kandemir, D., and Eng, T-Y. (2017). The role of horizontal and vertical new product alliances in responsive and proactive market orientations and performance of industrial manufacturing firms. *Industrial Marketing Management*, 64, 25–35.

Peters, L., and Karren, R.J. (2009). An examination of the roles of trust and functional diversity on virtual team performance ratings. *Group & Organization Management*, 34, 479–504.

Petrunia, R. (2007). Persistence of initial debt in the long-term employment dynamics of new firms. *Canadian Journal of Economics*, 40(3), 861–880.

Petrunia, R. (2008). Does Gibrat's law hold? Evidence from Canadian retail and manufacturing firms. *Small Business Economics*, 30, 201–14.

Provost, F., and Fawcett, T. (2013). Data science and its relationship to big data and data-driven decision making. *Big Data*, 1(1), 51–9.

Rindfleisch, A., and Heide, J.B. (1997). Transaction cost analysis: past, present, and future applications. *Journal of Marketing*, 61(4), 30–54.

Rothaermel, F.T., and Deeds, D.L. (2004). Exploration and exploitation alliances in biotechnology: a system of new product development. *Strategic Management Journal*, 25(3), 201–21.

Schoenherr, T., and Speier-Pero, C. (2015). Data science, predictive analytics, and big data in supply chain management: current state and future potential. *Journal of Business Logistics*, 36(1), 120–32.

Schroeck, M., Shockley, R., Smart, J., Romero-Morales, D. and Tufano, P. (2012). Analytics: the real-world use of big data (IBM Institute for Business Value – Executive Report), IBM Institute for Business Value.

Sena, V., and Ozdemir, S. (2020). Spillover effects of investment in BDA in B2B relationships: what is the role of human capital? *Industrial Marketing Management*, 86(April), 77–89.

Shmueli, G., and Koppius, O.R. (2011). Predictive analytics in information systems research. *MIS Quarterly*, 35(3), 553–72.

Sivarajah, U., Kamal, M.M., Irani, Z., and Weerakkody, V. (2017). Critical analysis of Big Data challenges and analytical methods. *Journal of Business Research*, 70, 263–86.

Slater, S.F., and Narver, J.C. (1995). Market orientation and the learning organization. *Journal of Marketing*, 59(3), 63–74.

Stinchcombe, A.L. (1965). Social structure and organizations. In J.P. March (ed.), *Handbook of Organizations*, Chicago, IL: Rand Mcnally, pp. 142–93.

Stubbs E. (2014). *Big Data, Big Innovation: Enabling Competitive Differentiation through Business Analytics*, Hoboken, NJ: Wiley.

Sutton, J. (1997). Gibrat's legacy. *Journal of Economic Literature*, 35(1), 40–59.

Szulanski, G. (1996). Exploring internal stickiness: impediments to the transfer of best practice within the firm. *Strategic Management Journal*, 17, 27–43.

Tsai, K., Chou, C., and Kuo, J. (2008). The curvilinear relationships between responsive and proactive market orientations and new product performance: a contingent link. *Industrial Marketing Management*, 37(8), 884–94.

Tsai, W. (2001). Knowledge transfer in intraorganizational networks: effects of network position and absorptive capacity on business unit innovation and performance. *Academy of Management Journal*, 44(5), 996–1004.

Tsai, W., and Ghoshal, S. (1998). Social capital and value creation: the role of intrafirm networks. *Academy of Management Journal*, 41, 464–76.

Urga, G., Geroski, P., Lazarova, S., and Walters, C. (2003). Are differences in firm size transitory or permanent? *Journal of Applied Econometrics*, 18(1), 47–59.

Van Wijk, R., Jansen, J.J.P., and Lyles, M.A. (2008). Inter- and intra-organizational knowledge transfer: a meta-analytic review and assessment of its antecedents and consequences. *Journal of Management Studies*, 45, 830–53.

Wamba, S.F., Gunasekaran, A., Akter, S., Ji-fan Ren, S., Dubey, R., and Childe, S.J. (2017). Big data analytics and firm performance: effects of dynamic capabilities. *Journal of Business Research*, 20, 356–65.

Wang, Y., Kung, L., and Byrd, T.A. (2018). Big data analytics: understanding its capabilities and potential benefits for healthcare organizations. *Technological Forecasting and Social Change*, 126, 3–13.

Wedel, M., and Kannan, P. (2016). Marketing analytics for data-rich environments. *Journal of Marketing*, 80(6), 97–121.

Williamson, O.E. (1985). *The Economic Institutions of Capitalism*, New York: The Free Press.

Williamson, O.E. (1989). Transaction cost economics. In R. Schmalensee and R. Willig (eds), *Handbook of Industrial Organization*, Amsterdam: North-Holland, pp. 135–82.

Wills, M.J. (2014). Decisions through data: analytics in healthcare. *Journal of Healthcare Management*, 59(4), 254–62.

Zahra, S.A., and George, G. (2002). Absorptive capacity: a review, reconceptualisation, and extension. *Academy of Management Review*, 27(2), 185–203.

Zeng, D.D., Lusch, R., and Chen, H-C. (2010). Social media analytics and intelligence. *Intelligent Systems, IEEE*, November/December, 12–16.

PART II

Capabilities: getting digitization right

4. Value-creation for Industry 4.0 and SMEs' data-driven growth: strategies and resource alignment

Bieke Struyf, Wouter Van Bockhaven and Paul Matthyssens

4.1 INTRODUCTION

Since its introduction at the Hannover Fair in 2011, the idea of Industry 4.0 (I4.0) has taken the world by storm. Variations of the strategic initiative, launched by three engineers aimed at rendering the German manufacturing industry competitive (again), have since popped up in the USA (Industrial Internet of Things), China (Made in China 2025) and the 2016 World Economic Forum's meeting held in Davos (Pfeiffer, 2017; Tao & Qi, 2019).

I4.0 is presented as a new industrial stage in which information and communication technology, the Internet of Things (IoT) and machines are combined into cyber-physical systems. Increased product connectivity and advanced integration of manufacturing operations systems are key to the new opportunities offered. Expected benefits include, among others, flexible manufacturing processes, strategic innovation and improved operational decision-making. Real-time collected and analyzed *big data* are quoted to be the basis of these gains (Dalenogare et al., 2018; Kagermann et al., 2013).

Indeed, high integration of systems which characterizes I4.0 allows organizations to collect large volumes of data (*volume*), which are updated quickly and frequently (*velocity*) and stem from different sources leading to a huge range of different formats and content (*variety*) (Alharthi et al., 2017). Big data analytics allow companies to translate collected data into meaningful and actionable insights (Mikalef et al., 2018). These insights can inform decision-making in a descriptive, predictive or prescriptive manner (Lamba & Dubey, 2015) or lead to the creation of entirely new products and services (Müller, 2019). Big data thus hold potential for both increased internal efficiency and improved customer experience, enhancing both profitability and competitiveness (Alharthi et al., 2017; Sivarajah et al., 2017).

Technology in itself, however, does not *generate* value (Mueller & Jensen, 2017; Yunis et al., 2018). Gathering massive amounts of data without a clear idea as to what company objectives the management wants to realize could easily turn technology potential into a "white elephant": a useless and expensive to maintain asset (Marr, 2017). Big data and big data analytics can however *enable* value creation. Basic requirements? A clear strategy and the proper resource configuration to turn this strategy into a reality (Amit & Han, 2017; Black & Boal, 1994; Coreynen et al., 2017).

Contrary to technological optimism found in engineering literature, the strategic exercise linked to the introduction of I4.0 technology is said to be challenging. Financial, organizational, technological and market barriers (Constantiou & Kallinikos, 2015; Horváth & Szabó, 2019; Schneider, 2018) as well as lack of insight into strategic options and their critical success factors are listed as the main reasons for the restraint companies show towards the introduction of these technologies in their businesses (Arcidiacono et al., 2019; Coleman et al., 2016; Kiangala & Wang, 2018; SERV, 2019).

For small and medium enterprises (SMEs) in particular, which struggle with limited and specialized resources (Coleman et al., 2016; Horváth & Szabó, 2019), answers to the strategy question are vital since unfortunate investment decision-making and poorly executed strategies can considerably affect market and financial performance or even their survival (Rahman et al., 2016). Given that SMEs make up 99.8 percent of all enterprises in the EU-28 non-financial business sector and represent 54.5 percent of the EU-28 GDP (European Commission, 2019), clarifying strategic options does not only seem relevant for individual companies but also for the greater health of the entire European economy.

One could of course wonder if it is even worth their while. What big data opportunities are there, after all, for SMEs? Horváth and Szabó (2019) found that SMEs had lower driving forces and higher barriers to Industry 4.0. Human and financial resources, profitability and management reality revealed themselves to be the top three hindrances to implementation – and consequently the benefits – of Industry 4.0 in SMEs. According to Simon (2013), SMEs "are often intimidated by the cost and complexity of handling large amounts of digital information." Yet, a decrease in data storage costs (Del Vecchio et al., 2018) and technological advancements such as cloud computing solutions (Vajjhala & Ramollari, 2016) have considerably lowered the costs of upfront investment in big data-enabling infrastructure (Polkowski et al., 2017), making it more feasible for SMEs to embark on their own I4.0 journey. Indeed, opportunities for SMEs with regard to big data have been demonstrated (Del Vecchio et al., 2018; Frank et al., 2019a; Müller et al., 2018). Even more so, Dong and Yang (2020) showed that big data do not necessarily need to be harvested by or proprietary to the SME itself. Big data analytics based on social media data – externally procured and publicly accessible data – can already lead to an increase in market performance for SMEs, an increase which was found to be even more salient for SMEs than for larger companies (Dong & Yang, 2020).

Currently, most companies looking to transform their business through I4.0 technology are banking on *low road* strategies (Arnold et al., 2016; Flanders Make, 2019; Sivarajah et al., 2017). In these strategies, the focus lies on reducing costs and gaining efficiency (Dessers et al., 2019). These results are not surprising. After all, the business case for increased efficiency is easily made, thanks to elaborate research on the topic (Lu, 2017; S.Y. Wang et al., 2016). On top of that, companies' preferences for rational investments grounded on hard numbers are more easily fed by carefully calculated savings than by wild guesses about the grandeur of possible future new income streams (Papadakis et al., 1998).

The aim of this chapter is to add to the I4.0 strategic options of SMEs by specifically focusing on non-priced-based differentiation (Matthyssens & Vandenbempt, 2008) or *high road* strategies (Aiginger & Vogel, 2015; Dessers et al., 2019). Rather than looking for cost reductions, these strategies focus on value creation for both the customer and the company. The reason to investigate these strategies is threefold. Firstly, gaining insight in this less-trodden path might prove to lead to a more substantial contribution for literature. Secondly, given that

Table 4.1   Low road versus high road data-driven growth strategies

Low road *Efficiency*		High road *Effectiveness*	
Cost-oriented		Value-oriented	
Optimization of processes related to		**Customer-** oriented value creation	
Core product	*Supporting services*	*Improved offer*	*New products/services*
e.g. quality monitoring and error reduction during production process of core product	e.g. optimization of inventory through tracking and automatic ordering	e.g. guided self-order system offering advice	e.g. co-creation with customer; optimization of customer's processes
Case: Daimler Group	Case: Eriks (Dutch B2B wholesaler)	Case: Xerox document management	Case: Daimler Moovel
(mostly affects back office)		(mostly affects front office)	
Independent solution			Networked solution

customer satisfaction is an important driver for SMEs to implement I4.0 technology (Horvath & Szabo, 2019), it seems important to investigate strategies which affect the front office of organizations and are focused on truly adding value for customers. Finally, value innovation might be necessary to keep away from the margin squeeze following price competition linked to the digital commodity magnet (Rangan & Bowman, 1992). After all, if companies implement efficiency-oriented strategies only, the way to distinguish oneself is through pricing. Price competition can easily lead to the destruction of value created for businesses (Shaked & Sutton, 1982). In the digital commodity magnet, digitization does not only exert pressure on prices. It also raises customers' expectations leading to additional costs without room to raise prices. By focusing on non-price-based differentiation strategies, SMEs can avoid being sucked into the digital commodity magnet, allowing them a chance at sustained profitability (Krämer et al., 2016). Table 4.1 summarizes both types of data-driven growth strategies.

Thus, the goal of this chapter is to answer the following research questions:

1. Which **non-price-based strategic options** are available to SMEs for the implementation of I4.0 technology and the use of big data analytics?
2. Which **resource configurations** are deemed necessary to execute data-enabled strategies?
3. What **gaps** can be expected in SMEs' resource configurations and how can these gaps be closed?

By doing so we intend to contribute in several ways. Firstly, by concentrating on non-price-based strategic options, we aim to enrich I4.0 strategy literature, which so far has mainly highlighted opportunities for efficiency gains, at the expense of more innovative, value creating alternatives. Secondly, since extant research into I4.0 strategies has mostly focused on large firms and only to a limited extend on SMEs, taking up strategic options for SMEs allows us to challenge and tailor current knowledge to fit the specific characteristics and needs of small and medium enterprises. Finally, it is our goal to facilitate and improve the adoption of I4.0 in SMEs by expanding the strategic options available to them and outlining which resource configurations support effective implementation.

The chapter is structured as follows. Section 4.2 briefly reviews the current literature on non-price-based strategic options linked to the adoption of I4.0 technology, as well as the capabilities and resources which make up their supporting resource configurations. A preliminary framework is introduced. In Section 4.3, the methodology used and the case study's background are outlined. Section 4.4 illustrates the evolution of Sanders Material[1] from service minded vendor of components to initiator of a brand new digital platform. In Section 4.5, the company's evolution is discussed based on the preliminary framework. Section 4.6 presents the conclusion, highlighting implications of and limitations to the study.

4.2 LITERATURE OVERVIEW AND THEORETICAL BACKGROUND

4.2.1 Non-Price-Based Strategic Options

We consider non-price-based competitive strategies to be differentiation strategies (Porter, 1980) with a focus on the creation of new customer value (Matthyssens & Vandenbempt, 2008). Customer intimacy and product leadership are two value disciplines which bank on boosting customer satisfaction in order to raise profits (Anderson & Mittal, 2000; Treacy & Wiersema, 1993). Customer intimacy, on the one hand, centers on the development of tailored offerings which match the exact demands of niche markets. Product leaders, on the other hand, concentrate on creating an infinite series of cutting-edge products and services, continuously raising the bar for competitors. According to Banker et al. (2014), technology-enabled differentiation strategies allow companies to sustain their financial performance to a greater extent than cost leadership.

The introduction of I4.0 technology nowadays offers companies new possibilities for differentiation and value creation (Amit & Han, 2017; Matthyssens, 2019; Mueller & Jensen, 2017). Big data analytics facilitate the discovery of specific customer needs and the segmentation of clients to customize actions (Reddy & Reinartz, 2017; Wamba et al., 2015). High integration of systems, supporting closeness to customers and the wider network, allows for novel ways to create and deliver innovative products and services (Amit & Han, 2017). While value generation in former non-price-based strategies was mainly oriented at the client and often costly (Porter, 1980, 1985), I4.0 technology now allows companies to reduce the costs of delivery and capture value in transactions with clients as well. Swift data collection and analysis made possible through cyber-physical systems and increased connectivity facilitate optimization of internal processes while supporting idea generation for new products and services (Frank et al., 2019b).

High road strategies focus on value generation for both the customer and the company. The strategies are chosen for their boost in effectiveness rather than their increase in efficiency. Given the strong focus on customer value creation, front office operations are mostly affected. Within the group of high road strategies, we distinguish two different options: one oriented towards *improved offerings*, and a second one aimed at the realization of entirely *new products and/or services* (Table 4.2). In the first case, incremental value is found in the increased *convenience* of the purchase process. Big data solutions are applied to "upgrade" companies'

Table 4.2   Framework on data-enabled value creating strategies based on literature review

High road options towards effectiveness	
Convenience	*Experience*
Improved offer	**New products and/or services**
Incremental value creation	Radically new value creation
Basic servitization	Advanced servitization
e.g. B2B e-commerce related services leading to quicker, more accurate order processes and faster delivery thanks to facilitated online processes hosted at a platform or through cloud services which improve the flow of information.	e.g. advanced services (manufacturer delivers services critical to the core business of its customer), predictive maintenance, total solution offer in which cross-industry partners are approached to co-create brand new products/services.
References: Sousa and da Silveira (2017); Li, Tian, and Tian (2018); Baines et al. (2011)	References: Alharthi et al. (2017); Baines and Lightfoot (2014); Coreynen et al. (2017)
Mass customization	Mass personalization
Highly customized products and services are made available to customers without considerable trade-off in cost, delivery, and quality.	Advanced stage of mass customization. Customers are intensively integrated in the product design and production process. Products and services rendered can be increasingly delivered electronically.
References: Da Silveira et al. (2001); Sandrin et al. (2018)	References: Kumar (2007); Tiihonen and Felfernig (2017); Torn and Vaneker (2019); Yi Wang et al. (2017)
	Digital platform strategy
	Novel, total solutions emerge from co-creation with an extending ecosystem of autonomous agents.
	References: Rietveld et al. (2019); Wan et al. (2017); Yablonsky (2018)
Apply technology to **best answer** your customer's requests.	*Use technology to think beyond* what your customer is asking of you.
Independent solution	
	Networked solution

responses towards customer requests. In the second case, radically new value is offered and realized through thinking beyond what the customer is asking (Arnold et al., 2016; Rachinger et al., 2019; Reddy & Reinartz, 2017).

4.2.1.1   Evolutionary pathways and combined strategies

Of course, companies can combine both options and move from one strategy to the next. Literature shows that the most frequent movement occurs from the left-hand side towards the right-hand side of Table 4.2 (Frank et al., 2019a). A possible explanation could be that the process of learning how to best answer your customers' requests can provide you with deeper insights into their operations and needs, allowing you to reason beyond their explicit requests.

4.2.1.2   From independent to networked solutions

Taking on the creation of radically new solutions often requires looking outside the organization for capabilities and resources (McEvily & Marcus, 2005; Moonen et al., 2019). After all, the more complex the proposition, the more likely it is that some of the necessary expertise can either not be found in-house or be more efficiently sourced from an external network partner (Moonen et al., 2019). Thinking beyond the customer's request might easily entail thinking beyond one's own expertise. Especially for SMEs, known to be challenged by specialized knowledge (Coleman et al., 2016), relying on the surrounding network is often the solution (Mei et al., 2019). We therefore expect successfully implemented experience-oriented data strategies to have a higher degree of network involvement. However, being able to co-create and collaborate with the extended network requires specific capabilities on its own (Saunila et al., 2019; Vesalainen & Hakala, 2014). We come back to this when we look at resource capabilities for the realization of high road data strategies.

4.2.2   Data-Enabled Value Creating Strategies

A review of the most relevant literature, presented in Table 4.2, revealed the following strategies as high road options related to I4.0 implementation: digital servitization, mass customization and personalization, and digital platform strategy. The strategies are briefly discussed below.

4.2.2.1   Digital servitization

A first value creating data-enabled strategy is digital servitization (Coreynen et al., 2017; Kohtamäki et al., 2019; Vendrell-Herrero et al., 2017). This emerging strategy focuses on new servitization opportunities offered by the digitization of manufacturing companies. Servitization describes the addition of services to manufacturers' core product offerings to create additional customer value (Raddats et al., 2019; Vandermerwe & Rada, 1988). On top of improvements made in front- and back-end operations, digitization enables the creation of new offerings in which physical and digital products are combined (Coreynen et al., 2017). Today, the introduction of I4.0 technology amplifies the opportunities offered by digitization. For firms, exponential growth of real-time data, which are increasingly captured automatically in transactions with customers, boosts their ability to understand, respond to and even anticipate customers' needs. Acting on real-time data insights allows companies to enhance the quality of their services even faster and offer increasingly tailor-made solutions to customers, who can in turn benefit from an improved customer experience (Alharthi et al., 2017; Matthyssens, 2019; Opresnik & Taisch, 2015).

Servitization knows a wide variety of forms (Baines et al., 2009). For this chapter we use the classification by Coreynen et al. (2017) who combined the dimensions of service orientation and value proposition into a servitization pyramid consisting of six dimensions: product life cycle services, product performance services, product result services, process support services, process delegation services and hybrid solutions.

4.2.2.2   Mass customization and mass personalization production

The literature points towards mass customization (Davis, 1989; Pine, 1993) or mass personalization production (Kumar, 2007; Torn & Vaneker, 2019; Yi Wang et al., 2017) as a second high road strategy supported by I4.0 technology. Mass customization refers to a company's ability to offer *customized products and services that fulfill each customer's idiosyncratic needs* through high process flexibility and integration *without considerable trade-offs in cost, delivery, and quality* (Da Silveira et al., 2001; Sandrin et al., 2018). Increased customization potential and improved quality would follow from the implementation of 3D printing, cyber-physical systems, seamless integration of the supply chain and machine learning capabilities, to name a few (Zhong et al., 2017).

Even though "mass customization" and "mass personalization" are interchangeably used, certain authors clearly differentiate between both (Kumar, 2007; Yi Wang et al., 2017). According to them, I4.0 enables an evolution from mass customization towards a more advanced mass personalization. Increased involvement of the customer into the creation and design process is seen as the distinguishing factor. The degree to which a company can move towards mass personalization depends on the extent to which the offered products can be produced and delivered electronically.

With mass customization, value for the customer is found in the preference fit as well as the feeling of accomplishment experienced through the co-development of customized products (Franke et al., 2010). Business value, on the other hand, can be found in the facility of high customization of products at a relatively low cost.

4.2.2.3 Digital platform strategy

A third high road strategy enabled by I4.0 technology is the digital platform strategy (Rietveld et al., 2019; Wan et al., 2017; Yablonsky, 2018). Firms which successfully pursue a platform strategy coordinate *an ecosystem of autonomous agents* with which they *co-create value* while offering them value in return (Hein et al., 2019). Platform initiators invest in the necessary infrastructure, draw up the rules and often provide supporting services to facilitate interactions between the different network members (Yablonsky, 2018). Rather than focusing on competition for control of the value chain, digital platform strategists concentrate on selecting and attracting profitable, cross-industry value partners befitting their platform (de Reuver et al., 2018; Rietveld et al., 2019).

Advancements made in big data and big data analytics are making the adoption of digital platforms more attractive (Cenamor et al., 2019). At the same time, the implementation of I4.0 technology expedites the creation of ecosystems by nature through its emphasis on horizontal and end-to-end integration (Savastano et al., 2018; L.D. Xu et al., 2018; Yablonsky, 2018). Companies can bank on these opportunities by opting to take the lead in the development of a new platform ecosystem, and positioning themselves at the center of value creation and capture (Hein et al., 2019). According to Gawer and Cusumano (2008), platform leadership is available to all, including small companies. If only they take the right business and technology decisions.

Following a platform strategy can lead to advantages for many actors involved. Customers can profit from easy access to an expending product and services portfolio, which is likely to be compatible with previous purchases and tailored to their specific needs and preferences (Wan et al., 2017). Original suppliers of the platform sponsor and complementors can partake in innovative initiatives, enjoy the benefits of investments made in platform infrastructure, and gain access to new markets (Rietveld et al., 2019). The latter is also true for the leading firm, for which additional returns can be found in, among others, a strengthened competitive position (Cenamor et al., 2019), market power (Graef, 2015), and opportunities for novel value creation following cross-contamination between ecosystem partners who do not necessarily belong to the same traditional industry realm (Teece, 2018). Even more so, as platform architect, the leading firm gains access to an abundance of privileged data, which in turn can support the improvement of its current offer as well as the expansion of it (Eisenmann et al., 2011).

Iansiti and Lakhani (2017), however, point towards the importance of balancing invest-ments in the health of the ecosystem with value capture and creation by the focal firm. Indeed, challenges are involved in realizing a digital platform strategy. The same holds up for the implementation of mass customization and servitization (Coreynen et al., 2017; Tiihonen & Felfernig, 2017). Since technology only generates value through proper *translation* into strat-egy, effective implementation of the data-enabled strategies is essential to reaping potential benefits of digital technologies.

4.2.3 Resource Configurations

For a strategy to be well executed, specific resources and capabilities are required (Helfat & Peteraf, 2003). Resources, like technology infrastructure and analytical tools, are inputs to the company's processes and can often be bought on the market (Amit & Schoemaker, 1993). Capabilities, however, are developed in-house and consist of *internal technological, organizational and managerial firm processes* which enable firms to transform their resources into valuable outputs (Amit & Schoemaker, 1993; Teece et al., 1997). Research shows that it is certain configurations of resources rather than one resource alone which make up compet-itive advantage (Black & Boal, 1994). Especially capabilities would in times of high-speed technological change greatly contribute to a company's sustainable competitive advantage (Moonen et al., 2019; Teece et al., 1997). With our literature research we therefore focused on uncovering capabilities that contribute to organizational mixes of resources and capabilities, or resource configurations (RC), which support the realization of data-enabled strategies (Borch et al., 1999).

Table 4.3 presents the distillated supporting capabilities. We distinguish advanced digital capabilities, network capabilities, emotional capabilities and innovation and learning capabil-ities. In what follows, the different capabilities are discussed.

As stated earlier, digital technologies only lead to value creation when they are properly translated into a strategy which is then effectively realized (Mikalef et al., 2018; Müller, 2019; Yunis et al., 2018). **Advanced digital capabilities** are essential to the translation of data into value, since they bring together technological and business intelligence with an advanced IT-architecture and well-managed data.

Big data analytics capability (BDAC) is a multidimensional capability which refers to an organization's capacity to capture, integrate and analyze big data, and generate meaningful insights from them, allowing improved decision-making and extraction of value in a timely manner (Mikalef et al., 2018; Yichuan Wang et al., 2018). BDAC thus entails both a talent and a technology component (Akter et al., 2016; Sivarajah et al., 2017; P. Xu & Kim, 2014). The technology component consists of a flexible, scalable and reliable IT-infrastructure which carefully procures high quality data. Expertise in sensemaking, manipulation and acquisition of data complemented with knowledge on legal and ethical issues related to data analytics make up the talent element.

Since I4.0 benefits depend on the vertical and horizontal integration of manufacturing systems which characterize the industrial stage, *interconnectivity and integrative capabili-*

Table 4.3   Supporting capabilities for the successful realization of data-enabled strategies

Capability Set	Components	References
Advanced Digital Capabilities	• Big Data Analytics Capability • Interconnectivity & IT-integration Capability • Software Development Capability	Yichuan Wang et al. (2018); Wamba et al. (2017); Moonen et al. (2019); Mikalef et al. (2018); Akter et al. (2016); Sivarajah et al. (2017); Günther et al. (2017); Kim et al. (2013); Müller and Voigt (2017); Rußmann et al. (2015)
Network Capabilities	• Relational Network Capability • Cocreation Capability • Framing • Coopetition Capability • Network Orchestration	Kohtamäki et al. (2013a); Marcos-Cuevas et al. (2016); Raffaelli et al. (2019); Van Bockhaven and Matthyssens (2017); Brusoni and Prencipe (2013); Hannah and Eisenhardt (2018); Niemczyk and Trzaska (2020); Bengtsson et al. (2016); Hurmelinna-Laukkanen and Nätti (2018); Möller and Svahn (2003)
Emotional Capabilities	• Organizational Emotional Capability • Emotional Balancing • Emotional Aperture • Emotional Regulation • Emotional & Cognitive Framing	Q.N. Huy (1999); Akgün et al. (2011); N. Vuori et al. (2018); T.O. Vuori and Huy (2016); Huy (2002); Huy (2010); Sanchez-Burks and Huy (2009); Q.N. Huy and Zott (2019); Hodgkinson and Healey (2014); Raffaelli et al. (2019)
Innovation & Learning Capabilities	• Absorptive Capacity • Ambidexterity • Continuous Alignment Capability • Innovative Organizational Culture • Management Committed to Data Strategy	Cohen and Levinthal (1990); Limaj and Bernroider (2019); Müller et al. (2020); Lubatkin et al. (2006); Ko and Liu (2019); Yeow et al. (2018); Günther et al. (2017); Akter et al. (2016); Pisano (2019); Agostini and Filippini (2019); Upadhyay and Kumar (2020); Alharthi et al. (2017); Mittal et al. (2018)

ties which enable firms to connect their systems with and extend them towards the broader network are particularly relevant (Kim et al., 2013).

Finally, *software development capability* can enable an SME to differentiate itself even more. Standard solutions may be found in cloud computing and Software as a Service (Liu et al., 2020). However, firms looking to distinguish themselves through the design of total digital solutions might find that understanding the basics of software development or becoming fluent in it can facilitate cooperation with external software partners and lead to new value creating opportunities (Rüßmann et al., 2015).

A second set of capabilities which we found to be important for the effective implementation of data-enabled strategies concerns **network capabilities**. After all, the implementation of I4.0 technology is said to enable and speed up the creation of ecosystems (Amit & Han, 2017; Schneider, 2018). Within such highly interdependent business environments, the success of an individual company becomes intertwined with the overall health of the ecosystem in which it is embedded (Adner & Kapoor, 2010; Subramaniam et al., 2019; L.D. Xu et al., 2018). Being able to navigate this complex environment, source capabilities from it, or even influence and shape it, might lead to a significant increase in competitive advantage (Aarikka-Stenroos & Ritala, 2017; Hurmelinna-Laukkanen & Nätti, 2018; Kohtamäki et al., 2013a; Mei et al., 2019; Mittal et al., 2018). Hence, we consider network capabilities to be capabilities that enable organizations to survive and thrive in today's increasingly interconnected, cross-industry business environment.

SMEs in particular have a lot to gain from being able to manage and leverage their network (Cenamor et al., 2019; Horváth & Szabó, 2019). *Relational network capabilities* allow them to access external resources which can compensate for their often limited financial resources, specialized knowledge and capacity constraints (Kohtamäki et al., 2013a; Moonen et al., 2019). Given that novel value creation frequently depends on collaboration with ecosystem partners, *co-creation capability*, or the ability to co-create value with customers and other actors in ecosystem environments will be an essential capability for the realization of experience-oriented data-enabled strategies (Dugstad et al., 2019; Marcos-Cuevas et al., 2016). *Framing* can support firms in the mobilization of external partners through careful interpretation, packaging and "organizing of information" towards them (Raffaelli et al., 2019). Since high integration of systems encourages cross-industry collaborations, being able to convince unfamiliar actors of the mutual benefits of collaboration becomes increasingly important (Van Bockhaven & Matthyssens, 2017). Equally relevant is the ability to manage the tension that arises from the simultaneous pursuit of cooperation and competition with other firms, or coopetition capability (Bengtsson et al., 2016). After all, the increase in interdependencies can make it interesting or even necessary to collaborate with competitors, especially in settings where firms depend on each other for the collective provision of components to realize customer value (Hannah & Eisenhardt, 2018). Finally, network orchestration capability refers to a firm's ability to influence the evolution of the ecosystem in which it is embedded (Hurmelinna-Laukkanen & Nätti, 2018; Möller & Svahn, 2003). Having a clear vision, as well as strong communication and persuasive skills are a prerequisite to being able to orchestrate fellow actors without the explicit mandate to manage them (Möller et al., 2005). Since SMEs are inclined to have fewer suppliers and thus tend to be more dependent on their partners (Mittal et al., 2018), having great network capabilities could decrease this dependency or afford SMEs a stronger position within their network – which in turn could help them mobilize the network more easily.

Emotional capabilities enable a firm to effectively manage individual and collective emotions in order to facilitate learning and change (Huy, 2002; Q.N. Huy, 1999; Sanchez-Burks & Huy, 2009). Recently, strategy literature has started to recognize the importance of incorporating an emotional perspective in strategy development and execution related to radical innovation (Healey & Hodgkinson, 2017; Hodgkinson & Healey, 2014; Q.N. Huy & Zott, 2019). After all, strategic change which challenges organizational identity and routines, established work roles and interests often triggers intense emotions (Healey & Hodgkinson, 2017; N. Vuori et al., 2018). The disruptive character of I4.0 technology in particular is expected to feed opposition to change (Horváth & Szabó, 2019). Research shows that acceptance problems and resistance can lead to negative change outcomes when left unattended (Healey & Hodgkinson, 2017; Huy et al., 2014; T.O. Vuori & Huy, 2016). Possessing the capability to actively manage emotions could therefore facilitate strategic change within the context of I4.0.

Five components are distinguished. Firstly, a company's *organizational emotional capability* or its ability to "acknowledge, recognize, monitor, discriminate and attend to its members' emotions" increases the likelihood for organizations to realize radical change (Q.N. Huy, 1999, p. 325). Secondly, *emotional balancing capability* supports change by providing the organization with champions dedicated to the change project, on the one hand, and managers devoted to change recipients' emotions, on the other (Huy, 2010). Like the divide and conquer strategy, this organizational capability allows managers to focus, while assuring both organizational needs are met. Thirdly, emotion aperture or the ability to recognize the composition of diverse emotions in a collective (e.g. group or business unit) allows management to respond timely and appropriately to shared emotions leading to improved change outcomes (Sanchez-Burks & Huy, 2009). Finally, *emotion regulation*, or the extent to which individual organizational members can modify their own and other people's emotions, and *emotional and cognitive framing* which also play a role in external mobilization, both affect internal mobilization or the degree to which companies succeed in getting employees "on board" with the change project (Q.N. Huy & Zott, 2019; Raffaelli et al., 2019). Since the implementation of I4.0 is said to be a long-term change effort, being able to continuously motivate employees and encourage their willingness to learn are essential to realizing data-enabled strategies (Agostini & Filippini, 2019; Schuh et al., 2017).

The fourth and final set of supporting capabilities consists of *innovation and learning capabilities*. Since working with I4.0 technology is still novel to many firms, the successful implementation of data strategies will considerably depend on organizations' *absorptive capacity* or the ability to "recognize the value of new, [external] information, assimilate it, and apply it to commercial ends" (Cohen & Levinthal, 1990, p. 128; Limaj & Bernroider, 2019; Müller et al., 2020). *Ambidexterity*, or the capacity to combine the maximization of current business profits with the exploration of new opportunities, facilitates the integration of new knowledge and has been proven to positively affect firm performance (Lubatkin et al., 2006). Recent literature shows that digitization might boost SMEs' ambidextrous capacity (Ko & Liu, 2019). Indeed, Wan et al. (2017) found that applying a platform approach enabled firms to manage exploitation and exploration simultaneously.

As an invisible hand behind organizational behavior, *organizational culture* considerably enables knowledge creation and innovation related to I4.0 implementation (Alharthi et al., 2017; Horváth & Szabó, 2019). A strong innovative culture which encourages disciplined exploration (Pisano, 2019) and accepts innovation as a fundamental organizational principle

(Hartmann, 2006) can support *continuous (re)alignment*. The ability to iteratively realign work practices, organizational structure and stakeholder interests as a response to internal and external tensions is quoted to be "a journey of continuous adaptation and change" and essential to realizing big data benefits (Akter et al., 2016; Günther et al., 2017; Yeow et al., 2018).

A final element which significantly contributes to a climate for innovation and learning, which was found to be wanting in SMEs, is *management's commitment* to data strategy (Alharthi et al., 2017; Mittal et al., 2018). By developing a clear data vision, dedicating a specific function to the advancement of I4.0 related projects, and trusting data rendered insights, management can set the tone for an organizational data mindset.

Based on our literature review, we expect the different sets of capabilities to be required for the successful implementation of all the identified high road strategies. In the following sections, we examine this assumption for the Sanders Material case. Firstly, we introduce the methodology and sketch the case study's background. Next, we illustrate Sanders Material's evolution from the company's Pre-Industry 4.0 era to its I4.0 Maturity state today.

4.3 METHODOLOGY

A longitudinal case study was chosen based on the following arguments. Firstly, case studies are considered most appropriate for the exploration of new phenomena and their underlying key variables (Eisenhardt, 1989; Yin, 2011). Given the slow adoption of I4.0 technology, opportunities to empirically research implemented data-enabled strategies have been scant so far (Müller, 2019; Schuh et al., 2017). By applying an explorative approach and focusing on a single, in-depth case study, richness in data is achieved which enables the understanding of the relationship between the studied phenomenon and its context (Dubois & Gadde, 2002; Woodside & Wilson, 2003). Considering the context seems specifically desirable given the increasing embeddedness of companies in their surrounding ecosystem. Secondly, a longitudinal approach was used in order to capture process dynamics, allow for the identification of main sequences throughout the company's evolution over time, and achieve a causal perspective on behavior (Eisenhardt, 1989; Quintens & Matthyssens, 2010; Stevens & Dimitriadis, 2004). Sanders Material was selected through purposeful sampling, as this allowed us to maximize learning through the identification of an information-rich case (Patton, 2005).

4.3.1 Research Background

Our case study focuses on a Belgian manufacturing SME, which offers products and services destined for the construction industry. Founded in 1965, Sanders Material [2] grew from a small enterprise to a leader in its business, recognized by its peers and known for its innovative and sustainable solutions. Nowadays, counting over 2,200 employees spread out over 40 countries, the company services over 70 countries worldwide. Most of the company's clients are SMEs. As one of our interviewees stated:

> Since we understand their mindset, and most value can be offered to them, it is our goal to help them grow. (INT 1)

Throughout the years, Sanders' strategy evolved from selling hardware solutions to a fully-fledged digital servitization strategy in which optimization of the client's processes

Table 4.4   *Overview of management interviews*

	Number of interviews	Length of interviews
Chief Product Officer	1 separate, 1 collective interview	2 x 1 hour
VP/CTO	1 collective interview	50 mins
Product Manager I4.0	2 separate, 1 collective interview	1 hour, 1 hour 30 mins

and the processes of their clients' clients is central to their value proposition. Over the last 20 years, the company has experienced exponential growth, registering +200 percent growth from 2008 to 2018 – despite the financial crisis. A true success story, which only seems to continue as 2019's numbers indicate.

Yet, the integration of I4.0 and big data didn't happen overnight. We take a closer look at each phase as we zoom in on the barriers encountered and the critical success factors that allowed Sanders to overcome these challenges and evolve towards I4.0 Maturity and data-driven growth.

4.3.2   Data Collection and Analysis

This illustrative case study is built on a combination of document analysis and three different interviews (three separate, one collective) lasting from 30 minutes up to an hour, in which the Chief Product Officer (CPO), Vice President (VP) and Chief Technical Officer (CTO), and the I4.0 Product Manager (PM) were involved (Table 4.4). The virtual interviews followed a semi-structured format, allowing us to gather rich qualitative data necessary to reconstruct the case and present it vividly, as is typical for illustrative case studies. Specific attention was paid to the company's evolution with regards to the implementation of I4.0 and the key challenges and critical success factors which accompanied this evolution.

Three out of four interviews were recorded and carefully transcribed. During the other interview, notes were taken by both the interviewer and the transcriber. These proceedings were afterwards combined.

Additional information was collected consisting of news items, reports, video testimonials and data found on the company's website as well as its social media accounts. These secondary data sources allowed for the triangulation of findings from diverse sources safeguarding substantiated interpretation (Charmaz, 2006). Consecutive content analysis enabled the distinction of major themes (Patton, 2005) which will be presented later in the discussion section.

4.4   FINDINGS

Throughout the evolution of Sanders Material (SM) we distinguish four different phases, all with their own challenges. We follow the company from its Pre-Industry 4.0 years (stage 0) over its first experiments with automation in I4.0: Embryonic Stage (stage 1) and its advanced I4.0 efforts: Adolescence (stage 2) to I4.0: Maturity (stage 3). In the following sections we describe the distinct phases while focusing on the strategy followed and challenges encountered. To facilitate understanding of the case the different stages are summarized in Table 4.5.

4.4.1 Pre-Industry 4.0 (1965–2006)

Emile Sanders set up a company in semi-finished products in 1965. Incidentally, his neighborhood friend, Joris Baelen, dealt in tools and small machines which facilitated the production of end-products for which Emile sold parts. And so, Emile set out not only offering parts but also tooling which could aid his customers in the fabrication of their own products. From the very start, the SME owner was not so much focused on simply selling products but rather on providing solutions to even the smallest enterprise.

> In the old days, a small customer could start making products with an investment of only 20–30.000 EUR. Emile Sanders responded to that market. It was his goal to simplify the production process and accelerate it. (INT 1)

This story matters as it explains the strong SME mentality and strong customer-oriented focus which seem to have become engrained in the company's DNA. That service-oriented mindset is a huge part of the foundation on which Sanders built its growth, as the following quote illustrates:

> We aim to lift our clients. If their business grows, we can benefit from this as well. (INT 2)

In 1999, the company began with the optimization of its back-end processes by implementing an electronic ordering system or EOS, allowing clients to electronically submit their orders. Since they did not yet have the proper software capabilities in-house, they needed help. Agodata became their software partner and would remain so for the next 20 years. The I4.0 PM stated that they "are supplier and customer but even more so, they are partners improving the program or the product together."

Around the same time, stemming from a shared interest in technological innovation, the I4.0 PM started looking for new solutions together with Sanders' top salesperson.

> That's how the automation department originated. It's in our DNA. (INT 1)

Years before, employees at Sanders already knew how to automatically control a saw but the company's automation story only truly kicked off when they started offering automation solutions to its clients. The company evolved from selling parts and tooling to providing advice to fabricators[3] on how to automate their production.

Since Sanders itself did not produce the machines necessary for the automation of the production, the company once again needed a partner. They found one in Temran, a family-owned business, known for its outstanding German quality. SM distinguished itself from machine vendors, their brand new competitors in this strategy, by offering fabricators a total solution. Rather than simply dropping the machines on site, the company promised its clients the production would be up and running once they left. The guaranteed fit with the parts sold – inputs to the fabricators' production process – as well as the simplicity of the solution offered helped SM stand out and even allowed the company to charge higher prices compared with machine vendors. "Customers were willing to pay the extra fee" (INT2) for the added value found in the expert advice, the guided installation and the assurance of compatibility with their production input.

During this first stage, challenges were encountered. Linking machines in a DOS-environment was incredibly difficult. Deciding on the right associates to team up with, no less so. Even though the criteria on which to base partner selection seemed clear initially, in the years to come, opportunities available to SMa – as well as their own stability – would prove to be affected by choices made in this preliminary stage.

4.4.2   I4.0: Embryonic Stage (2007–14)

Working with the software and experimenting with automation, allowed SM to grow its own digital capabilities and discover potential for new ways in which they could facilitate clients' processes. By now, orders were running electronically, and part of the clients' production process was automated. Yet again, the company saw room for improvement. The I4.0 PM explains:

> There was no flow, no optimization of their production environment and planning. There was no information flowing from one production step to the next.

The company decided to encourage clients to move towards a paperless production environment. Together with their software developer Agodata, they co-developed a first application which they branded SANDOPRO. The configurator which consisted of a web-based platform supported customers in three ways.

Firstly, it facilitated the generation of "attractive, clear and accurate proposals." By optimizing their customers' back end, SM increased both the fabricators' efficiency and their competitive advantage. After all, with the growing competitiveness following the popularization of the Internet, "the process of generating prices offers needed to speed up" (INT1).

A second way in which the tool offered value was through integration with the fabricator's production environment. Bar codes which rolled out of SANDOPRO could be applied to the production parts. The previously implemented machines would scan the bar code and, by reading it, know exactly how to process the parts.

Finally, by linking SANDOPRO to the existing EOS-module, Sanders contributed to an optimization of its end-to-end flow. The tool generated the bill of material itself, allowing Sanders to respond faster and more accurately to fabricators' orders.

SM recognized integration as key to I4.0 realization. By opting for standard machines and software, they increased compatibility with the existing IT-systems and eased integration. The ROI sought in the SANDOPRO investment was in customer bonding, rather than in sales margin. This differentiated SANDOPRO's approach from competitors.

> We do not intend to present ourselves as a software company but rather as a company that offers software and machines to its clients so that they can process our products, our core business in a more efficient way and bigger volumes can be realized. (INT 1)

Rolling out a solution which surpassed Sanders' core expertise posed challenges. Start-up problems faced in the early launch stage left initial clients somewhat dumbfounded. The reputation damage influenced purchasing decisions of potential new clients. This put extra pressure on the support team. After all, the deep integration of Sanders' software system into the customers' processes made it even more important for clients to have issues resolved quickly. With the introduction of EOS, only the fabricators' back end got affected. Now, when the software did not work, the production process itself could be put at risk. Thankfully, SM could count on a great support team, as the following quote illustrates.

> For the moment, the support works very good for me. I am not an easy client for them either because when I have a problem, I immediately grab the phone, get assistance, let them take over my screen. It is important that your machines continue to run and that the production does not come to a halt when there's a problem. And they help you immediately. (CL 2)

It did help SM that it could count on customers who were willing to take the plunge and were prepared to put in the time necessary to perfect the software tool together with the company.

> There have been some start-up problems with regards to lay-out of price offers etcetera, so we have spent some time on it together with Sanders Material and now that's running rather well too. (CL 1)

4.4.3 I4.0: Adolescence (2014–19)

With SANDOPRO up and running at some of its customers' sites, SM realized it could optimize its clients' production process further by redesigning their workflow and by adding work instructions. To accomplish this, they needed to create an additional layer to SANDOPRO. Yet again, a solution was co-developed with software supplier Agodata. SANDOFLO, the resulting web-based Manufacturing Execution System (MES), was set up to be tested in a pilot with 12 customers. The solution ran on Sanders' server and was in fact an extension of the previous SANDOPRO configurator. Catalogues which had been inputted for the configurator before now became available to workers on the factory floor.

SANDOFLO optimized jobs by providing highly detailed and visualized step-by-step instructions displayed on screens to the workers. Throughout the process, they would press "start" and "stop" to confirm the start and end of a job. Gathered data were presented to CEOs and owners by means of an in-house developed dashboard. The I4.0 PM explained why they opted for proprietary software:

> The standard dashboard for SANDOFLO was insufficient. Since we know the managers and foremen, understand what they need the tool for, and how they use it, we developed our own dashboard which allows them to stay on top of what happens in the production without having to be connected to the server. We built connections with SANDOPRO and SANDOFLO in the back so the information can be fed straight into the web-based dashboard. (INT 1)

The dashboard not only provided managers with increased insights into quality issues and progress made. It also assisted fabricators in improved communication with their clients. Most of the fabricators still collected information on paper. Answering requests for project updates was a time-consuming activity which involved walking into the production area and asking around. SANDOFLO offered CEOs the advantage of always knowing immediately how their production was doing. This deep integration into the customers' processes, however, came at a price. Both internally and externally, numerous barriers were encountered.

Internally, software development and sales posed the biggest challenges. Given the novelty and the complexity of the solution, a lot of time was spent at the fabricator's site. Three to four days were devoted to gathering information on the existing production process and the initial lay-out of the manufacturing unit, after which the new lay-out was designed and discussed. Co-creating the solution together with the client took time.

Since the company continued building systems on systems, its choice of software partner became increasingly important. After all, the reliability of Sanders' overall system and future opportunities for extending it would be influenced by the capacity, maturity and reliability of the underlying software. Thinking ahead, the company investigated the possibility of co-creating SANDOFLO with a new software partner. The MES-tier, however, still needed to be able to communicate seamlessly with SANDOPRO and EOS, both Agodata systems. Since the new layer "needed so much information from the current calculation software, which was already controlling machines" (INT 1), a smooth information flow from one system to the next mattered even more. Unfortunately, according to the I4.0 PM, "back then [Agodata] was not ready to facilitate this." Hence, the company decided to stick with its initial supplier.

A third challenge was found in the development of a system flexible enough for all types of customers. Even though the 12 customers of the SANDOFLO pilot project produced similar end-products, made use of the same catalogues and executed similar processes, the order in which they did things still differed. On top of that, the novelty of the solution made it almost impossible to get it right the first time. There were "no terms of reference, no clear manual in which was exactly explicated how things worked. We only had a lay-out of a couple of pages describing what had to happen" (INT 1).

Hence, constructing the MES became a venture of ongoing improvement. Problems with software connectivity, speed and flexibility, tempered the initial enthusiasm of Sanders' sales team. They started selling less, resulting in a temporary halt in the recruitment of new customers. Customers who did embark on the journey strongly relied on the support of the automation team to keep their core business running smoothly. The introduction of SANDOPRO had taught SM that implementing novel solutions which were deeply integrated into the client's core business made clients more dependent on its assistance. The I4.0 PM stated that, since they were now "not only involved with the machines but with the entire production, things were more critical."

Being able to quickly respond to and resolve issues, often from a distance, required experience. Sanders could count on a great automation team with 15+ years of experience, who "will surely help you out if you can't find what you're looking for" (CL 2), according to clients. In order to scale up, however, the team needed to grow. Finding and training adequate people turned out to be difficult and time-consuming. The lack of a sufficiently large support team led to a temporary slowdown in the roll-out of SANDOFLO.

Externally, barriers were encountered in the sales process of the novel solution as well as the mobilization of a diverse set of involved actors. A first challenge consisted of convincing fabricators of the value of the solution. SM tried to persuade early customers by pinpointing the potential efficiency gains upon reorganization of the production process. This did not always work, however. The I4.0 PM explicated that "not every client who is interested in SANDOFLO will eventually start, because some of them don't believe us or think that they are already operating at sufficiently efficient levels." Convincing customers could become easier, with the results of the pilot project rolling in, confirming the promised efficiency gains.

> Most [pilot project] customers say they observe a 10–30% increase in efficiency or that they can produce more with the same amount of people. We've gained a client three years ago. His order

volume raised from 1,1 MIO to 1,5 MIO. Can this increase be entirely contributed to the implementation? That is always difficult to say with 100% certainty but most of the customers do say so. (INT 1)

The biggest challenge, however, was found in convincing customers to change their ways of working. Compared with the implementation of the automated machines, SANDOFLO was not a simple plug-and-play solution. For companies to fully benefit from the implementation, a reorganization of the workflow was required or at least suggested.

> They need to agree with the different way of working too … Each and every one of those 12 clients who have already started had to change their lay-out … It's not just a couple of screens which are added to the production floor. (INT 1)

Reorganization came on top of the job and entailed not only optimization of the factory floor lay-out, but also the instalment of increased levels of division of labor. For workers who were used to constructing a product from start to finish, this was a big change. Even more so, they feared increased control since SANDOFLO traced every move they made. Foremen were not always too excited about the prospect of the extra start-up work, especially when they did not see the added value.

The I4.0 PM stressed the importance of adequate change management at the client's site for successful implementation of SANDOFLO. After all, for the company's solution to come to realization, cooperation was required from all whom were affected by and essential to its operationalization. "Technology is only one part of it" (INT 1). Within the SANDOFLO pilot group, the I4.0 PM spotted a divide between two groups, as he sees "3–5 out of the 12 [pilot] companies picking things up rapidly, with the others lagging slightly behind." According to the product manager, having a key person responsible for the implementation of I4.0 projects is essential. Next to that

> the different levels need to be on board so that the system gets implemented and used quickly. They need to understand the advantages and receive the necessary time to familiarize themselves with the system. (INT 1)

Overall buy-in and clear commitment from management were stated to be prerequisites for successful implementation.

Simultaneously with the roll-out of SANDOPRO and SANDOFLO, SM started offering services to installers, the clients of its clients. Protest followed from fabricators who were afraid SM would start reaching out to their clients directly, causing them to lose business. By showing fabricators the services for installers would boost their own revenue, Sanders managed to convince them. Consequently, installers who were frequent customers of one of Sanders' fabricators could count on SM for marketing tools, training and access to an information platform which supported the installers in better servicing their clients. The foundation for Sanders' digital platform strategy was laid.

4.4.4   I4.0: Maturity (2020)

While planning to scale up SANDOFLO, SM continued optimizing its internal processes. Its EOS-system evolved from a simple ordering system to an extended client portal. Regular updates of SANDOPRO enabled continuous alignment with evolving customer needs and the

Table 4.5   *Sanders Material's gradual growth towards I4.0 Maturity*

	PRE-INDUSTRY 4.0 (1965–2006)	EMBRYONIC I4.0 (2007–14)	I4.0 ADOLOSCENCE (2014–19)	I4.0 MATURITY (2020)
High road strategy	Servitization *Convenience/Experience*	Digital Servitization *Convenience*	Digital Servitization *Experience*	Digital Platform Strategy *Experience*
Description	Optimization of the company's back end through implementation of an electronic ordering system (EOS). Simplification of the client's production process through automation of his/her production.	Installation of a paperless production environment at the fabricator's site aimed at the optimization of his/her planning, production environment and information flow.	Advanced optimization of the customer's production process through reorganization of his/her workflow lay-out and the adding of work instructions to facilitate workers in the production process. Services are extended to clients' clients.	Evolution towards a digital platform strategy through the extension of the SANDOPRO platform with newly in-house built tools and the development of the Digital Passport project.
Systems	Implementation of an EOS. Fabricator's machines are linked in DOS-environment.	Development and implementation of price offer generator SANDOPRO. Integration of SANDOPRO with the customer's existing software systems and production environment.	Development and implementation of SANDOFLO and the proprietary dashboard which are both integrated with SANDOPRO. Development of an information platform for installers.	Finalization of SANDOPRO Element Installer and Element Installer Online. Integration of SANDOPRO with REVIT, an external application. Proof of concept and pilot of the Digital Passport platform.

	PRE-INDUSTRY 4.0 (1965–2006)	EMBRYONIC I4.0 (2007–14)	I4.0 ADOLOSCENCE (2014–19)	I4.0 MATURITY (2020)
Barriers	• Linking machines in a DOS-environment is difficult • Machine partner selection seems obvious but will jeopardize operations in a later stage	• Start-up problems with the software cause a temporary drawback in sales • Increasing pressure on the support team	• Co-creation of complex solutions with customers is time-consuming • Initial problems with the development of a flexible MES discourage the sales team • Limited size of support team hinders scale up • Clients need persuasion regarding the value of the novel solution and the accompanying workflow reshuffle • Implementation is met with resistance from a divergent set of involved actors at the client's side • Customers initially refuse to let Sanders offer services to their clients (installers)	• Introduction of a new integrated tool might negatively affect clients' operations in case of software instability upon launch • Timely development of software could be hindered by complexity of the solution and the need for customization • Finding the right partners for the Digital Passport project will influence Sanders' future innovation capacity • Search for highly advanced IT-knowledge takes time
Co-creating partnerships	machine supplier Temran	machine supplier Temran, customers, software supplier Agodata	machine suppliers Temran and Risker, customers, software supplier Agodata,	machine suppliers Temran and Risker, customers, software supplier Agodata and brand new software partner Vibe
Beneficiaries of value creation	customers and machine vendor Temran	customers, machine vendor Temran and software supplier Agodata	customers, machine vendors Temran and Risker, software supplier Agodata and installers	customers, machine vendors Temran and Risker, software supplier Agodata and installers, architects, new value partners and clients of the Digital Passport project
I4.0 Maturity	Independent solution			Networked solution

extension of use towards new actors. An example of this is the integration of SANDOPRO with REVIT, a building information modeling software used by architects. Additionally, Sanders is looking into the optimization of the catalogues behind SANDOFLO. The catalogue generator, developed based on the logic of paper catalogues, would be reorganized following insights generated by SM's internal document management system. Adding novel ways of presenting the information on the screens (e.g. videos) would allow SM to make the MES-system even more user-friendly.

Finally, the company is thinking about leveraging data gathered at its software platform. Analytics could help Sanders optimize internal workings, spot new market trends and align its offer with prevalent market needs. Currently, no analyses are being run but the long-term intention is there. In order to be ready for when that time comes, SM has already asked their clients to sign a new contract related to General Data Protection Regulation (GDPR) and the use of data.

Parallel to the internal optimization track, the company continues extending its software platform. The CPO explains how they are currently building new applications around the software platform focused on visualization. The goal is to eventually build and develop Sanders' branded solutions. SANDOPRO Element Installer (SEI), for example, is an application aimed at installers which is being grafted onto SANDOPRO today. The software is a web-based simplified version of SANDOPRO, which supports installers in the quick generation of professional price offers. Proactively boosting the efficiency of its clients' clients as well as strengthening ties between fabricator, installer and itself are Sanders' main objectives related to the implementation of SEI.

Next to these continuous innovation projects, the blueprints for an entirely new trajectory have been drafted. With the Digital Passport project Sanders intends to create brand new services, which extend far beyond their core offering and initial value chain. By adding a QR-code to the finalized product at the fabricator's site, the company plans to collect data about the product's entire life cycle. By simply scanning this QR-code the data should be easily accessible to everyone. "The Digital Passport should be able to stand on its own" (INT 2). SANDOFLO will not be a prerequisite to accessing the platform but the I4.0 PM assured "integration would of course be provided."

The Digital Passport offers many opportunities. Collaborations with novel partners might expose SM to brand new markets. Tracing products throughout their life cycle is likely to supply the company with extra data allowing for additional analyses. Not to mention that being central to the creation of a new digital platform ecosystem will not hurt their negotiating power.

According to the I4.0 PM, Sanders' first concern is now the successful and timely finalization of the newly developed SEI. History has taught them about the instability of neonatal software applications. Malfunctioning of fresh tools might affect the workings of already implemented systems. Since "SANDOPRO is our entire digital link with our client, from the start to the end of their entire process" (INT 1), having the new tool work flawlessly upon implementation becomes increasingly important. Nervousness about the timely development of the software is due to the complexity of the complete value chain integration with different parties to be linked and the need to customize the solution to each partner's specific application.

Secondly, realizing the Digital Passport project will require a central database which needs to be managed well. Setting up a strong data platform and gathering the right partners to team up with will be essential to the project's success.

Finally, developing more complex solutions as well as taking on more software development in-house increasingly necessitates advanced IT knowledge. Finding knowledgeable employees who fit SM's mindset will become increasingly important.

4.5   DISCUSSION

SM's progress from the start of their automation offer to the roll-out of its digital platform strategy today, has been described in the Findings section. In this section, we dive deeper into the characteristics of the specific strategy followed and the resource configuration which enabled the company to implement its strategy effectively. Linking the insights gained from the case back to our initial theoretical framework allows for deeper reflection and the fine-tuning of our original model.

4.5.1   Gradual Growth Towards Maturity

Even though the solution offered to clients today might seem radically new, SM clearly built both the knowledge and systems which allow them to do so in a steady and gradual way. Capabilities and systems were gathered along the road in an incremental process towards maturity.

4.5.1.1   Evolutionary pathways and combined strategies

The evolution from a focus on increasing internal efficiency (EOS) towards boosting customers' convenience (SANDOPRO), before moving onto radically new value creation (SANDOFLO, Digital Passport) follows our initial expectations of a movement from convenience to experience as illustrated in Table 4.5. The case also illustrates that combining different strategies is an option. The fact that SM is nowadays thinking about improving the EOS and upgrading the organization and display of their catalogues (MES-system) might even suggest that such a combination is necessary to continue building novel, advanced solutions. After all, in I4.0 environments "systems are built on systems" (Frank et al., 2019a). New technology does not substitute older technology but rather depends and builds on former configurations. Hence, the maturity grade of your base technology influences the maturity grade and potential complexity of front-end value propositions. Following this logic, going back and forth between optimization of the internal processes and the development of new solutions is no more than an illustration of the continuous alignment quoted to be necessary to reap benefits from digitization (Günther et al., 2017; Yeow et al., 2018).

4.5.1.2   From independent to networked solutions

A movement from left to right in Table 4.2 insinuated an evolution towards more complex, network embedded solutions in which an increasing number of differentiated actors is involved. Indeed, Sanders evolved from co-designing a solution with their software supplier to co-creating value with and to the advantage of suppliers, clients and clients' clients. For newer applications they are teaming up with a software developer outside their original value chain.

One could say that they are moving on from end-to-end (vertical) integration towards more cross-industry (horizontal) collaboration. By becoming increasingly embedded in an extended network, Sanders is able to boost its service innovation performance (Hsueh et al., 2010), since gaining access to expert knowledge not only enables the company to create ground-breaking solutions, but also to reach a brand new set of potential beneficiaries.

4.5.2   Critical Success Factors

A strong innovation culture and the development of state-of-the-art, total solutions aided by network capabilities and gradually developed advanced digital capabilities allowed Sanders to grow from selling industrial parts and tools to laying the groundwork for a brand new digital platform. The following paragraphs focus on key resources and capabilities which facilitated Sanders in its growth towards maturity.

4.5.2.1 Lock-in through superior solutions and service rather than systems
SM follows a customer process-oriented advanced servitization strategy in which hybrid solutions are offered that promise fabricators growth through the optimization of their production processes and back end (Coreynen et al., 2017). With the deep integration down the value chain and high customization of the offered solutions, the company aims to strengthen its customer relationships and increase its competitive advantage rather than boost financial performance directly. Growth in profits is believed to follow from increased demand for their core product. That is why they adhere to competitive pricing for their added services, or as the CPO stated: "We sell premium products with a high service level. We do not intend to present ourselves as a software company."

By focusing their servitization offer on the optimization of their clients, SM counters the "servitization paradox," a situation in which revenues increase with greater servitization while profits decrease (Baines & Lightfoot, 2014). Through raising the efficiency of the fabricators, Sanders helps them grow their capacity which in turn leads to higher purchases of their own products.

For the creation of their hybrid solutions, SM relies on standard software and standard machines which are company branded. This is in comparison with their main competitor, which solely works with its proper machines and systems. The literature points towards the importance of standardization and integration capabilities for effective I4.0 implementation (Müller & Voigt, 2017). Standardization facilitates integration with the customers' systems and contributes to ease of use. Standardization, however, also considerably lowers switching costs, allowing customers the freedom to leave whenever they want to, but "they know that if they switch, they would have to take a step back" (INT 1). The I4.0 PM is convinced of the superiority of their solution and states that even though customers "don't feel bound to us, they are because the solution works well."

Being first to come up with a total solution did not harm the company either. Sales of novel service solutions can be challenging (Coreynen et al., 2017). The market might not be ready to understand the value of the solution offered, as this case illustrates. However, in a world where systems are built on systems, laying the first stone can pay off. After all, familiarizing themselves with integrated system solutions requires a significant investment from the customers as well.

> If you are the first one to come up with a solution and you offer a total solution which works, customers say "Maybe I can find the parts elsewhere at a discount, but we'd still be missing out on Sanders' service." … It is not only about pricing but also about the expert advice and the total service offered. (INT 1)

Sanders' support team turned out to play an essential role in the realization of that total service. The efforts of the team allowed the company to keep customers engaged throughout its start-up problems with SANDOPRO and added to the fine-tuning of solutions in co-creation with customers. Its role only increased with the growing interdependencies and profound integration into the customers' core processes. Surprisingly, our literature review did not point out the importance of the support team in the realization of hybrid solutions.

4.5.2.2 A highly innovative spirit

A strong innovation culture turns out to be the main driver behind SM's continuous stream of innovations. Engrained in their DNA rests a desire to unceasingly develop solutions to simplify their customers' operations, following the initial ideology of Emile Sanders who in 1965 decided that even the smallest clients should be able to process SM's parts into final products.

Customers are stated to be Sanders' main source of innovation. Frequent client interactions with both the sales and the automation team facilitate informal knowledge transfer. The automation team spends one-third of their time on site with the fabricators. Many of the sales team have a background in automation, allowing them to truly understand the technical challenges, reason with the clients and co-create solutions with them. The encouragement of "horizontal moves" in which employees switch from one department to the next is part of Sanders' HR policy. It allows for the development of a broad range of knowledge and experiences, which enables synergies and information absorption throughout the organization. Informal channels are complemented with formal initiatives, such as workshops, in which market and industry trends as well as recurring questions from clients are presented to key players in order to gain more in-depth insight. Closeness with the client, a varied background of expertise and an active take on collecting novel ideas all seem to contribute to Sanders' well-developed absorptive capacity.

Another important role is said to be played by the CEO and the board of directors who are highly supportive of innovation initiatives. "Linda Sanders permits experiments and is not afraid to take quick decisions. She has always supported me, which allowed me to develop many positive innovations" (INT 1). The appointment of a project manager dedicated to I4.0 initiatives demonstrates management's commitment and reveals a belief in the importance of I4.0 for the company's future.

Support from management sets the tone for an experimental mindset which enabled Sanders to acquire its advanced digital capabilities. Try-outs with linking machines in a DOS-environment laid the groundwork for their interconnectivity and IT-integration capability. Continuous linking of machines and software platforms led to the company being the center of a new digital platform today. Co-developing software solutions with Agodata helped SM develop its own software development capability, which nowadays allows them to realize proprietary applications in-house. From sourcing capabilities externally to soaking up knowledge and developing the capabilities yourself. Another great example of Sanders' absorptive capacity. Today, being sponsor of the digital platform, Sanders has access to an exponential amount of data. This offers an opportunity for the company to further build its big data analytics capability, which SM fully intends to do. Sanders is currently thinking about how it might leverage data gathered on its software platform and through customer interactions, to better align its offer with the needs of the market. The fact that SM is only now starting out with BDAC confirms the findings by Frank et al. (2019a), who listed BDAC as a final destination in the growth towards maturity. This makes sense, since systems are being built on top of systems and big data require highly integrated, reliable systems.

Twenty years of experience with innovation has led to the development of advanced digital capabilities and has reinforced the company's ambidexterity, allowing Sanders to continue designing and realizing several innovative solutions simultaneously. It is a great illustration of how *path dependency* or the gathering of capabilities throughout the years can open up an avenue for advanced strategy making (Schreyögg & Koch, 2009).

4.5.2.3 Ecosystem mindset

The results of an individual company are said to become intertwined with the overall health of the ecosystem in which it is embedded (Adner & Kapoor, 2010; Subramaniam et al., 2019). SM seems to understand this as it explicitly invests in the development of its fabricators, clients of clients and its suppliers. Through co-creation and expert advice, the company aims to lift its partners and boost their competitiveness while strengthening ties throughout its emerging ecosystem.

This allows Sanders to continue creating cutting-edge solutions. After all, having ecosystem partners lag behind can lead to a misfit between the company's innovation goals and the potential for realized value creation. Indeed, Kim et al. (2013) found that IT-alignment between interdependent partners facilitated customer value creation.

Increasing interdependencies unfortunately make the firm more vulnerable to failure of a value partner. Sanders decided to put a stop to 13 years of collaboration when its initial machine vendor ran into financial issues, thereby endangering its own value delivery. According to the I4.0 PM, "the situation became very critical" since the company still needed to provide support to its clients' systems, not knowing whether the machine vendor would be able to deliver on its part. Following the split, the company switched to Risker, a machine vendor under the umbrella of a holding "worth almost 1MIA EUR which seems to be very stable" (INT1). High integration into the customer's core processes urged Sanders to select partners based on stability rather than on a shared SME background. Incidentally, Risker also happened to offer advanced automated machines, precisely in line with SM's own growth in maturity.

Strong network capabilities contributed to SM's steady growth. Sanders' total solution is the result of nonstop co-creation with customers, machine vendors and software suppliers which all played a vital role in the growth of the company. Strong ties aided by framing capabilities allowed the company to convince partners to support its novel ideas. An example could be found in the persuasion of fabricators to allow Sanders to approach their installers directly. Sanders knows when to compete and when to collaborate. Coopetition capability also shows from their numerous co-creations with suppliers, who afterwards could implement the co-developed solutions at competitors' sites. What probably sets the company aside most, however, is its future vision. The integration of the supply chain on which the brand new digital platform gets embroidered today sprung from Sanders' minds. The company's network orchestration capability allowed it to carry out this vision and mobilize both familiar and unfamiliar ecosystem partners to turn its vision into a reality.

Contrary to our expectations, little to no explicit mention of emotional capability was registered throughout the interviews. This could be explained by the limited number of interviews which allowed insufficient depth to investigate such mechanisms. Yet, the I4.0 PM did stress the importance of change management at the customer's site. Frequent interactions with customers suggest the human factor is being considered throughout the co-creation and implementation phases. Further research will be needed, however, to gain proper insight.

To sum up, Sanders succeeded in its gradual growth towards I4.0 Maturity thanks to its highly innovative spirit supported by management, 20 years of experience and co-creation which led to the development of highly advanced digital capabilities, and the company's aptness at mobilizing and leveraging its surrounding ecosystem.

4.6   IMPLICATIONS FOR PRACTITIONERS

In this chapter we have touched upon opportunities and barriers that SMEs experience regarding the implementation of Industry 4.0 and big data as well as what this technology might entail in terms of strategic options for SMEs. In general, two strategic options can be distinguished: a high road and a low road. Both are not mutually exclusive. Hybrid strategies in which efficiency-oriented projects are combined with an effectiveness-oriented focus are possible. Even more so, their combination might be essential to ensuring continuous growth as our case shows.

Changing strategies, however, does not happen overnight. For a successful transition to take place, gaps need to be surmounted often through the development of additional capabilities. An overview of the process is sketched out in Figure 4.1. Companies willing to benefit from I4.0 will first have to *sense* the potential of I4.0 and recognize their own barriers before being able to move on to *seizing* the opportunities presented to them. Understanding the current strategic position and its relation to the desired strategic goal is step one to crafting an effective I4.0 strategy. Based on the size of the divide between both, adjusting the strategic objective or setting intermediate goals might be useful. Next, resource configurations will need to be revised to fit and support the *realization* of the chosen strategy. Continuous improvement loops resulting from the need for internal and external alignment enable organizations to gradually leverage I4.0 technology for competitive advantage.

To support managers in drawing up their own I4.0 strategic roadmap, an evaluation tool is outlined below. We suggest managers apply this tool to identify gaps and make well-founded strategic decisions in order to smooth their transition towards I4.0.

4.6.1   Towards I4.0

4.6.1.1   Step 1: evaluating current strategic position and future strategic options for fit

A first step towards developing an I4.0 strategy is the assessment of the current strategic position. Only that way can the strategic fit with the desired I4.0 strategic option be evaluated. Literature shows that, in general, the larger the gap between the present and future strategy, the

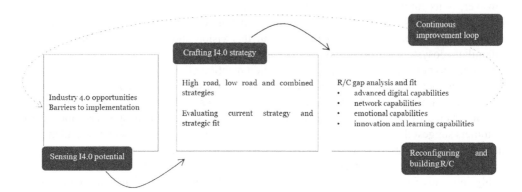

Figure 4.1   Sensing, seizing and realizing I4.0 strategies

Table 4.6   Evaluation tool: current strategic position

Low road	**High road**
Basic technology-enabled option	*Advanced technology-enabled option*
Our business logic is rather product-oriented. We distinguish ourselves mainly through product, price and quality. When services are presented, they are so in support of our product offer.	Our business logic is rather service-oriented. We distinguish ourselves mainly through the offering of advanced services and/or cutting-edge products and our close relationship with customers.
1 2 3 4 5	
The market is requiring mainly standardized products and/or services at competitive prices.	The market is mainly looking for tailored, customized products and/or services.
1 2 3 4 5	
I4.0 technology is mainly applied to save costs and increase efficiency.	I4.0 technology is mainly aimed at generating new customer value and raising effectiveness.
1 2 3 4 5	
We are at the starting point of our digitization journey. Data are not yet being collected in a consistent manner.	We have experience with digitization and are looking to expand further. Data collection and analysis are the basis of product and service improvements.
1 2 3 4 5	

more barriers will have to be faced during transition. This does not necessarily mean a certain strategy is out of reach. Understanding the starting point can help in identifying intermediate goals bridging the gap between today's and tomorrow's strategy.

The statements in Table 4.6 can help the decision maker determine the organization's current strategic position. Remember that the implementation of low road strategies is an often necessary step towards developing capabilities which allow access to more advanced technology-enabled value creating strategies in the long run.

For the evaluation of the current strategic position, four components are taken into account: the intrafirm dominant logic (products vs. services), market demands (standardized vs. customized products and services), the objective of previous technology implementations (cost reduction and efficiency vs. value creation and effectiveness), and experience with digitization.

Table 4.7   *Role of I4.0 technology in different strategic positions*

Current strategic position	Description	Average score
Low road – no (digital) services	Experiments with I4.0 technology are planned or have taken place. Digitization is aimed at increasing efficiency. The idea of utilizing services to boost competitive advantage is rather new.	1–1.5
Low road plus – supporting services	I4.0 technology facilitates the optimization of internal processes. Some (digital) services have been added to improve the lifespan and/or functioning of the sold products.	2–2.5
High road – basic services	I4.0 technology supports the offering of services aimed at improving customer experience. Some data are being collected in a structured manner.	3–3.5
High road plus – advanced services	I4.0 technology enables the creation and delivery of advanced services which exceed customer expectations/explicit customer requests. Data analysis is used as a tool to improve the company's offering.	4–5

The more a company's current situation leans towards a statement on the left, the lower the number that must be encircled and vice versa. Upon completion, an average score can be calculated. Considering the insights gained from literature, we expect the relationships presented in Table 4.7.

In a next stage, based on the obtained average score, potential future strategic options can be evaluated. Alignment theory dictates that with every internal and external shift strategy, resources, the company's offer, leadership and the external environment need to be re-harmonized (Alghisi & Saccani, 2015; Chorn, 1991). The bigger the chasm between the current and the novel situation, the more efforts are required to realign the different aspects. Therefore, immediately transferring from a low road strategy to a high road plus strategy (3–4-point difference) is expected to be increasingly more challenging than it is to transition from a 'low road plus' strategy towards a high road track (1-point difference).

Furthermore, specific resource configurations are required for strategies to be rolled out successfully. True differences in competitive advantage are mainly made through the development and collection of distinct, company-specific capabilities. Step 2 presents a gap analysis tool which decision makers can use to evaluate their present resource configuration as well as the gap with the capability set required for the desired strategy.

Based on the literature, we expect firms which follow a low road strategy to score a 1–2 on average in the capabilities' evaluation tool. Higher scores are indications of high road potential already being present in the organization. Vice versa, companies which are on a high road (plus) track, are likely to score 4–5 on average on capabilities. Subcategories of capabilities which are scored lower might be indicators of misalignment and an explanation of potential difficulties the company is experiencing in realizing its high road strategy.

4.6.1.2   Step 2: evaluating the present resource configuration and fit with the desired strategic option

Our research identified advanced digital capabilities, network capabilities, emotional capabilities and innovation and learning capabilities as essential to the implementation of high road strategies. Table 4.8 can be used to assess the extent to which these capabilities are currently present in the organization. Upon completion, an average score can be calculated to reflect the current capability set.

Following alignment theory, we expect more advanced capabilities to be required to support the offering of advanced services. In Table 4.9, an overview is given of average resource configurations scores and strategic options which, based on the literature, are expected to be a good fit. The table can be interpreted as follows: companies looking to roll out a low road plus strategy would do well to score a 3 on average on every subsection (advanced digital capabilities, relational capabilities, innovation and learning capabilities) of the capabilities' evaluation tool.

In a final stage, the gap between the current strategy and the desired strategy as well as the present capabilities and future capability requirements should be analyzed. When the gap is larger than 1 point, defining intermediate goals might help to facilitate the transition towards the new digital strategy.

To recapitulate, SMEs wanting to leverage I4.0 for strategic advantage best start with a gained understanding of their current strategic position and resource base before crafting their I4.0 strategy. Based on literature, we expect larger gaps between the existing and the desired strategy, and the present and required resource configuration, to boost the chances of the servitization paradox (Baines & Lightfoot, 2014).

Firstly, the bigger the divide between the current and the desired strategy, the larger investments will have to be made to attune the resource configuration to the new direction. Significant investments made in a short period of time, however, reduce the potential return on investment for extra services rendered. Additionally, congruence theory shows that an underestimation of gaps between strategy, resources, the (service) offering and the external environment boost internal and external alignment challenges (Alghisi & Saccani, 2015; Matthyssens & Vandenbempt, 2008). Inefficiencies inherent to misalignment might further hinder the realization of returns (Chorn, 1991). Therefore, taking incremental steps towards a radically new strategy is advised.

Iterative improvement loops and intermediate goals can facilitate the alignment process and support the realization of profits (Yeow et al., 2018). Researchers are invited to further investigate the profitability of the different strategic options (low road, low road plus, high road, high road plus) and the extent to which the size of the gap between the present and aimed for strategy contributes to and/or hinders effective strategic change.

4.7   CONCLUSIONS

With this study we explored strategic options and supporting resource configurations available to SMEs regarding the implementation of I4.0 as well as potential gaps which might be encountered.

A first contribution of our study lies in the confirmation of the findings of Frank et al. (2019b) who presented I4.0 Maturity as the end-result of *a gradual growth trajectory*. Its progressively built technological backbone allowed Sanders to increasingly benefit from I4.0 opportunities. The systematic development of advanced digital capabilities points towards the importance of experimenting with I4.0 today in order to be able to implement value creating strategies tomorrow. The Sanders' case shows that *co-creation* can speed up the development of advanced digital capabilities. By partaking in initiatives from innovative ecosystem

Table 4.8 Evaluation tool: current resource configuration

ADVANCED DIGITAL CAPABILITIES

Siloed systems	*Integrated systems*	*End-to-end integration*	Scale
Our data are dispersed across different places of the organization.	Our data are gathered in a central database.	Our systems seamlessly integrate with supplier and/or customer systems allowing access to network partner data.	1 2 3 4 5
Business insights and decision-making are based on the analysis of historical data.	Business insights and decision-making are based on the analysis of real-time internally gathered data.	External data sources and customer usage data are integrated and employed to optimize business insights and decision-making in real-time.	1 2 3 4 5
Operations are focused on *standardization*, e.g. customers can order standard products via a web shop.	Operations support *high degrees of customization*, e.g. customers can customize their products via a web-based interface.	High degrees of customization are *facilitated by autonomous systems*, e.g. customized orders are automatically being processed from start to finish. OR predictive maintenance(?)	1 2 3 4 5

RELATIONAL CAPABILITIES

Strong operational capabilities	*Strong value creating/relational/market capabilities*	Scale
We mainly depend on our own organization for the creation and delivery of products and services.	We are close to our customer and/or are used to working together with suppliers, complementors and technology partners for the creation and delivery of novel solutions.	1 2 3 4 5
Traditional industry relations — Relationships with external parties consist mainly of contractual, transactional, procurement-dominated interactions with value chain partners. Cost management is central to these interactions.	*Partnership collaborations* — Collaborative relationships extend beyond the traditional value chain. Technology, innovation and value creation are central to the interactions which are based on trust and a partnership mindset.	1 2 3 4 5

INNOVATION & LEARNING

Product-oriented						*Market-oriented/Customer-specific solutions*
Innovation starts rather internally from our product and/or current service offer.	1	2	3	4	5	Innovation starts mostly from customer interactions, feedback and analysis of customer data and processes.
Reactive						*Proactive*
We respond to expressed customer needs and trends spotted in the market.	1	2	3	4	5	We aim to answer/anticipate unexpressed customer needs.
Business units mainly engage in knowledge exchange in formal reporting cycles and working processes. Optimizing execution is the main focus of these conversations.	1	2	3	4	5	As an organization, we excel at cross-business unit collaboration. (In)formal knowledge exchanges with a focus on innovation and improvement are common practice.
Our management is not yet familiar with/committed to implementing I4.0 technology into our business.	1	2	3	4	5	Our management team is highly committed to implementing I4.0 into our business. A management position has been created to follow up on I4.0 projects.
Innovation budgets are revised on a strict quarterly/yearly basis.	1	2	3	4	5	Budget can be allocated flexibly towards technology-enabled innovative projects.
We are rather unfamiliar with technology-enabled innovation projects.						We are constantly combining daily operations with technology related proof of concepts.

Note: a. With relational capabilities, we refer to the combination of emotional and network capabilities.

Table 4.9   *Strategic options and advised average R/C scores*

Current strategic position	Advised average R/C score
Low road – no (digital) services	1–2
Low road plus – supporting services	3
High road – basic services	3.5–4–5
High road plus – advanced services	5

partners, SMEs might through co-creation not only source capabilities in the short term but develop capabilities in-house in the long term. The case does illustrate that with rising interconnectedness *careful partner selection* is advised.

Secondly, the strategic commitment of Sanders' *management* to innovativeness, experimentation and entrepreneurial effectuation was found to spur on the continuous exploration of novel ideas (Berends et al., 2014; Garms & Engelen, 2019). SMEs might benefit from developing *flexible investment decision-making processes*. With technological advancements speeding up exponentially, being able to quickly decide on innovation projects could considerably contribute to the seizing of opportunities.

Thirdly, radically new value creation at Sanders followed from high degrees of *customer-intimacy*. This generated a willingness in customers to share proprietary knowledge, leading to heightened insight into the clients' operations and their unpronounced needs, which in turn enabled the development of market-driving solutions (Berghman et al., 2006). Co-creation might have enhanced trust (Franklin & Marshall, 2019) facilitating the implementation of nearly perfected software, a necessary step in the fine-tuning of Sanders' innovative solutions. The vital role played by Sanders' support team seems currently underexposed by literature. Future research might profit from investigating the support team's characteristics, especially since integrated software solutions are expected to become prevalent for manufacturing (Keller et al., 2014), making this a relevant topic for other companies attempting similar implementations.

SMEs looking to differentiate themselves through the offering of highly innovative services would do well to foster customer-intimacy. As the case illustrates, customers can be a valuable source of novel ideas. Furthermore, closeness to the client could provide SMEs with the insight necessary to develop efficiency-boosting solutions. Banking on the provision of such services might help SMEs to differentiate themselves and counter the servitization-paradox. Additionally, implementation of ICT-supported efficiency-oriented solutions may boost IT-alignment between interconnected partners, which has been shown to enhance value creation (Kim et al., 2013).

Finally, Sanders' ecosystem mindset and strong network capabilities braced the company in the mobilization of powerful network partners necessary for the realization of their innovative ideas. Growing interconnectedness compels SMEs to develop their network capabilities in order to prosper in future I4.0 ecosystems.

Notwithstanding the contributions made, this study has its limitations. Despite rich interviews our vision on the company's evolution remains rather one-sided. Given that Sanders is becoming increasingly embedded in its brand new ecosystem, a multi-actor perspective (Story et al., 2017) might considerably add to our understanding. Additionally, the case could be extended towards exploring the evolution of fabricators who too are in the process of developing their own I4.0 capabilities. Building an embedded case could facilitate the discovery of characteristics which made Sanders' support team stand out and might add to the clarification of the role emotional capabilities played in the development of Sanders' digital platform.

ACKNOWLEDGMENTS

This chapter was written in the context of the Paradigms 4.0 project. The authors are grateful for the financial support received by the Flanders Research Foundation (FWO) which made this research possible.

NOTES

1. For confidentiality reasons, the name of the company is disguised.
2. The name of the company, its employees and partners, and specific technologies have been disguised to ensure confidentiality. The precise names of the rolled-out software programs have been changed as well, although we tried to maintain their spirit. Some numbers and calendar dates were altered for privacy reasons. The interpretation of the data, however, was not affected by these alterations in the display of the data.
3. The company offers services to both clients and clients of their clients. When we talk about fabricators, we refer to the original clients of Sanders. Installers, on the other hand, are clients of the fabricators which now have become part of Sanders' extended value chain.

REFERENCES

Aarikka-Stenroos, L., & Ritala, P. (2017). Network management in the era of ecosystems: Systematic review and management framework. *Industrial Marketing Management, 67*(September), 23–36. doi: 10.1016/j.indmarman.2017.08.010

Adner, R., & Kapoor, R. (2010). Value creation in innovation ecosystems: How the structure of technological interdependence affects firm performance in new technology generations. *Strategic Management Journal, 31*(3), 306–33.

Agostini, L., & Filippini, R. (2019). Organizational and managerial challenges in the path toward Industry 4.0. *European Journal of Innovation Management, 22*(3), 406–21. https://doi.org/10.1108/EJIM-02-2018-0030

Aiginger, K., & Vogel, J. (2015). Competitiveness: From a misleading concept to a strategy supporting beyond GDP goals. *Competitiveness Review, 25*(5), 497–523. https://doi.org/10.1108/CR-06-2015-0052

Akgün, A.E., Keskin, H., Byrne, J.C., & Gunsel, A. (2011). Antecedents and results of emotional capability in software development project teams. *Journal of Product Innovation Management, 28*(6), 957–73. doi:10.1111/j.1540-5885.2011.00845.x

Akter, S., Wamba, S.F., Gunasekaran, A., Dubey, R., & Childe, S.J. (2016). How to improve firm performance using big data analytics capability and business strategy alignment? *International Journal of Production Economics, 182*, 113–31.

Alghisi, A., & Saccani, N. (2015). Internal and external alignment in the servitization journey – overcoming the challenges. *Production Planning & Control, 26*(14–15), 1219–32.

Alharthi, A., Krotov, V., & Bowman, M. (2017). Addressing barriers to big data. *Business Horizons, 60*(3), 285–92.

Amit, R., & Han, X. (2017). Value creation through novel resource configurations in a digitally enabled world. *Strategic Entrepreneurship Journal, 11*(3), 228–42. doi:10.1002/sej.1256

Amit, R., & Schoemaker, P.J. (1993). Strategic assets and organizational rent. *Strategic Management Journal, 14*(1), 33–46.

Anderson, E.W., & Mittal, V. (2000). Strengthening the satisfaction-profit chain. *Journal of Service Research, 3*(2), 107–20.

Arcidiacono, F., Ancarani, A., Di Mauro, C., & Schupp, F. (2019). Where the rubber meets the road. Industry 4.0 among SMEs in the automotive sector. *IEEE Engineering Management Review, 47*(4), 86-93. doi: 10.1109/EMR.2019.2932965

Arnold, C., Kiel, D., & Voigt, K.-I. (2016). How the industrial internet of things changes business models in different manufacturing industries. *International Journal of Innovation Management, 20*(8), 1640015.

Baines, T., & Lightfoot, H.W. (2014). Servitization of the manufacturing firm. *International Journal of Operations & Production Management, 34*(1), 2–35. htts://doi.org/10.1108/IJOPM-02-2012-0086

Baines, T.S., Lightfoot, H.W., Benedettini, O., & Kay, J.M. (2009), The servitization of manufacturing: A review of literature and reflection on future challenges. *Journal of Manufacturing Technology Management, 20*(5), 547–67. https://doi.org/10.1108/17410380910960984

Baines, T., Lightfoot, H., & Smart, P. (2011). Servitization within manufacturing. *Journal of Manufacturing Technology Management, 22*(7), 947–54. https://doi.org/10.1108/17410381111160988

Banker, R.D., Mashruwala, R., & Tripathy, A. (2014). Does a differentiation strategy lead to more sustainable financial performance than a cost leadership strategy? *Management Decision, 22*(7), 947–54. https://doi.org/10.1108/17410381111160988

Bengtsson, M., Raza-Ullah, T., & Vanyushyn, V. (2016). The coopetition paradox and tension: The moderating role of coopetition capability. *Industrial Marketing Management, 53*, 19–30. doi:10.1016/j.indmarman.2015.11.008

Berends, H., Jelinek, M., Reymen, I., & Stultiëns, R. (2014). Product innovation processes in small firms: Combining entrepreneurial effectuation and managerial causation. *Journal of Product Innovation Management, 31*(3), 616–35.

Berghman, L., Matthyssens, P., & Vandenbempt, K. (2006). Building competences for new customer value creation: An exploratory study. *Industrial Marketing Management, 35*(8), 961–73.

Black, J.A., & Boal, K.B. (1994). Strategic resources: Traits, configurations and paths to sustainable competitive advantage. *Strategic Management Journal, 15*(S2), 131–48.

Borch, O.J., Huse, M., & Senneseth, K. (1999). Resource configuration, competitive strategies, and corporate entrepreneurship: An empirical examination of small firms. *Entrepreneurship Theory and Practice, 24*(1), 49–70.

Brusoni, S., & Prencipe, A. (2013). The organization of innovation in ecosystems: Problem framing, problem solving, and patterns of coupling. *Advances in Strategic Management, 30*(July), 167–94. doi: 10.1108/S0742-3322(2013)0000030009

Cenamor, J., Parida, V., & Wincent, J. (2019). How entrepreneurial SMEs compete through digital platforms: The roles of digital platform capability, network capability and ambidexterity. *Journal of Business Research, 100*(December 2018), 196–206. doi:10.1016/j.jbusres.2019.03.035

Charmaz, K. (2006). *Constructing Grounded Theory: A Practical Guide through Qualitative Analysis*. London, Thousand Oaks, CA, New Delhi: Sage.

Chorn, N.H. (1991). The "alignment" theory: Creating strategic fit. *Management Decision, 29*(1), 20–4. https://doi.org/10.1108/EUM0000000000066

Cohen, W.M., & Levinthal, D.A. (1990). Absorptive capacity: A new perspective on learning and innovation. *Administrative Science Quarterly, 35*(1), 128–52. https://doi.org/10.2307/2393553

Coleman, S., Göb, R., Manco, G., Pievatolo, A., Tort-Martorell, X., & Reis, M.S. (2016). How can SMEs benefit from big data? Challenges and a path forward. *Quality and Reliability Engineering International, 32*(6), 2151–64.

Constantiou, L.D., & Kallinikos, J. (2015). New games, new rules: Big data and the changing context of strategy. *Journal of Information Technology, 30*(1), 44–57. doi:10.1057/jit.2014.17

Coreynen, W., Matthyssens, P., & Van Bockhaven, W. (2017). Boosting servitization through digitization: Pathways and dynamic resource configurations for manufacturers. *Industrial Marketing Management, 60*, 42–53. doi:10.1016/j.indmarman.2016.04.012

Da Silveira, G., Borenstein, D., & Fogliatto, F.S. (2001). Mass customization: Literature review and research directions. *International Journal of Production Economics, 72*(1), 1–13.

Dalenogare, L.S., Benitez, G.B., Ayala, N.F., & Frank, A.G. (2018). The expected contribution of Industry 4.0 technologies for industrial performance. *International Journal of Production Economics, 204*, 383–94.

Davis, S.M. (1989). From "future perfect": Mass customizing. *Planning Review, 17*(2), 16–21. https://doi.org/10.1108/eb054249

de Reuver, M., Sørensen, C., & Basole, R.C. (2018). The digital platform: A research agenda. *Journal of Information Technology, 33*(2), 124–35.

Del Vecchio, P., Di Minin, A., Petruzzelli, A.M., Panniello, U., & Pirri, S. (2018). Big data for open innovation in SMEs and large corporations: Trends, opportunities, and challenges. *Creativity and Innovation Management, 27*(1), 6–22.

Dessers, E., Dhondt, S., Ramioul, M. et al. (2019). Towards a multidisciplinary research framework for studying the digital transformation of industry. *European Journal of Workplace Innovation, 5*(1), 3–19.

Dong, J.Q., & Yang, C.-H. (2020). Business value of big data analytics: A systems-theoretic approach and empirical test. *Information & Management, 57*(1), 103124.

Dubois, A., & Gadde, L.E. (2002). Systematic combining: An abductive approach to case research. *Journal of Business Research, 55*(7), 553–60. doi:10.1016/S0148-2963(00)00195-8

Dugstad, J., Eide, T., Nilsen, E.R., & Eide, H. (2019). Towards successful digital transformation through co-creation: A longitudinal study of a four-year implementation of digital monitoring technology in residential care for persons with dementia. *BMC Health Services Research, 19*(1), 1–17. doi:10.1186/s12913-019-4191-1

Eisenhardt, K.M. (1989). Building theories from case study research. *Academy of Management Review, 14*(4), 532–50.

Eisenmann, T., Parker, G., & Van Alstyne, M. (2011). Platform envelopment. *Strategic Management Journal, 32*(12), 1270–85.

European Commission (2019). Annual report on European SMEs 2018/2019 – Research & Development and Innovation by SMEs.

Flanders Make (2019). *Industry 4.0 after the hype. Where do we stand today?* https://cdn2.hubspot.net/hubfs/2449418/200109%20Rapport%20Industry%204.0%20survey.pdf?__hssc=250892825.1.1580801994139&__hstc=250892825.684aab292660e6902bd441a8809ca13f.1580801994137.1580801994138.1580801994138.1&__hsfp=2890650767&hsCtaTracking=f1f61b62-09d3-45aa-8f03-2032cac315b2%7C144b92e6-ba75-41ba-9cb4-9933aecbebad (accessed June 2, 2021).

Frank, A.G., Dalenogare, L.S., & Ayala, N.F. (2019a). Industry 4.0 technologies: Implementation patterns in manufacturing companies. *International Journal of Production Economics, 210*, 15–26.

Frank, A.G., Mendes, G.H., Ayala, N.F., & Ghezzi, A. (2019b). Servitization and Industry 4.0 convergence in the digital transformation of product firms: A business model innovation perspective. *Technological Forecasting and Social Change, 141*, 341–51.

Franke, N., Schreier, M., & Kaiser, U. (2010). The "I designed it myself" effect in mass customization. *Management Science, 56*(1), 125–40.

Franklin, D., & Marshall, R. (2019). Adding co-creation as an antecedent condition leading to trust in business-to-business relationships. *Industrial Marketing Management, 77*, 170–81.

Garms, F.P., & Engelen, A. (2019). Innovation and R&D in the upper echelons: The association between the CTO's power depth and breadth and the TMT's commitment to innovation. *Journal of Product Innovation Management, 36*(1), 87–106.

Gawer, A., & Cusumano, M.A. (2008). Platform leaders. *MIT Sloan Management Review; MIT Sloan School of Management: Boston, MA, USA*, 68–75.

Graef, I. (2015). Market definition and market power in data: The case of online platforms. *World Competition, 38*, 473.

Günther, W.A., Mehrizi, M.H.R., Huysman, M., & Feldberg, F. (2017). Debating big data: A literature review on realizing value from big data. *The Journal of Strategic Information Systems, 26*(3), 191–209.

Hannah, D.P., & Eisenhardt, K.M. (2018). How firms navigate cooperation and competition in nascent ecosystems. *Strategic Management Journal, 39*(12), 3163–92. doi:10.1002/smj.2750

Hartmann, A. (2006). The role of organizational culture in motivating innovative behaviour in construction firms. *Construction innovation, 6*(3), 159–72.

Healey, M.P., & Hodgkinson, G.P. (2017). Making strategy hot. *California Management Review, 59*(3), 109–34. doi:10.1177/0008125617712258

Hein, A., Schreieck, M., Riasanow, T. et al. (2019). Digital platform ecosystems. *Electronic Markets*, 1–12.

Helfat, C.E., & Peteraf, M.A. (2003). The dynamic resource-based view: Capability lifecycles. *Strategic Management Journal, 24*(10), 997–1010.

Hodgkinson, G.P., & Healey, M.P. (2014). Coming in from the cold: The psychological foundations of radical innovation revisited. *Industrial Marketing Management, 43*(8), 1306–13. doi:10.1016/j.indmarman.2014.08.012

Horváth, D., & Szabó, R.Z. (2019). Driving forces and barriers of Industry 4.0: Do multinational and small and medium-sized companies have equal opportunities? *Technological Forecasting and Social Change, 146*, 119–32.

Hsueh, J.-T., Lin, N.-P., & Li, H.-C. (2010). The effects of network embeddedness on service innovation performance. *The Service Industries Journal, 30*(10), 1723–36.

Hurmelinna-Laukkanen, P., & Nätti, S. (2018). Orchestrator types, roles and capabilities – a framework for innovation networks. *Industrial Marketing Management, 74*(October), 65–78. doi:10.1016/j.indmarman.2017.09.020

Huy, Q.N. (2002). Emotional balancing of organizational continuity and radical change: The contribution of middle managers. *Administrative Science Quarterly, 47*(1), 31–69. doi:10.2307/3094890

Huy, Q.N. (2010). Emotion management to facilitate strategic change and innovation: How emotional balancing and emotional capability work together. *Emotions in Organizational Behavior*(February), 295–316. doi:10.4324/9781410611895

Huy, Q.N., Corley, K.G,. & Kraatz, M.S. (2014). From support to mutiny: Shifting legitimacy judgments and emotional reactions impacting the implementation of radical change. *Academy of Management Journal, 57*(6), 1650–-80.

Huy, Q.N. (1999). Emotional capability, emotional intelligence, and radical change. *Academy of Management Review, 24*(2), 325–45. doi:10.5465/AMR.1999.1893939

Huy, Q.N., & Zott, C. (2019). Exploring the affective underpinnings of dynamic managerial capabilities: How managers' emotion regulation behaviors mobilize resources for their firms. *Strategic Management Journal, 40*(1), 28–54. doi:10.1002/smj.2971

Iansiti, M., & Lakhani, K.R. (2017). Managing our hub. *Harvard Business Review,* September–October, 84–93.

Kagermann, H., Wahlster, W., & Helbig, J. (2013). Recommendations for implementing the strategic initiative INDUSTRIE 4.0. *Final report of the Industrie 4.0 WG,* April.

Keller, M., Rosenberg, M., Brettel, M., & Friederichsen, N. (2014). How virtualization, decentrazliation and network building change the manufacturing landscape: An Industry 4.0 perspective. *International Journal of Mechanical, Aerospace, Industrial, Mechatronic and Manufacturing Engineering, 8*(1), 37–44.

Kiangala, K.S., & Wang, Z. (2018). Initiating predictive maintenance for a conveyor motor in a bottling plant using industry 4.0 concepts. *The International Journal of Advanced Manufacturing Technology, 97*(9–12), 3251–71.

Kim, D., Cavusgil, S.T., & Cavusgil, E. (2013). Does IT alignment between supply chain partners enhance customer value creation? An empirical investigation. *Industrial Marketing Management, 42*(6), 880–9.

Ko, W.W., & Liu, G. (2019). How information technology assimilation promotes exploratory and exploitative innovation in the small- and medium-sized firm context: The role of contextual ambidexterity and knowledge base. *Journal of Product Innovation Management, 36*(4), 442–66. doi:10.1111/jpim.12486

Kohtamäki, M., Partanen, J., & Möller, K. (2013a). Making a profit with R&D services – the critical role of relational capital. *Industrial Marketing Management, 42*(1), 71–81.

Kohtamäki, M., Parida, V., Oghazi, P., Gebauer, H., & Baines, T. (2019). Digital servitization business models in ecosystems: A theory of the firm. *Journal of Business Research, 104*, 380–92.

Krämer, A., Jung, M., & Burgartz, T. (2016). A small step from price competition to price war: Understanding causes, effects and possible countermeasures. *International Business Research, 9*(3), 1.

Kumar, A. (2007). From mass customization to mass personalization: A strategic transformation. *International Journal of Flexible Manufacturing Systems, 19*(4), 533.

Lamba, H.S., & Dubey, S.K. (2015). *Analysis of Requirements for Big Data Adoption to Maximize IT Business Value*. Paper presented at the 2015 4th International Conference on Reliability, Infocom Technologies and Optimization (ICRITO) (Trends and Future Directions).

Li, H., Tian, G., & Tian, Y. (2018). Servitization: Its preferred organization and impact on firm performance. *Human Systems Management, 37*(2), 181–93.

Limaj, E., & Bernroider, E.W. (2019). The roles of absorptive capacity and cultural balance for exploratory and exploitative innovation in SMEs. *Journal of Business Research, 94*, 137–53.

Liu, Y., Soroka, A., Han, L., Jian, J., & Tang, M. (2020). Cloud-based big data analytics for customer insight-driven design innovation in SMEs. *International Journal of Information Management, 51*, 102034.

Lu, Y. (2017). Industry 4.0: A survey on technologies, applications and open research issues. *Journal of Industrial Information Integration, 6*, 1–10.

Lubatkin, M.H., Simsek, Z., Ling, Y., & Veiga, J.F. (2006). Ambidexterity and performance in small-to medium-sized firms: The pivotal role of top management team behavioral integration. *Journal of Management, 32*(5), 646–72. doi:10.1177/0149206306290712

Marcos-Cuevas, J., Nätti, S., Palo, T., & Baumann, J. (2016). Value co-creation practices and capabilities: Sustained purposeful engagement across B2B systems. *Industrial Marketing Management, 56*, 97–107. doi:10.1016/j.indmarman.2016.03.012

Marr, B. (2017). *Data Strategy: How to Profit from a World of Big Data, Analytics and the Internet of Things*. London, UK: Kogan Page Publishers.

Matthyssens, P. (2019). Reconceptualizing value innovation for Industry 4.0 and the Industrial Internet of Things. *Journal of Business & Industrial Marketing, 34*(6), 1203-9. https://doi.org/10.1108/JBIM-11-2018-0348

Matthyssens, P., & Vandenbempt, K. (2008). Moving from basic offerings to value-added solutions: Strategies, barriers and alignment. *Industrial Marketing Management, 37*(3), 316–28. doi:10.1016/j.indmarman.2007.07.008

McEvily, B., & Marcus, A. (2005). Embedded ties and the acquisition of competitive capabilities. *Strategic Management Journal, 26*(11), 1033–55.

Mei, L., Zhang, T., & Chen, J. (2019). Exploring the effects of inter-firm linkages on SMEs' open innovation from an ecosystem perspective: An empirical study of Chinese manufacturing SMEs. *Technological Forecasting and Social Change, 144*(March), 118–28. doi:10.1016/j.techfore.2019.04.010

Mikalef, P., Pappas, I.O., Krogstie, J., & Giannakos, M. (2018). Big data analytics capabilities: A systematic literature review and research agenda. *Information Systems and e-Business Management, 16*(3), 547–78.

Mittal, S., Khan, M.A., Romero, D., & Wuest, T. (2018). A critical review of smart manufacturing & Industry 4.0 maturity models: Implications for small and medium-sized enterprises (SMEs). *Journal of Manufacturing Systems, 49*, 194–214.

Möller, K., Rajala, A., & Svahn, S. (2005). Strategic business nets – their type and management. *Journal of Business Research, 58*(9), 1274–84.

Möller, K., & Svahn, S. (2003). Managing strategic nets: A capability perspective. *Marketing Theory, 3*(2), 209–34.

Moonen, N., Baijens, J., Ebrahim, M., & Helms, R. (2019). *Small Business, Big Data: An Assessment Tool for (Big) Data Analytics Capabilities in SMEs*. Paper presented at the Academy of Management Proceedings.

Mueller, S.D., & Jensen, P. (2017). Big data in the Danish industry: Application and value creation. *Business Process Management Journal, 23*(3), 645–70. https://doi.org/10.1108/BPMJ-01-2016-0017

Müller, J. (2019). Business model innovation in small- and medium-sized enterprises: Strategies for industry 4.0 providers and users. *Journal of Manufacturing Technology Management, 30*(8), 1127–42. https://doi.org/10.1108/JMTM-01-2018-0008

Müller, J., & Voigt, K.-I. (2017). *Industry 4.0 – Integration Strategies for Small and Medium-sized Enterprises.* Paper presented at the Proceedings of the 26th International Association for Management of Technology (IAMOT) Conference, Vienna, Austria, pp. 2–17.

Müller, J., Buliga, O., & Voigt, K.-I. (2018). Fortune favors the prepared: How SMEs approach business model innovations in Industry 4.0. *Technological Forecasting and Social Change, 132,* 2–17.

Müller, J., Buliga, O., & Voigt, K.-I. (2020). The role of absorptive capacity and innovation strategy in the design of industry 4.0 business models – a comparison between SMEs and large enterprises. *European Management Journal, 39*(3), 333–43.

Niemczyk, J., & Trzaska, R. (2020). Network approach in Industry 4.0: Perspective of coopetition. In *Contemporary Challenges in Cooperation and Coopetition in the Age of Industry 4.0.* Cham: Springer, pp. 139–54.

Opresnik, D., & Taisch, M. (2015). The value of big data in servitization. *International Journal of Production Economics, 165,* 174–84.

Papadakis, V.M., Lioukas, S., & Chambers, D. (1998). Strategic decision-making processes: The role of management and context. *Strategic Management Journal, 19*(2), 115–47.

Patton, M.Q. (2005). Qualitative research. In *Encyclopedia of Statistics in Behavioral Science,* Hoboken, NJ: John Wiley & Sons.

Pfeiffer, S. (2017). The vision of "Industrie 4.0" in the making – a case of future told, tamed, and traded. *Nanoethics, 11*(1), 107–21.

Pine, B.J. (1993). *Mass Customization: The New Frontier in Business Competition.* Cambridge, MA: Harvard Business Press.

Pisano, G.P. (2019). The hard truth about innovative. *Harvard Business Review, 97*(1), 62–71.

Polkowski, Z., Khajuria, R., & Rohadia, S. (2017). Big data implementation in small and medium enterprises in india and poland. *Scientific Bulletin-Economic Sciences, 16*(3), 149–61.

Porter, M.E. (1980). *Techniques for Analyzing Industries and Competitors. Competitive Strategy.* New York: Free Press.

Porter, M.E. (1985). *Competitive Advantage.* New York: Free Press, pp. 33–61.

Quintens, L., & Matthyssens, P. (2010). Involving the process dimensions of time in case-based research. *Industrial Marketing Management, 39*(1), 91–9.

Rachinger, M., Rauter, R., Müller, C., Vorraber, W., & Schirgi, E. (2019). Digitalization and its influence on business model innovation. *Journal of Manufacturing Technology Management, 30*(8), 1143–60.

Raddats, C., Kowalkowski, C., Benedettini, O., Burton, J., & Gebauer, H. (2019). Servitization: A contemporary thematic review of four major research streams. *Industrial Marketing Management, 83,* 207–23.

Raffaelli, R., Glynn, M.A., & Tushman, M. (2019). Frame flexibility: The role of cognitive and emotional framing in innovation adoption by incumbent firms. *Strategic Management Journal, 40*(7), 1013–39. doi:10.1002/smj.3011

Rahman, N.A., Yaacob, Z., & Radzi, R.M. (2016). An overview of technological innovation on SME survival: A conceptual paper. *Procedia – Social and Behavioral Sciences, 224,* 508–15.

Rangan, V.K., & Bowman, G.T. (1992). Beating the commodity magnet. *Industrial Marketing Management, 21*(3), 215–24.

Reddy, S.K., & Reinartz, W. (2017). Digital transformation and value creation: Sea change ahead. *Marketing Intelligence Review, 9*(1), 10–17.

Rietveld, J., Schilling, M.A., & Bellavitis, C. (2019). Platform strategy: Managing ecosystem value through selective promotion of complements. *Organization Science, 30*(6), 1232–51.

Rüßmann, M., Lorenz, M., Gerbert et al. (2015). Industry 4.0: The future of productivity and growth in manufacturing industries. *Boston Consulting Group, 9*(1), 54–89.

Sanchez-Burks, J., & Huy, Q.N. (2009). Emotional aperture and strategic change: The accurate recognition of collective emotions. *Organization Science, 20*(1), 22–34. doi:10.1287/orsc.1070.0347

Sandrin, E., Trentin, A., & Forza, C. (2018). Leveraging high-involvement practices to develop mass customization capability: A contingent configurational perspective. *International Journal of Production Economics, 196*, 335–45.

Saunila, M., Ukko, J., & Rantala, T. (2019). Value co-creation through digital service capabilities: The role of human factors. *Information Technology & People, 32*(3), 627–45. https://doi.org/10.1108/ITP -10-2016-0224

Savastano, M., Amendola, C., & D'Ascenzo, F. (2018). How digital transformation is reshaping the manufacturing industry value chain: The new digital manufacturing ecosystem applied to a case study from the food industry. In *Network, Smart and Open*. Cham: Springer, pp. 127–42.

Schneider, P. (2018). Managerial challenges of Industry 4.0: An empirically backed research agenda for a nascent field. *Review of Managerial Science, 12*(3), 803–48. doi:10.1007/s11846-018-0283-2

Schreyögg, G., & Koch, J. (2009). Organisational path dependence. *Academy of Management Review, 34*(4), 689–709.

Schuh, G., Anderl, R., Gausemeier, J., ten Hompel, M., & Wahlster, W. (2017). Industrie 4.0 maturity index. In Günther Schuh, Reiner Anderl, Roman Dumitrescu, Antonio Krüger, Michael ten Hompel (eds), *Managing the Digital Transformation of Companies*. Munich: Herbert Utz, pp. 1–64. White paper, online via https://en.acatech.de/wp-content/uploads/sites/6/2020/04/aca_STU_MatInd _2020_en_Web-1.pdf (accessed June 6, 2021).

SERV (2019). *Rapport Industrie 4.0 onder de loep in vijf sectoren*. https://www.serv.be/sites/default/ files/documenten/SERV_20190617_Industrie_4.0_ADV.pdf (accessed June 6, 2021)

Shaked, A., & Sutton, J. (1982). Relaxing price competition through product differentiation. *The Review of Economic Studies, 49*(1), 3–13.

Simon, P. (2013). Even small companies can tap big data if they know where to look. *Harvard Business Review*. https://hbr.org/2013/12/even-small-companies-can-tap-big-data-if-they-know-where-to-look (accessed June 6, 2021).

Sivarajah, U., Kamal, M.M., Irani, Z., & Weerakkody, V. (2017). Critical analysis of Big Data challenges and analytical methods. *Journal of Business Research, 70*, 263–86.

Sousa, R., & da Silveira, G.J. (2017). Capability antecedents and performance outcomes of servitization. *International Journal of Operations & Production Management, 37*(4), 444–67. https://doi.org/10 .1108/IJOPM-11-2015-0696

Stevens, E., & Dimitriadis, S. (2004). New service development through the lens of organisational learning: Evidence from longitudinal case studies. *Journal of Business Research, 57*(10), 1074–84.

Story, V.M., Raddats, C., Burton, J., Zolkiewski, J., & Baines, T. (2017). Capabilities for advanced services: A multi-actor perspective. *Industrial Marketing Management, 60*, 54–68.

Subramaniam, M., Iyer, B., & Venkatraman, V. (2019). Competing in digital ecosystems. *Business Horizons, 62*(1), 83–94.

Tao, F., & Qi, Q. (2019). New IT driven service-oriented smart manufacturing: Framework and characteristics. *IEEE Transactions on Systems, Man, and Cybernetics: Systems, 49*(1), 81–91. doi:10.1109/ TSMC.2017.2723764

Teece, D.J. (2018). Profiting from innovation in the digital economy: standards, complementary assets, and business models in the wireless world. *Research Policy, 47*(8), 1367–87.

Teece, D.J., Pisano, G., & Shuen, A. (1997). Dynamic capabilities and strategic management. *Strategic Management Journal, 18*(7), 509–33.

Tiihonen, J., & Felfernig, A. (2017). An introduction to personalization and mass customization. *Journal of Intelligent Information Systems, 49*(1), 1–7.

Torn, I., & Vaneker, T.H. (2019). Mass personalization with Industry 4.0 by SMEs: A concept for collaborative networks. *Procedia Manufacturing, 28*, 135–41.

Treacy, M., & Wiersema, F. (1993). Customer intimacy and other value disciplines. *Harvard Business Review, 71*(1), 84–93.

Upadhyay, P., & Kumar, A. (2020). The intermediating role of organizational culture and internal analytical knowledge between the capability of big data analytics and a firm's performance. *International Journal of Information Management*, 102100.

Vajjhala, N.R., & Ramollari, E. (2016). Big data using cloud computing – opportunities for small and medium-sized enterprises. *European Journal of Economics and Business Studies, 2*(1), 129–37.

Van Bockhaven, W., & Matthyssens, P. (2017). Mobilizing a network to develop a field: Enriching the business actor's mobilization analysis toolkit. *Industrial Marketing Management, 67*(July), 70–87. doi:10.1016/j.indmarman.2017.08.001

Vandermerwe, S., & Rada, J. (1988). Servitization of business: Adding value by adding services. *European Management Journal, 6*(4), 314–24.

Vendrell-Herrero, F., Bustinza, O.F., Parry, G., & Georgantzis, N. (2017). Servitization, digitization and supply chain interdependency. *Industrial Marketing Management, 60*, 69–81.

Vesalainen, J., & Hakala, H. (2014). Strategic capability architecture: The role of network capability. *Industrial Marketing Management, 43*(6), 938–50.

Vuori, T.O., & Huy, Q.N. (2016). Distributed attention and shared emotions in the innovation process: How Nokia lost the smartphone battle. *Administrative Science Quarterly, 61*(1), 9–51. doi:10.1177/0001839215606951

Vuori, N., Vuori, T.O., & Huy, Q.N. (2018). Emotional practices: How masking negative emotions impacts the post-acquisition integration process. *Strategic Management Journal, 39*(3), 859–93.

Wamba, S.F., Akter, S., Edwards, A., Chopin, G., & Gnanzou, D. (2015). How "big data" can make big impact: Findings from a systematic review and a longitudinal case study. *International Journal of Production Economics, 165*, 234–46.

Wamba, S.F., Gunasekaran, A., Akter, S., Ren, S.J.-f., Dubey, R., & Childe, S.J. (2017). Big data analytics and firm performance: Effects of dynamic capabilities. *Journal of Business Research, 70*, 356–65.

Wan, X., Cenamor, J., Parker, G., & Van Alstyne, M. (2017). Unraveling platform strategies: A review from an organizational ambidexterity perspective. *Sustainability, 9*(5), 734.

Wang, S.Y., Wan, J.F., Zhang, D.Q., Li, D., & Zhang, C.H. (2016). Towards smart factory for industry 4.0: A self-organized multi-agent system with big data based feedback and coordination. *Computer Networks, 101*, 158–68. doi:10.1016/j.comnet.2015.12.017

Wang, Y., Ma, H.-S., Yang, J.-H., & Wang, K.-S. (2017). Industry 4.0: A way from mass customization to mass personalization production. *Advances in Manufacturing, 5*(4), 311–20.

Wang, Y., Kung, L., & Byrd, T.A. (2018). Big data analytics: Understanding its capabilities and potential benefits for healthcare organizations. *Technological Forecasting and Social Change, 126*, 3–13.

Woodside, A.G., & Wilson, E.J. (2003). Case study research methods for theory building. *Journal of Business & Industrial Marketing, 18*(6/7), 493–508. https://doi.org/10.1108/08858620310492374

Xu, L.D., Xu, E.L., & Li, L. (2018). Industry 4.0: State of the art and future trends. *International Journal of Production Research, 56*(8), 2941–62.

Xu, P., & Kim, J. (2014). *Achieving Dynamic Capabilities with Business Intelligence.* Paper presented at the PACIS.

Yablonsky, S. (2018). A multidimensional framework for digital platform innovation and management: From business to technological platforms. *Systems Research and Behavioral Science, 35*(4), 485–501.

Yeow, A., Soh, C., & Hansen, R. (2018). Aligning with new digital strategy: A dynamic capabilities approach. *The Journal of Strategic Information Systems, 27*(1), 43–58.

Yin, R.K. (2011). *Applications of Case Study Research.* Los Angeles, CA, London and New Delhi: Sage.

Yunis, M., Tarhini, A., & Kassar, A. (2018). The role of ICT and innovation in enhancing organizational performance: The catalysing effect of corporate entrepreneurship. *Journal of Business Research, 88*, 344–56.

Zhong, R.Y., Xu, X., Klotz, E., & Newman, S.T. (2017). Intelligent manufacturing in the context of industry 4.0: A review. *Engineering, 3*(5), 616–30.

5. Analyzing and developing digitization capabilities for data-driven projects in SMEs

Carsten Lund Pedersen and Thomas Ritter

5.1   INTRODUCTION

The world has become increasingly "datafied"—everything from location (GPS) to words (digital books) to even friendships (Facebook) has been transformed into massive piles of data that organizations can collect and commercialize.[1] As a result, some have argued that "every company operating today is a data company."[2] While becoming digital is a top priority for many CEOs,[3] surprisingly few companies have the capabilities required to deal with this new reality. Perhaps even more perplexing is the fact that many SMEs do not have clear insights into what they want to achieve through the utilization of data. In fact, our many years of research on data-driven growth in small- and medium-sized enterprises (SMEs) (see "About the research") suggest that capability gaps are more the rule than the exception. Consequently, the predominant barrier to successful data utilization typically lies within SMEs themselves. This is problematic, as SMEs' success increasingly relies on data utilization and as SMEs comprise a substantial part of the global economy.

Consequently, there is arguably significant, untapped potential for SMEs to embark on data-utilization journeys in which they initiate transformational projects with the aim of better exploring and exploiting data for commercial purposes. Based upon our ongoing research conducted in collaboration with Danish SMEs, we provide guidance for data-utilization journeys in this chapter. We contend that analyzing and developing a digitization capability is a crucial point of departure for any SME seeking data-driven growth. As a digitization capability entails three dimensions (data, analytics, and permission), establishing the right foundation for data-driven growth is a complex task. Moreover, SMEs are typically better in one dimension and worse in the others, and success in one dimension may blind the organization to shortcomings in other dimensions. Hence, it is necessary to analyze the SME's maturity level in relation to its digitization capability before engaging in concrete data-utilization projects that build on that digitization capability and use it to create value. Such projects will not only drive performance but also support the further development of the underlying digitization capability. In order to assess the likelihood of project success, we propose a framework for locating data projects and uncovering potential shortcomings. This process will alert SMEs to the need for capability development.

The chapter is laid out as follows. First, we explore the disadvantages and advantages of being small in relation to data-driven growth. Then, we explain the digitization capability construct and how it can be utilized to analyze a firm. Thereafter, we propose a framework for analyzing data-driven projects and conceptualize how SMEs can assess their maturity level in terms of their data-utilization journeys. Finally, we suggest ways in which SMEs can assess and develop their digitization capabilities and data-driven projects through a series of workshops.

5.2 THE DISADVANTAGES AND ADVANTAGES OF BEING SMALL

A small size comes with both disadvantages and advantages. When making strategic decisions on data-related matters, it is crucial for SMEs to know both their relative weaknesses and strengths. One characteristic of SMEs is that they are relatively small in size. Their "liability of smallness" (e.g., Aldrich & Auster, 1986) is reflected in financial constraints as well as difficulties in finding qualified employees and business partners. These aspects are particularly important within a data-related domain, as initial investments can be substantial, returns on investments may be uncertain, and the war for talent is extensive (Davenport & Patil, 2012). Moreover, data-related activities may depend on partnerships that also require investments. Therefore, many SMEs face barriers in the initial phase of their data-utilization journey. Notably, these differences in the initial conditions between SMEs and their larger counterparts may increase along the way, thereby creating substantial competitive disparities. Together, these stylized facts point towards the contention that SMEs are forced to work with and within constraints, and that they are ill-suited to compete head-to-head with larger firms. In sum, the main disadvantages can be summarized as follows:

1. SMEs have financial constraints and may struggle to attract the right talent.
2. The liability of smallness makes initial investments in digitization difficult.
3. Over time, differences in the initial conditions of small and large firms may increase, resulting in substantial performance disparities in the domain of big data.

Despite the fact that being small is often referred to as a liability, it also entails advantages. In the strategy and economics literature, the advantages of being small have been detailed under the headings of "judo strategy" or "judo economics," where some smaller companies succeed in defeating bigger and stronger opponents by applying principles from the martial art of judo, such as avoiding competition that favors larger counterparts, and relying upon speed, agility, and creativity (Yoffie & Kwak, 2002). Unlike most martial arts, judo is based on the notion of leveraging the strengths of the opponent, such as weight and power, against themselves, whereby you turn your opponent's strengths to your advantage. As a philosophical anchor, SMEs can use this concept as inspiration for their strategic discussions on data-enabled growth. In the field of industrial marketing, judo strategies have been identified in the context of entrepreneurs applying soft power strategies (Bockhaven, Matthyssens, & Vandenbempt, 2015). The innovation and economics literature has also long been preoccupied with why and how small entrants with fewer resources (i.e., "underdogs") can beat incumbents with significant resources (i.e., "giants") at their own core business (e.g., Bower & Christensen, 1995; Wernerfelt, 2020). While the underlying patterns and reasons vary slightly, they often revolve around how small firms focus on an overlooked niche with an inferior product that the incumbent does not perceive as a threat. These studies show how the small firms subsequently scale up the business to take more of the mainstream customers and, thereby, challenge the incumbent.

These views point to three important advantages of being small:

1. Being small makes an SME seem like less of a threat to incumbents in the beginning. This insight can be utilized strategically as a "puppy dog ploy" (Yoffie & Kwak, 2002).
2. Being small can make an SME flexible, faster, and more agile than its larger competitors (Yoffie & Kwak, 2002).
3. Being small implies losing less than larger competitors, as those competitors have often invested heavily over a longer period of time and are consequently tied to a certain path-dependent trajectory (e.g., Wernerfelt, 2020). Therefore, the incumbent's "strength" can be utilized against it (Yoffie & Kwak, 2002).

The bottom line is that SMEs have both advantages and disadvantages in utilizing their data for growth. Consequently, they should focus on their unique strengths and apply judo strategies based on speed, creativity, and agility instead of simply copying larger firms' data efforts. It is counterproductive to think of all of the resources and data that an SME does not have. Instead, an SME should think of all the things it can do that large firms cannot. SMEs need to find unique ways to utilize data, and they have to uncover their own paths and projects. However, such applications of data can only thrive when an underlying foundational capability for digitization is developed.

5.3   A FIRM'S DIGITIZATION CAPABILITY

Based on our prior work on data-driven growth in SMEs (e.g., Pedersen & Ritter, 2020; Ritter & Pedersen, 2020; Ritter, Pedersen, & Sørensen, 2017), we have developed a conceptualization of a firm's "digitization capability." We define a "capability" as "a firm's ability to perform repeatedly a productive task which relate[s] either directly or indirectly to a firm's capacity for creating value through affecting the transformation of inputs into outputs" (Grant, 1996, p. 377). In so doing, we highlight that a firm must be able to repeatedly conduct an activity (as opposed to a lucky, one-off event) and that the performance of that activity must relate to the firm's core business (as opposed to being isolated and unrelated). Both criteria must be met to derive a sustained competitive advantage. The application of data necessitates the development of a core capability within this domain—a digitization capability.

In our research, we have found that a digitization capability entails three dimensions that the organization must master: *data*, *permission*, and *analytics* (Ritter & Pedersen, 2020). In the following, we briefly describe, explain, and illustrate each of these dimensions.

5.3.1   Data

Data refers to the organization's capacity to generate, collect, store, secure, and share data. Most organizations collect a variety of data from a multitude of sources, such as sensors, apps, and websites. They also collect data from and through their salespeople and accounting systems. Organizations need to be proficient in securely storing this data and providing access to it. In other words, they need to make it available internally when necessary (for a discussion and measure of "data availability," see, e.g., Cao, Duan, & El Banna, 2019; Gupta & George,

2016). Data generation, collection, and storage activities also need to address the fact that data differs in terms of *volume, velocity,* and *variety* (McAfee & Brynjolfsson, 2012), as well as potential cybersecurity risks (Jalali, 2018). For instance, Gupta and George (2016) draw on the resource-based view of the firm to suggest a need for a capability to deal with big data. They emphasize the capacity to, for instance, capture every bit of data regardless of size, structure, or speed. Jalali (2018) argues that proactive decision-making and resource allocation are important for developing a cybersecurity capability.

Several cases of successful data activities exist. For instance, telecommunications companies, such as Verizon, Deutsche Telekom, and Telefónica, collect, store, and share a multitude of data through their daily operations.[4] Moreover, John Deere has created a new source of revenue for itself by collaborating with Cornell University to access farm data.[5] But data is not only a big-firm phenomenon—many, if not all, SMEs have data in various forms, formats, and databases. However, the ability to generate, collect, store, and access data is only part of a digitization capability. An organization also needs to be able to analyze it.

5.3.2   Analytics

"Analytics" refers to the organization's capacity to analyze, visualize, and report data. Data in itself rarely provides any value. Instead, it is the analysis of data that fosters insights that can provide a competitive advantage. Analytics range from simple descriptive statistics to more elaborate predictive models drawing on inferential statistics. Increasingly, analytics include machine learning and artificial intelligence. SMEs need to process data (Ackoff, 1989) using a variety of novel and sophisticated techniques (e.g., Bertsimas, O'Hair, & Pulleyblank, 2016; Siegel, 2013). In this regard, Ackoff (1989) suggests that there are differences among data, information, knowledge, and wisdom, and that individuals should seek to obtain wisdom in this taxonomy. Bertsimas and colleagues (2016) posit that companies can derive a competitive edge by being proficient in the use of analytical tools to gain unique insights that allow for improved decision-making. Siegel (2013) concurs with these arguments and stresses the importance of predictive analytics in business.

Many interesting examples of new analytics developments are emerging. For instance, automated email solutions in which software automatically analyzes inbound leads, reaches out to them, and engages in two-way conversations have seen the light of day.[6] Other developments include software that transcribes and analyzes sales calls, and subsequently provides suggestions for improvements.[7] Despite the many opportunities that possession of data and the capacity to analyze it can offer SMEs, these opportunities will not come to fruition in the long run if SMEs do not have permission to collect and analyze data.

5.3.3   Permission

Permission refers to the organization's capacity to obtain legal, contractual, and societal permission to collect, combine, and use data. Data can be *open* (i.e., belongs to everyone) or needs to be *negotiated* (i.e., belongs to another party). Alternatively, it can be the organization's *own* data. Each situation entails different requirements and possibilities for usage. As numerous high-profile scandals have shown in recent years, the collection and use of data requires permission that is both legally and ethically valid. Not only do organizations need to live up to current legal frameworks (e.g., Europe's General Data Protection Regulation (GDPR)), but they also need to negotiate contracts for data ownership and usage rights with their business partners. Moreover, they must comply with society's sentiments concerning data usage and the right to privacy (e.g., Do consumers think the data collection is "creepy"?).

In other words, SMEs need to pay attention to the regulatory context (e.g., Tankard, 2016), their negotiated frameworks (e.g., Geiger, 2017), and ethical issues (e.g., Zwitter, 2014). For instance, Tankard (2016) explains the new regulatory context created by the GDPR, where compliance is mandatory. Geiger (2017) presents a model of negotiation revolving around issue-based tactics, which is also relevant for contractual issues related to data. Zwitter (2014) suggests that the speed of data development has surpassed the individual-level understanding of consequences. Therefore, ethics considerations need to focus on actions taken by those who are unaware that their actions may have unintended consequences for others.

Many companies have sought to strengthen their permission capabilities with varying results. For instance, Equifax has extensively considered whether its data resources are aligned with its ethical and legal responsibilities.[8] Accenture has identified a new job category within artificial intelligence (AI) dedicated to monitoring the fairness of AI systems.[9] However, permission is a complex phenomenon, as what is legal can conflict with ethics and vice versa. SMEs can lose their license to operate in their ecosystems due to shortcomings with their permissions—permissions are important but potentially overlooked in digitization efforts that typically focus more on data and analytics.

While the digitization capability forms the backbone of SMEs' data-utilization journeys, these journeys will typically be materialized through a "living" portfolio of data-related projects.

5.3.4   A Project View

When companies have data, analytics, and permission skills, we argue that they have a *digitization capability*. That is, they have data to use, analytical skills to understand it, and permission to use it, thereby creating a solid foundation for data utilization. A digitization capability can be analyzed at the firm level by asking how good a firm is in performing the tasks involved in the three dimensions. However, as digitization can affect all parts of a business model (Ritter & Pedersen, 2020) in very different ways and as different areas of an organization may be at different levels, we propose taking a project view when analyzing data-utilization journeys. In other words, the three dimensions should be assessed for each project or potential project.

While a digitization capability is an organizational phenomenon, the proficiency of the dimensions entailed in the construct may vary according to the specific project. That is, one project may be particularly challenged in the analytics domain, while another project may be challenged in the permission domain. Both projects can draw upon the firm's general digitization capability for project support but they may also operate beyond the capacity inherent in the digitization capability in different ways. We expand on these points in the following section.

5.4 ANALYZING DIGITIZATION CAPABILITY FOR YOUR PROJECTS

As explained above, success requires proficiency in all three dimensions of a digitization capability—not only for the organization as a whole, but also for each project. Our research indicates that most organizations tend to have a blind spot in at least one of the dimensions, which results in suboptimal performance. This is most apparent with individual projects. We define projects as "intentional and temporary resource-committing actions that occur alongside an organization's ongoing operations to achieve new outcomes" (Pedersen, Ritter, & Andersen, 2021). In the data-utilization context, we focus on projects using data in order to either better exploit their business models (typically related to resource optimization) or explore new business opportunities (e.g., newly developed digital value propositions, the use of digital formats to interact with customers). For each project, one can assess:

1. Is the necessary data available in a useful format?
2. Are the correct algorithms, software, and/or visualizations available?
3. Are all permissions given? Are we legally and ethically allowed to use this data in this way?

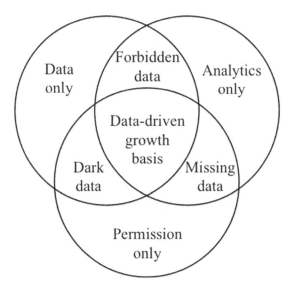

Figure 5.1   *Classification of data-driven projects*

With this assessment in hand, each project (past, ongoing, and future) can be placed into Figure 5.1. At the center, we find projects with all dimensions in place. These projects are well positioned to utilize the organization's digitization capability to ensure success. In the three outer areas where only one dimension is given, we find weakly positioned projects—situations in which the organization's digitization capability is too weak to support the projects. Typically, these projects fail, as they cannot progress on such weak grounds. The possession of data without the other necessary dimensions means that nothing happens with the data. Possession of only analytics skills implies that nothing happens due to a lack of data, possession of permission alone cannot lead to action either. These projects simply fail—and implied and expected contributions to performance will not be realized.

The three overlapping areas with only two dimensions in place are also problematic for an organization. When companies have data and analytics skills but no skills in obtaining permission, we argue that they have *forbidden data*. That is, they have data and they can analyze it, but they do not have the permission needed to do so. A particularly high-profile example of such a case was the *Cambridge Analytica scandal* in which 50 million Facebook profiles were harvested, analyzed, and utilized for political marketing.[10] Thus, these types of projects can be threatening to an organization.

When companies have data and permission skills but no skills in analytics, we argue that they have *dark data*. This term is inspired by dark matter, which is matter that exists but cannot be observed and analyzed (e.g., science.nasa.gov). For these projects, the analytics skills required to use the data in relevant ways are lacking, resulting in permitted data lying idle. According to one estimate, 60 percent of executives believe that more than 50 percent of their data lies in the dark.[11]

When companies have permission and analytics skills but no skills to collect and handle data, we argue that they have *missing data*, which results in important organizational capacities lying idle. While most companies have access to data in some form, it is becoming increasingly difficult to collect data that is not only valuable but also unique. In particular, SMEs may have difficulties in competing against larger firms in collecting unique, large datasets through, for instance, sensors in an installed base across large numbers of customers. They may also struggle to purchase data access. Yet, as highlighted in Section 5.2, the success of SMEs often does not lie in competing like large firms but rather against them as small firms. In that respect, SMEs might be able to build completely different datasets that are relevant and unique (rather than large) based on their detailed and hands-on customer insights.

This analysis will typically reveal why projects fail and what to do to ensure that projects do not fail (i.e., which capabilities to build). This should prevent major crises, as SMEs will be alerted to the pieces they lack to continue their data-utilization journeys. As such, there are interesting mutual dependencies among the three dimensions of digitization capability and data-driven projects—the projects depend on capabilities but they also contribute to the development of those capabilities.

5.5   ASSESSING AN ORGANIZATION'S MATURITY LEVEL

The maturity of SMEs in relation to their work on data can be unfolded further, as one needs to consider both the SME's excellence with regards to digitization capability and its success with data-driven projects. This can be illustrated in a 2x2 matrix with one dimension considering *digitization capability* (i.e., the extent to which the digitization capability is well developed) and the other dimension relating to *project success* (i.e., the return on investments in data-driven projects). This distinction is in line with Grant's (1996) definition of capabilities and value creation. Thus, the matrix explicates the development of an organization's maturity within the domain of data utilization. When the two dimensions are combined, four scenarios can be distinguished (Figure 5.2): "baby steps," "stuck on a treadmill," "on the right foot," and "up and running."

5.5.1   Baby Steps

If an SME does not have a well-established digitization capability or successful data-driven projects, it is taking the initial *baby steps*. Rarely do SMEs completely lack experience in working with data, as they typically have data saved in Excel sheets as a minimum level. Many SMEs that deal with European customers have recently been forced to address the requirements of the GDPR. However, most SMEs that belong in this category are focused on the physical production of tangible products or the provision of services—and they have more data available than they utilize. They rely, at best, on descriptive analyses. Consequently, major success stories cannot be found among such SMEs. In other words, they are walking but they are only taking small, insecure baby steps.

5.5.2   Stuck on a Treadmill

If an SME has a well-established digitization capability but no successful projects, it is *stuck on a treadmill*. In our research, we have encountered various SMEs that belong in this category. These SMEs had the foresight to focus on data utilization early on, but they had not enjoyed any notable success. In this case, the SME runs faster and faster, but it fails to get anywhere. In some cases, although the three dimensions of digitization capability are developed, individual projects regularly fail to transform sufficient levels of capability into performance. This emphasizes the advantages of analyzing a digitization capability and projects in combination as challenges are vested in projects, not in the underlying capabilities. Not only is this status quo situation similar to the characteristics of a treadmill, but data initiatives may also gain traction and gain a life of their own, making it nearly impossible for these SMEs to get off the treadmill.

5.5.3   On the Right Foot

If an SME has successful projects but it does not yet have a fully developed digitization capability, it is *on the right foot*. Some SMEs are lucky in their first few attempts at data utilization. These SMEs launch a couple of projects that become great successes. In order to maintain momentum and to ensure continued success in data utilization, these SMEs need to institutionalize and routinize their workflows and enable organizational learning. In other words, they need to move from random project success to development of a digitization capability that can ensure success. As such, they are on the right foot—they have achieved enough balance that they will not fall, but they are not yet running because the other leg is not sufficiently developed.

5.5.4   Up and Running

If an SME has both a digitization capability and success, it is *up and running*. SMEs belonging to this category have built up a sustainable digitization capability and they also have successful projects that justify their efforts. In other words, they find important projects that they can successfully implement utilizing their digitization capability. Up-and-running SMEs still run the risk of making mistakes, as success is never guaranteed. However, their chances of success are higher, as their digitization capability and their strategic choices of projects have a proven track record.

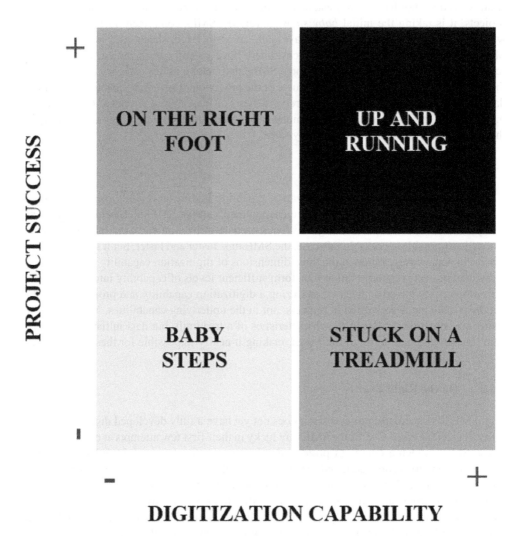

Figure 5.2   Data-utilization journey

The 2x2 matrix is in line with our core recommendation: in their data-utilization journeys, SMEs should take small but progressive steps aimed at moving towards the upper right-hand corner. As is evident in the matrix, the normative ideal for an SME is the scenario entitled "up and running." It follows that SMEs should assess where they are in the matrix (i.e., their maturity level) and then determine what they need to do today to reach the upper right-hand corner.

Necessary actions are predicated on the organization's current position in the matrix. That is, if an SME is "stuck on a treadmill," its Achilles' heel is the lack of return on investment

(ROI). Therefore, it will need to prioritize projects based on a commercial (rather than a technical) logic. It should not ask whether something *could* be done, but rather whether something *should* be done. Similarly, if an SME is "on the right foot," it needs more experience and time to build up the digitization capability needed to institutionalize the successful projects that it has already undertaken. If an SME finds itself in the "baby steps" quadrant, the managerial options are many. These SMEs may want to first build up some experience (via the "on a treadmill" scenario) or aim for a few small wins (via the "on the right foot" scenario). Alternatively, they may want to combine elements from both scenarios in small, incremental steps (a kind of tit-for-tat scenario). All three options may be viable depending on the SME's resource base and opportunities.

5.6   ASSESSING AND DEVELOPING YOUR DIGITIZATION CAPABILITY AND DATA-DRIVEN PROJECTS

Throughout this chapter, the concepts of digitization capability and projects have been used in combination. Yet they are very different phenomena: a digitization capability refers to organizational routine(s) for dealing with data, while a data-driven project is an initiative with a delimited timeframe with a beginning and an end (Pedersen, Ritter, & Andersen, 2021). However, both are necessary to ensure success with data utilization, and they complement each other (Figure 5.3). In other words, a well-developed digitization capability can support your data-driven projects (as specified in Section 5.4) by providing the foundation for data-driven projects. Moreover, if your organization has a living portfolio of data-driven projects, those projects will reinforce your digitization capability (as specified in Section 5.5).

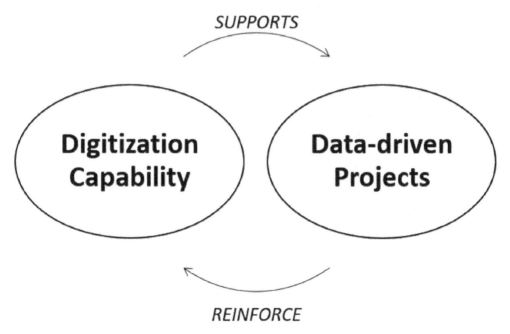

Figure 5.3   *Capability-project interaction*

To utilize both perspectives and their interactions, we suggest that SMEs should introduce a set of three workshops to start their journeys towards the up-and-running quadrant:

1. *Workshop 1* should focus on the SME's digitization capability and on assessing the three dimensions on a scale of –3 to 3, with –3 indicating very poor performance, major barriers, and a position that lags the competition; 0 indicating some experience, some but no major obstacles, and a position on par with competitors; and 3 highlighting excellence and peer-group leadership. All ratings should be supported by concrete examples that illustrate the advantages or disadvantages the SME faces. Differences in the ratings assigned by participants will typically emerge and should be discussed.
2. *Workshop 2* should focus on current and planned projects. Participants should place each project in Figure 5.1 and then discuss what can be done to support projects in non-optimal positions.
3. *Workshop 3* should apply Figure 5.2 as a basis for a discussion about how to develop the organization towards up and running. In other words, where is the organization in the matrix and which trajectory should it take to move towards the up-and-running quadrant?

This workshop series is not a one-off. It should be repeated regularly in order to track developments, integrate new knowledge, and update the project portfolio.

As the world becomes increasingly digitized, it is pivotal for companies to follow suit if they wish to maintain or develop a competitive edge. However, developing and maintaining a digitization capability is not an easy task, and neither is the management of a project portfolio. Both require managerial attention in a variety of areas as well as interdepartmental collaboration and coordination. Consequently, building a digitization capability and managing a project portfolio are substantial tasks. At the same time, these tasks are too important to be delayed or downplayed. In a winner-takes-all digital world, those who fail to develop their digitization capabilities and project portfolios will fall victim to those who don't fail to do so.

ABOUT THE RESEARCH

This chapter partly draws on a three-year research project on data-driven growth that covered an industry core group as well as interactions with more than 100 companies. The results of this project inspired the development of the digitization capability concept. They are further explained in the following publications:

Ritter, T., & Pedersen, C.L. (2020). Digitization capability and the digitalization of business models in business-to-business firms: past, present, and future. *Industrial Marketing Management*, *86*(4), 180–90.
Pedersen, C.L, & Ritter, T. (2020). Use this framework to predict the success of your big data project. *Harvard Business Review*, Digital Articles, https://hbr.org/2020/02/use-this-framework-to-predict-the-success-of-your-big-data-project.
Ritter, T., Pedersen, C.L., & Eibe Sørensen, H. (2017). *Dataprofit: A Capability Map for Data-driven Growth*. Frederiksberg: CBS Competitiveness Platform.

NOTES

1. https://heinonline.org/HOL/LandingPage?handle=hein.journals/fora92&div=46&id=&page= (accessed February 25, 2021).

2. https://sloanreview.mit.edu/article/demystifying-data-monetization/ (accessed February 25, 2021).
3. https://www.gartner.com/en/newsroom/press-releases/2018-05-01-gartner-survey-reveals-that-ceo -priorities-are-shifting-to-embrace-digital-business (accessed February 25, 2021).
4. https://sloanreview.mit.edu/article/demystifying-data-monetization/ (accessed February 25, 2021).
5. Ibid.
6. https://sloanreview.mit.edu/article/five-ai-solutions-transforming-b2b-marketing/ (accessed February 25, 2021).
7. Ibid.
8. https://sloanreview.mit.edu/article/using-unstructured-data-to-tidy-up-credit-reporting/ (accessed February 25, 2021).
9. https://sloanreview.mit.edu/article/will-ai-create-as-many-jobs-as-it-eliminates/ (accessed February 25, 2021).
10. https://www.theguardian.com/news/series/cambridge-analytica-files (accessed February 25, 2021).
11. https://blog.datumize.com/infographic-what-is-dark-data-and-why-it-matters (accessed February 25, 2021).

REFERENCES

Ackoff, R.L. (1989). From data to wisdom. *Journal of Applied Systems Analysis, 16*(1), 3–9.
Aldrich, H., & Auster, E.R. (1986). Even dwarfs started small: liabilities of age and size and their strategic implications. *Research in Organizational Behavior, 8*, 165–98.
Bertsimas, D., O'Hair, A., & Pulleyblank, W. (2016). *The Analytics Edge*. Charlestown, MA: Dynamic Ideas.
Bockhaven, Wouter Van, Matthyssens, Paul, & Vandenbempt, Koen (2015). Empowering the underdog: soft power in the development of collective institutional entrepreneurship in business markets. *Industrial Marketing Management, 48*, 174–86.
Bower, J.L., & Christensen, C.M. (1995). Disruptive technologies: catching the wave. *Harvard Business Review, 73*(1), 43–53.
Cao, G., Duan, Y., & El Banna, A. (2019). A dynamic capability view of marketing analytics: evidence from UK firms. *Industrial Marketing Management, 76*(1), 72–83.
Davenport, T.H., & Patil, D.J. (2012). Data scientist. *Harvard Business Review, 90*(5), 70–6.
Geiger, I. (2017). A model of negotiation issue-based tactics in business-to-business sales negotiations. *Industrial Marketing Management, 64*, 91–106.
Grant, R.M. (1996). Prospering in dynamically-competitive environments: organizational capability as knowledge integration. *Organization Science, 7*(4), 375–87.
Gupta, M., & George, J.F. (2016). Toward the development of a big data analytics capability. *Information & Management, 53*(8), 1049–64.
Jalali, M.S. (2018). The trouble with cyber security management. *MIT Sloan Management Review* (Online October 8, 2018).
McAfee, A., & Brynjolfsson, E. (2012). Big Data: the management revolution. *Harvard Business Review, 90*, 60–8.
Pedersen, C.L., & Ritter, T. (2020). Use this framework to predict the success of your big data project. *Harvard Business Review*, Digital Articles, https://hbr.org/2020/02/use-this-framework-to-predict-the -success-of-your-big-data-project.
Pedersen, C.L., Ritter, T., & Andersen, T.J. (2021). A project-based perspective on strategic renewal. *Strategic Management Review*, forthcoming.
Ritter, T., & Pedersen, C. L. (2020). Digitization capability and the digitalization of business models in business-to-business firms: past, present, and future. *Industrial Marketing Management, 86*(4), 180–90.
Ritter, T., Pedersen, C.L., & Sørensen, H.E. (2017). *DataProfit: A Capability Map for Data-driven Growth*. Frederiksberg: CBS Competitiveness Platform.
Siegel, E. (2013). *Predictive Analytics: The Power to Predict Who Will Click, Buy, Lie, or Die*. Hoboken, NJ: Wiley.
Tankard, C. (2016). What the GDPR means for businesses. *Network Security, 2016*(6), 5–8.

Wernerfelt, B. (2020). When does the underdog win? *MIT Sloan Working Paper.*

Yoffie, D.B., & Kwak, M. (2002). Mastering balance: how to meet and beat a stronger opponent. *California Management Review*, *44*(2), 8–24.

Zwitter, A. (2014). Big data ethics. *Big Data & Society*, (July–December), 1–6.

6. How a glass-processing SME developed its big data competence

Joel Mero, Heikki Karjaluoto and Tanja Tammisalo

6.1 INTRODUCTION

The extant literature offers extensive discussions of the resources and capabilities that are needed to make big data valuable for businesses (see, e.g., Barton & Court, 2012; McAfee & Brynjolfsson, 2012; Mikalef et al., 2019). While big companies may be able to advance big data initiatives by simply acquiring the necessary human skills, know-how, and technical infrastructure, small and medium-sized enterprises (SMEs) with limited funds and limited technical expertise need to take more innovative routes to build big data competence.

Although the proficient use of data is associated with business performance in SMEs (Ferraris et al., 2019; O'Connor & Kelly, 2017), the literature does not provide actionable insights into the capabilities that foster the development of big data competence over time. To fill this void, this study describes how Glaston, a glass-processing SME, has overcome the constraints many SMEs face in their big data journeys. While describing Glaston's journey, the study focuses on the dynamic capabilities (i.e., market listening and business imagination, open innovation, and a culture of experimentation) that have stimulated Glaston's development of its big data competence. We elaborate on the impact of these capabilities using an illustrative example—the creation of the Glaston Siru, a mobile application that uses unstructured image data.

6.2 THEORETICAL BACKGROUND

In order for businesses to make big data valuable, they must have a versatile set of capabilities. Brinch et al. (2020) identify 24 types of big data capabilities related to IT, process, performance, human, strategic, and organizational practices. However, the extant research on big data in business has primarily focused on *analytics* capabilities that provide firms with the technical competence needed to refine data into insights (Sivarajah et al., 2017; Wang & Hajli, 2017). Although analytics know-how is a clear antecedent for big data usage, it does not guarantee that a firm can turn big data into a competitive advantage and business value. Accordingly, Mikalef et al. (2020) show that the relationship between big data analytics capabilities and a firm's competitive performance is mediated by the firm's dynamic capabilities. In other words, the business value of big data analytics capabilities is determined by the firm's ability to develop organizational routines that advance data-driven business renewal.

"Dynamic capabilities" refer to the capacity of the firm to sense opportunities and threats, seize opportunities, and transform organizational routines by reconfiguring organizational resources and assets (Teece, 2007). A number of studies have demonstrated the important role of dynamic capabilities in leveraging big data to improve business performance (Erevelles et al., 2016; Gupta et al., 2020; Shams & Solima, 2019). Our theoretical approach builds on the notion that dynamic capabilities are needed to make the most out of big data initiatives. In particular, we propose that dynamic capabilities play a critical role in big data usage, especially in terms of ensuring that the firm focuses on relevant business opportunities that can be seized via advanced use of big data. However, although the extant research has demonstrated the impact of big data analytics capabilities and dynamic capabilities on business performance, it fails to provide in-depth insights into the specific dynamic capabilities that nurture the development of big data competence over time. We address this shortcoming by presenting an in-depth description of Glaston's dynamic capabilities, which not only have stimulated its big data competence but also resulted in a number of practical applications that have brought value to Glaston and its customers.

6.3   DESCRIPTION OF THE CASE COMPANY: GLASTON

Glaston is a glass-processing technology company headquartered in Finland and listed on the Nasdaq Helsinki Oy exchange. In 2020, the company had about 800 employees and annual revenue of about EUR 200 million. Glaston roughly doubled its size in 2019 via the acquisition of Swiss-German Bystronic glass. Notably, the big data journey described in this chapter is primarily focused on the time before the acquisition when the company was half of its current size.

Glaston's history dates back to the nineteenth century paper-mill industry, but its glass-processing technology business emerged in 1970. In 2007, the company changed its name from Kyro to Glaston. Today, Glaston has four factories on two continents (Europe and Asia) and customers around the world. Glaston produces glass-processing machinery and technologies that serve the needs of glass manufacturers in the architectural, automotive, solar, and appliance industries.

The company's strategy is to seek growth by offering high-quality glass-processing machinery that is augmented by digital services. It differentiates itself from its competitors through its status as the industry's innovative technology leader, and it works to help its customers efficiently realize their ambitions in glass processing. A technological orientation has been at the core of Glaston's strategy throughout its existence. It has closely followed advances in technology and continuously tried to capitalize on those developments. For decades, Glaston has adopted the latest technologies, thereby ensuring that its customers have been able to enjoy the benefits of, for instance, increased automation and a reduced need for human resources in glass processing. Glaston was also an early adopter of enterprise resource planning (ERP) customer relationship management (CRM) systems, and it has been able to integrate customer relationship, sales, and logistics data into a unified cloud database, which provides it with better visibility for its marketing, sales, and product-delivery processes. However, the most recent leaps in the use of data and technologies have occurred in relation to the Internet-of-Things (IoT) and the big data that Glaston's machinery produces on the customer's end. The remainder of this chapter focuses on these developments.

6.4   GLASTON'S BIG DATA JOURNEY

Glaston's big data journey began in the mid-2010s when the company recognized the potential value of collecting big data from its machinery. The company realized that by connecting its machinery to a cloud service, it could remotely access data on how customers used its machinery. Although Glaston was not sure how it could transform that data into business value, it started to implement IoT and cloud-service solutions as soon as it signed agreements with customers. In the early phase, data were collected on, for instance, the types, sizes, and thicknesses of processed glass; the extent to which machines were used efficiently; and how and when the machines were maintained.

As the data accumulated, Glaston began to evaluate what it could do with that data and what other data points should be added to derive meaningful insights that would improve the customer experience. Careful consideration led Glaston to envision a fully automated processing line that could produce standardized, high-quality glass that meets specific customer needs as efficiently as possible with minimal human intervention. The rationale behind this vision was that the quality and efficiency of glass processing is highly dependent on the skills of the individual processing the glass. Thus, the introduction of highly automated, standardized processes would allow almost anyone to produce high-quality glass products, leading to significant benefits for customers. The vision was ambitious, but Glaston was convinced that this was the right direction and started to take steps to reach its goal.

An important step on the journey was the launch of the *MyGlaston Portal*. The portal was a digital interface offering customers access to product-related information that could help them maximize the efficiency of production with Glaston's machinery. In addition to relevant information regarding product features and user manuals, the portal included real-time data on the operation of the machines owned by the customer (e.g., how many loads per hour, the amount of glass in each load, and the glass types and products that were processed). The second significant step was the introduction of *iLook* data to the portal. iLook is an industrial measurement tool that provides data on the quality of glass processing by detecting whether the production of different glass products meets the customer's quality standards (i.e., measurement thresholds). For example, it can recognize quality defects, such as waviness on the surface of the glass.

Recently, Glaston had begun to develop and pilot a new feature entitled *Machine Health*. This function was expected to build on the iLook feature and holistically examine the various functionalities of the machinery that affect product quality. Thus, while iLook detected quality errors, Machine Health was being designed to provide data that is useful for analyzing the causes of quality errors. Consequently, it would allow Glaston and its customers to predict needs for maintenance and spare parts.

The MyGlaston Portal provided customers with visibility into their production processes. Equipped with this information, they could optimize the energy efficiency and quality of the production process. More specifically, by monitoring the differences between machine usage and the quality of output at various times, customers could identify which operators produced the best efficiency and quality. In turn, this knowledge could be shared with others via training programs and the creation of optimal glass-processing recipes for specific glass types. Increased energy efficiency offered a direct monetary benefit for the customers because energy consumption represents a sizeable share of costs in the glass-processing industry.

Table 6.1   *Timeline of key developments in Glaston's big data journey*

Timeline	2015	2016	2017	2018	2019	2020
Big data application	IoT and cloud services	MyGlaston Portal	iLook online feature	Glaston Siru	AI assistant	Machine Health
Description	Machines connected to cloud database	Digital interface to access product-related information	Tool for detecting quality defects	Mobile application for performing tempered glass-fragmentation test	Guidance for machinery users	Detection of machinery malfunctions
Benefits for customers		Optimization of energy efficiency	Improved quality of production	Time and cost savings	Optimization of machinery usage	Shorter maintenance breaks
Benefits for Glaston		Product-development insights via data on customers' use of the machinery	Remote detection of quality defects and faster responses to customer queries	Improved brand image	Step towards fully automated, standardized processing lines	Prediction of maintenance and spare-parts orders

Moreover, quality is important for end users and it is another a significant cost factor, as the glass products need to meet specific quality standards. The higher the proportion of products that meet quality standards, the better the productivity.

Glaston has benefitted from its big data development projects in multiple ways. First, the projects have enabled the company to derive insights into how their machinery is used by customers and to harness those insights in product development by, for instance, adding, removing, or modifying features. Second, Glaston can remotely detect malfunctions, respond to customer queries quickly (even proactively), and provide maintenance guidance. Finally, it can predict customers' needs for spare parts and repair services, leading to higher cost-efficiency and significantly shorter maintenance breaks, both of which are costly for customers.

By the end of 2020, Glaston had connected more than 150 machines located around the world to its cloud. In addition, it had gathered data on about three million glass-processing loads, each of which involved hundreds or even thousands of data points. As manually analyzing such data would be practically impossible, Glaston began implementing artificial intelligence (AI) solutions (e.g., machine learning and neural network algorithms) to create automated and intelligent processing lines that would serve customer needs. Glaston perceived the smart use of big data as its key competitive advantage, and it wanted to stay ahead of the competition by continuously developing its processing lines. In 2019, Glaston piloted an AI assistant that notified machinery operators of quality errors and potential reasons for those errors (e.g., "Did you notice that …?").

The next step is to move from assistance to giving recommendations (or even commands) on how the operator should change the processing recipe (e.g., "I recommend that you make the following changes to the recipe."). If successful, Glaston will be close to realizing its vision of a fully automated, standardized process in which the machine will be allowed to make changes to processing recipes and then notify the operator of the changes made (e.g.,

"Please note that the recipe has been changed as follows."). A summary of key developments in Glaston's big data journey is provided in Table 6.1.

6.5   DYNAMIC CAPABILITIES FOR TURNING BIG DATA INTO BUSINESS APPLICATIONS

For Glaston, the fundamental driver of successful big data usage has been a genuine desire to create the best possible product—a product that exceeds customers' expectations and differentiates Glaston from its competitors. However, there is a significant gap between this abstract desire and its fulfillment. Glaston's core strength in terms of fulfilling that desire stems from three co-existing dynamic capabilities that support each other (Figure 6.1). The first, *market listening and business imagination*, focuses on sensing technological opportunities and adapting them to Glaston's business context. The second, *open innovation*, refers to Glaston's collaboration and knowledge sharing with external partners, which produces new ideas and implementation insights related to big data initiatives. The third, the *culture of experimentation*, refers to Glaston's tendency to test and validate big data applications before their full-scale implementation. These three capabilities explain the development of Glaston's big data competence primarily because they foster continuous organizational learning. In the following, we describe the roles of these capabilities in Glaston's product-development processes.

6.5.1   Market Listening and Business Imagination

As Glaston's business strategy implies, the company believes that the leaders in the glass-processing industry will be those capable of identifying relevant technological advances

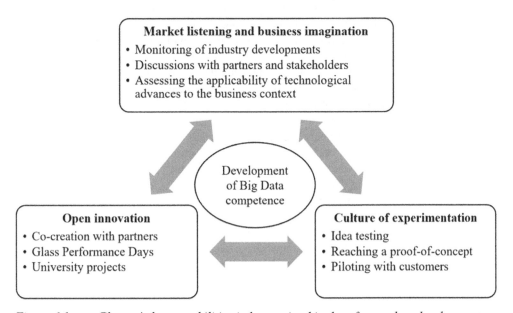

Figure 6.1   Glaston's key capabilities in leveraging big data for product development

and applying them in ways that create value for customers. In many companies, such a vision might be shared by members of top management, but it may be difficult to implement and communicate to employees. At Glaston, however, the technology strategy is primarily driven by engineers and designers, who are self-motivated to devote time and energy to monitoring technological developments and to identifying market trends and emerging signals of new opportunities. In addition to monitoring broader industry developments, they continuously listen to partners and stakeholders, and follow the emergence of new startups with fresh ideas.

For an SME, it is important to recognize that the resources it has available may not allow it to create big data solutions from scratch. By keeping an eye on the solutions that the large Silicon Valley technology companies produce, Glaston can reap the benefits of new solutions by adapting them to its business. An important part of this work involves business imagination, which revolves around analyzing which developments can be adapted to support Glaston's product development and how such steps could be accomplished. Business imagination is further fostered by matching technological expertise with product expertise:

> Often, we just meet with processing-line designers, explain how neural networks work, and ask for ideas for use cases. Then we collect and model the data produced by processing lines, and we discuss the findings with the designers. Through active discussions, we continually generate new ideas and patent applications.[1]

6.5.2   Open Innovation

The second key capability is open innovation. This is particularly important for an SME that has limited resources and skills for internal development. From the beginning, Glaston's big data strategy has been based on extensive collaboration with suppliers, partners, universities, and other companies. One platform for such collaboration is Glass Performance Days (GPD). GPD is a conference organized by Glaston every two years that brings together actors involved in the glass industry around the world. During the conferences, industry experts and practitioners present recent developments in the industry and discuss challenges that they are facing. GPD is a central part of Glaston's identity—a firm that is willing to share ideas and solve problems with other companies.

Glaston has also incorporated formal partnerships into its big data projects. These partnerships have allowed Glaston to shift its focus from technical issues (e.g., maintenance of big data infrastructure) to ways of creating more value for customers through big data. The company's collaboration with universities has been a major factor in the success of its big data projects. The university projects have provided access to expertise and a peer network encompassing a broad range of companies from other industries that have had similar ambitions. Joint learning and knowledge sharing have been extremely fruitful in terms of gaining insights into the types of big data solutions that other companies are developing, and which ones might be beneficial for Glaston. Collaboration has also made Glaston more confident that it is moving in the right direction with its big data development. Furthermore, university projects have provided Glaston with new expertise in the form of commissioned thesis projects. Many of Glaston's successful big data projects have been designed by university thesis writers who familiarized themselves with Glaston's big data challenges and developed actionable solutions. In fact, Glaston has hired several of these writers after completion of their theses, which has increased the company's skills and competence in such fields as coding and neural networks. These new talents have been crucial in designing and implementing new big data projects:

> If you handle big data projects internally, you are on your own and in your own little silo. Therefore, I think that collaborative projects with universities and other companies are extremely important. They connect firms from different industries and, as we are not competitors, we can openly share everything we do and together consider what we could do better. It is a kind of peer-to-peer mentoring, and it is important because you get the feeling that you are doing the right thing.
>
> Thesis projects have been also very productive. On the one hand, we provide young talents with challenging tasks. On the other hand, they have surprisingly strong coding and neural network skills. Often, what we consider challenging has been relatively easy for these students, as they undertake similar tasks during their studies. The projects give us plenty of new knowledge thanks to these young talents.

6.5.3 Culture of Experimentation

The third important capability is the culture of experimentation. Business imagination does not help a firm unless the firm has the courage to test ideas. Glaston wants to be a frontrunner in its industry, and to experiment with all new technologies that might create valuable data or otherwise be relevant for its business. Careful testing in big data projects is particularly important in terms of enabling companies to identify the relevant data points and ensuring that the data is of high quality. Only then is it possible to use machine learning and neural networks for the selected use cases.

Status as a frontrunner means that failures are inevitable, but those failures must be transformed into learning. Nevertheless, Glaston tries to avoid failures that would affect the customer experience. Therefore, a typical experiment goes through several phases. First, an idea is tested using simulators to evaluate its validity until a theoretical proof of concept is reached. Second, the idea is tested and optimized in internal showrooms until an empirical proof of concept is reached. Third, the proof of concept is piloted with a *"friendly user"* customer. Thus, before launching a new feature or service for customers, Glaston requires strong proof that the new feature actually works as intended. The need for a proof is also a part of the organizational culture:

> If we just go to our service-maintenance employees and present them with cool, new features for machinery, they would tell us that we need to prove that they work before they can be implemented. Seeing is believing, and that is what we have to do.

6.6 THE GLASTON SIRU—A BIG DATA APPLICATION

To illustrate the impact of Glaston's dynamic capabilities, we discuss how Glaston leveraged them in developing the Glaston Siru. The Glaston Siru is a mobile application based on big data that uses image recognition to perform tempered glass-fragmentation tests. The test is used to ensure that the glass fragmentation meets regulations and quality standards. In other words, when glass breaks, it must fragment into small pieces for safety reasons. Traditionally, fragmentation tests have been conducted either by manually counting the pieces of glass or by using massive industrial scanners that cost tens of thousands of euros and are very slow. In contrast, with the Glaston Siru, a user can take a picture of a fragmented glass and the app automatically conducts the test using neural networks. The app can be downloaded for free, and the goal is to give users a taste of Glaston's big data and AI competences.

The project that developed Glaston Siru illustrates the capabilities that enabled Glaston to progress on its big data journey. The preliminary idea for Glaston Siru emerged in late 2017 at a Glaston Hackathon event that was organized together with Business Tampere (an organization offering support for local businesses). Glaston invited startups, engineering students, and university researchers to come up with a new product-development idea for glass processing with a prize of EUR 10,000 for the winner. The open invitation attracted 24 teams (72 participants in total). The hackathon included a presentation on glass processing given by Glaston in its showroom and a discussion of some of the challenges that Glaston wanted to overcome through digitalization and big data. In response, the teams presented ideas and solutions for the challenges. The winning team was made up of researchers from the local university (Tampere University), who came up with the idea for the Glaston Siru.

The hackathon resulted in a research project led by Tampere University that allowed Glaston to access a broader network of companies that were dealing with big data challenges. Moreover, Glaston commissioned a thesis on transforming the idea for a mobile app into reality. After completing theoretical research related to the use case, the thesis writer spent one summer on the empirical research, which included breaking glass, taking pictures of fragmented glass, drawing the fragmentation patterns, and training neural networks to detect those patterns. The thesis provided a strong theoretical proof of concept. When the thesis was finished, Glaston hired the thesis writer. The task given to this employee was to move from the theoretical proof of concept to its practical implementation. It took only a couple of weeks for the employee to present the first version of the Glaston Siru. At that point, Glaston involved an external partner to design a functioning and aesthetically appealing user interface, which was a fast and straightforward process. Soon thereafter, the application was ready to be launched.

The entire development process took approximately one year and the results exceeded expectations. By late 2020, the app had been downloaded thousands of times and it was actively used by hundreds of people around the globe. As such, interest in the app was significant, especially given that the target group was composed of those responsible for glass-fragmentation tests. As a direct benefit, Glaston was able to use the app to showcase its big data and AI competences, and to build an image of itself as a technological frontrunner in the industry. The Glaston Siru was also selected as a finalist in the *Best Mobile Service* category of the *Grand One 2020* competition, which presents awards to the best work related to digital media in Finland. This was a notable achievement for an industrial SME, as the other finalists had developed apps targeting consumers.

> When customers see that we are able to use functional neural networks in a mobile app, they believe that we can do the same thing with our machinery at scale. The Siru app showcases our competence and increases customers' interest in our products.

The app's indirect benefits were even greater. Prior to the Siru app project, Glaston knew very little about neural networks. The project opened the company's eyes to how it might be able to use knowledge of neural networks in the development of its machinery. Moreover, the company realized how straightforward and easy it was to conduct big data and AI projects after suitable use cases were uncovered. This realization remarkably increased Glaston's confidence and its desire to engage in other development projects. Moreover, the costs of developing the app were low thanks to the company's approach to open-innovation learning and its collaboration with the university. Glaston learned that it could derive remarkable business benefits despite its limited resources if it generated new ideas, had the courage to experiment with them, and was willing to collaborate with other parties.

> The Siru app is a great story because we knew very little about neural networks before the project. We learned that they are surprisingly easy to use if you simply find a suitable use case or problem that they can solve. Many firms feel that AI solutions are difficult. We did not know how difficult it would be, but we had to start somewhere. As we were lucky to find a good thesis writer who did most of the work, the app cost us next to nothing to develop.

6.7 FUTURE DEVELOPMENT

Glaston has long been committed to developing its big data competence and it has persistently moved towards its vision of creating automated and standardized glass-processing lines. The company has learned that big data projects are relatively straightforward to complete given an open, curious, and experiment-driven organizational culture. Glaston is devoted to continuing along its chosen path and to leading the way in the glass-processing industry. However, as its big data usage has become more advanced, it is now facing a new set of challenges that it must overcome.

Glaston has adopted a highly customer-centric approach in its big data development, as it has focused on designing big data services that create value for customers. It is reaching a point at which it must carefully consider how all of those value-adding services can be transformed into a new business model. Glaston currently produces most of its revenue by selling machinery and maintenance services. Although some of the features of the MyGlaston Portal are premium features that produce revenue, the company is assessing new revenue models that would create a more constant stream of revenue. One alternative is a subscription model through which the company could generate recurring revenue via software licenses on a monthly or yearly basis:

> It is a matter of how well we can bundle these new services into packages that our customers would be willing to pay for.

The challenges of changing a business model are not limited to bundling new services into offerings for customers. Such changes require a significant organizational transformation. Moving from a focus on hardware to a focus on software is a significant challenge for a company that has focused on selling machinery for decades:

> We have a lot of people who have extensive experience in the industry. They are used to thinking that we are a hardware company that sells machinery. Now we are trying to change our identity from a hardware company to a software company. It is difficult for people to change their perspective, even though none of our existing machines have worked without software for a long time.

6.8 CONCLUSIONS AND MANAGERIAL IMPLICATIONS

This chapter highlights how a manufacturing SME has harnessed big data for product development. The study identifies three dynamic capabilities that Glaston has used to turn big data

Table 6.2   Fostering the development of big data competence—key questions for managers

Dynamic capability	Question 1	Question 2	Question 3
Market listening and business imagination	How do we sense new opportunities created by data-rich environments and new technologies?	How do we share the identified opportunities across the organization?	What do we need to do to capitalize on the identified data opportunities? What adaptations are needed in our business context?
Open innovation	How do we currently collaborate with external partners to develop big data initiatives?	Who could help us advance our big data journey? (Companies with similar interests? Universities? Experts? Others?)	How do we convince external partners to collaborate with us? What do we offer them in return?
Culture of experimentation	How does our organizational culture encourage people to test big data applications?	What criteria need to be fulfilled before an experiment proceeds to implementation?	How do we react if an implementation fails even though the experimentation criteria have been fulfilled?

into value-added services for its customers: market listening and business imagination, open innovation, and a culture of experimentation. These capabilities are closely aligned with the concept of adaptive marketing capabilities (i.e., vigilant market learning, adaptive market experimentation, and open marketing), which enables companies to leverage environmental changes in order to create customer-oriented competitive advantages in a data-rich environment (Day, 2011). Previous research has highlighted the importance of big data analytics capabilities (Ferraris et al., 2019; Yasmin et al., 2020) and the importance of dynamic capabilities (Cao et al., 2019; Gupta et al., 2020; Mikalef et al., 2020) for harnessing big data. This study contributes to this stream of literature by showing how an SME can harness dynamic capabilities for developing a big data competence over time. As such, the study has relevant managerial implications, especially for SMEs that are in the early phases of their big data journeys.

First, market listening and business imagination can serve as the cornerstones of big data competence development. We recommend that managers devote time and effort to actively monitoring technological developments across industries in order to identify big data applications that could have value. Furthermore, managers should encourage cross-functional knowledge sharing related to potential applications as well as imaginative thinking regarding how applications could be adapted to a given business setting.

Second, few SMEs possess the human resources and knowledge needed to design and implement big data initiatives. Therefore, we recommend that SMEs foster open innovation with external partners in order to share best practices and gain collective wisdom for designing and implementing big data initiatives. As Glaston's case demonstrates, the peer networks of other companies that are developing big data applications can be a source of significant competitive advantage. In particular, university projects that bring together companies with similar interests can be great opportunities to advance big data initiatives and acquire the talents needed to implement them.

Finally, idea generation must be complemented with continuous experimentation in order to test and validate the actionability and business value of those ideas. Managers should foster a culture of experimentation by empowering employees to run tests and offer clear criteria that must be met before implementation. Many projects will fail, but managers should treat failures as learning opportunities instead of blaming employees for disappointing results.

To synthesize the managerial implications, Table 6.2 presents the key questions that managers should ask when developing the dynamic capabilities identified in this study. We hope that by answering these questions, managers will uncover potential pitfalls in their current practices and be better able to advance their big data competence.

NOTE

1. All citations are taken from a two-hour interview with Glaston's digitalization manager, Kai Knuutila. The case description is based on this interview and a range of material from company archives.

REFERENCES

Barton, D., & Court, D. (2012). Making advanced analytics work for you: A practical guide to capitalizing on big data. *Harvard Business Review*, *90*(October), 78–83.

Brinch, M., Gunasekaran, A., & Wamba, S. (2020). Firm-level capabilities towards big data value creation. *Journal of Business Research*, 131, 539–48.

Cao, G., Duan, Y., & El Banna, A. (2019). A dynamic capability view of marketing analytics: Evidence from UK firms. *Industrial Marketing Management*, *76*, 72–83.

Day, G.S. (2011). Closing the marketing capabilities gap. *Journal of Marketing*, *75*(July), 183–95.

Erevelles, S., Fukawa, N., & Swayne, L. (2016). Big Data consumer analytics and the transformation of marketing. *Journal of Business Research*, *69*(2), 897–904.

Ferraris, A., Mazzoleni, A., Devalle, A., & Couturier, J. (2019). Big data analytics capabilities and knowledge management: Impact on firm performance. *Management Decision*, *57*(8), 1923–36.

Gupta, S., Drave, V.A., Dwivedi, Y.K., Baabdullah, A.M., & Ismagilova, E. (2020). Achieving superior organizational performance via big data predictive analytics: A dynamic capability view. *Industrial Marketing Management*, *90*, 581–92.

McAfee, A., & Brynjolfsson, E. (2012). Big data: The management revolution. *Harvard Business Review*, *90*(October), 61–8.

Mikalef, P., Boura, M., Lekakos, G., & Krogstie, J. (2019). Big Data analytics capabilities and innovation: The mediating role of dynamic capabilities and moderating effect of the environment. *British Journal of Management*, *30*, 272–98.

Mikalef, P., Krogstie, J., Pappas, I.O., & Pavlou, P. (2020). Exploring the relationship between big data analytics capability and competitive performance: The mediating roles of dynamic and operational capabilities. *Information and Management*, *57*, 1–15.

O'Connor, C., & Kelly, S. (2017). Facilitating knowledge management through filtered big data: SME competitiveness in an agri-food sector. *Journal of Knowledge Management*, *21*(1), 156–79.

Shams, S.M.R., & Solima, L. (2019). Big data management: Implications of dynamic capabilities and data incubator. *Management Decision*, *57*(8), 2113–23.

Sivarajah, U., Kamal, M.M., Irani, Z., & Weerakkody, V. (2017). Critical analysis of Big Data challenges and analytical methods. *Journal of Business Research*, *70*, 263–86.

Teece, D.J. (2007). Explicating dynamic capabilities: The nature and microfoundations of (sustainable) enterprise performance. *Strategic Management Journal*, *28*(13), 1319–50.

Wang, Y., & Hajli, N. (2017). Exploring the path to big data analytics success in healthcare. *Journal of Business Research*, *70*, 287–99.

Yasmin, M., Tatoglu, E., Kilic, H.S., Zaim, S., & Delen, D. (2020). Big data analytics capabilities and firm performance: An integrated MCDM approach. *Journal of Business Research*, *114*, 1–15.

7. Big data in and for small business: data excellence in SMEs through engagement in university partnerships

Shirley Y. Coleman

7.1 INTRODUCTION

Data is in abundance more than ever before. Not only is there an appetite within business to capture measurements but there is also a wide variety of equipment available with sensors that feed back data allowing a new wave of digital communication between processes. The term Industry 4.0 has been coined to represent the way that machines and processes are increasingly able to talk with each other and to share data. Industry 4.0 means that processes can act on the values of the data to continually improve output. This sea change in the way production and services function means that there are opportunities to be grasped by analysing data. Unfortunately, it is often the case that data appreciation and analytical skills are out of the skill-set of small and medium-sized enterprise (SME) personnel and are far from the expertise that was used to set up the SME.

Data has become important in all companies. Using data and statistics equalizes the differences between large and small companies; small start-ups with small numbers of staff but high usage of data can compete with large companies and make an impact in the business world. These counter-intuitive claims are justified by solid examples in a range of sectors. For example, the online company Zoopla (www.zoopla.co.uk) started out by utilizing publicly available information on the value of house sales and has grown into a massive industry leader offering sales, rentals, property valuations, area appraisals and many other related services. An agile data-wise SME can make use of massive databases from large conglomerates and create a business from interpreting and showcasing the data and providing insight (Coleman, 2016).

SMEs can read in their trade magazines all about the marvellous benefits their smart competitors are realizing from analysing their data. The data is already available from the processes making up the business such as stock control, operations, human resources and marketing. SMEs have the advantages of being flexible and agile but amongst a range of barriers and challenges (Coleman et al., 2016) they have the disadvantage of a more limited pool of in-house expertise. The question is how to tap into this new source of wealth.

As for large companies, the first step is to find out if using data would help the business, and if so, what benefits can be expected, what is involved in getting started and what it will cost.

SMEs have a number of options to help them answer these questions, and if they decide to go ahead, how they can develop their data science skills. The options include training up their own staff, employing ready-trained data-proficient staff, bringing in consultants, making partnerships with more advanced non-competitor larger companies or SMEs, and teaming up with universities.

In this chapter we explore the pros and cons of SMEs working with universities to embed data science capabilities. The chapter reviews what can be offered and what can be learnt from these partnerships. It is written from personal experience of working in a self-funding university unit dedicated to helping SMEs and larger organizations make use of statistics. Initially and latterly, the unit has worked extensively with knowledge transfer partnerships with part funding from an external funder; most recently these projects have focused on using data science to monetize SME big data.

The process of engagement follows a number of stages:

1. SME explores the motivation to participate. SME is aware of advances in its specialty, can read glowing articles in the trade press and discuss in networks. University boasts knowledge of state-of-the-art and shares exemplars of engagement via websites, popular articles and case studies, roadshows, showcases and informal meetings with SME. The input from both sides is equal but SME and university bring different knowledge.
2. SME decides how to engage; they consider using consultants, in-house personnel, and so on. Universities offer their options: student projects, consultancy, training courses, funded partnerships. Both sides have equal engagement. SME decides on a funded knowledge transfer partnership.
3. SME chooses the university partner based on reputation and past experience; SME wants value for money, university wants an interesting project with a reliable partner; they require assurance of SME commitment and access to staff and data, an external funder wants value for money. The balance of need is equal.
4. The project is fully scoped and a work plan is designed with SMART objectives, milestones and deliverables. Usually, the university and funder have more experience at this than the SME.
5. Research Associate (RA) is appointed. SME and university have equal say in who is appointed.
6. Project commences and is monitored by the funder. All stakeholders, SME, university, RA and funder work together to keep project on track.
7. Project concludes and is summed up in a final report. SME has to complete the paperwork to ensure all funding is secured; university academics want publications and quantified impact; RA wants to complete the project for future career prospects and may get a finishing bonus and/or a job; funder wants statistics for their credibility.
8. Ongoing, SME may want support but not so much as the university wants ongoing access to the SME for student projects and publications. The RA and funder move on to new prospects.

These stages are summarized in the flowchart presented in Table 7.1.

Table 7.1   Flowchart of process of engagement

Process stage	SME input	University input	Symmetry of input
1. Motivation	Trade press, network discussions	Exemplars, roadshows, showcases	Equal
2. How to engage	Review past experience, new offers	Presentation of options	Equal
3. Choose partner and timescale	Consider links and relationships with universities	Check credentials of SME	Equal
4. Design project	Based on strategy, personnel, future plans	Ensure research integrity and depth	University may have more experience. Funders check value for money.
5. Appoint Research Associate (RA)	Human resource management	Follow employment policies	Equal
6. Run project	Find way to embed and work with RA	Support RA	Funder monitors project for benefit of all stakeholders.
7. Project concludes	Report on outcomes and may employ RA	Ensures academic publications are achieved	Both partners aim for high grade.
8. Ongoing	Develop new skills	Continue with research and further projects	Depends on direction taken by each partner.

In accordance with the flowchart, the next section on Theoretical Background considers stages 1 to 4, including the motivation for SMEs to engage with universities, and the types of engagement on offer. We describe how projects are designed, set up and monitored. We then give Empirical Insights regarding stages 5 to 8 via examples of data science knowledge transfer partnerships in a number of different sectors with their outcomes and ongoing impact. The final section is Managerial Implications in which we review the process in terms of what works and what doesn't and what lessons can be drawn for SMEs.

7.2   THEORETICAL BACKGROUND

7.2.1   Motivation for Engaging with Universities

The options available to SMEs for implementing the necessary skills to enable them to carry out data analytics and take advantage of the new digital environment include training up their own staff, employing ready-trained data-proficient staff, bringing in consultants (or other external agents, such as software vendors), making partnerships with more advanced non-competitor larger companies or SMEs, or teaming up with higher education providers, namely universities, as these are the most prolific example of higher education providers.

When wanting to acquire new expertise, engaging with a university is a sound option. The alternatives have considerable down-sides. Training staff presupposes that someone is available with the necessary skills to do the training; not only do they need the technical skills, but they also need the teaching skills. Identifying staff who can be trained via full- or part-time external courses is an option but the courses are likely to be too widely focused and take too long to complete. In addition, this option is risky as it takes the staff away from their usual duties, thus impairing the company before any benefits are realized. Employing ready-trained staff can be expensive and the SME needs to be really confident that the new skills are the right choice before the expense is committed. Consultants are also expensive and ensuring their work leaves a legacy is an important issue as embedding the new skills can take a long time. Partnerships with other non-competitor companies are a good option if suitable partners can be found (Stewardson and Coleman, 2003). However, there is always a danger of losing the newly skilled staff to the mentor company. Engagement with universities is a way of addressing SME difficulties in terms of access to knowledge and its transfer to business and also bringing benefits to the universities.

In most countries, governments acknowledge the need to support knowledge transfer between business and academia. However, the extent of supportive funding varies depending on the economic climate. Without assistance SMEs tend to underinvest in research and innovation projects (DIUS, 2008). The rationale for government to invest in engagement as a vehicle to promote knowledge transfer, innovation and skills development has a strong basis in the UK and there is a long tradition of part funding which is especially generous for SMEs.

7.2.2   Types of Engagement

7.2.2.1 Consultancy and research projects

There is an increasing enthusiasm in universities for engagement (Ferguson, 2014), not least because it is a requirement of government funding that engagement is demonstrated. Many academics have ongoing relationships with industry which are mutually beneficial but because they are informal the work must fit in whenever the academic has time for their research amongst teaching and other duties. Universities often offer consultancy services provided by their academic staff. Unless these consultancy episodes are affordable and lead to longer term engagements, they do not, however, meet the need of embedding new skills in an SME.

Student projects are an excellent way of forging business-academia links. Most universities have data-centric courses that include short or longer projects usually in the final year of undergraduate studies or as a larger part of a Master's degree. Students studying for a doctorate (PhD) may also be interested in interspersing a period of real world experience within their research activities and be able to take time out to undertake a short 3–6 month project in industry or business. These student projects may explore some useful area of potential new expertise but do not necessarily aim at retaining the student as a future employee and may be too short to embed the skills.

Engagement can take many forms. Someone has to do the work and the question is who? Academics have heavy workloads, teaching, carrying out fundamental research and administering the functions of the university. They may be reluctant to take on more commitments, even though their engagement work may be paid. Whilst the knowledge that they can impart to industry is new, there are many basic steps that have to be taken before ground-breaking innovation can happen. These steps provide excellent on-the-job learning for a graduate. It makes sense, therefore, to employ the knowledge and skills of the academic in a supervisory role and employ a graduate research associate to do the work. This is the model used in UK government part-funded knowledge transfer partnerships.

7.2.2.2 Knowledge transfer partnerships

Knowledge transfer partnerships (KTPs) are a form of engagement that actively addresses the needs of SMEs to acquire and embed new skills and new ways of working that will be sustainable beyond the duration of the project.

KTPs link companies with a university and a graduate to work on a substantial project of strategic importance to the company. The university will help to recruit a suitable graduate, who is employed by the university as a research associate but who then works nearly full time at the company for the duration of the project. KTPs therefore enable businesses to bring in new skills and academic thinking without the risk of employing a new person. The company does, however, have to commit to the full length of the project which can be between 12 and 36 months depending on the project and needs of the company. Two-year projects are very common as these give sufficient time to develop the transfer and offer stable employment to the research associate but they are not prohibitively long for any of the participants.

Typically, the KTP will be to help the company develop a new offering and income stream, learn new skills, develop new products or change the way they work (KTP-UK, 2020). There are four stakeholders each with their own personal motivation, aims and objectives. These are:

- The SME that wishes to improve its business, open up new areas of expertise, develop new products and keep ahead of competitors.
- The university that wishes to put its research into practice as a means of testing it and eliciting new ideas to pursue or implement old ideas whose usage is not widely established. Universities wish to show the impact of their research in terms of changing society and the wider business community for the better and to add to their prestige through publications, higher degrees and staff development.
- The research associate (RA) who does the work and wishes to gain experience not only from putting their theoretical learning into practice but also from interacting with other people and understanding the world of business.
- The funder who needs to show return on investment.

It is important that the company has a well-formulated idea of what they want from the project. A clear work plan with milestones and deliverables helps make the RA feel confident that they are achieving as they are on the right track. There should be regular meetings at different levels to monitor the progress of the project.

The UK Knowledge Transfer programme has been running for over 40 years and its longevity is testimony to its effectiveness (Gov.UK, 2020). At the end of the KTP the research associate is highly skilled and experienced and in high demand. In 75 per cent of cases in recent years, the RA has been offered a job within the company, providing a tried-and-tested employee with valuable skills, tailored to the needs and culture of the company. It is a joint decision between the RA and the company as to whether a job is offered and accepted. In most cases, when the RA does remain with the company they start in a more senior role and will usually lead a team of people in the new field of expertise.

Taking part in a KTP definitely helps a company to develop their business. The SME can tap into academic expertise that doesn't exist in-house. This can improve business performance and help the SME to become more competitive and productive. There is a requirement from the funder that KTP work is disseminated widely. One or more papers are written for the academic and trade press. Often work is presented at conferences and to the company staff. These deliverables as well as company reports are valuable legacy resources for the company.

Not all countries have such a well-established knowledge transfer scheme as the KTP programme. Other countries may allocate funds for job creation schemes and industry-university linkage projects, but the KTP programme is particularly targeted at SMEs and could be beneficial worldwide.

7.2.2.3 Mentoring schemes

One other project type of engagement is the group-mentoring project. In these a large 'host' company acts as mentor to a number of SMEs, usually around eight of these, supported by expert facilitators from the university. A technology-transfer company, funded by government, for example a Manufacturing Advisory Service (MAS) Regional Centre for Manufacturing Excellence, acts as the broker of the scheme. These schemes are highly successful and have led to many longer ongoing projects funded from public sources. The benefits to the participants of these types of group schemes cannot be underestimated, bringing with them a balance of practical help supported by the more academic or technical skills of the university, all set in context by the mentor company. Some SME staff feel more comfortable with this structure as the host company staff have valuable skills but without the distance and aura sometimes associated with academics. An example is described more fully in Coleman et al. (2001).

7.2.3 Motivation for an SME to Use Their Big Data

This chapter is based on our experience of working with SMEs to help them to realize the value of their company internal big data by using statistics and the wider application of data science. We first consider what data science is and then consider what can be done with it.

7.2.3.1 Data science

With the rise of massive amounts of accessible data, the ability to manipulate data and extract meaning has become highly valued. Data science is recognized as a combination of information technology (IT), statistics and business knowledge. All three aspects are important and it is the strength of this combination of methods and skills that is producing so many interesting findings. Data scientists are in hot demand and can earn high salaries.

Data arises from all operations of a company as part of the day to day business and includes transaction records, logistics, stock control, administration and financial data. Job scheduling, for example is a common task for SMEs and job lists include date and time of request, location and job category. After the job has been addressed, details of the action taken, the arrival date and time of the operator, duration of job, findings and follow-up are associated with the job, making a rich source of data. In retail, data is available on the date and number of customers entering the premises, the volume, value and type of purchases, the personnel on duty, weather and external environmental conditions. In a more digitally connected or smart outlet there may also be information on the customer journey through the premises, including time in, out and duration of stay, sequence of interest in different products purchased; and where a loyalty card is used there is information about age, sex, address, employment and many other things for each customer.

Internal company data can be enriched by a variety of external data from official statistics and open data sources and also from the mass of useful data arising from social media. Information plays a crucial role in a company's competitiveness. Companies that use innovative technologies are able quickly and flexibly to adapt to rapidly changing market conditions and customer requirements, enabling them to achieve a strong competitive advantage. Information depends on data and innovative technologies need data.

Essential information is often not available to decision makers at the critical point of need, or at least the information is not in a form necessary for creative analysis and decision making. Data science is the means of making meaningful data available quickly in a usable form. For example, using data science it should be straightforward to find valuable business information such as the location and number of new prospective customers whenever the information is needed, and to answer basic questions such as:

- Which customers place the largest numbers of orders?
- What service is most profitable?
- How seasonal are our sales?
- What turnover can be achieved next year?
- How can new customers with high lifetime values be attracted?
- What is the risk that we lose a customer?

Having data available to answer key questions represents a major strategic advantage. Some questions can be answered by taming company data. The answers to other questions, however, do not lie in a single set of figures or customer features, but in the right combination of a variety of different bits of information. Thus, for example, the risk of losing a customer depends on characteristics such as customer age, demographic typologies, previously purchased products, interest shown in the product, payment practices and business environment. Thus, SMEs need to develop their data science skills in the context of their business and this does not happen overnight.

7.2.3.2 Project design

Companies see the need for data science, and in particular statistics, and are very open to using engagement with a university where there are staff dedicated to helping SMEs. As with any project, it is vital that the aims and objectives are well defined. Six Sigma project management gives valuable guidance (Coleman, 2008). The Define phase of the Six Sigma methodology ensures that partners consider what it is that they want to achieve, the relevant timescales and whether the appropriate people are available to be involved in the partnership.

Having settled this, before starting an engagement with data analytics, it is important to consider how ready the business is regarding the availability, accessibility, quantity and quality of appropriate data. A data readiness scale focuses attention on the condition of datasets required for the project. It provides a constructive way of communicating between the academics and the specialists within the company. In particular, it can help in the difficult area of releasing funds and IT personnel, who often have other priorities, to improve the data resource (Ahlemeyer-Stubbe and Coleman, 2018). IT departments may be reluctant to share data for non-operational projects, leading to considerable delays.

7.2.3.3 Data analytical software
Data analysis carried out during the engagement can make use of freeware such as Python or R. Or a company may have its own bespoke software, or may choose to buy new proprietary software. The advantage of this is that the software is auditable and (probably) reliable. On the other hand, it is expensive. The SME has to decide what methods of analysis can be continued with after the partnership is completed.

7.3   EMPIRICAL INSIGHTS

7.3.1   Case Studies from SMEs

SMEs in all sectors are enthusiastic to start using their big data. Many are attracted to the KTP programme and the results have been very positive. The aims are to embed data science capability in the company to increase new products and create new revenue streams.

The examples below are based on our experience and include references to where further details can be found. Sectors such as healthcare, pharmaceuticals and chemical process industries have massive amounts of big data but tend to be larger organizations rather than SMEs. The examples below are from a range of sectors where SMEs are common.

7.3.1.1   Automotive aftersales
A project in the automotive aftersales sector aimed at developing new products and services from big data such as the masses of daily look-ups in online catalogues of automotive parts. Insight from this project is described in Coleman (2019) where a funnel plot is used to illustrate the variation in return rates between parts. Insight from garage services in the same project is discussed in Smith et al. (2019) where a cumulative distribution function of mileage shows how the reliability of vehicle models differs. Each of these insights is of value to different stakeholders in the business and can be offered by the SME as new products and services.

Statistical and machine learning techniques were effectively embedded within the company allowing it to enhance existing services as well as produce more saleable products such as car part failure predictions, vehicle coverage trends, catalogue gap analysis. The company was a start-up and it took some time to fully embed the KTP outputs into company processes and to realize the potential of their big data analysis in the automotive after-market. However, the company is confident of marketable products from the work of the KTP associate who is now a full-time employee.

7.3.1.2   Shipping
In the shipping sector, a company manufactures a customized sensor that is attached to a ship's engine to record its fuel consumption. Analysis of the big data returned by the sensor can be used to indicate the condition of the engine, to show the cost implications of tide and weather (Coleman, 2019) and to suggest an economic speed for the engine, optimal routes and the best time to set off (Vicario and Coleman, 2020).

The SME aims to provide insight from the data analysis and offer consultancy. The company initially found it difficult to market the new products, however, and so there was not an immediate positive effect on turnover. However, commercialization is being achieved through offering the products to existing customers and marketing them as part of the core product externally. The marine industry internationally faces major challenges in cost control and environmental footprint. The new products established during the KTP have been designed to help customers meet these challenges in a proactive way using the new systems to monitor fuel use and emissions. They will enable an ECO approach for each journey using knowledge from the data captured and offer the SME a competitive edge.

7.3.1.3 Assistive technology

An expert system created by an SME to recommend suitable assistive technology collects big data from its users, including details of challenges in activities of daily living and environmental circumstances. There are many stakeholders in such a business and all can benefit from anonymized analysis of this data (Ahlemeyer-Stubbe and Coleman, 2018, section 10.12). For example, the data gives insight into what and where the problems are, thus aiding localized planning and policy making; which assistive technology products and services are most widely applicable and in what combinations, enabling suppliers and retailers to ensure adequate stocks; and which challenges and circumstances have few solutions, indicating where new products and services need to be developed. The KTP aimed at diversifying the revenue streams and, as a result of developing data science capability, the SME can now offer a broader range of services, allowing them to become an insight-based business.

The company is now far more aware of the value and importance of research in general and of data analytics in particular. In addition, when considering new developments such as software applications, all staff are aware of the value and importance of the data generated, which means that they are mindful of the need to ensure the high quality of data required for fruitful analytics. As part of this heightened awareness, the company has now allocated specific budgets to both research and data analytics. These are major changes in the company's culture, which was previously highly operational and prescriptive and is now far more flexible, innovative and capable of responding to the rapidly changing policy-base and commercial marketplace within which it operates. A bespoke protocol has been created and implemented within the company to facilitate access to operational and research data required for analysis, which resolved the challenge of lengthy waits for data encountered at the start of the KTP.

7.3.1.4 Social housing

The social housing sector aims to secure accommodation for under-privileged families. Large numbers of properties are owned by local councils or housing associations for this purpose. An SME provides the information systems to deal with the big data related to rent collection, property repairs and maintenance. This data is a valuable resource which can give insight into many aspects of the properties and the people who live in them. Cluster analysis of rent balance profiles was described in Vicario and Coleman (2020). The likelihood of a property being empty and the typical length of time before it is reoccupied can also be examined using regression analysis and random forests. The engagement project focused on the development of data analytics capacity to make use of the massive database of housing rental data for the benefit of the landlords and tenants alike.

In the social housing sector, there are few competitors delivering high end analytic solutions, and therefore a large market opportunity. The KTP has addressed this by proving the value of analytic solutions in the sector. The company will continue to develop these solutions, in many cases being first to market. This not only strengthens the company position in the sector, but also brings new products to the sector which will help with increasing demands to cut costs. The new analytics product set is a rapidly developing revenue stream and a key component for forecast growth in revenues over the next three years.

7.3.1.5 Manufacturing

Plastic pipes are manufactured by forcing softened material through a shaped orifice to produce a continuous length of consistently shaped pipe when solidified. Enough pressure must be used to feed the material, at the right temperature, into the die and it must be pulled out at the right speed. Components of the raw material must be mixed completely and in the right proportions. Sensors on all parts of the manufacturing process produce big data with potential for valuable insight.

The KTP introduced quality improvement techniques including failure mode and effect analysis, house of quality and fault tracking to identify key factors leading to defects, waste and non-conformance of the product. Statistically designed experiments using orthogonal arrays were conducted aimed at minimizing scrap levels. The KTP helped transfer knowledge of quality measurement, cause and effect analysis, experimental design and how to select appropriate target variables, in this case the roughness of the internal wall of the pipe as well as the tensile strength of the pipe.

The output of the KTP was improved production processes and a reduction of waste. The company was hit by a downturn in the sector, however, and much of the good work was lost.

7.3.1.6 Processing

A soft drinks company were enthusiastic to undertake a KTP but had a very vague problem area, defined as general improvement, and the company were more or less taking part in a quality improvement programme to please the programme organizers rather than definitely expecting some benefit. This was reflected in their rather mediocre outcomes.

Prior to the KTP, there was little knowledge of statistics within the company. The KTP successfully introduced the company to quality improvement techniques including reliability analysis of measurements made in the bottling plant and statistical process control monitoring and improving the fill levels. The KTP introduced flow charting and the use of data presentations such as scatterplots to look for relationships between variables, histograms to look for distributions and outliers, and Pareto charts to prioritize causes of disruptions to the plant.

7.3.1.7 Retail

The SME business rationale was to source clothing and retail them through a catalogue and a few strategically placed shops. Before the KTP, the big data relating to customers, sales and of high and low worth were used for marketing campaigns. These levels were based on a poorly understood RFM method of categorizing customers in terms of Recency, Frequency of purchases and Monetary value.

The KTP explored the use of data mining techniques, including data presentation in graphs, tables and dashboards. Relationships between sales and customer characteristics were analysed using principal components and analysis of means. Useful patterns in the data were discovered that could improve targeted marketing. The segmentation of customers by worth was put onto a more scientific footing (Coleman and Smith, 2007). The KTP outcomes cut the costs of marketing by improving targeting and increasing response rate to promotional campaigns. However, further exploitation of the results was curtailed by a severe recession in the sector and the closure of the company.

7.3.1.8 Digital marketing

The shipping SME referred to above had two previous successfully completed KTPs with our university. The first KTP was aimed at designing and manufacturing new products and resulted in a bespoke fuel consumption sensor. The company then embarked on a second KTP to make use of the big data from the fuel consumption sensor and this again was an effective way to make innovative new products based on the data. The company then decided to undertake a third KTP to maximize their digital marketing to promote their products and services. Each of these three KTPs involved an academic team of experts in different areas, from marine engineering to statistics and marketing.

Finding a research associate for the digital marketing project with skills in marketing as well as data competency proved difficult and there were several rounds of recruitment before an excellent candidate was appointed.

7.3.2   Similarities and Differences

7.3.2.1 Recruitment

The SMEs were able to recruit a skilled specialist into the company to try out new methods, products and services with minimum financial risk. The academic partners transferred considerable knowledge and expertise to the SME via the RA. In five of the case studies, the RA became a permanent employee. This is particularly important where the SME is in a niche market, such as shipping and requires someone with a lot of background knowledge. In other cases, such as assistive technology and retail, no prior experience of the sector was needed but the RA was able to build on statistical skills acquired as a student to develop data science applications bespoke for the SME and become a valuable staff member.

In some cases, there was a mismatch between the expectations and ambitions of the RA and the opportunities offered by the company. Nevertheless, the two-year KTP was completed successfully and the RA moved onto a more demanding data science role.

7.3.2.2 Project conduct

SMEs tend to be particularly vulnerable to economic changes and need to be agile and flexible to move with the market. In one case the promising results from the KTP were influenced by the world events around the coronavirus pandemic. However, the RA was simultaneously working on a PhD based on the KTP, and this could continue whilst the company was affected. The projects were generally able to follow the KTP work plan but some of the details about specific activities had to be adjusted.

There are a lot of similarities between the sectors as regards what works and what doesn't. The main differences are due to the size of the company; smaller companies tend to be more focused on the specific project and are happy to follow the KTP work plan whereas larger companies with a lot of different functions can see the wider application of academic expertise and expect a greater degree of flexibility in the activities.

7.3.2.3   Closure

In all but one of the case studies, the two-year programme was completed. In two of the case studies, the SME was disrupted by economic downturns. In one case, the project had to be discontinued after a year, but in the other case, the RA continued in the project as an employee of the university, but was unable to continue in the company on completion. In all of the other case studies, the projects were completed successfully and, in all but one, the RA stayed on as an employee. All projects were highly rated by the funder, the SME was in possession of an excellent collection of reports and presentations and the academics were able to present the research at conferences and in academic papers.

7.3.2.4   Ongoing

All SMEs were pleased to have taken part in the projects. The continuation of RA employment generally means that the innovation and knowledge exchange can continue to develop and the university can maintain ongoing relations. SMEs usually just have one funded KTP but where the subject matter is distinctly different more are allowed, as was the case in the digital marketing case study. The ongoing connection with the SME is vitally important to the university as it is a source of future student projects, speakers at university events, further funding bids and the all-important demonstration of research impact. The academic's experience working with the company adds realism to their lectures and often data can be used to teach methods and demonstrate the relevance of data science techniques.

7.4   MANAGERIAL IMPLICATIONS

Each of the case studies has its own special features and issues that had to be considered to make it go well. In addition, there are many similarities. It has become clear to us over the last few years that certain patterns of work are better than others when helping industry, especially the smaller companies, and there are certain dos and don'ts. The following is a synopsis of the main findings.

7.4.1   Collaboration

One main factor in successfully helping SMEs is to aid them without the university staff looking too good. It is important that gains for the company are perceived as won by the SME staff themselves, with the academics simply seen as facilitators. Whenever company staff perceive that it is the 'outsiders' who have achieved success they are less likely to adopt the new methods that are used to create the gains. By helping them to own the 'win' the self-esteem of the staff is raised and they are happier to learn and use the new techniques.

It is also important not to rely too much on training alone. Hands-on help or mentoring is essential if gains are to be maintained. This is partly because SME staff in particular tend to be short of time in which to organize and change the way they work without this adversely affecting immediate work patterns. The academics act as an extra resource and must involve the SME staff fully in the project decision making so that they feel empowered and are enabled to 'own' the changes. When this is done, the company benefits are more quickly apparent and the new skills are more likely to be adopted.

7.4.2   Team Working

Company cultures regarding ways of working vary enormously. In some cases, the RA is micro-managed and works in the company office apart from regular visits to the university. At the other extreme to micro-management, some KTPs are extremely loose with no fixed working place and most meetings conducted electronically. This has the disadvantage that the RA does not meet face to face and interact with other staff and can be a shock to a fresh graduate starting their first job after university.

Working in teams is nearly always a better idea than working alone. Change can sometimes appear threatening and shared projects always seem to work better. Commitment from the top is also essential to ensure the project is driven through. This was one of the well-known arguments of W. Edwards Deming in his work on quality management (Deming, 2018).

An important aspect of team working is trust. One of the common pitfalls in big data projects is not assiduously checking the quality of historical data before it is analysed. The academic supervisor may feel uncomfortable pressing for details of data provenance, but it is always vital to check historical data, and in particular the definitions of the variables recorded. Operational definitions may have changed, or the data may have been collected for a different purpose in the past, or with less attention to detail. These checks are easier to make if everyone in the team trusts that the data analysts know what they are doing.

7.4.3   Communication

Breaking the work plan down into easily digested chunks of five to ten days of effort is also a good idea. What doesn't work is just ploughing away without reporting back to the main decision maker. The regularity of management and supervisory team meetings in KTPs helps guard against this. Continuous communication is always advisable.

One of the difficult issues is gaining access to company data. Precious IT personnel are rightly concerned with the security and confidentiality of their data and may be reluctant to share with KTP personnel unless kept fully informed of the planned usage of the data. The special position of the RA being embedded in the company is helpful and it is not uncommon for them to be the only university personnel allowed full data access. Effective communication between RA and academic supervisor then becomes of paramount importance.

Case studies help SMEs who are beginning or continuing to use their big data to improve their business. These demonstrate how engaging with a university in a KTP can lead to tangible benefits with new skills embedded, new revenue streams, increased sales, new products and services, increased output, efficiency and profitability.

7.4.4   Presentation of Results

Publicizing the wins themselves, throughout the company, having first properly quantified them is also a very good idea, both boosting the 'winners' esteem and encouraging others to use successful methods. Posters and articles in newsletters are helpful (see, for example, Coleman and Stewardson, 2002). Training in using graphical methods is of key importance and provides a good way to start the engagement. We usually encourage the company to examine a sample of their data early on and see what insight can be extracted by plotting histograms, time series charts, scatterplots and quantified geographical displays.

7.4.5   Open Data

Another effective early activity is to look for publicly available sources of data that are relevant to the company. SMEs are often amazed by the richness of official statistics sources, such as www.Eurostat.eu and a variety of sector-specific providers. These data are usually free to use and can add enormous value to the more specific company datasets.

7.4.6   What Can Go Wrong

The main failure we have found is the failure to embed effectively. Companies are happy to work in a new way and employ new methods whilst they are in contact with the academic partner, but once they are on their own there is a tendency to slip back to their old ways.

A recurring feature of engagement with SMEs is the company being hit by recession and downturn. Company closure is always very upsetting but in a way is not surprising because government intervention is aimed at trying to revitalize and support companies that have good prospects but which need help. Sometimes even though the KTP is successful in terms of producing the planned outputs of new products, ways of working or revenue streams, the company fails through external circumstances.

One of the most difficult problems to overcome is the middle manager who hinders the project in mid-flow. People who resist change are difficult to deal with and special care should be taken to get buy-in from all pivotal personnel. Open discussion and inclusive meetings are a good start combined with convincing presentation of expectations and results.

Sometimes the KTP is created to respond to a specific perceived opportunity and it can happen that an alternative solution is found or the opportunity disappears so that the importance of the new knowledge decreases. This can result in the RA finding themselves in a job that differs from the subject area of the KTP. This can be acceptable for some RAs but not others and they need to move on and find themselves a new job.

There is always a tendency for companies to want to maximize the usefulness of the RA, particularly if they are competent, and to use them for work outside of the KTP. The RA should be flexible enough to cope with a certain amount of loyalty duty but may need to learn how to say no or to bring things out into the open at a management meeting.

We have identified the following managerial implications:

- Method of engagement and project partners should be selected with care after reviewing all the options, reading trade press and discussing with business network.
- Projects must be well defined with clear stages, milestones and deliverables. This ensures legacy documents and helps hold the gains after the project has ended.
- Although collaboration is fundamental to a project, meetings and discussions should be mindful of addressing the diverse needs of all stakeholders, the SME, the academics, the RA and the funder.

7.5   SUMMARY

The chapter has promoted the value of integration between SMEs and universities. The engagement process can be summarized in a flowchart (Figure 7.1) which illustrates the elements described in the chapter.

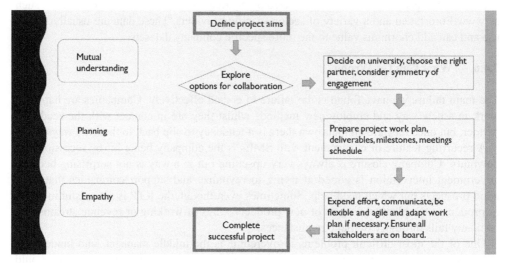

Figure 7.1   Flowchart of engagement process

Both parties can offer a lot and both gain by interacting; SMEs gain valuable knowledge and potential new recruits and universities gain practical experience and case studies to use in teaching. There are various types of collaboration and engagement methods and the SME has to decide exactly what it is that they need and what method is best for them. Experience over many years and projects has shown that mutual communication is important, as are planning and mutual respect. These findings are demonstrated in case studies from a variety of different business and industry sectors.

There are a lot of insights and experiential advice in this chapter. We now reiterate and prioritize the main conclusions and give three key take-aways for SME practitioners as we sum up the chapter.

- Mutual understanding between SME and university: In all sectors certain ways of working are effective including solid collaboration, team working, good communication and presentation of results in a meaningful and easily digestible form. The partnership can fail if the company doesn't keep to the business case, or the academics don't appreciate the importance for the SME of maintaining and increasing income.
- Planning: The partnership and project need to be well defined and captured in a detailed work plan with responsibilities clearly stated, so that any divergence can be discussed and all the stakeholders can get what they need from the partnership.

- Empathy: SMEs in all sectors should look for a university partner whose staff are knowledgeable and also have a proven ability to communicate, understand business issues and empathize with company personnel. In this way, the SME feels they own the new expertise and can further develop it after the engagement is completed.

It is hoped that the findings, some more obvious than others, will help SME-university partnerships to work well and avoid some of the pitfalls that can occur, and that this will lead to better and more structured help for SMEs to improve their data excellence generally.

REFERENCES

Ahlemeyer-Stubbe, A. and Coleman, S.Y. (2018). *Monetising Data – How to Uplift Your Business*, Chichester: Wiley,

Coleman, S.Y. (2008). Six Sigma – an opportunity for statistics and for statisticians. *Significance*, 5, 94–6.

Coleman, S. (2016). Data mining opportunities for small to medium enterprises from official statistics. *Journal of Official Statistics*, 32(4), 849–66, https://www.degruyter.com/view/j/jos.2016.32.issue-4/issue-files/jos.2016.32.issue-4.xml

Coleman, S.Y. (2019). Data science in Industry 4.0. In I. Faragó, F. Izsák, and P. Simon (eds), *Progress in Industrial Mathematics at ECMI 2018. Mathematics in Industry*, vol. 30. Cham: Springer, https://doi.org/10.1007/978-3-030-27550-1_71

Coleman, S. and Smith, K (2007). Data mining sales data for Kansei Engineering. In D.T. Pham, E.E. Eldukhri, and A.J. Soroka (eds), *Innovative Production Machines and Systems*. Caithness, Scotland: Whittles Publishing, pp. 268–73.

Coleman, S.Y., Francis, J., Hodgson, C., and Stewardson, D.J. (2001). Helping smaller manufacturers implement performance measurement – a regional group mentoring programme. *Industry & Higher Education*, 15(6), 409–14.

Coleman, S.Y., Gob, R., Manco, G., Pievatolo, A., Tort-Martorell, X., and Reis, M. (2016). How can SMEs benefit from big data? Challenges and a path forward. *Quality and Reliability Engineering International*, 32(6), 2151–64, http://onlinelibrary.wiley.com/doi/10.1002/qre.2008/full

Deming, W.E. (2018). *Out of the Crisis*, reissue edn. Cambridge, MA: MIT Press.

DIUS (2008). UK Government Department of Innovation, Universities and Skills. Innovation Nation White Paper, March.

Ferguson, M. (2014). Knowledge exchange between universities and the creative industries in the UK. *Industry & Higher Education*, 28(3), 177–83.

Gov. UK (2020). Knowledge Transfer Partnerships: what they are and how to apply, https://www.gov.uk/guidance/knowledge-transfer-partnerships-what-they-are-and-how-to-apply (accessed 2 June 2021).

KTP-UK (2020). About KTP, https://www.ktp-uk.org/about-ktp/ (accessed 2 June 2021).

Smith, W., Coleman, S., Bacardit, J., and Coxon, S. (2019). Insight from data analytics with an automotive aftermarket SME. *Quality and Reliability Engineering International*, 35(5), 1396–407, https://onlinelibrary.wiley.com/doi/full/10.1002/qre.2529

Stewardson, D.J. and Coleman, S.Y. (2003). Success and failure in helping SMEs, a three-year observational study. *Industry and Higher Education*, 125–30.

Vicario, G. and Coleman, S. (2020). A review of data science in business and industry and a future view. *Applied Stochastic Models in Business and Industry*, 1–13, https://onlinelibrary.wiley.com/toc/15264025/2020/36/1

PART III

Functions: getting all business areas into big data mode

8. Capitalizing on human capital analytics in small and medium-sized enterprises

Frederikke Amalie la Cour Nygaard and Dana Minbaeva

Human capital analytics (HCA) has become increasingly popular over the last few decades for several reasons. First, companies have gradually become aware of the value of their human capital and its impact on performance in the context of hypercompetitive markets. Second, the digitalization of business processes has made a great deal of data available for computational analysis. Lastly, the development and popularity of data science and the related fields of artificial intelligence, machine learning, and big data have led to countless discussions in corporate boardrooms and a generally positive attitude towards analytics.

In both the academic literature and the practitioner-oriented popular press, HCA is predominantly discussed in the context of large and complex organizations. Hence, many mistakenly think of it as a capability suitable only for those types of organizations. This might be the result of the false assumption that a human resource management (HRM) department must act as the anchor and driver of HCA processes ("We do not have an HR department to work with HCA"). Another possible false assumption is that the firm needs to own and/or be able to produce a large sample for the analytical process ("We do not have enough data"). Finally, small and medium-sized enterprises (SMEs) usually do not invest in data infrastructure and they seldom collect data documenting changes in the organization. As a result, even those SMEs that possess a substantial amount of data often fail in implementing formal, centralized coordination of data collection ("I know that we have a lot of HR data, but I do not know what kind of data we have"). This situation makes it impossible to combine different datasets, creates unexplained breaks in time-series (i.e., longitudinal) data, and leads to data inconsistencies due to the proliferation of various metrics, coding systems, and timeframes.

In this chapter, we discuss the misconceptions of what HCA is and is not, and the value it delivers to SMEs. In the following, we start with a definition of HCA and then explain the relevance of HCA for SMEs. We then provide guidelines and examples of how SMEs can capitalize on HCA to drive value creation and, ultimately, build a competitive advantage.

8.1 DEFINITION OF HCA

Let us start with the definition of HCA. In general, analytics refers to "the use of analysis, data and systematic reasoning to make decisions" (Davenport et al., 2010, p. 4). Building on this definition, Minbaeva (2017) defines HCA as the process of answering questions, providing insights, and making recommendations to assist decision-making related to an organization's human capital. Van Vulpen (2016, p. 11) refers to HCA as people analytics and defines it as "analyzing organizations' people problems." As van der Togt and Rasmussen (2017) explain, the ultimate objective is to create an HR organization that balances "intuition, experience, and beliefs with hard facts and evidence, and [is grounded] in the vast knowledge of organizational behavior" (p. 128).

HCA uses a broad spectrum of people-related data, often including, but not limited to, demographic data, data about HR practices (e.g., compensation and development), and soft performance data (e.g., engagement, satisfaction, turnover, and absences). Huselid and Minbaeva (2019) argue that discourse regarding the kind of data needed for HCA should not be concerned with the "bigness of data" but rather with the concept and definition of *smart data* (George et al., 2014)—the valuable insights that the data can reasonably provide. Accordingly, instead of gathering data on a large number of individuals (i.e., vertically large datasets), HCA could provide many more insights from horizontally large datasets that cover the same individuals over the period of their employment in the company.

However, as highlighted by Levenson and Fink (2017), having more or smarter human capital data does not automatically result in actionable insights. While the availability of data is paramount, it does not necessarily lead to a competitive advantage. The data must be transformed and aggregated into useful information with meaning and form, and then understood in relation to a problem area (Minbaeva, 2017). Only then can we consider it as providing deep understanding or knowledge. Generally, decision risk is lower when the decisions are based on knowledge, rather than descriptive data (Figure 8.1). That is, with the progression from data to information and ultimately to knowledge, organizations could lower the risk in their data-driven decisions.

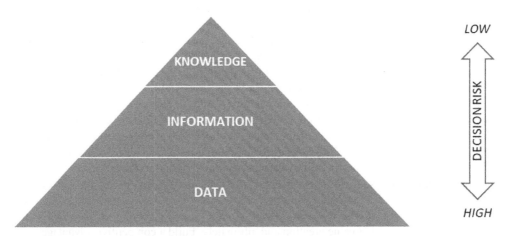

Figure 8.1   Data-Information-Knowledge hierarchy

Accordingly, HCA is about asking the "right questions." An analytics process should always take its point of departure in a critical business outcome or a specific business-related problem (Davenport, 2013; Mondore et al., 2011: Rasmussen, 2013). In relation to HCA, critical business outcomes can include productivity, employee turnover, customer satisfaction, or safety. Furthermore, organizations need a deep understanding of how individual and collective interactions (human capital as defined by Ployhart et al., 2014) drive these organizational results

(Boudreau & Cascio, 2017; Minbaeva, 2017). Van der Togt and Rasmussen (2017) suggest asking two questions before conducting an analysis: (1) Will top management appreciate the insights and proposed interventions given our strategy? and (2) What would it take to suspend long-held beliefs in light of our new data?

As such, much of HCA is about framing the analysis in a way that has an impact on the business ("telling the story"). For example, when presenting the findings from an HCA project, a statistical methods story ("First, we ran a t-test, then we did multiple OLS regressions, and then we lagged the economic data by a year") is rarely interesting and does not invite action (Davenport, 2013). In contrast, a focus on the urgency behind the results ("We have seen an increase in safety incidents in recent years, which our analysis suggests is limited to certain departments, and can be predicted by leadership scores and training") and on suggesting a plan of action ("We have to increase training opportunities in that department and create mentorships for our managers") is much more powerful. Therefore, any high-impact analytics project is also a change-management process, as it is about changing attitudes, behaviors, processes, and cultures. Any HCA project needs to be interpreted and understood within the organizational context (Minbaeva, 2018), and it needs to establish a sense of urgency by, for instance, creating a "burning platform" around the problem and framing it as a major opportunity (Kotter, 2012). In other words, an HCA project must be compelling to both the head and the heart. It is important to speak to people's genuine desire to contribute to positive change, as change processes require extra energy and brainpower. People must therefore see how engaging in the process provides their work with meaning and purpose (Kotter, 2012). In addition, Kotter (2012) argues that it is important to build a guiding coalition around the project and to identify HCA champions who can act as change agents across the organization. These two steps can help to qualify the problem, develop a vision for change and subsequent initiatives, and empower broad-based actions. As such, they are essential for bringing about change (Kotter, 2012).

In summary, HCA is the process of answering questions, providing insights, and making recommendations through the use of analytics, all of which can serve as inputs for evidence-based decisions related to an organization's human capital. The impact of that process depends on the ability to recognize the right questions, and on the ability to engage in change management to ensure that the process and the resulting recommendations have an impact on the organization.

8.2 WHY HCA IS RELEVANT FOR SMES

We argue that SMEs could benefit even more from the insights delivered by HCA than their large counterparts. As SMEs have fewer employees, they are more dependent on variations in individual performance. HCA helps identify the sources of such variations. Furthermore, the talent pool in SMEs provides a foundation for the development of firm-level capabilities. Investments in human capital to ensure, for instance, growth or successful internationalization (Benfratello & Razzolini, 2008; Mefford, 2009; Onkelinx et al., 2016) will be higher in SMEs. HCA helps track "the return on investments." Finally, SMEs typically position themselves as niche differentiators (Miller & Toulouse, 1986), and they derive their competitive advantages from superior innovation or superior quality, and from careful specialization within an industry's value chain. Consequently, they rely on higher levels of knowledge, abilities, and skills, which allow employees to engage in complex and non-routine tasks, and to perform them efficiently (Onkelinx et al., 2016). However, the Organisation for Economic Co-operation and Development (OECD, 2019) found that SMEs generally have lower labor productivity, although there are some geographical and sector-based exceptions.[1] As such, there is room for improvement. Furthermore, the OECD found that apart from workforce skills, the main internal determinants of SME productivity are managerial skills, innovation, business networks, information and communication technologies (ICT), and digitalization (Marchese et al., 2019). HCA is a capability that plays into many of these determinants. For example, the digitalization of people practices with the help of ICT can help organizations more easily incorporate remote workers, create new opportunities for cooperation, and make it easier to analyze the productivity outcomes of different ways of working. As Pete Jaworski, a management consultant specializing in HR analytics and related fields, explains:

> A perception often shared with me is: "people analytics is only relevant for very large organizations." This implies that smaller organizations do not have the same general need for or interest in analyzing their HR data as large companies do. While this may be true among the smallest of businesses, I would argue that as soon as an organization employs even a few hundred people, its executives will have a desire to accurately understand the macro-level trends and costs related to workforce talent inflow, outflow, development, and internal movements. They will also want overviews on workforce diversity, performance, and compensation. Such insights can immediately inform workforce-management priorities and highlight opportunities to improve HR practices, such as program policies, design, and delivery. Thus, they will help the business identify and select relevant human capital management KPIs for annual business cycles or longer-term planning periods.

Therefore, we argue, that SMEs should exploit the opportunities HCA offers to solve business challenges related to their workforces and make educated decisions about those workforces. In the next section, we take this argument one step further to claim that, in comparison with large enterprises, SMEs have some significant advantages in terms of successfully implementing HCA as organizational capability (Minbaeva, 2017).

8.3   THE WAY FORWARD: HOW SMEs CAN CAPITALIZE ON HCA

As an organizational capability, HCA comprises three dimensions: data quality, analytical competencies, and a strategic ability to act (Minbaeva, 2018).

8.3.1   Data Quality

Data quality is the backbone of all good and useful analytics. What quality of data should we be expecting in the context of SMEs?

Since the 1980s, large firms have increasingly relied on human resource information systems (HRIS) to store information on their employees (van den Heuvel & Bondarouk, 2017). This information normally includes master data on employees (e.g., name, age, gender, nationality, geographical location, pay level, and type of employment). There are differences in the sophistication of the systems, the extent to which the systems have been kept up to date, and the amounts companies have invested in these systems over the years. HRIS are not always set up for data integration or data export, and they do not necessarily offer reports on organizational structure or log changes in that structure. Furthermore, firms might not have designed processes to keep the information updated and they may lack organization-wide agreement on data definitions. At the same time, large companies have invested significant resources in their systems, which may make them reluctant to move to other, more effective and efficient solutions. Consequently, they may struggle to ensure the data quality and availability needed for HCA (Minbaeva, 2017, 2018). As such, what initially appears to be an advantage might actually be the opposite.

McKinsey & Company (Petzold et al., 2020) states that data governance still poses significant challenges for companies. In its 2019 Global Data Transformation Survey, McKinsey found that an average of 30 percent of organization's total enterprise time was spent on non-value-adding tasks because of poor data quality and availability. Could that also be the case for SMEs? Yes, but let us break down the opportunities for SMEs. With regard to human capital, ensuring data quality for 250 entries is quite different from ensuring it for 25,000 entries.[2] At the same time, SMEs often find it easier to develop, implement, and switch IT structures (Deloitte, 2015), and they usually do not have existing, organically grown, complex systems to consider.

According to an OECD report on the use of data analysis in SMEs, small businesses are 15 percent more likely than large businesses to buy cloud-based software for finance or accounting purposes. The OECD finds that such systems can lead to significant savings and reduce the need for specialized personnel (Bianchini & Michalkova, 2019). However, SMEs are more reluctant to invest in information systems for their human capital, at least until they reach a certain size. This is unfortunate, as there are gains to be made in this regard. Pete Jaworski emphasizes this point:

> Many good, impactful things can begin to fall into place when an organization of just a few hundred people moves toward a more data-driven HR path, whether by implementing descriptive analytics to gain new workforce insights or by applying advanced analytics to improve the accuracy of workforce projections. There is an iterative effect. The desire to better understand workforce costs creates an imperative to link workforce data with financial data (e.g., payroll costs, HR-program and employee-development expenditures) and to establish effective data governance. KPIs for human capital management and other workforce metrics may be visualized in management dashboards or reports, which can be coupled with essential financial and operational metrics. Taking on some or all of these activities at an early stage—while the organization is small—helps build the foundation for more sophisticated analytics (e.g., deeper workforce segmentation within predictive modelling) by the time … predictive analytics can be performed on larger sub-populations with robustness and validity, and by the time the HR function has built a capability for handling such advanced analytics on its own.

With regard to data quantity for analytics, while there are some limitations in the context of a smaller workforce, there are also plenty of possibilities. First, not all statistics require a big sample. While a statistical analysis with small samples is like making an astronomical observation with binoculars, it can still be helpful to see the broad lines. For instance, t-tests can be used to tell how significant the differences between groups are by letting you know whether differences in means could have happened by chance. Second, one can utilize longitudinal data (i.e., observations about fewer employees but over multiple time points). In this regard, we can consider a couple of examples.

8.3.2   Case 1: Sales Practices and Outcomes[3]

In a small company with 42 employees, the sales team was discussing the best technique for driving sales. While some team members emphasized the frequency of communication, others argued that it was important not to bother the clients too often, as doing so would have a negative effect. The team engaged the HR analyst to help settle this question. The analyst collected data from three salespeople who were similar in terms of age, education, experience, performance (e.g., closing ratios), and territory. As the company used a customer relationship management (CRM) system, the analyst had access to data on two years' worth of interactions and customers' net promoter scores (cNPS). The analyst looked at whether increased contacts by phone and mail had a positive effect on sales volume, perceived service quality, perceived value for money, and overall customer satisfaction. For each of the three salespeople, she included 140 customers. She first divided the customers into two groups: customers that the salespeople contacted once per month (control group), as was customary, and customers they contacted more frequently (test group). The analyst then ran an analysis of variance (ANOVA), which is a statistical test of whether two or more population means are equal (similar to t-tests). The results indicated that there was an increase in all parameters for customers contacted more than once per month.

8.3.3   Case 2: Does Leadership Matter?

A medium-sized event organizer with approximately 200 full-time employees had varied levels of engagement across teams for several years. Some teams had increasingly shown low engagement, while others had consistently shown medium or high scores. The company had been in existence for 20 years and had low turnover among managers. Members of top management valued loyalty and, in general, they trusted their managers to continuously develop their leadership skills. Twenty-one managers led teams of 3 to 12 people and around half of those managers had been with the organization for more than ten years. For the past five years, the managers had received leadership scores—a combined evaluation of a performance score given by each manager's immediate supervisor and a performance score given by a randomly chosen peer.

An HR analyst decided to look for a link between these leadership scores and team engagement. She started by plotting the leadership-score data to see whether scores were normally distributed, and whether there were any correlations between leadership scores and team engagement across the five years of data. Some interesting patterns emerged (Figure 8.2).

She then ran a regression analysis with engagement as the dependent variable and the leadership score as the independent variable. She controlled for manager age, gender, and tenure, and she tried to accommodate the effect of time (e.g., controlled for the level of engagement in the previous year and used leadership scores from the previous year in connection with engagement results for the next year). The results showed that engagement could be predicted by the leadership scores for both the current year and the previous year. Furthermore, manager tenure had a significant negative impact on the engagement score, while age and gender were insignificant. This confirmed what the analyst had expected: that managers with longer tenures were not taking their employees' experiences seriously. Instead, they had adopted a leadership style along the lines of "it worked in the past, it will work in the future." She used these

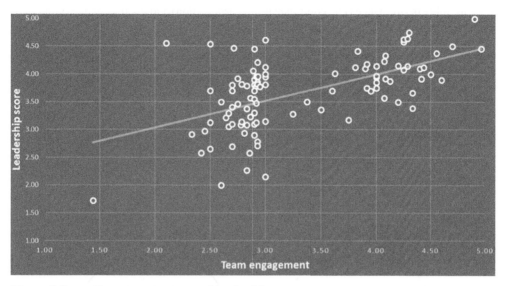

Figure 8.2   Team engagement and leadership score

findings to add "leadership" to top management's agenda, especially in terms of determining which actions should be taken to boost team engagement.

When it comes to soft performance data, like data on engagement, the literature shows that engaged employees perform better on the job regardless of whether performance is measured in terms of production, sales, customer satisfaction, or safety (e.g., Christian et al., 2011; Rich et al., 2010). Engagement is also a good predictor of voluntary turnover (Harter et al., 2002). For example, in Case 2, the correlation between the engagement scores and the intention to leave was between 0.73 and 0.87. Unfortunately, SMEs often disregard formal measurements of engagement, claiming that "everyone is visible in a small workplace." This is unfortunate, as collecting and analyzing such data over time could offer interesting insights (see Case 3). Cloud-based engagement solutions (e.g., Peakon)[4] often work with SMEs, as their use of norm groups normalizes the responses. SMEs could also consider bundling engagement or satisfaction surveys in networks with other SMEs. While this comes with some limitations, it can be helpful as long as a control for the organizational context is included.

8.3.4   Case 3: Safety, Training, and Engagement[5]

A medium-sized construction company active in an environment characterized by high physical risk was continually working to make its employees safer. In fact, it had "safety" as a core value and as an important performance indicator, and it had intensified its safety-related training programs. However, top management wondered what actually influenced safety incidents and whether the company's training programs had an impact. An HR analyst set out to investigate this issue. By talking with colleagues who were specialized in safety as well as examining consulting research, the analyst found that organizational safety measures and commitment relate to personal safety attributes (e.g., knowledge and motivation), which in turn relate to safety performance (i.e., compliance and participation) and, thereby, safety violations and injuries (Figure 8.3).

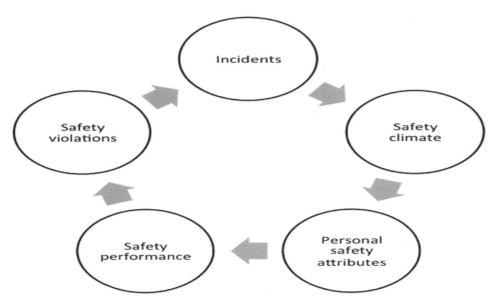

Figure 8.3   Safety and incidents: causal relations

The analyst determined that, in addition to training, he should include employees' level of engagement as an independent variable to determine whether engagement was linked to safety-related personal motivation and participation. He assumed that an employee could either experience an incident or not, and that an incident could have two outcomes: an injury or no injury. He undertook two analyses using logistic regressions. The first analysis had safety incidents that did not result in an injury as the dependent variable. The second analysis had safety incidents that resulted in an injury as the dependent variable. Both dependent variables took the value of 1 when an employee had experienced an incident, or 0 otherwise. He knew that some of the employees had undergone a safety course in Q2 2018, and that the employee-engagement survey was collected and analyzed in Q3 each year. Therefore, he included only incidents from Q1 to Q3 2019. The analyst also thought that seniority might affect safety-related outcomes, as employees who had been with the company for a longer period were more familiar with the safety rules. Therefore, he added tenure as a control variable. As incidents with no injuries indicated safety violations, he also added this variable as a control in the analysis of incidents with injuries.

From the analyses, the HR analyst learned that while training had an impact on incidents with injuries, engagement scores helped predict both types of incidents. Incidents without injuries also helped predict those with injuries (Figure 8.4). While this analysis highlighted the importance of training, it also pointed to a need for additional emphasis on increasing employee engagement.

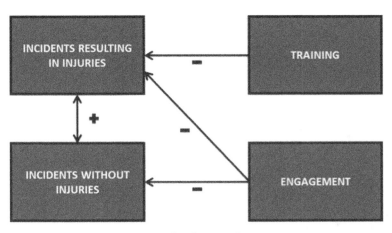

Figure 8.4   Training, engagement and safety incidents

Another type of analysis that is useful in relation to human capital in SMEs is organizational or social-network analysis. Social networks are defined as a set of nodes (or network members) that are tied together by one or more types of relations (Marin & Wellman, 2014). Organizational network analysis refers to a structured way of analyzing how communication, information, and decisions actually flow through an organization (Deloitte, n.d.). While SMEs might be able to easily map out their formal organization, informal processes and structures can be more difficult to grasp, especially if the individuals are not co-located. However, these processes and structures can be important when planning change processes and attempting to improve collaboration. Jeppe Vildstup Hansgaard, CEO of Innovisor, a consultancy specialized in organizational network analysis, explains:

> Analytics is not only for large enterprises. Some of our most successful assignments have been with teams of only 30–40 people, where the leaders have acted quickly on the evidence and successfully introduced organizational changes within two or three months. These leaders eliminated blind spots and organizational risks. They knew where to start and where to focus.

8.3.5   Case 4: Getting Everyone Onboard with Strategic Change[6]

The CEO of a car-repair company with 150 employees across different locations wanted to implement a new strategy. However, he was unsure of how to engage his employees in the change process. When he had previously tried to implement changes, they had fallen flat. Therefore, he wanted to perform an organizational network analysis in order to understand the organization's informal structure, locate key influencers, and determine how the workforce and, more specifically, the influencers related to the planned strategic direction. As this would be a one-off analysis and as he did not have the necessary competencies in-house, he engaged a consultancy specialized in organizational network analysis.

The consultant helped identify the key influencers (marked as large dots in Figure 8.5) and provided clarity on the location of the barriers to strategic change efforts. She also helped the CEO develop a plan for making certain employees change-champions.

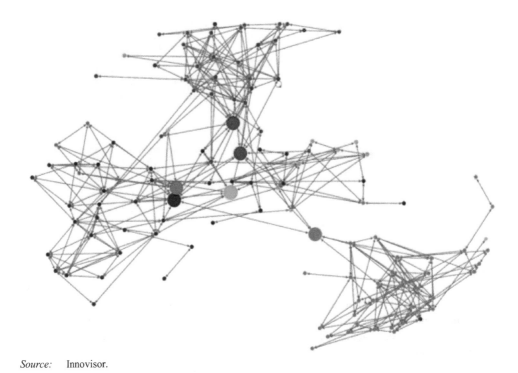

Source: Innovisor.

Figure 8.5   Organizational network

8.4   ANALYTICAL COMPETENCIES (INDIVIDUAL, PROCESSES, AND STRUCTURES)

Large companies often have the advantage of specialized analytics or business-intelligence teams that can support their HCA projects. However, depending on an organization's structure, there can be significant red tape in the way of accessing those capabilities. Furthermore, it can be difficult to figure out who to ask for assistance. In SMEs, if the analytics capabilities are there, cooperation efforts are often much simpler. However, if individual-level analytical capabilities are lacking, SMEs need to look for more creative solutions. For example, if someone in the organization has a general understanding of HCA gained through courses, seminars, or readings on the subject, the organization can solicit the help of a student worker with data-science experience. The student will need guidance on the conceptual relationships and key metrics, but he or she will understand the statistical aspects and know how to use relevant software. While consultants can be used, there is a need to have a good idea of what to look for in advance. Collaboration with local universities offers opportunities to bond and to lift the level of analytical capabilities. In fact, practitioner-academic collaboration is becoming more prevalent. Even the pioneers of the HCA field—the analysts at Google—are in close contact with academia in every HCA project they undertake. As Prasad Setty, Google's Vice President of People Analytics & Compensation, states:

> [W]henever we are faced with a new people issue at Google now, we don't ask ourselves, what does successful organization X do with this topic? Instead, we ask ourselves, what does the literature say? And if I have one piece of advice to give all the businesses that are in the audience out here, it is to develop better relationships with academics.[7]

8.4.1 Case 5: A Tech Start-up's Growing Pains

Over a span of two years, a Danish company specialized in cloud-based software for accounting had grown from four employees situated in the same location to 62 employees situated in three locations. The company had remote workers as well as two overseas departments, through which it could access the best (and most affordable) qualified human capital and be closer to its customers. The employees' job areas largely corresponded to their locations with seven salespeople in the Danish office, 25 software engineers in the Ukrainian office, and 30 service-support employees in Poland. Although the company had been running efficiently, the manager noticed that orders were getting mixed up and productivity was declining. Initial conversations with local supervisors revealed that there had been some bottlenecks in terms of workflow among the three locations. This led the manager to wonder which employees were the bottlenecks and why.

She contacted researchers at a local university who helped her with an organizational network analysis of the three locations. The aim of the analysis was to map out interactions among network members and help identify connectors, influencers, bottlenecks, and other key employees who served as gatekeepers to parts of the organization. The results showed low connectivity between teams in different locations. They did not connect with each other very often and, therefore, the transfer of knowledge and experience across the company was limited. In fact, the few cross-collaboration connections had become bottlenecks.

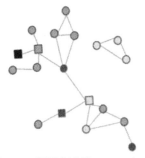

Source: Innovisor, https://www.innovisor.com/2020/08/25/how-team-leader-created-wellbeing-performance-productivity-in-environment-of-chaos/ (accessed September 20, 2020).

Figure 8.6   Organizational network of a low connected team

After the researchers had helped the manager identify the bottlenecks, she distributed a survey to the whole organization focused on understanding the current situation. One of the researchers had a background in organizational behavior and highlighted the possibility of a cultural reason for the employees' behavior in the different locations. Therefore, the manager included location-specific questions in the survey. The employees in Ukraine responded that, in addition to the lack of transparency, they struggled to directly connect with their colleagues on the other teams because they were used to and more comfortable with a top-down way of management with clear mandates. This surprised the manager, as she had assumed that the software engineers wanted more autonomy—she had not considered the cultural implications of working across European countries. In response to these insights, she created clear roles and responsibilities for the employees in the Ukrainian office and their connections in the other departments. In addition, she introduced weekly virtual company meetings during which the teams took turns presenting themselves and a challenge they faced in order to increase transparency.

SMEs can also bundle together to tap into shared services offered especially for them. For example, in Singapore, where competition is high and a data-driven approach is necessary, a small company provides HR analytics to 92 SMEs for a monthly fee. The subscription provides the SMEs with HR analytics dashboards and talent-assessment software that compares the answers of potential candidates with those of high performers. As the job market in Southeast Asia is very active, this helps the organizations stay efficient.[8]

However, analytical competencies are not only at the individual level—they are also procedural and structural. The results of analytics projects, especially those regarding human capital, need to be linked to existing organizational processes in order to be effective. This means asking a key question: How should the findings affect the way we do things? How can we make sure that the necessary changes are made? This is also an analytical exercise. In this regard, SMEs can capitalize on the advantage of their size, as SMEs usually have a centralized structure with the owner/manager making most of the major decisions (Cragg & King, 1993). SMEs are often connected with innovation and entrepreneurship (Deloitte, 2015; OECD, 2010), but they also tend to be more concerned with survival than their large counterparts. Therefore, growth can sometimes be assigned a lower priority (Gray, 2002). This has been associated with SMEs being "time poor" and, therefore, tending to focus on operational activities (Garengo et al., 2005). However, being "time poor" is another argument for using HCA in the long term, as it can help optimize processes, limit bad decision-making, and ensure that the people practices that actually make a difference are prioritized.

Nevertheless, HCA requires an investment. For example, in Case 1 above, the analyst actually went one step further. More specifically, she ran regression analyses in which sales volume and overall customer satisfaction were used as the dependent variables, call frequency was an independent variable, and controls for the length of the relationship were included. She found that the effects of call frequency diminished as relationships became longer. After looking into research on the subject, she found that this was probably because uncertainty about the seller diminishes as knowledge is gained over the course of a relationship. Consequently, increases in communication frequency no longer have the same effect. The company could have used these findings to make decisions about its way of working by, for instance, putting more emphasis on communication early in relationships. However, the company was much more focused on market growth and pushed for continuous increases in call frequency, regardless of the type of customer.

8.5   STRATEGIC ABILITY TO ACT

"Strategic ability to act" refers to whether the results are actionable in the sense that top management supports HCA projects and whether the results of HCA projects are used in change management (Minbaeva, 2018). This is where large companies often struggle, as they are more complex in terms of their existing, organically grown structures. They often struggle with red tape that lies between insights and implementations. SMEs have a unique advantage—they can more easily act upon insights, as their set-up is typically more centralized. Jeppe Vildstup Hansgaard, the CEO of Innovisor, also mentions the pace of reaction among smaller entities. Furthermore, due to their centralization, SMEs are more aware of the challenges they face and will face in the coming years. The main internal barrier that prevents adoption of data analysis in SMEs is a lack of managerial awareness and skills (OECD, 2019). The shift from intuition-driven to data-driven decision-making requires a strong commitment from management.

8.5.1   Case 6: Retention Problems Addressed through Management Buy-in[9]

A data-consultancy company with slightly fewer than 50 employees had an employee-retention problem in a highly competitive environment. Due to its size, it could not compete on compensation to attract and keep the right talent. Like a lot of small firms, it also had cases of long-term sickness due to stress, which affected profits. Management noticed that when female employees returned from maternity leave, they solved their tasks as well as their colleagues but managed to leave the office not only earlier than they had prior to their leave but also earlier than their colleagues. At the same time, the company's leaders were very interested in evidence-based management. Therefore, they looked into the research on productivity and time spent at work, and found theories and case studies supporting the hypothesis that there was not necessarily a linear relationship between work input and outcomes (e.g., Keynes, 2010: Pencavel, 2015).

Inspired by Parkinson's Law that work expands until it fills the time allotted to it (Parkinson, 1957), members of management set out to investigate whether working in a more optimized manner could limit actual work hours and increase productivity. They looked into which tasks took a lot of time but did not add value, and tried to either eliminate, automatize, or outsource those tasks to virtual assistants. They also analyzed meetings, which took up much of the employees' time. These investigations involved every employee. Management then continuously evaluated the various initiatives using relevant metrics, which meant that initiatives that did not have the desired effect were discontinued. Moreover, management continuously measured different satisfaction and engagement constructs as well as sick leave and earnings. These steps were only possible because of the complete buy-in from management and because the CEO was the project's champion. Providing employees with a benefit (a four-day work week) that was unusual in the current work climate gave the company a competitive advantage in retaining the top talents in the field, which again led the company to win awards and maintain profitability.

Although this might be an extreme example, it shows that a great deal is possible in SMEs if the CEO is engaged and the organization possesses a strategic ability to act on insights regarding human capital. In this case, this occurred through boundary-spanning behavior, which served to engage all employees in changing the work culture (for their own benefit). Those initiatives were based on, for instance, data on the employee workday, and they encouraged employees to collectively experiment with ways of working smarter and to develop follow-up initiatives.

The dimensions of HCA presented here—data quality, analytical competencies, and a strategic ability to act—could be used to map and continuously assess[10] own organizational capabilities relevant for HCA. In general, employees with strong technical skills, the right data analytics and IT backgrounds should be prioritized in recruitment and selection. Investment in data processes will always pay off: for any analysis the data must be valid and reliable. But most importantly, analytics should produce actionable insights. However, even that is not sufficient. What, then, facilitates HCA? Is there a certain culture that not only permits the organization to ask the right questions but also links strategies, people, and performance? Is there a culture in which acting upon insights is encouraged? We discuss these questions in the next section.

8.6   CULTURE, NOT SIZE, COUNTS

As we have highlighted throughout this chapter, size is not what stands between a company and successful HCA. What does success depend on? We focused on three areas that should be considered—data quality, analytical capability, and strategic ability to act—all of which transcend the individuals, processes, and structures within an organization (Minbaeva, 2018). However, decisions about processes and structures, especially when it comes to strategic ability to act, are based in cultural norms and values. For instance, investments are often a matter of priorities based on both values and strategy. This is evident when looking at, for example, IIH Nordic or Google. Minbaeva (2018) argues that the value of HCA lies in changing mindsets, attitudes, and habits associated with the use of evidence for decision-making.

The role of culture is particularly visible in two extreme cases: start-ups and family businesses. In contrast to SMEs in general, start-ups are highly growth oriented (Breschi et al., 2018; Picken, 2017). In OECD countries, they contribute disproportionally to job creation, and start-ups backed by venture capitalists are characterized as innovative and fast-growing (Breschi et al., 2018). Often, the end goal of start-ups is to be acquired (Picken, 2017). However, not all start-ups succeed in expanding. The OECD highlights that start-ups' success critically depends on their founders' experiences and incentives, and the ways in which they manage the knowledge and ideas flowing through their organizations (Breschi et al., 2018). As a start-up is a new organization, the cultural clues stem from the founders, and the start-ups' organizational culture depends on those clues, at least in the beginning. As we mentioned above, although start-ups typically have a structure that is somewhat centralized around the founder/owner, those that capitalize on innovation often use more flexible forms of governance to promote creativity, motivation, and productivity. Mintzberg (1993) termed this an "adhocracy," but it is often referred to as "agile organization and management" (Birkinshaw & Ridderstråle, 2015). Agile management, which stems from practices within software development (i.e., SCRUM), has grown increasingly popular in recent years (Rigby et al., 2016). This innovative and collaborative environment is often what attracts talents to start-ups and their founders are keen to keep it that way, even when the organization starts to grow and increasingly needs strategic alignment and an effective infrastructure (Picken, 2017).

With regard to HCA, one assumption regarding tech-oriented start-ups is that they work with an array of digital tools and solutions that complement their agile way of working. If that holds true, they should be better equipped for analytics in terms of data availability. One could also argue that these organizations are used to work that is based on data and that, therefore, they should be more open to initiatives like HCAs, while they could show resistance to other, more traditional management practices (Garvin, 2013). In Google's early days, the highly trained data engineers were highly skeptical of their managers. They felt that the managers distracted them from their real tasks and micromanaged them (Garvin, 2013). While Google tried a completely flat hierarchy for a period of time, it found it needed managers in order to run effectively and to, for instance, communicate strategies, facilitate collaboration, and prioritize projects. However, Google still needed to persuade the engineers. Therefore, it established a people analytics team that examined employee surveys, performance reviews, and double-blind interview responses using, among other tools, multivariate analyses and applying analytical rigor—all to verify that management mattered. The team gathered evidence of managerial successes to make the case for skeptics, and it identified eight behaviors shared by high-scoring managers. Google used those insights to develop behavioral guidelines for all managers, thereby lifting the level of leadership (Garvin, 2013). As such, HCA helped Google to not only legitimize management in the eyes of its employees but also to identify the kind of leadership that helped its employees reach their full potential.

The agile culture favored by start-ups can be contrasted with the culture of family businesses. In general, family firms are assumed to have a long-term orientation and centralized decision-making. Therefore, SMEs in this category have an excellent opportunity to implement HCA initiatives. While these firms are often assumed to be behind on digitalization, they recognize that the adoption of technology in the workplace is the top issue influencing private-company markets, and that agility in adapting to changing environments is important for their business (Deloitte, 2019). However, Deloitte (2019) found that some family businesses are risk-averse and unwilling to innovate, even when they have the resources to do so, due to concerns about possible negative outcomes or reductions in the family's wealth. Furthermore, Deloitte (2019) showed that family members may not be aligned in their goals for the business, including goals other than financial success. They might therefore face some cultural obstacles as they attempt to introduce HCA. Bazerman and Chugh (2006) highlighted the critical problem of bounded awareness in management, arguing that most people fail to bring the right information into their conscious awareness at the right time. The absence of contradictory evidence is an indication of highly bounded awareness, which leads managers (and everybody else) to make the wrong decisions. Family business management is no different. In fact, given the likelihood of homogeneity in the composition of decision-makers (because the management teams in these firms tend to consist of a majority of family members), the risk could be even higher. With regard to their human capital, therefore, they could capitalize on HCA if they manage to achieve the necessary data quality and obtain the required analytical capabilities.

8.7   CONCLUSIONS

In this chapter, we argued that SMEs have a unique opportunity to capitalize on HCA. SMEs can easily ensure the data quality and availability needed for HCA, and they would benefit from starting down this path sooner rather than later, especially if they plan to grow. HCA can also help SMEs keep track of their human capital and determine which efforts to prioritize if they are time poor. We propose that the flexible and centralized nature of SMEs should make it easier to harvest the organization's analytical capabilities, and to enhance the strategic ability to act upon insights gained from HCA.

NOTES

1. The gross value added in current prices per person employed.
2. Regardless of the size, all employees' data processes should be GDPR compliant. See more at https://www.bernardmarr.com/default.asp?contentID=1430 (accessed 29 September 2020).
3. Inspired by Román and Martín (2008).
4. https://peakon.com/ (accessed September 15, 2020).
5. Inspired by Hartmann (n.d.)
6. Inspired by Innovisor (2020).
7. https://www.analyticsinhr.com/blog/benefits-collaboration-academia-people-analytics/ (accessed September 29, 2020).
8. https://www.computerweekly.com/news/450281609/Singapore-SME-makes-HR-analytics -affordable-for-other-small-companies (accessed September 29, 2020).
9. Inspired by IIH Nordic (Abildgaard, 2019).
10. See guidelines for the self-assessment here: http://www.nhca.dk/ (accessed 29 September 2020).

REFERENCES

Abildgaard, P. (2019). *Manden der knuste kalenderen for at gøre sine medarbejdere lykkelige.* Frederiksberg: Frydenlund.

Bazerman, M.H. & Chugh, D. (2006). Decisions without blinders. *Harvard Business Review, 84*(1), 88.

Benfratello, Luigi & Razzolini, Tiziano (2008). Firms' productivity and internationalisation choices: Evidence for a large sample of Italian firms. Centro Studi Luca d'Agliano Development Studies Working Paper No. 236. http://dx.doi.org/10.2139/ssrn.1313707

Bianchini, M. & Michalkova, V. (2019). Data analytics in SMEs: Trends and policies. *OECD SME and Entrepreneurship Papers*, No. 15, Paris: OECD Publishing. https://doi.org/10.1787/1de6c6a7-en

Birkinshaw, J. & Ridderstråle, J. (2015). Adhocracy for an agile age. *McKinsey Quarterly*, December 1.

Boudreau, J. & Cascio, W. (2017). Human capital analytics: Why are we not there? *Journal of Organizational Effectiveness, 4*(2), 119–26. https://doi.org/10.1108/JOEPP-03-2017-0021

Breschi, S., Lassébie, J., & Menon, C. (2018). A portrait of innovative start-ups across countries. *OECD Science, Technology and Industry Working Papers*, 2018/02. Paris: OECD Publishing, http://dx.doi .org/10.1787/f9ff02f4-en

Christian, M.S., Garza, A.S., & Slaughter, J.E. (2011). Work engagement: A quantitative review and test of its relations with task and contextual performance. *Personnel Psychology, 64*(1), 89–136.

Cragg, Paul & King, Malcolm (1993). Small-firm computing: Motivators and inhibitors. *MIS Quarterly, 17*, 1.

Davenport, T.H. (2013). Keep up with your quants. *Harvard Business Review, 91*(7–8), 120–3.

Davenport, T.H., Harris, J.G., & Morison, R. (2010). *Analytics at Work: Smarter Decisions, Better Results*. Cambridge, MA: Harvard Business Press.

Deloitte (n.d.). Perspectives—Organizational network analysis–gain insight, drive smart. Accessed September 27, 2020, from https://www2.deloitte.com/us/en/pages/human-capital/articles/ organizational-network-analysis.html

Deloitte (2015). Industry 4.0—challenges and solutions for the digital transformation and use of expo- nential technologies. Accessed September 15, 2020, from https://www2.deloitte.com/ch/en/pages/ manufacturing/articles/manufacturing-study-industry-4.html

Deloitte Private (2019). *Long-term Goals, Meet Short-term—Global Family Business Survey 2019*. A Deloitte Insights Publication.

Garengo, Patrizia, Biazzo, Stefano, & Bititci, Umit (2005). Performance measurement systems in SMEs: A review for a research agenda. *International Journal of Management Reviews*, 7(1). doi:10.1111/j .1468-2370.2005.00105.x

Garvin, David A (2013). How Google sold its engineers on management. *Harvard Business Review*, 91(12), 74–82.

George, G., Haas, M., & Pentland, A. (2014). From the editors: Big data and management. *The Academy of Management Journal*, 57(2), 321–6. Accessed October 1, 2020, from http://www.jstor.org/stable/ 43589260

Gray, C. (2002). Entrepreneurship, resistance to change and growth in small firms. *Journal of Small Business and Enterprise Development*, 9(1), 61–72.

Harter, K.J., Scmidt, L.F., & Hayes L.T. (2002). Business-unit-level relationship between employee satisfaction, employee engagement, and business outcomes: A meta-analysis. *Journal of Applied Psychology*, 87(2), 268–79.

Hartmann, P. (n.d.). How I did it: Understanding the relationship between employee engagement and safety. Accessed September 20, 2020, from https://www.cbs.dk/files/cbs.dk/how_i_did_it _understanding_the_relationship_between_employee_engagement_and_safety.pdf

Huselid, M.A & Minbaeva, D.B. (2019). Big data and human resource management. In Wilkinson, A., Bacon, N., & Snell, S. (eds), *The SAGE Handbook of Human Resource Management* (pp. 494–507). London: SAGE Publications. https://doi.org/10.4135/9781529714852.n29

Innovisor (2020). Don't forget your employees in your transformation. Accessed September 15, 2020, from https://www.innovisor.com/2020/04/29/dont-forget-your-employees-in-your-transformation/

Keynes, J.M. (2010). Economic possibilities for our grandchildren. In *Essays in Persuasion*. London: Palgrave Macmillan. https://doi.org/10.1007/978-1-349-59072-8_25

Kotter, J.P. (2012). Accelerate. *Harvard Business Review*, 90(11), 45–56.

Levenson, A. & Fink, A. (2017). Human capital analytics: Too much data and analysis, not enough models and business insights. *Journal of Organizational Effectiveness*, 4(2), 145–56. https://doi.org/ 10.1108/JOEPP-03-2017-0029

Marchese, M., Giuliani, E., Salazar-Elena, Juan C. and Stone, I. (2019). Enhancing SME productivity: Policy highlights on the role of managerial skills, workforce skills and business linkages. *OECD SME and Entrepreneurship Papers*, No. 16, OECD Publishing, Paris. https://doi.org/10.1787/ 825bd8a8-en

Marin, A. & Wellman, B. (2014). Social network analysis: An introduction. In Scott, J. & Carrington, P.J. (eds), *The SAGE Handbook of Social Network Analysis* (pp. 11–25). London: SAGE Publications. doi: 10.4135/9781446294413

Mefford, R.N. (2009). Increasing productivity in global firms: The CEO challenge. *Journal of International Management*, 15(3), 262–72.

Miller, D. & Toulouse, J.M. (1986). Chief executive personality and corporate strategy and structure in small firms. *Management Science*, 32(11), 1389–409.

Minbaeva, D. (2017). Human capital analytics: Why aren't we there? Introduction to the special issue. *Journal of Organizational Effectiveness*, 4(2), 110–18. https://doi.org/10.1108/JOEPP-04-2017-0035

Minbaeva, D.B. (2018). Building credible human capital analytics for organizational competitive advantage. *Human Resource Management*, 57(3), 701–13.

Mintzberg, H. (1993). *Structure in Fives: Designing Effective Organizations*. Englewood Cliffs, NJ: Prentice Hall.

Mondore, S., Douthitt, S., & Carson, M. (2011). Maximizing the impact and effectiveness of hr analytics to drive business outcomes. *People and Strategy*, 34(2), 20–7. http://hrps.site-ym.com/resource/ resmgr/p_s_article_preview/ps_34.2_hranalytics.pdf (accessed 29 September 2020).

OECD (2010). *SMEs, Entrepreneurship and Innovation*, OECD Studies on SMEs and Entrepreneurship. Paris: OECD Publishing. https://doi.org/10.1787/9789264080355-en

OECD (2019). *OECD Compendium of Productivity Indicators 2019*. Paris: OECD Publishing. https:// doi.org/10.1787/b2774f97-en

Onkelinx, J., Manolova, T., & Edelman, L. (2016). The human factor: Investments in employee human capital, productivity, and SME internationalization. *Journal of International Management*, *22*(4), 351–64.

Parkinson, C. Northcote (1957). *Parkinson's Law: Or, the Pursuit of Progress*. Boston: Houghton.

Pencavel, J. (2015). The productivity of working hours. *Economic Journal*, *125*(589), 2052–76. https://doi.org/10.1111/ecoj.12166

Petzold, Bryan, Roggendorf, Matthias, Rowshankish, Kayvaun, & Sporleder, Christoph (2020). Designing data governance that delivers value. Accessed September 3, 2020, from https://www.mckinsey.com/business-functions/mckinsey-digital/our-insights/designing-data-governance-that-delivers-value

Picken, J. (2017). From startup to scalable enterprise: Laying the foundation. *Business Horizons*, *60*(5), 587–95.

Ployhart, R.E., Nyberg, A.J., Reilly, G., & Maltarich, M.A. (2014). Human capital is dead; long live human capital resources! *Journal of Management*, *40*(2), 371–98.

Rasmussen, T.H. (2013). *Målbar HR: En praktisk guide til datadrevet HR-ledelse*. Kbh.: Dansk Psykologisk Forlag A/S.

Rich, B.L., Lepine, J.A., & Crawford, E.R. (2010). Job engagement: Antecedents and effects on job performance. *Academy of Management Journal*, *53*(3), 617–35.

Rigby, D., Sutherland, J., & Takeuchi, H. (2016). Embracing agile. *Harvard Business Review*, *94*(5), 40–50.

Román, S. & Martín, P. (2008). Changes in sales call frequency: A longitudinal examination of the consequences in the supplier–customer relationship. *Industrial Marketing Management*, *37*(5), 554–64.

van den Heuvel, S. & Bondarouk, T. (2017). The rise (and fall?) of HR analytics: A study into the future application, value, structure, and system support. *Journal of Organizational Effectiveness*, *4*(2), 157—78. https://doi.org/10.1108/JOEPP-03-2017-0022

van der Togt, J. & Rasmussen, T.H. (2017). Toward evidence-based HR. *Journal of Organizational Effectiveness: People and Performance*, *4*(2), 127–32. https://doi.org/10.1108/JOEPP-02-2017-0013

van Vulpen, E. (2016). *The Basic Principles of People Analytics: Learn How to Use HR Data to Drive Better Outcomes for Your Business and Employees*. CreateSpace Independent Publishing Platform.

9. How experimental data can optimize e-learning

Camilla Nellemann and Torben Pedersen

9.1 INTRODUCTION

Experiments and big data are often associated with analysis of complex data in larger companies that have the capacity to track and analyze experimental data. However, smaller companies can also benefit from collecting experimental data. In this chapter we will show how a smaller company has benefitted greatly from conducting experiments in collaboration with Copenhagen Business School. The company is QualiWare (approximately 30 employees in Denmark and 80 employees globally), which is offering a software system that handles all information processes in larger organizations, so the right people in the company have access to the right information at the right time. Customers are large organizations like the Department of National Defence Canada, Equinor and GKN Aerospace (Volvo Aero). As such, QualiWare needs to be at the forefront when it comes to understanding and analyzing data as they are making a business out of tracking, systematizing and presenting organizations' data in a smart way.

The specific case we focus on in this chapter is the collection and use of experimental data to support the training activities conducted by QualiWare. QualiWare sells customers an extensive software package that simulates the enterprise architecture and includes many modules and features. Therefore, QualiWare needs to train their customers in using the platform properly. The training is part of the services offered to customers. QualiWare has formed the QualiWare Academy that provides a number of courses to customers on the different modules of the software package. To date, the courses have mainly been offered as in-person teaching, but QualiWare want to take the teaching further and make it more virtual and move into e-learning mainly because they will be able to scale it and offer more courses. However, QualiWare is not sure about how to do this as e-learning can be done in many different ways. Many questions arise like: Can they go fully online? Should they combine e-learning with a managed online dialog? Should the online modules include incentives like tests? More reward like diplomas? More gamification and playing? Or how should the online modules be structured? Will learners have the same respect for e-learning as in-person learning? In order to learn what is working and what is not, QualiWare and CBS joined forces in conducting experiments with different features in the e-learning modules.

We believe the case is a very good illustration of how small and medium-sized enterprises (SMEs) can use experimentation and more scientific methods rather than "gut feelings" when making strategic decisions. Here we illustrate the use of experimentation in a training case, but the same method can be used in many other cases, for example, when SMEs have to decide on which product features to offer or how to best communicate with customers. In all cases, the experimentation allows one to make better informed decisions. In the following we will unfold how the e-learning experiments were conducted in QualiWare and the takeaways from the experiments.

9.2   THEORETICAL BACKGROUND AND E-LEARNING EXPERIMENTS

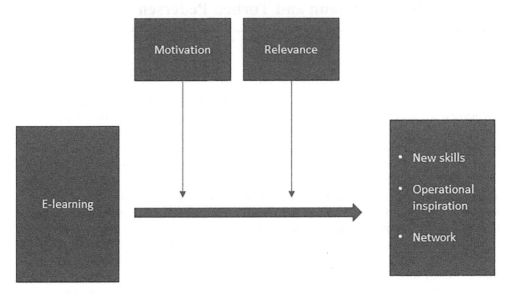

Figure 9.1   Theoretical model

The literature on e-learning in corporate training points to the outcome of training as being multifaceted and typically including individual learning, gaining operational inspiration and building networks among like-minded people. It also highlights that the outcome is determined in an interaction between the technical features in terms of the e-learning platform and the human characteristics in terms of learners' perception, ability and willingness to learn. There needs to be a fit between the human characteristics and the technology. A perfect technology is worthless, without motivated users who are willing to apply the technical features. Along these lines, we hypothesize that individual motivation and perceived relevance moderate the outcome of the e-learning. This leaves us with a model where we analyze how different e-learning experiments (technical features) affect the individual cognitive outcome in terms of new skills, operational inspiration and network – and how this relationship is moderated by individual motivation and perception of relevance. The underlying model of the study is illustrated in Figure 9.1.

We carried out the e-learning initiative in the fall of 2019. The courses focused on how to use the QualiWare platform in relation to process management, risk management, General Data Protection Regulation (GDPR), customer journey mapping, capability mapping, enterprise architecture and a new version of the platform called QualiWare X. QualiWare decided

Table 9.1   *The experiment's sequence of events*

Step	Action
1	Literature review and interviews with potential course participants
2	Develop hypotheses and theoretical model
3	Recruit participants through a pre-survey
4	Develop course materials incorporated with post-survey
5	Execute the course
6	Analyze platform data and the pre-survey and post-survey replies
7	Conduct and analyze interview with QualiWare
8	Adapt the theoretical model based on research results

on these topics based on the outcome of our interviews with a number of QualiWare's customers in Denmark and Norway regarding their need for learning.

In the interviews the respondents stressed that they need a timely and comprehensive online environment where they can learn on the fly. "When I need help, I need it immediately. I can't move on before it is sorted out," explained one interviewee. Customers need training often as QualiWare frequently launches new features and functionalities to the platform. That includes employees who have been working with the platform for years. "My boss criticizes that I don't know everything about the platform. After all, they hired me as their QualiWare expert," said an interviewee when she explained to us why she needed flexible, online training.

Table 9.1 shows the sequence of events of the experiment. We performed the sequence twice; first, an internal pilot among QualiWare staff and later an experiment among QualiWare customers. The internal pilot served as a test we could learn from and thus conduct a more effective experiment for the customers.

The learners would have to spend between 10 and 15 hours to complete the course, which was available online from October 1 to November 11, 2019. It featured many experimental features like video tutorials, a forum for online discussion, a quiz after each module, a digital coach, live webinar and a certificate for completion as listed in Table 9.2. Data were collected during the course on user behavior in relation to the experimental features, learning path and experiences.

When signing up for the course, participants had to fill in a pre-survey to gain access to the course materials. The pre-survey asked abour the learners' year of birth, place of work, experience with the QualiWare platform, how they learned to use the platform, which topics they were interested to learn about, to what extent they were already familiar with the topics covered in the course, their experience with and attitude toward e-learning and their motivation(s) for enrolling in the course. The 140 learners who filled in the pre-survey are representative of QualiWare's customer base given their differences in nationality (Europe, North America, South Africa and South East Asia), age (born between 1947 and 1995) and experience with QualiWare (from less than a year to more than 20 years). The learners worked in public and private organizations, respectively. They were using QualiWare's platform from zero up to 12 different modules.

In order to measure the outcome, we analyzed the quiz results to check their learning, and monitored the activity in the online forum to analyze learner-learner and learner-instructor interaction. Twenty learners were invited to an e-mail interview on their experience and

Table 9.2   *Applied experimental features in the e-learning course*

Activity	Benefit
Videos	Instruction in specific QualiWare features. The learners may see the videos as many times as they like during and after the course.
Quizzes	Learner-content interaction which highlights key learnings and provides a knowledge check. The instructor can track the learners' progress.
Discussion forum	Knowledge sharing, co-creation and community building through learner-learner and learner-instructor interaction.
Digital coach	Learner support through daily e-mail about course activity, an e-mail with quiz result, a pop-up window appearing on the screen in case of inactivity, and e-mail support from the instructor.
Live webinar	Online talk by QualiWare's CEO. Opportunity for learners to post questions through a live chat.
Certificate	The learners receive a reward for completion.

learnings from the course, the opportunity to network and how they completed the course. The selected informants were those who indicated in their pre-survey that they looked forward to providing their feedback to QualiWare after the course. This could imply a bias. On the other hand, we know from experience that trying to collect information from respondents who are not keen to provide it tends not to be worthwhile. Finally, we recorded QualiWare's perception on learnings, successes and failures in relation to the e-learning initiative through a semi-structured interview of about two hours in February 2020 with the QualiWare employee who was responsible for executing the e-learning initiative.

9.3   EMPIRICAL INSIGHTS

In the following we outline the descriptive statistics for the key variables that we are studying (motivation, perception and learning outcomes) and relate the obtained findings to the existing literature. The first part on motivation and learners' perception is based on data from the pre-survey, the completion rate is discussed based on data obtained from the platform, while the learning outcome is assessed and grounded on the post-course interviews. As such, different sources have been triangulated to obtain more reliable results.

9.3.1   Motivation

Motivated learners are more inclined to complete e-learning; motivation mediates the relationship between perceived barriers and enablers of e-learning (Garavan et al., 2010). Perceiving e-learning as essential to perform one's job is motivating, according to Hanssen et al. (2017) who found that 140 Norwegian nurses and care workers were more motivated for e-learning when it appeared as on-the-job training. Along similar lines, Joo et al. (2012) identified perceived usefulness as a crucial factor for e-learning success. Drivers of e-learning acceptance include job duties requiring new skills, as well as e-learners appreciating the training and feeling it pays off (Rabak & Cleveland-Innes, 2006). Of the 140 learners responding to our pre-survey, 97 percent indeed indicated they enrolled to learn more about QualiWare. "I need to learn to be able to do my job," elaborated one learner.

The second motivating factor in our pre-survey was wanting to experience e-learning, with 27 percent of the respondents selecting this option. The finding is encouraging in light of research identifying e-learning acceptance problems (e.g. Kimiloglu et al., 2017; McKay & Vilela, 2011; Paulsen, 2009). On the other hand, data from 976 Brazilian e-learners showed high acceptance of e-learning (Stadler et al., 2017). An increasing rate of e-learning acceptance was observed in Slovenia (Markovic-Hribernik & Jarc, 2014), while the evaluation of a Mexican organization's virtual corporate university showed that employees perceived e-learning as effective corporate training (Rodriguez & Armellini, 2013). Only 9 percent of 312 bank employees and managers questioned about their attitude toward e-learning expressed a negative opinion (Skrtic et al., 2012). E-learners tend to emphasize the immediate feedback and the self-paced format as advantages of e-learning over in-class training (Herzberg et al., 2017). Our survey result indicates that QualiWare's customers are open to e-learning. It justifies QualiWare's transition from blended learning to pure e-learning.

Twenty-one percent responded that the course certificate was important for them (pre-survey, 2019). QualiWare's corporate trainer in fact heard from a manager of some of the e-learners taking the course that he would use QualiWare's certificate as a key performance indicator for his employees (interview, 2020). These results are in line with research suggesting that meaningful rewards and recognitions are important (Rabak & Cleveland-Innes, 2006), and linking course completion to career development has a positive effect on the course completion rate (Seraphim, 2010). The result shows that providing a certificate is worthwhile for QualiWare.

Fourteen percent responded in our pre-survey that they had been encouraged to take the course by their boss. It suggests the presence of organizational support, which is motivating for e-learners (Hanssen et al., 2017; Montgomerie et al., 2016; Sarabadani et al., 2017; Schultz & Correia, 2015; Wang, 2018).

Twenty-one percent of our respondents were eager to expand their network. Previous research on e-learning in organizations suggests it can improve the internal communication by giving a common experience to build on (Paulsen, 2009; Stephens, 2013). It might strengthen the communication between learners and QualiWare as 15 percent of the respondents looked forward to providing their feedback to QualiWare.

Nine percent reported other reasons, for example, researching QualiWare to consider whether to adopt the platform or not. Research on open e-learning indeed shows that online courses can act as marketing and branding channels (Dodson et al., 2015).

9.3.2   Perceived Relevance

The pre-survey showed that enterprise architecture was the most popular topic with 60 percent of the learners indicating their interest. QualiWare X was the second most popular topic (57 percent) followed by process management (54 percent), capability mapping (49 percent), diagrams in QLM (49 percent), dashboards (49 percent), customer journey mapping (44 percent), risk management (43 percent), application portfolio management (40 percent) and GDPR (38 percent). The difference in learning interest among the learners is because they use QualiWare for different purposes.

9.3.3   Completion Rate

Thirty-seven learners completed 100 percent of the course, 28 learners completed 22 to 89 percent of the course, 40 learners completed 11 percent of the course while 35 learners never

Table 9.3   *Attitude to e-learning compared with completion rate*

	Like a great deal (%)	Like a moderate amount (%)	Like a little (%)	Neither like nor dislike (%)	Dislike (%)
Total (83 learners)	37	52	8	2	–
100% course completion	52	43	4	0	–
11% course completion	38	46	12	–	–
0% course completion	–	21	58	16	5

Table 9.4   *Interaction with QualiWare and QualiWare users compared with completion rate*

	Learned through correspondence with QW (%)	Learned through QW events (%)	Learned through knowledge sharing with QW users in other organizations (%)
Total (140 learners)	21	11	19
100% course completion	24	14	24
11% course completion	18	10	13
0% course completion	18	8	15

got started. It is important to bear in mind that the learners use QualiWare for different purposes and thus, some may not find all the course modules relevant. As mentioned previously, learners are inclined to drop out if they find the learning irrelevant. Furthermore, two patterns emerged from the data. First, the learners who had experienced e-learning before and who completed 100 percent of the course indicated a positive attitude toward e-learning in their pre-survey. Those who had tried e-learning before and completed 11 percent or less of the course reported a less positive attitude toward e-learning. See Table 9.3.

Second, the learners who completed 100 percent of the course tend to communicate with QualiWare, share knowledge with other QualiWare users, attend QualiWare events to a higher degree than the learners who completed 11 percent or less of the course. See Table 9.4.

The learning outcomes that we focused on in this study were: (1) new skills; (2) operational experience; (3) networking. The learning along these dimensions was partly assessed by the obtained results in the platform (e.g. from quizzes) and partly from the interviews conducted among participants after the course was completed. In the end, four participants agreed to the interview after the course. This is not a very high number, but the qualitative interviews mainly served as a supplement to the quantitative data obtained from the platform.

9.3.4 New Skills

Based on the quizzes that were built into the platform as an integrated part of the learning, we conclude that the course succeeded in teaching new skills to the learners. Thirty-seven learners took the quiz two or three times before getting it right. A number of learners retook the quiz to achieve the maximum score although they had already passed the quiz.

Furthermore, the interviews with two interview respondents confirmed they had learned new skills while two other interview respondents were more skeptical. See the replies below:

1. "Yes."
2. "… the course gave me a very useful insight in how enterprise architecture can be implemented in QLM."
3. "It helped for me to understand better the platform, but I have the feeling that our solution is too customized and not that much can be applied."
4. "No, I was aware of most of the content that was provided."

The mixed results from the interviews can be explained by the fact that the learners' prior understanding of QualiWare and the way they use the platform in their organization vary significantly.

9.3.5 Operational Inspiration

The course also succeeded in providing operational inspiration to the learners as all four interview respondents replied positively as follows:

1. "Definitely, I was impressed about the business ecosystem and the business capability model."
2. "It was very useful to get an overview of all the different modules of QualiWare (X). Hopefully, my company will upgrade to X during the next months."
3. "Yes, especially around the capability modelling and the views around that concept."
4. "Yes."

9.3.6 Networking

The tool to facilitate networking was an online discussion forum. It received only one post during the entire period of the course. The post was a critical statement concerning the course content. QualiWare decided to make a phone call to the learner in order to clear the misunderstanding and avoid lengthy comments to the post in the discussion forum (interview, 2020). The result was that the post appeared unanswered to the other learners in the forum and they refrained from posting. An interviewee explained: "The forum was completely dead both from the users and from QualiWare's side."

Companies aspire to deliver more collaborative e-learning, for instance, through asynchronous discussions. But it requires significant time and resources to construct and maintain discussion threads (Czeropski, 2012). QualiWare realized during the course that it would be difficult to facilitate discussion in the forum given the amount of resources available (interview, 2020). The discussion forum thus turned out to be inactive and failed in fostering networking among the participants.

9.4   WHAT HAVE WE LEARNED?

The goal of our study was first to test the learning outcomes of different experimental features in an e-learning course. More specifically, to analyze whether the e-learning features successfully (a) taught the learners new skills; (b) provided them with operational inspiration; and (c) helped them develop a network.

The experimental features were generally very well received by the learners and helped improve the learning outcomes; for example, the quizzes, which were attempted more than needed. The only exception was the discussion forum that was not used properly during the course. As such, the experiment was successful in relation to (a) and (b) but failed in relation to (c) due to the lack of facilitation in the discussion forum. We conclude there is no point in having a discussion forum without a dedicated community manager who facilitates discussion and encourage learners to interact with each other through posts and comments. Yet, we stress the potential benefit of an active discussion forum and recommend QualiWare to include a discussion forum as part of their e-learning if the firm should dedicate resources for a community manager in the future. An active discussion forum may maximize the potential of QualiWare's e-learning, as a discussion forum or a chat function might provide a bit of individualization in the course. For instance, two interviewees found the course content too general. They could have benefitted from posting follow-up questions in the forum and starting a discussion among peers and instructors. The fact that 21 percent of the 140 respondents to the pre-survey indicated networking as a motivation to enroll in the course also highlights the usefulness of an active discussion forum. There already exists an informal network among a number of QualiWare users in different organizations in Denmark who help each other and exchange experiences on an ongoing, ad hoc basis. A member of the network informed us: "I often turn to the QualiWare group for help."

Another way to maximize the potential of QualiWare's e-learning would be to increase the completion rate. A mere 26 percent completed the course entirely, while another 20 percent completed between 22 and 89 percent of the course. Distractions to study and interruptions tend to keep learners from completing their e-learning (Seraphim, 2010). This was also the case in our learning experiment, where interviewees explained their lack of participation in the discussion forum and/or drop-out of the course because of other, unexpected, obligations. It turned out that several of these learners completed the course after our study had ended (interview, 2020). This suggests that online training should always be accessible as opposed to taking place during a fixed period of time. Flexibility is the key.

Table 9.3 reveals that learners with a positive e-learning experience are more inclined to complete another e-learning course. Thus, it is important for QualiWare to not only focus on course content but also ensure a high degree of user-friendliness and technical support. Table 9.4 shows a higher completion rate among learners who interact more with QualiWare and other QualiWare users in general. Hence, efforts to develop the QualiWare community seem worthwhile.

As a future study, we recommend investigating the potential for increasing sales through e-learning. In our study, e-learning spurred an interest in using the QualiWare platform for more purposes (operational inspiration). By analyzing sales to customers having completed the e-learning, it might be possible to determine whether and to what extent e-learning can contribute to QualiWare's sales.

9.5   WHAT ARE THE MANAGERIAL IMPLICATIONS?

The obvious question then is what can other SMEs learn from this story? This is not a story about QualiWare, but a story about conducting experiments in order to be on safer ground when conducting strategic decisions. All firms irrespective of size can benefit from a more scientific approach when making strategic decisions.

The problem is that there are so many confounding factors for each decision you want to make that it is very difficult to know exactly what works and what does not work unless you apply a more experimental design. The key in an experimental design is that you manipulate different features (you control the manipulation rather than the other way around), while other things are kept constant, so you can clearly sort out the effect of the specific manipulation. The experimental design can be used in relation to most decisions like how to optimally communicate with customers by experimenting with different ways of doing so or different ways of organizing the product line, the distribution system, the service features and so on. The opportunities for applying the experimental design are endless. The experimental design can further be strengthened by combining it with surveys and interviews as in the outlined case.

REFERENCES

Czeropski, S. (2012) Use of asynchronous discussion for corporate training: a case study. *Performance Improvement, 51*(9), 14–21.

Dodson, M.N., Kitbury, K. & Berge, Z.L. (2015) Possibilities for MOOCs in corporate training and development. *Performance Improvement, 54*(10), 14–21.

Garavan, T.N., Carbery, R., O'Malley & O'Donnell, D. (2010) Understanding participation in e-learning in organizations: a large-scale empirical study of employees. *International Journal of Training and Development, 14*(3). 155–68.

Hanssen, H., Norheim, A. & Hanson, E. (2017) How can web-based training facilitate a more career friendly practice in community-based health and social services in Norway? Staff experiences and implementation challenges. *Health and Social Care in Community, 25*(2), 559–68.

Herzberg, T.S., Rosenblum, L.P. & Robbins, M.E. (2017) Teachers' experiences with literacy instruction for dual-media students who use print and Braille, *Journal of Visual Impairment & Blindness, 111*(1). https://doi.org/10.1177/0145482X1711100105

Joo, Y.J.Y.J, Lim, K.Y. & Kim, S.M. (2012) A model for predicting learning flow and achievement in corporate e-learning. *Educational Technology and Society, 15*(1), 313–25.

Kimiloglu, H., Ozturan, M. & Kutlu, B. (2017) Perceptions about and attitude toward the usage of e-learning in corporate training. *Computers in Human Behavior, 72*, 339–49.

Markovic-Hribernik, T. & Jarc, B. (2014) The importance and prevalence of modern forms of staff training in the corporate environments of transition countries: the case of Slovenia. *South East European Journal of Economics and Business, 8*(2), 16–31.

McKay, E. and Vilela, C. (2011) Corporate sector practice informs online workforce training for Australian government agencies: towards effective educational learning systems design. *Australian Journal of Adult Learning, 51*(2), 302–28.

Montgomerie, K., Edwards, M. & Thorn, K. (2016) Factors influencing online learning in an organsational context. *Journal of Management Development, 35*(10), 1313–22.

Paulsen, M.F. (2009) Successful e-learning in small and medium-sized enterprises analysis of the case descriptions. *European Journal of Open, Distance and E-learning, 12*, 1–9.

Rabak, L. and Cleveland-Innes, M. (2006) Acceptance and resistance to corporate e-learning: a case from the retail sector. *Journal of Distance Education, 21*(2), 115–34.

Rodriguez, B.C.P. & Armellini, A. (2013) Interaction and effectiveness of corporate e-learning programmes. *Human Resource Development International, 16*(4), 480–9.

Sarabadani, J., Jafarzadeh, H. & ShamiZanjani, M. (2017) Towards understanding the determinants of employees' e-learning adoption in workplace. *International Journal of Enterprise Information Systems, 13*(1), 38–49.

Schultz, T. L. & Correia, A. (2015) Organizational support in online learning environments: examination of support factors in corporate online learning implementation. *International Journal on E-learning, 14*(1), 83–95.

Seraphim, K.G. (2010) Entivers and barriers to e-learning-based distance corporate training: the case of a Greek bank. *Turkish Online Journal of Distance Education, 11*(4), 109–20.

Skrtic, M.M., Horvatincic, K. & Tisma, S. (2012) E-learning in banking. *Croatian Journal of Education, 14*(March), 257–74.

Stadler, A., de Camargo, R.T.M. & Maioli, M.R. (2017) E-learning as a training tool for civil servants: a case in the state of Parana – Brazil. *Turkish Online Journal of Distance Education, 18*(2), 94–105.

Stephens, M. (2013) Exemplary practice for learning 2.0: based on a cumulative analysis of the value and effect of "23 things" programs in libraries. *53*(2), 129–39.

Wang, M. (2018) *E-learning in the Workplace*. Cham: Springer Cham. https://doi.org/10.1007/978-3-319-64532-2

10. How do big data impact business market relationships?

Poul Houman Andersen

There is a lively debate about what big data means for the business operations of the future. An anchor point in this debate is the disruption potential of big data. Will unlimited access to an expanding and increasingly diverse "sea" of real-time data fundamentally change how most organizations and markets will function in the future? Or is the potential impact of big data on a more evolutionary nature, adding efficiency and effectiveness to the existing organization and market exchange practices in some contexts and not in others? There is no simple answer to these questions. Partly because they build on the premise that concepts such as markets, business operations, and organizations are static, and clear-cut ideas present a clear division of work among market participants and that big data represents a relatively easy predictable force of change. However, technologies like the big data phenomenon are not an external disruptive macro-level force. They work through existing exchange relationships. This contribution takes the relational perspective and assumes that buyer-seller relationships as a concept persist despite digital upheavals, but existing market exchange processes gradually change through big data enablement.

One crucial issue concerns the marketing effectiveness of small versus large businesses. When it comes to establishing and managing business relationships, entrepreneurs and other small business owners are fundamentally different creatures from their large-scale counterparts (Donnelly et al., 2015; Florén, 2006). Over time, the market relationships and networks of small and medium-sized business consistently follow a pattern, where a handful of customers in the customer portfolio are responsible for a large share of the turnover (Drejer et al, 2015; Kalwani & Narayandas, 1995; Håkansson, 1986). Hence, given their comparatively weak resource base for conducting sales and marketing efforts, small and medium-sized enterprises (SMEs) depend on developing and maintaining long-term relationships with specific customers, and may, for this reason, emphasize the ability to target and flexibly match offerings to the exact demands of their customers to a relatively higher degree than more substantial counterparts. Therefore, big data's impact on small business practices most likely depends on the interaction patterns between buyers and sellers – moves and countermoves as they unfold in a continuous and dialectical interactive market process.

Therefore, we pose the research question: How does big data impact the possibilities for creating a market relationship presence for small business operations? By market relationship presence, we mean a company's ability to establish, develop, maintain, and defend valuable exchange relationships with customers and suppliers. This concept builds further on the notion of a marketing environment; an idea conventionally used to describe how suppliers may create a conducive atmosphere supporting their sales efforts as an integral part of the value offering

(Kotler, 1974; Langeard et al., 1981). The reason to replace the term marketing environment with market relationship presence is not only a question of semantics. The traditional notion of an environment suggests a macro-level force to which companies can only adjust, and the abstract notion fails to address the complexity and emergent qualities of a business context, which partly is shaped through the actions and interactions of a firm with its constituents (Möller et al., 2020). The notion *relationship presence,* on the other hand, emphasizes that the context is co-produced through buyer-seller interaction, suggesting that the firm's efforts toward staging a specific interaction to co-create value with customers is at the center as a capability. Still, it maintains the notion that value creation unfolds in a customer context and that utility ultimately is defined by the customer – and not an inherent quality of the offering itself (Pine & Gilmore, 2011). The focus on value creation in customer contexts is in line with more recent marketing approaches, assuming customers are empowered, rather than passive, and that value creation is co-created in the interaction between buyer and seller (Pine & Gilmore, 1998; Vargo & Lusch, 2004).

The purpose of this chapter is to explore and further conceptualize the idea of relationship marketing presence, to create prescriptive insights for managers and inspiration for further research. Methodologically, the chapter follows a rationalist approach, inspired by the tradition of strategic management (Schoemaker, 1993). Ontologically, the chapter builds on existing theory, and the epistemological objective is to conceptualize a rational model with crucial variables of use for decision-makers. Case examples and other data are used mainly for illustrative purposes and to drive a point. Although using examples from large enterprises, the chapter presents illustrative case examples from a range of predominantly small Danish firms. The cases have not been used before in the literature and therefore provide novelty concerning specific challenges related to using big data to enable relationship presence. These cases include small enterprises such as Burd Delivery, Sol & Strand, Amager Bryghus, Okholm Masking Fabrik, Uggerhøj, Billy, and Hapti.

To move from a general level of understanding into specifically addressing big data's potential impact on market relationship presence, we start by discussing the nature of big data as a resource. We then critically match the specific problematics, tasks, and concerns of small business owners with the potential services rendered by big data, building on small business and entrepreneurship literature and using several illustrative examples. In the concluding part, we return to our opening question and discuss the principal ways in which big data is a valuable tool (or not) for entrepreneurs.

10.1   BIG DATA AS A RESOURCE FOR MARKET RELATIONSHIP PRESENCE IN SMALL (AND LARGE) BUSINESSES

It is becoming increasingly common to refer to big data as a resource. *Wired Magazine* even compares data to the digital economy's new oil – a potential source for endless uses – to derive value from it (*Wired*, 2014). Laney (Fan & Bifet, 2013) has defined it more precisely as data streams that conform with the three V's: "High volume, high variety, and high velocity information assets." High volume refers to a large and exponentially growing amount of data that makes it possible to search for correlations and fine-tuning contexts in ways other than what has previously been possible. Thus, relationships can be detected, and decisions made on an informed basis better than before. Variety relates to the diversity of data and the possibility of interconnecting these to uncover patterns not previously revealed (such as identifying new ways of describing and reaching target groups in a market). Velocity is the speed – often real-time – at which data are available. The development in volume variety and velocity means having a faster reaction time for decision-makers, thus creating utterly new market offerings and product features. In many ways, big data forms the basis for a market economy dominated by services shaped by customer desires and actions and where companies provide services (something a product can) rather than physical products (ownership).

Market relationship presence is an essential concept for this discussion. It considers how you, as a seller are present in the flow of experiences that constitute an exchange relationship. Basically, being present is not only a question of whether you are physically located some-where, but much more complicated, whether the customer experiences you as being present. Customers' experience attempts toward creating market relationship presence ("we are here for you") both on digital and analog touchpoints throughout their buying journey. In the eyes of a customer, your presence includes the series of events representing how you meet and interact with them and where in their travels through the digital and physical decision space you meet them and – for instance, in organizational buying where several individuals are involved – who you meet. The experience is partly the outcome of how you stage a market relationship presence. Formally, creating a market relationship presence must be seen as a firm's capability in staging interactions to shape the possibilities for valuable cooperation.

The qualities of big data in creating a relationship market presence context are undeniable, but the literature discussing these in more practical terms is scant (Guenzi & Habel, 2020). Access to data increases information reach and richness in developing a deep insight into *granular* customer behavior and consumption patterns across a much broader scope of cus-tomers than otherwise possible. However, thinking that information is inherently valuable is a mistake. Resources are commodities, but it is the capability of using them in staging relationship presence that creates possibilities for value creation. Large companies such as Netflix and Amazon have deployed algorithms on big data to unearth micro-market segments and consumption patterns no one had thought about previously. Hence, from information such as which movie scenes we like to replay, they can build customer intimacy to an extent where they use predictive analytics to form extremely educated guesses concerning customers' preferences and use this insight for developing new productions (or buying up existing movie material). Moreover, they can develop this without the traditional trade-off between *reach*, reaching many customers at the same time, and *richness*, engaging in considerable depth with each customer to learn and adapt market offerings which traditionally are associated with customer intimacy as a market discipline (Treacy & Wiersema, 1993). Figure 10.1 illustrates the relationship between reach and richness and how big data-enhanced relationship market presence challenges the conventional resource trade-off.

The figure portrays two drivers of resource consumption in marketing and sales efforts. Reach describes the number of customers a company can contact with its products and ser-vices. Evans and Wurster (1999) further explain reach in terms of "access" and "connectivity" and define it as the volume of customers a business can connect with, and how many products it can offer to those customers. Richness concerns the depth and detail of information that the business exchanges with the customer. Conventionally, there is a trade-off between these activities as sales management is a scarce resource. However, big data can be used to enable both reach and richness and, thus, in reality, digitally boost sales management and marketing

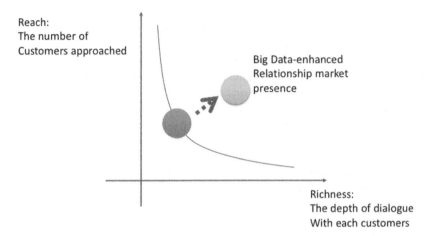

Figure 10.1　　The trade-off between reach and richness in customer interaction

activities. Some data can be used in Customer Relationship Management (CRM) tools to address customer needs more accurately, thus reducing the time spent on pinpointing the right need and reducing the cost of creating rich dialogues. Others may create reach by automating sales and contact tasks during an interaction and increase the volume of customers reached. Others, such as active use of Social Media Management (SoMe) tools, such as LinkedIn, can make networking with the company's resource persons easier for potential clients, and in this sense reduce both reach and richness, as the customers take on the active role of engaging the company in a potential value creation process. Take as a case the accounting software service company Billy.dk, which is a small Danish enterprise with 20 employees. The company provides an accounting software service to entrepreneurs and owners of small businesses. The standard software used for accounting purposes is free of charge. However, it still creates value for the company. When users are interfacing with Billy's software, it generates a constant flow of data and makes it possible for the salespersons at Billy.dk to use real-time data on customers' usage of their software solutions. They can address customers in real-time, and commoditize a service, which used to require a more in-depth dialogue between an external accountant and a firm. A bot drives much of the customer dialogue staged by Billy. Only when things become too hairy and difficult will an employee step in, and the bot will step aside. This process is automated as well, flagging difficult dialogues (for instance, when the customer keeps asking the same question, as he or she is not satisfied with the answer). Billy. dk has about 40,000 company users of its accounting software, amounting to 2000 clients per employee in Billy. Not surprisingly, the productivity of chartered accountants is skyrocketing (FSR, 2019).

A way of portraying the potential gains from big data in enhancing relationship market presence for small (and for larger) firms is to think of these in terms of increasing supplier and buyer insights or reducing buyer or supplier costs of interacting (Table 10.1).

Building supplier and buyer insights through big data potentially boosts the ability to match the needs of buyers and suppliers better. This means more efficiency (reach) and more effectiveness (richness) in buyer-supplier dialogues. In terms of actions, Guenzi and Habel (2020) suggest a route of potential digital pathways to follow that can also create a better utility

Table 10.1   Potential gains

	Buyer	Supplier
Insights	Big data and analytics driving need predictability (for instance, artificial intelligence applications)	Big data and analytics driving transparency (for instance, third-party evaluation sites of suppliers)
Actions	Big data and analytics empowering sales efforts (for instance, digital displaying or application in customer contexts)	Big data and analytics enhancing accessibility (for instance, professional SoMe)

function in the sales efforts: digital presence can substitute physical sales presence; it can supplement it, it can simplify it, it can support it or create and enhance servicing of it.

However, digitalization of relationship market presence is no panacea. Companies easily end up in a trap of overwhelming their customers with attention and probes, simply because it is almost cost free for the supplier to "push the button." The overall challenge for the supplier who realizes the potentials of big data and digitalization of sales efforts is to provide a relationship presence without intimidating the prospective customer. Also, automated payment and costing services, akin to sticking your hand out too many times during your interaction with customers, and asking for nickels and dimes at every turn, can create a sense of being trapped, as many customers of low-price airlines have addressed in their customer complaints. A cross-national study of sales digitalization in companies shows that few companies in fact have a clear strategy of what they are doing and why they are doing it (Guenzi & Habel, 2020). Broadly, the research suggests two overall strategic approaches when it comes to the digitization of sales efforts: sales enablement or sales replacement.

In this sense, we concur with Porter (2001) in claiming that big data is a strategic enabler of existing business, more than a transformative force. In many ways, the advent of digitalization is offsetting scale advantages. For instance, international reach costs, such as the ability to contact (or be contacted by) international customers and engage in exchange with them, have been dramatically reduced. Still, these possibilities are only proactively pursued to a minor extent by small businesses. As we use their services, the buying behavior algorithms learn more about our needs and wants through our search strategies and by tracking all sorts of activities. How do late-night shoppers move their shopping trolley around in a superstore? What aisles do they stop at? How long do they spend at each section of the store? What is on their mobile device when they shop and ponder about a specific item? Insights on customer behavior may lead to better targeting possibilities and, in the end, more sales for the progressive seller.

Similarly, in business-to-business (B2B) markets, insights about when, how, and why members of the buying organization search for ideas and what insights they search for can enable sales efforts and create better customer journeys. Challenging and not debated further in this context is, of course, that the drivers of relationship presence are not exclusive to small firms. The qualities of creating intimacy and trustworthiness, which was a hallmark and a somewhat protected competitive advantage of SMEs, is likely to be eroded by large enterprises with the ability to emulate the ambiance of relationship presence, generally attributed to small firms. Hence, the small-firm virtue of knowing the client can be easier emulated by a larger firm. Consider the story of sales enablement in a large building and construction firm by providing the right information at the right time (Guenzi and Habel, 2020, p. 65):

> the typical problem was that these clients oftentimes have more information on the relationship than our sales people, especially because the members of our sales force change over time as a consequence of turnover and job rotation … Now, thanks to digital innovation, this situation has been rebalanced, since our CRM system gives our sales force the opportunity to get a comprehensive picture of the history of the relationship.

Paradoxically, on the buying side, it seems that increased access to information in the digital age has complicated rather than helped employees involved in B2B buying. As digitization has caused the amount information available to explode, traditional sales methods of providing customers with more information to make better-informed decisions may have the opposite effect. Due to the buyers' sense of information overload, they can find themselves overburdened and decide to withdraw or anchor on what they have decided already, to avoid the psychological pain of more bewilderment and uncertainty (Kahneman, 2011). We can imply from research carried out by the Gartner Group management consulting firm that B2B buying is becoming increasingly complicated as more voices and information are present for the buyer. On average, the number of people involved in B2B buying journeys increases and the B2B buying journey is less driven by traditional sales and increasingly by individuals searching for online information (Gartner Group, 2020). In other words, customers process much information before meeting with the supplier. Gartner estimates than, on average, buying centers have treated more than half of the information they will transform throughout the entire buying journey before meeting the supplier.

Furthermore, the trustworthiness of insights obtained from online sources such as other customer reviews seem to dominate over information from, for instance, supplier interaction (Jiménez & Mendoza, 2013). At the same time, we also know that the information load requires increasing amounts of time to process and may confuse rather than help a buying team make decisions, by continually introducing new concerns and parameters to factor into the decision. Research on collective decision-making in organizational units often calls for a collective decision-making process, which can breed mutual confusion or myopia, rather than clarity (Knudsen & Srikanth, 2014). Hence, the sales rep's role in the supplying company is changing – from a specialist information provider to an under-informed customer to being a representative that can be drilled by a knowledgeable team of representatives from the buying company. This change in market behavior calls for a shift in market presence for the selling company if they want to stay relevant and valuable. One crucial insight here is that complexity reducing rather than complexity enhancing is a way to provide value. To develop a significant relationship market presence in a B2B context, reducing complexity, and making sales a smoother experience for a group through understanding their journey and digitally tracking their progress may be a way to engage buyers in a new way.

These insights on the recursive impacts on data on the B2B buying behavior are also interesting from a small business perspective. Understandably, big data looks more like another buzzword for a small business owner on the surface. The churn of new business and marketing concepts to learn (and forget) seems endless. However, below the stream of thoughts hides a critical but straightforward truth for small business owners. Customers are increasingly converting to digital means and away from analog business. The amount of web-based business transactions is only increasing, and a theory of the market based solely on analog handshakes and personal trust is fading. Small businesses can take advantage of the sales enablement benefits of deriving big data insights on B2B customers' buying and consumption processes. Take as a case the subcontractor Okholm Maskinfabrik in Southern Denmark. This small machine workshop delivers processed metal components to manufacturers in a broad range of Denmark and Germany industries. To increase process transparency, they have digitalized workflow processes, which means that customers can follow production activities and contract employees working with their components. As the CEO of the company Kristian Kvistgaard-Persson emphasizes:

> We can easily deliver the customer's requirements for traceability and documentation, because all information is stored on our tablets. It has been a crucial parameter for the customer.

By creating a real-time insight into customers' activities, big data provides new opportunities for designing and developing market presence and the ability to quell customer concerns as they arise. This insight relates to the notion of the touchpoints that makes up the digital market presence. Matching customers' needs throughout ideation, information and search, and decision-making situations provides a way to take out complexity and ease commitment to a provider of services and products. A few simple tricks may go a long way in creating marketing insight (Boxes 10.1 and 10.2).

BOX 10.1 TRICK 1: OBSERVE HOW CUSTOMERS INTERACT WITH YOU DIGITALLY

Does your company host an active website for selling and marketing purposes? Try to follow the experience by observing how someone might navigate on your website. An MBA student of mine who also happened to be the CEO of a small company, selling courses online, learned an invaluable lesson when he saw how customers could not follow the website's logic as they browsed for information.

BOX 10.2 TRICK 2: DEVELOP A CUSTOMER JOURNEY MAP

Mapping customer journeys is a powerful way to visualize when, how, and under what circumstances customers meet your company during their decision journey. Customer journeys are individual experiences, and there are no two journeys which are precisely alike. Still, it is possible to find patterns and identifiable situations, and there are ways to design positive customer experiences from them. A small example of a high-level customer journey map may look like this.

With each high-level activity, numerous events typically involve a touchpoint between a customer's want and an offering supplied by an organization. Take as a case, arrival at the theatre by car and learning there are no parking spaces nearby. Each experience creates thoughts and feelings. Each presents an opportunity for improving the interaction with the customer and to develop "sweet spots." See Pennington (2019) for much more information on how to draw journey maps.

Being present in a customer's buying process is an ongoing activity, which extends beyond the sales event. A necessary lesson for marketing and sales, which is also backed up by extensive research, is that satisfied customers tend to be more loyal and even willing to work as a faithful ambassador for your company and its offerings. There has been a tendency for marketing and sales to zoom in on a net promoter score.[1] It is a single performance indicator for the success (or failure) of relationship-based marketing and most of marketing efforts are tailored to increase this score. Satisfaction is typically discussed as a judgment achieved through a calculus between expected pre-purchase and realized pro-purchase benefits and costs. If pre- and post-purchase expectations balance, customer satisfaction is moderate but does not necessarily lead to loyalty (repeated buying). When positively disconfirmed, customer attitude is also positive, which contributes to preference and loyalty.

On the other hand, negative disconfirmation drives dissatisfaction, which means no future buying and possibly a negative word-of-mouth effect (Oliver & Swan, 1989). This attitude formation model assumes that customers are articulate regarding their expectations concerning a market offering they can remember. Second, when consuming the offering, customers can distinguish the consumption experience from other distractions in the bewildering array of contextual impressions around specific consumption experiences. No doubt, this portrait of satisfaction-building is sometimes real. However, customer satisfaction can be a much more complicated concept than an initial inspection would lead us to believe. First, from a marketing perspective, what motivates our purchases is to satisfy a need. The need can range from being quite clear and necessary, but it can also be vague and complex – mixed with desires, uncertainties, and wishful thinking (Fournier & Mick, 1999). These differences make the expected benefits from buying complicated and hard to understand. Customers sometimes buy because they want to acquire a desired skill (for instance, to play a music instrument) or out of a desire to solve a domestic issue, such as buying an electric lawn mower to have more time with the family and maintain a level of social acceptance in the neighborhood. In these cases, options for relationship marketing presence to chauffeur the experience toward a satisfying outcome involve multiple touchpoints and alerts. Big data backs up insights when customers might show signs of dissatisfaction (through net search behaviors, etc.) and can open a direct dialogue. Or it creates unexpected, pleasant surprises by engaging customers on levels that they did not expect. Take as a case the brand community activities evolving around (typically middle-aged men) buying a weber grill. Besides selling the grill, Weber has developed the

Weber academy for gathering grill aficionados and it hosts events to build companionship and fun around the weber grilling experience. Furthermore, keeping market presence through social media, sending text messages and e-mails, and so on are part of digitalizing existence. Similarly, small businesses may use big data to engage in a dialogue with their customers.

An important lesson for small and large businesses for utilizing the potential of big data is that it can provide insight into the current state of relational presence. It also offers opportunities to select possible customer touchpoints and engage digitally in a fashion that spells richness for customers and is valuable. One obvious strategy for this is to use existing social media platforms to create market presence – and possibly mix this with online and hybrid experiences. Take the case of Amager Bryghus, a Danish, internationally recognized craft brewer. Big data insights from specialized search engines (such as RateBeer.com) and hits on their web page can support communication and postings and create global awareness about new beers, collaboration with world-known brewers, and building brand experiences in alignment with customer expectations. These activities are all part of creating a market presence. An example is the cartoon-like labels used by Amager Bryghus, created by an artist associated with the brewery. They stir discussions and sometimes also create issues that provide a brand experience. One case concerns a label in the "Sinners" beer series labeled *Lust* and portraying a lady. Systembolaget, the state-controlled Swedish alcohol monopoly, found the combination of the name of the beer and the drawing of the lady inappropriate and censored the label in 2013. They allowed the beer into the Swedish market but required that the beer was presented to the sensitive Swedish audience with a black label only. The story went viral as beer bloggers started writing about it. The story gained international recognition and global online media such as the *New York Daily News*, *Huffington Post*, *Asian News*, and even the *Daily Bhaskar* in India covered the story. CEO Henrik Papsø, Amager Bryghus says:

> It was invaluable marketing for us, no doubt about it. We deliberately set out to focus on the ban and create publicity, but I must say that we are a little surprised at how much the story has spread.

Perhaps not surprisingly, Swedish customers flocked to Danish stores and websites to collect the Lust beer.

A big data-supported market presence for small business also extends beyond traditional selling and into co-creation of value. Value co-creation can take many forms, blurring the traditional boundaries between sellers and buyers, and the value proposal may include other dimensions than monetary value. Big data can support relating to these market actors and in creating national and international market presence, as in the case of Sol & Strand (a company specializing in mediating contacts between summer cottage owners in Denmark and tourists) and Burd delivery (a small company, specializing in adaptive logistical services for shops and other B2B customers) (Boxes 10.3 and 10.4). In both cases, the abilities to co-create a dialogue regarding shared social and societal values and to use big data in support of these efforts are central.

BOX 10.3 CASE IN POINT: SOL & STRAND

Sol & Strand is a company owned by a charity foundation. It rents out and services summer cottages in Denmark for approximately 6500 owners and matches these with patrons from Denmark and nearby countries such as Germany, Sweden, and Norway. The cottage owners receive most of the rental income, except for a service and administration fee. The operations of this company are a combination of off- and online market presence. Potential customers search and find summer houses online, and most of the contracting business happens this way. Also, cottage owners can follow renting out efforts online, using the platform. They can choose to cancel or act otherwise on available rental weeks. They can rent out themselves using services such as Airbnb, and so on. Customers and summer cottage owners experience offline presence through the 21 sales, destination, and service offices located in Denmark, Sweden, and Germany. Sol & Strand uses their knowledge about their patrons with a dedicated TV platform on all summer cottages to direct marketing messages from local events, grocery shops, and so on to their customers. In this way, they have developed a platform for selling advertisement space directly to patrons. An interesting additional issue is that summer cottage owners and guests are also offered the opportunity to decide what humanitarian activity the Sol & Strand foundation should support in their local region. This change provides the opportunity for another form of market presence and engaging customers differently from other businesses. As expressed by Per Dam, CEO of Sol & Strand: "We must think in sustainability and circularity. It is important both for the cottage owners and our patrons." Sol and Strand returns 75 percent of their revenues to local humanitarian initiatives. Big data is an essential facilitator of this summer cottage owners, and their patrons are involved in the online dialogue concerning this. They are asked to come up with suggestions, engage in discussions, and vote on specific initiatives, which are then eventually decided by the foundation's board.

BOX 10.4 CASE IN POINT: BURD DELIVERY

Burd is another startup company that has integrated big data to create market presence and interaction with all users. The company specializes in same-day distribution of small packages in the greater Copenhagen area. The group organizes deliveries of 50 distributors.

The company boasts of having the world's highest trust pilot score when it comes to package distribution. They have developed a digital platform through which they communicate schedules, route plans, and everything else needed. Also, Burd asks end-users to rate their delivery experience directly, which shows immediately on the employees' website and is used by Burd delivery for training and development purposes. The employees check in at the warehouse in Glostrup (a suburb in the greater Copenhagen area) to pick up the deliverables (or pick them up directly in the shops, from which the goods are sold). Employees are typically on the margin of the traditional job market and work late afternoons and evenings to deliver packages to people in person. The company owner has a strong focus on the sustainable development goal (SDG) regarding the development of an accessible and open labor market. The company has been able to mobilize and maintain people in employment where others have given up. This also means that the company has received numerous prizes and works jointly with the Copenhagen municipality to activate people who have difficulties in onboarding the labor market.

10.2   USING BIG DATA IN THE CREATION OF RELATIONAL MARKET PRESENCE

Departing from the discussion and the examples above, we propose a conceptual model to integrate the small business perspective insights on staging parts of the buyer journey and interacting with buyers. We draw on the relatively new literature of designing customer experience journeys in this respect (Johnston & Kong, 2011; Lemon & Verhoef, 2016; Trischler et al., 2018). Customers' "experience journey" is a way of describing the iterative information search and evaluation process customers traverse as they search for a way to satisfy a need. It entails consumers' pre-purchase, purchase, and post-purchase activities and involves multiple touchpoints with multiple vendors and other suppliers of information, insights, and support. A customer experience journey perspective has much in common with buying behavior approaches and differs in important respects. First, the customer experience perspective highlights the interactive, co-created experiences that unfold and adds to the customers' cumulative affective and emotional stage, and second, focuses on the individual's experience events. It is possible to map an iterative and dynamic rather than a linear sequence, as is often done in the buying behavior model. (By following what the customer does, the perspective helps to reveal the underlying activated ecosystem of actors involved in assisting customers in making up their minds.) Hence, it links to, but goes beyond what selling activities a prospective supplier is responsible for. Research suggests that customers spend less than 17 percent of the buying journey time with suppliers (Gartner Group, 2020). Embracing this perspective also suggests that buying companies must differentiate their selling efforts to be present, whereby customers are current, rather than assuming that their experience can be controlled. The derived value of creating market presence hinges on companies' ability to map customer journeys, meet and greet them, and accompany them in their journey. Ideally, small businesses can use big data to stage touchpoints in favor of executing these activities and thus digitally enable their sales and relationship-building efforts. However, as we shall return to in the final section of this chapter, there are also essential pitfalls to consider for small businesses venturing on big data. In the following, we discuss sales management practices for creating relationship presence throughout the customer experience journey and how big data can support them.

Figure 10.2 provides an overview of the customer journey. We use this to zoom in on three broad stages of interaction with customers (each containing multiple touchpoints) and some examples. The model does not claim to exhaust the possibilities or touchpoint situations. Most scholars would concur that sales broadly consists of three phases, with several sub-phases associated: a pre-selling phase (here named onboarding), a selling phase (here named interaction), and an after-sales phase (here called take-off) (Moncrief & Marshall, 2005; Plouffe & Barclay, 2007). The activities in the first part of the customer journey (marked with circles in Figure 10.2) are external to the selling firm, which happens before the prospective customer encounters the business enterprise's sales activities. They are essential for understanding what search and exploration activities came before the onboarding phase in the customer's experience journey, as they shape expectations and influence how digital interaction with prospective customers proceeds as SMEs seek to stage the customer experience. A survey with 750 respondents on information sources used by B2B buyers showed that on- and offline information search, and exploration dominated buying activities. Other major search activities involved discussing and interacting with peers. One of the least used sources for information

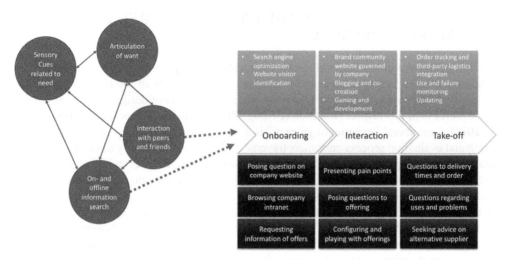

Figure 10.2   Customer decision journey and digital interaction with supplier

was meetings with potential suppliers (Gartner Group, 2020). This issue goes hand in hand with the changing attitudes and empowerment of customers generally witnessed in marketing (Wright et al., 2006). Hence, empowered customers approaching companies on their journey toward a purchase are typically well informed and have formed opinions about products and their uses already. The level of information that customers already have is a crucial aspect to bear in mind for designers of the journey touchpoints and interactions staged by the selling firm.

The latter part of the customer journey relates to the digital interaction between buyers and suppliers. For simplicity's sake, we divide this interaction into three phases: onboarding, interaction, and take-off. This three-step model broadly follows the convention used for classifying the main buyer-seller interaction phases in a customer journey design. Below each of the interaction phases, examples of digital touchpoints are provided, and further elaborated in the following discussion of each step. Again, these are typical examples rather than an exhaustive list. They are also generic. There are most certainly differences across industrial and cultural contexts. The box above each arrow mentions some of the possible big data enablers that can help the company develop a virtual reach/richness advantage. Again, the tools are in themselves only valuable when considering their utility in creating relationship presence.

The model is simplistic in several respects. First, it does not consider that customers may move back and forth and iterate between stages. Returning customers may also skip the initial steps. Second, it is essential to understand that customer personas differ, and that customer journeys can lead to the building of very different types of relationships. Fournier and Lee (2009) pointed out that relationship building has traditionally assumed that relationships always would end with a singular kind of buyer-seller commitment and closeness, sometimes referred to as a lifetime thing, akin to a marriage. However, from a relationship development perspective, we can think of numerous other types of relationships, which differ concerning norms and expectations. Customers don't expect the same connection to a provider of a commodity than customers who think of an offering as an essential part of an experience.

Furthermore, the same offering and corresponding journey activities may be considered differently by different customers. The model outlined here does, therefore, not pay heed to a specific type of relationship. Still, it does assume that relationships evolve based on foregone exchanges. Small business suppliers can utilize this along with digital cues derived from big data algorithms for creating, sustaining, and developing their relationship marketing presence. In the following, we will further elaborate on each phase.

10.2.1 Onboarding Prospective Customers

Unlike how they have typically been portrayed in consumer behavior models, they do not see themselves in the role of passive recipients of marketing communication. Still, they have researched for themselves and formed opinions. Today's customers are armed with an abundance of information when approaching suppliers. Research shows that four out of five buyers have done their Internet homework before contacting a prospective supplier (Shaver, 2007). Traditional, one-sided information and marketing communication models, which assume that the job is to persuade or inform, are often ineffective or even counterproductive. Customers most often think they are informed about market offerings and what they can provide (and at what price). They may focus on specific issues related to the offering and how it is performing and expect to interact with the supplier before they are ready even to consider exploring further the supplier as an opportunity. Relevant here is the notion of digital presence in the interaction. Does the supplier come across as an authentic dialogue partner? Testing this out through requesting information, asking questions, or browsing the company website are typical customer approaches. Treated the right way, they can lead to onboarding and further dialogue, resulting in relationship building and eventually a sale.

From the small business perspective, intelligent use of big data can help augment the prospective customer's experience in several ways. Still, few small businesses are actively using these sources of information. Danish society is considered one of the most digitized in Europe (Euromonitor, 2020). Still, the number of Danish companies using more advanced big data analytics is quite small. Among firms with fewer than 100 employees, less than 14 percent analyzed big data from social media and fewer from other sources. On a positive note, the proportion of companies using big data for analytical purposes has increased over the past five years (Danmarks Statistik, 2020).

There seem to be low-hanging fruits available for most small business (and many large businesses too). Two-thirds of all Internet search actions are carried out through the Google Chrome platform, and Google analytics is, therefore, a free source for an abundance of information for small businesses, useful for understanding the onboarding of a typical website user. Website visitor identification provides different kinds of information: repeat visiting, duration of stays on the site, how customers came to your site (landing), and where they left you are essential to assemble a picture of the customer persona you are dealing with, and helpful in further dialogue. Take, as a case, the small car dealer Uggerhøj, situated in Aalborg, which started using big data to trace existing customer responses to their campaigns. From broadcasting and developing leads to be contacted telephonically, they have built targeted dialogues with customers, based on their current information, and combined with their search data and other data about car buyers' behavior and search patterns. Data have enabled rather than replaced existing ways of creating relationship presence.

> Yes, it's an excellent example of big data. Because we have people who book online, people who just call in, who come into the system in different ways, and then we have people who have bought a car within some time, who have not been to the workshop yet. So, there are people who have been to the workshop, and then there are customer groups that we just must hit. So we join four different segments and say, "well, these are the ones we want to hit." We knew with 99 percent certainty that we would get a lot of bookings the first time because these are people who have booked online last time, and then we're off to them. (Olesen & Quist, 2019, p. 37)

10.2.2   Interacting with Prospective Customers

As customers engage in dialogue with small business supplier firms, they also commit time and resources, suggesting that they are willing to move from a purely transactional to a more relational based exchange. Engaging in dialogue is a critical step in relationship building because it requires investments in time and resources from both parties. In terms of marketing presence, this is a "moment of truth" situation, where customers are initially testing the authenticity and trustworthiness of a potential supplier. Customers may verify a supplier's authenticity, for instance, by posing a pain point or problem encountered and expecting involvement, or interactively, by "test driving" or experimenting with company offers. Concerning the former approach, small business owners may lend support from their online user community in interacting with customers and, in this way, enhance their digital presence beyond what would have been reachable from their limited offline resources. Liquor (Lakrids) by Johan Bülow and several other small companies have established and developed their social media presence on primary websites such as Instagram and Facebook to deal with this activity type. Users and other followers are attracted to blogging activity on the website, where they frequently post content. As prospective customers and brand followers enter and pose questions, others will typically greet them. Opening for gaming elements is another option, where customers – using or maybe trying out new products and offerings – are involved in a dialogue. Hapti.co (now bought up by a large company) is an example of a small business enterprise that develops online games. Knowing about gamers' age profile, and when they abandon games, they can adjust levels of difficulty or add content.

10.2.3   Take-off with Customers

The interactive model's final stage assumes that a transaction has taken place, and that supplier-customer interactions unfold on the premise that some form of contracting is in place. Buyer and supplier roles are pretty much set. Still, of course, for the relationship-building small company, it is necessary to understand how crucial this after-sales phase is for the prospects of building a customer relationship. The customer is, at this point, most vulnerable and potentially in doubt. Customers often search a lot of information after purchase to evaluate their own decisions (McKinsey, 2016). Should a customer experience that disappointment, for instance, that presence turns into absence, the customer feels disaffected, which can affect all other experiences. This, of course, also reflects on other customer relationships. In a company supplying software for shipping containers (for instance, systems for managing cooling equipment), a small Danish B2B supplier found that its relationships were damaged during customer complaints. A dominant customer, one of the largest shipping and sea transportation companies in the world, used this small-scale supplier for developing and equipping specialty type containers. Often, however, the supplier realized that parts of the buying center were highly dissatisfied. By analyzing the digital touchpoints with this customer, they learned that users of the services (which were not the same as the buyers) were interacting in parallel with the manufacturing and service unit. When they tried to answer delivery times, vague responses were given, and their fellow department blamed the sales department. Understanding the flows of data and digital interactivity helped remedy the problem and align customer expectations with responses. The issue here was not to solve the problem of late deliveries, but to provide reliable information that the customer could act upon. For instance, it turned out better to tell the customer that a specific repair would be finalized with 100 percent certainty at a specified date, even when this data was a conservative estimate. The customer would then know how to respond better than simply being told that a complaint would be processed "as fast as possible."

A related notion of customer complaints is customer regrets: a customer finding out after having purchased a good that this was not what they wanted. How to handle customer regrets and help prospective customers move on to a solution that may suit them better is, for some customers, an ultimate test of the supplier company's trustworthiness. Again, post-purchase behavior provides an excellent opportunity to demonstrate relationship market presence, which, perhaps at a later point, churned into a customer relationship.

Again, a range of solutions that integrate big data with internal data can help small businesses augment these situations. Big data, search patterns, and interactions provide rich insights into the opinions being formed and shared around business actors and their activities.

10.3 BIG DATA CHALLENGES FOR ENTREPRENEURS AND SMALL BUSINESS OWNERS

Having provided a reasonably positive and encouraging view of big data for small (and larger) businesses and how it might be used to yield market presence in business relationships, some cautionary words are needed. Big data offers a lot of opportunities and possibilities for following customers and to track performance on multiple levels. Big data is a time-killer, and the benefits of applying it to a specific problem are not always obvious. The benefits must be weighed against the costs. There is no doubt that designing, developing, and maintaining a relationship market presence is costly. Companies digitally present are always on and open – even when they are not. Customers expect to be able to contact and interact on a broad interface. Also, it may appear from this chapter that big data only works to the advantage of the small and agile firm, which may offset some big business advantages. It also works the other way around. It makes large companies able to appear as more intimate and knowledgeable than before. As customers are less bound to a supplier and are increasingly variety-seeking, this benefits a company with a much larger pool of relationships than for a smaller one. Supplier relationships are not what they used to be, and relationship advantages are more easily imitated by others these days.

10.4   CONCLUDING REMARKS

The purpose of this chapter has been to scrutinize the importance of big data for small businesses' ability to create market presence. We concur with Pine and Gilmore (2011) in stating
that the data and information are commodities rather than valuable goods. It is only when
they are matched with some capability that they can enhance the value-creating opportunities.
Also, with respect to creating market presence, big data in fact offers opportunities for large
enterprises to become as agile as their smaller competitors with respect to managing customer
interfaces and market presence. However, small firms cannot leave the impact of big data
aside. Increasingly, customers grasp the opportunities of using big data, and small enterprises
must find ways to match the new type of customer behavior they are facing. Hopefully, the
models and perspective in this chapter and the illustrative examples have offered some inspiration in this regard.

Table 10A.1   Self-assessment tool

		Customer		Your		Digitalization potential
		Benefit	Cost	Benefit	Cost	↓ Realized or irrelevant ↘ Minor potential → Some potential ↗ Major potential
Onboarding	Sub-process 1					
	Example: Weekly updating company LinkedIn and other SoMe profiles	Updates and insights	Wasted attention Irritation	Communication and fighting irrelevance Internal communication Engaging employees Knowledge about customers	Manpower Attention Potential exposure to negative word of mouth	Maybe potential for internal automatization?
Interaction						
Take-off						

APPENDIX: DIGITAL MARKET PRESENCE: SELF-ASSESSMENT TOOL

In the spirit of developing market practice, a self-assessment tool is suggested here. It consists of three steps with the purpose of structuring the managerial dialogue toward enhanced market presence.

- Step 0: Decide your overall market presence improvement target (Enablement (richness) or replacement (reach)).
- Step 1: Map your existing customer touch points and corresponding internal sub-processes.
- Step 2: Evaluate benefits and costs for customer and for you of each sub-process.

NOTE

1. Net promoter score is a measure for calculating the impact of customer satisfaction, where customers are asked to rate their willingness to recommend an offering (on a scale from 1 to 10 how likely is it that you would recommend this …).

REFERENCES

Danmarks Statistik (2020). Accessed July 26, 2021 at: https://www.dst.dk/da/

Donnelly, C., Simmons, G., Armstrong, G., and Fearne, A. (2015). Digital loyalty card "big data" and small business marketing: Formal versus informal or complementary? *International Small Business Journal*, *33*(4), 422–42.

Drejer, I., Andersen, P.H., Østergaard, C.R. et al. (2015). En kortlægning af underleverandører i Danmark, Report for The Industry Foundation (Industriens Fond).

Euromonitor (2020). Accessed July 26, 2021 at: https://www.euromonitor.com

Evans, Philip B., and Wurster, Thomas S. (1999). Getting real about virtual commerce. *Harvard Business Review*, *77*(6) (November–December), 84–94.

Fan, W., and Bifet, A. (2013). Mining big data: Current status and forecast to the future. *ACM SIGKDD Explorations Newsletter*, *14*(2), 1–5.

Florén, H. (2006). Managerial work in small firms: Summarising what we know and sketching a research agenda. *International Journal of Entrepreneurial Behavior & Research*, *12*(5), 272–88.

Fournier, S., and Lee, L. (2009). Getting brand communities right. *Harvard Business Review*, *87*(4), 105–11.

Fournier, S., and Mick, D.G. (1999). Rediscovering satisfaction. *Journal of Marketing*, *63*(4), 5–23.

FSR (Foreningen af Statsautoriserede Revisorer) (2019). Brancheanalyse. Accessed June 3, 2021 at: https://www.fsr.dk/Files/Files/dokumenter/Politik%20og%20analyser/Analyser/2019/ Brancheanalyse%202019%20FINAL.pdf

Gartner Group (2020). Various website information, publicly available on the Gartner Group website at: https://www.gartner.com/en

Guenzi, P., and Habel, J. (2020). Mastering the digital transformation of sales. *California Management Review*, *62*(4), 57–85.

Håkansson, H. (1986). The Swedish approach to Europe. In P.W. Turnbull and J.-P. Valla (eds), *Strategies for International Industrial Marketing*. London: Croom Helm Publishers.

Jiménez, F.R., and Mendoza, N.A. (2013). Too popular to ignore: The influence of online reviews on purchase intentions of search and experience products. *Journal of Interactive Marketing*, *27*(3), 226–35.

Johnston, R., and Kong, X. (2011). The customer experience: A road-map for improvement. *Managing Service Quality: An International Journal*, *21*, 1, 5–24

Kahneman, D. (2011). *Thinking, Fast and Slow*. New York: Macmillan.

Kalwani, M.U., and Narayandas, N. (1995). Long-term manufacturer-supplier relationships: Do they pay off for supplier firms? *Journal of Marketing*, *59*, 1–16.

Knudsen, T., and Srikanth, K. (2014). Coordinated exploration: Organizing joint search by multiple specialists to overcome mutual confusion and joint myopia. *Administrative Science Quarterly*, *59*(3), 409–41.

Kotler, P. (1974). Store atmospherics as a marketing tool. *Journal of Retailing*, *49*, 48–65.

Langeard, E., Bateson, J., Lovelock, C.H., and Eiglier, P. (1981). *Marketing of Services: New Insights from Consumers and Managers*. Cambridge, MA: Marketing Science Institute, pp. 81–104.

Lemon, K.N., and Verhoef, P.C. (2016). Understanding customer experience throughout the customer journey. *Journal of Marketing*, *80*(6), 69–96.

McKinsey (2016). How companies are using big data and analytics. Accessed June 3, 2021 at https://www.mckinsey.com/business-functions/mckinsey-analytics/our-insights/how-companies-are-using -big-data-and-analytics#

Moncrief, W.C., and Marshall, G.W. (2005). The evolution of the seven steps of selling. *Industrial Marketing Management*, *34*(1), 13–22.

Möller, K., Nenonen, S., and Storbacka, K. (2020). Networks, ecosystems, fields, market systems? Making sense of the business environment. *Industrial Marketing Management*, *90*, 380–99.

Olesen, C., and Quist, N.S. (2019). *Big Data: Brugbare Beslutningsindsigter eller Betydningsløse Bytes?* Kandidatspeciale, Aalborg Universitet

Oliver, R.L., and Swan, J.E. (1989). Consumer perceptions of interpersonal equity and satisfaction in transactions: A field survey approach. *Journal of Marketing*, *53*(2), 21–35.

Pennington, A. (2019). *The Customer Experience Book*. London: Pearson Education.

Pine, B.J., and Gilmore, J.H. (1998). Welcome to the experience economy. *Harvard Business Review*, *76*, 97–105.

Pine, B.J., and Gilmore, J.H. (2011). *The Experience Economy, Updated Version*. Cambridge, MA: Harvard Business Review Press

Plouffe, C.R., and Barclay, W. (2007). Salesperson navigation: The intraorganizational dimension of the sales role. *Industrial Marketing Management*, *36*(4), 528–39.

Porter, M. (2001). Strategy and the Internet. *Harvard Business Review*, *79*(3), March, 63–78.

Schoemaker, P.J. (1993). Strategic decisions in organizations: Rational and behavioural views. *Journal of Management Studies*, *30*(1), 107–29.

Shaver, D. (2007). Impact of the internet on consumer information search behavior in the United States. *Journal of Media Business Studies*, *4*(2), 27–39.

Treacy, M., and Wiersema, F. (1993). Customer intimacy and other value disciplines. *Harvard Business Review*, *71*(1), 84–93.

Trischler, J., Pervan, S.J., Kelly, S.J., and Scott, D.R. (2018). The value of codesign: The effect of customer involvement in service design teams. *Journal of Service Research*, *21*(1), 75–100.

Vargo, S.L., and Lusch, R.F. (2004). Evolving to a new dominant logic for marketing. *Journal of Marketing*, *68*(1), 1–17.

Wired (2014). Data is the new oil of the digital economy. *Wired Magazine*. Accessed July 13, 2020 at https://www.wired.com/insights/2014/07/data-new-oil-digital-economy/

Wright, L.T., Cova, B., and Pace, S. (2006). Brand community of convenience products: New forms of customer empowerment – the case "my Nutella the Community". *European Journal of Marketing*, *40*(9/10), 1087–105

11. Revenue blueprinting: identifying growth potential using customer data and customer insights

Henrik Andersen and Thomas Ritter

Human beings, who are almost unique in having the ability to learn from the experience of others, are also remarkable for their apparent disinclination to do so.
Douglas Adams

11.1 INTRODUCTION

It is a truism that any firm of any size has a best implemented practice—and that practice is not implemented throughout the organization. In other words, someone in the organization has found a way to achieve outstanding performance, but not everyone in the organization utilizes that way of working. Imagine a very small supplier with only two customers. One customer buys numerous offerings from the supplier's full product and service portfolio. Moreover, that customer only uses the focal supplier. The other customer buys only a limited selection of the supplier's offerings and only to a limited degree, as it procures most of its supplies from another supplier. From a revenue perspective, the supplier's best implemented practice is the practice implemented with the first customer. If the supplier could learn from that practice and transfer it to the other customer, revenue growth could be achieved.

Variations in practices, even in routinized tasks, occur in organizations because different people perform tasks differently, different circumstances result in different task executions, and different levels of dedication and motivation have different impacts (Feldman & Pentland, 2003). As such, even small and medium-sized enterprises (SMEs) can realize growth if they can spread their own best implemented practices from their current contexts (e.g., a salesperson in a given customer relationship) across the organization and, thereby, optimize performance. This strategic focus resembles Ansoff's (1957, p. 114) market-penetration strategy, which "is an effort to increase company sales without departing from an original product-market strategy" (i.e., customers and value propositions). Recently, such strategies have been referred to as focusing on the existing core business (e.g., Nagji & Tuff, 2012).

Our experiences have shown that SMEs and large organizations have pockets of customer knowledge and local practices to utilize that knowledge that are not commonly known and are not leveraged across the organization in its daily work. This underutilization relates to both explicit and tacit customer knowledge. Explicit knowledge is typically stored as accounting numbers in enterprise resource planning (ERP) systems and as "hard facts" (e.g., company name, address, industry, tax registration number) in customer relationship management (CRM) systems. Tacit knowledge relates to the customer insights held by individual, customer-facing employees. In relation to explicit customer knowledge, companies gather a wide range of customer data but they often lack knowledge about how to use it to develop the business. Tacit customer knowledge typically falls by the wayside because sales representatives are not involved in strategic decisions and, therefore, their intuitive understanding of customers' needs and expectations is excluded from judgements and prioritization.

Nevertheless, accelerating revenue growth requires the identification of the best implemented practice in the organization and the implementation of that practice across the organization. In this chapter, we describe how a supplier can realize significant revenue growth simply by learning from and applying its own best implemented practice across all of its customers. We explain how existing revenue data (i.e., explicit customer knowledge) can be used to calculate revenue blueprints, and how customer insights held by salespeople (i.e., tacit customer knowledge) can be used to verify and implement revenue blueprints. Notably, all one needs to start the revenue-blueprinting process is revenue data, a spreadsheet, and the participation of customer-facing employees. As such, revenue blueprinting utilizes both explicit and tacit customer knowledge to create a solid, realistic foundation for growth.

Revenue blueprinting is a data-driven growth method, as it utilizes data that is available in any firm to realize revenue growth potential. The use of revenue data allows for data-driven growth in SMEs that does not depend on expensive databases, large IT investments, or long return-on-investment horizons. Instead, revenue blueprinting is based on existing, readily available data and common spreadsheet analyses, and it has an immediate impact on performance.

The concept of a "blueprint" as "serving as a model or providing guidance" and as "a detailed plan or program of action" (merriam-webster.com) is widely used in architecture, software development, and service provision (e.g., Bitner et al., 2008, Shostack, 1984). We use the term "revenue blueprint" to refer to an estimation of potential customer revenue that is based on a supplier's best implemented practice. In other words, we identify a supplier's best implemented practice in terms of revenue derived from the best performing customers, and we project that practice onto other customers to estimate how revenues might look if that best practice is implemented in relation to all customers. These blueprints enable improvements in marketing strategy, which is defined as "an organization's integrated pattern of decisions that specify its crucial choices concerning products, markets, marketing activities and marketing resources" (Varadarajan, 2010, p. 119) by offering a tool for making better decisions and, thereby, enabling better use of marketing resources. Revenue blueprints build on customer knowledge capabilities, which are the "processes that generate and integrate information about specific customers" (Campbell, 2003, p. 376), and the notion that the active use of customer knowledge improves business performance (e.g., Campbell, 2003; Li & Calantone, 1998; see also the literature on market orientation, e.g., Jaworski & Kohli, 1993).

As such, revenue blueprints are based on established sales processes (i.e., best implemented practice) and adapted to a given customer's revenue history. This means that revenue blueprints are not illusions based on imagined future capabilities. Instead, they are calculations based on existing practice that are documented in revenue data. As salespeople's customer insights are indispensable for setting an implementation agenda and accounting for customer-specific variations, the blueprinting process includes the use of tacit customer knowledge for blueprint verification.

The blueprinting process is divided into the three steps:

- *Step 1* provides a calculation of customer-specific revenue blueprints based on a supplier's best implemented practice. Step 1 of the blueprinting process is solely based on the supplier's revenue data (i.e., the supplier's explicit knowledge regarding its past and current sales performance).
- *Step 2* consists of verification—a check of the calculated revenue blueprint performed by the supplier's customer-facing staff. As such, this step is based on customer insights (i.e., the customer-facing employees' tacit knowledge regarding their customer relations). Step 2 transforms the calculated revenue blueprint from step 1 into a verified revenue blueprint that indicates the accessible revenue potential of a customer. The accessibility mirrors the customer-facing staff's judgements of the potential revenue, which their customer insights suggest can realistically be achieved by applying the supplier's best implemented practice.
- *Step 3* provides a framework for prioritizing customer strategies in order to optimize top- and bottom-line growth when harvesting the revenue potential at the customer level identified in the revenue blueprints.

We have developed this revenue-blueprinting process over the course of many interactions with SMEs. It is easy to implement, as it is based on data and capabilities that every firm has. Consequently, it does not require specialized resources. Our experience suggests that applying the three steps of revenue blueprinting leads to immediate and sustainable growth in revenue.

In this chapter, we describe the revenue-blueprinting process in a business-to-business setting. We base it on a simplified, anonymized case in order to demonstrate the use of growth blueprinting and the benefits of applying it. While most of our work has been with business-to-business firms, the process works just as well in business-to-consumer settings. In the following section, we define a number of terms used in the blueprinting process. Thereafter, we outline the process in a step-by-step fashion. Finally, we offer an overview and our conclusions.

11.2 THEORETICAL BACKGROUND

11.2.1 Blueprint

A blueprint offers guidance on what to achieve. The idea of blueprints has been applied to both processes and outcomes to answer such questions as "How should a certain task be performed?" (e.g., in services, these are typically the processes used to successfully guide a customer through the customer journey) or "What should the end result look like?" (e.g., drawings of machines and buildings). We use the term "blueprint" in the latter interpretation (i.e., as a visualization of a result). In our case, a revenue blueprint illustrates the potential revenue that can be derived from a customer when the best implemented practice across customers is applied to that customer.

11.2.2 Revenue

From the supplier's perspective, active customers purchase a set of products and services. In fact, the act of buying from a supplier, which generates revenue, is the basis for status as an active customer. Revenue, which is also called "turnover" or "sales," captures the financial transfers between a supplier and its customers. Revenue data are readily available in most, if not all, firms. In fact, revenue data can typically be found in the supplier's ERP or CRM system. Revenues are specific for a given supplier, a given customer (e.g., customer A), and a given period of time (e.g., a month, a quarter, or a year).

11.2.3   Items and Categories

Category	Items
Desktop	Model 1
Desktop	Model 2
Laptop	Model A
Laptop	Model B
Laptop	Model C
Tablet	Model I
Operating	Software a
Video meeting	Software b
Video meeting	Software c
CRM	Software d
Onsite	Package i
Onsite	Package ii
Offsite	Package iii

Figure 11.1   Categories and items

The total revenue derived from a customer is typically spread across a portfolio of products and services. We refer to the individual products and services as "items." For a given customer, revenue can be divided into three levels (Figure 11.1):

* *Total revenue* (overall payments by a customer).
* *Revenue per category* (payments per product or service group).
* *Revenue per item* (revenue per individual product or service).

Revenue per item is the most detailed level of revenue data, and it is typically reported per unit (e.g., one drilling machine, one liter of machine oil, one hour of technician support, or one software license). Items are often listed on individual lines on invoices, where information on their individual product or service numbers is also provided.

Between total revenue and item revenue is the "category" layer. Categories are groups of items that share some characteristic. Examples of categories include:

- *Similar-item categories.* Supermarkets utilize this type of categorization, as they are built up around sections dedicated to fruits, vegetables, meat, dairy, and so forth. In industrial firms, similar-item categories could be steel products, aluminum products, and plastic products. In IT firms, categories could be desktop computers, laptop computers, and tablets (see Figure 11.1 for an illustration).
- *Quality categories.* This type of categorization is found, for instance, in the way airlines offer different classes of airfare, such as economy, business, and first class. In such categories, different items are combined into solutions, where the solutions differ in terms of their quality. Similar practices can be seen in industrial service contracts that range from basic to advanced or from standard to professional.

Many firms already have established categories, although they may refer to them as "product groups" or "industry portfolios." These categories are typically also reflected in item identification codes (e.g., part numbers), where the first few digits specify a category and the last few digits refer to the individual item. Different firms may operate with different category logics, as industry standards are rare in this regard.

11.2.4   Revenue Footprint

We refer to a customer's realized revenue as its "revenue footprint." Each revenue footprint is related to a specific customer, a specific supplier, and a specific time period. Footprints have two dimensions (Figure 11.2):

- *Footprint size* captures absolute revenue and is expressed in a currency.
- *Footprint pattern* captures the relative revenue of a category or item, and is expressed as a percentage.

As illustrated in Figure 11.2, Customer A's footprint is double the size of Customer B's footprint, but they both have the same footprint pattern. While Customer B and Customer C have the same size, their footprint patterns are very different.

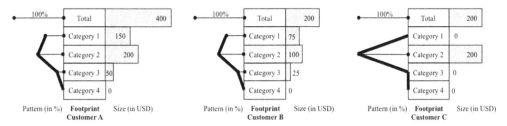

Figure 11.2   Illustration of customers' footprint sizes and patterns

11.2.5   Share of Wallet

Share of wallet is defined as "the percentage of money a customer allocates in a category that is assigned to a specific firm" (Cooil et al., 2007, p. 68). Customers can and often do split their purchases among different suppliers that are competing with each other. Thus, a supplier's revenue from a customer does not necessarily indicate the customer's total spending in that category. The share of wallet captures how much of a customer's demand within a category or for a single item is procured from the focal supplier. If the supplier is the only source, the customer fulfills 100 percent of its need using that supplier. However, customers often wish to reduce their dependence on single sources and, thus, split their procurement across a number of suppliers.

Customers can buy from all of a supplier's categories and items, or buy only a limited selection of items and categories. Consequently, the share of wallet can vary across categories and items. In other words, there is typically not a supplier-specific share of wallet (e.g., a customer fulfills 40 percent of its procurement needs across all relevant categories through a given supplier) that generally applies to all categories.

11.2.6   Best Implemented Practice

We use the term "best implemented practice" to highlight that we are interested in a practice that is already part of an organization's operation rather than an externally defined best practice against which the organization is benchmarking itself. Thus, the identification of a best implemented practice requires comparison of internal variations to determine which practice outperforms the others.

With regard to revenue generation from customers, we discussed the two versions of share of wallet above—one related to generating revenue across many, if not all, categories, and one related to supplying a large part, if not all, of one item or category. We recognize a best implemented practice by identifying those customers that buy across most, if not all, of a supplier's categories (i.e., the customers to whom the supplier is selling the most of its portfolio of products and services). These customers' footprint patterns provide an indication of the broadest item and category mix. We apply the logic of best implemented practice to each customer by identifying the item or category with which the supplier has created the highest revenue in relation to the expected revenue distribution. In other words, we identify the category in which the supplier has been the most successful with a given customer.

11.2.7   Customer Knowledge

Customer knowledge is a supplier's collective understanding of a given customer. This knowledge has explicit and tacit elements. Explicit customer knowledge is codified and, therewith, easy to transfer and use. Typically, a supplier's CRM system has plenty of explicit knowledge, including information on the customer's name, industry code, size, address, and contact persons. For revenue blueprinting, we consider revenue data as explicit customer knowledge.

Tacit customer knowledge refers to those insights about customers that are "difficult to codify or communicate across individuals or organizations" (Cui & Wu, 2016, p. 521; referring to Ganesan et al., 2005; Subramaniam & Venkatraman, 2001). Salespeople and other customer-facing employees possess much more knowledge about the firm's customers than is available in CRM systems. Salespeople who work with customers on a day-to-day basis combine all of their knowledge into judgements regarding what to offer to a customer and when to make that offer. Such tacit knowledge can only be utilized through its application (Nonaka, 1994). Thus, individuals with tacit knowledge need to partake in discussions and decision-making. With regard to revenue blueprinting, we enable the inclusion of salespeople's customer insights (i.e., their tacit customer knowledge) by involving salespeople in the verification of the calculated revenue blueprints (step 2). As such, step 2 turns the salespeople's tacit customer knowledge into explicit revenue blueprints that can be shared across the organization. Those verified blueprints, which provide explicit numbers for the realistic, accessible level of potential revenues, are based on tacit customer insights.

11.2.8 Customer Strategy Framework

All of the above-mentioned analyses result in the uncovering of a customer strategy that needs to be implemented. Ritter and Geersbro (2018) argue that there are four strategies for existing customers and four corresponding customer-management capabilities for implementing those strategies: maintaining, developing, reducing, and terminating. A major managerial issue is to allocate customers to the correct strategy and to ensure the implementation of that strategy.

Any verified revenue blueprint is only valuable when its realization can be assured or, in other words, when the organization can implement a customer strategy that turns potential revenue into realized revenue. To enable resource planning, we introduce a framework that allocates customers to customer strategies based on the current revenue footprint pattern and size of a customer relative to the verified revenue blueprints from step 2. As such, the framework highlights the resources the organization needs to implement the revenue blueprints. Customers can be classified into four categories according to their current footprint and their verified revenue blueprint (Figure 11.3):

- *Enthusiasts* buy across all categories and fulfill all of their demand for each item through the focal supplier. Consequently, these customers are enthusiastic about all of the supplier's categories and items, and they do not use other suppliers to a significant degree. As some firms may have procurement strategies that forbid, for instance, more than 80 percent of demand being met by one supplier, we also count customers who purchase an item "to the greatest extent possible" as enthusiastic. As such, enthusiasts have limited potential for revenue growth. This is indicated by the fact that the revenue blueprint for such a customer is (nearly) identical to the customer's current footprint. In this case, the main managerial task is to maintain the strong customer relationship to ensure that the customer's purchases remain on the same level. The footprint patterns of today's enthusiasts are a manifestation of the supplier's best implemented practice. Thus, their footprints serve as target revenue footprint patterns for all customers. While maintaining is the most likely customer strategy in this situation, enthusiasts may qualify for developing when they significantly grow their own business (e.g., through an active internationalization or acquisition strategy). Suppliers should focus on taking part in such growth and protecting their position as preferred suppliers. Alternatively, if salespeople foresee major disruptions in an enthusiast's business model (e.g., takeovers or recession), reducing strategies might be needed.

- *Supporters* are customers who buy from many but not all categories, or who buy less of selected items or from selected categories than possible. In this respect, their footprint patterns differ from those of enthusiasts and/or their footprint size is smaller than it could be. Typically, supporters miss out on less than 20 percent of categories and/or less than 20 percent of volume in a limited range of categories. For these customers, development strategies are needed in order to realize the potential indicated in the revenue blueprint. As the supplier already knows these customers and as business transactions already take place, the task of relationship development does not require significant resource allocations or sales efforts that go beyond the existing setup. Typically, minor adjustments are sufficient to increase the supplier's share of wallet and, thereby, turn supporters into enthusiasts (i.e., taking share of wallet from competitors). Again, alternative strategies may be relevant when customers are strategically focused on other issues or when a supplier's competitors are likely to win over a customer.
- *Spectators* are customers that only buy from a limited number of categories and they purchase only a limited volume. A supplier may be a minor safeguarding supplier that is only used to secure a small share of wallet or only activated when other suppliers fail to deliver. These customers exhibit confusing footprint patterns and sizes, and the reasons for their procurement behavior are typically varied. They may include dissatisfaction with parts of the supplier's offerings and a resulting hesitation to procure more. If the verified revenue blueprint is similar to today's footprint, the customer will remain "stuck in confusion" and, thereby, qualify for a maintaining strategy. Alternatively, a development strategy may be applied when additional business opportunities are identified in the blueprint. A reducing strategy may be utilized if the supplier is unable to provide satisfactory offerings or is not interested in the customer for strategic reasons.
- *Selectors* fulfill their full demand for only a limited set of items or categories through the supplier (i.e., 100 percent share of wallet or "to the extent possible"). Therefore, selectors have narrow footprint patterns, while their footprint size corresponds to 100 percent of the share of wallet for the chosen items or category. Selectors typically buy items that cannot be sourced from other suppliers. Within these "quasi-monopolies," selectors are forced to procure their full volume from the given supplier. If a selector's verified revenue blueprint indicates that additional items and categories can be sold to that customer (e.g., by bundling with the already procured items, or by claiming product and service leadership in other categories), that selector qualifies for a development strategy focused on selling specific items and categories and, thus, broadening its footprint pattern. Alternatively, a selector may remain steadfast in its procurement practices and, thus, should be maintained. Competitive pressures on the supplier's leadership position may also result in a verified revenue blueprint that is less than the current footprint. In such cases, a controlled reduction strategy needs to be implemented.

As illustrated in Figure 11.3, all customers in all four categories may fall under the develop, maintain, reduce, and terminate strategies. This is due to strategy and profit considerations that are not captured by the revenue considerations mentioned above. For example, enthusiasts may be located in an area or operate in an industry that has been deselected by a supplier's business strategy. Thus, the business will be reduced or terminated despite the customer's status as an enthusiast. While some of these arguments often enter the blueprint in the verification stage, it is important to explicitly consider them in step 3 to avoid implementing the wrong customer strategy.

Customers can be classified into a customer-strategy matrix (Figure 11.3) based on their footprints, blueprints, and overall judgements. The matrix serves as an implementation plan—a guiding tool for resource allocation and harvesting of revenue growth. The bars on the right-hand side of the matrix illustrate revenue development—developing strategies contribute more in the future (dark grey), maintaining strategies keep customer revenue about the same (mid grey), and reducing and terminating strategies lead to reductions (light grey).

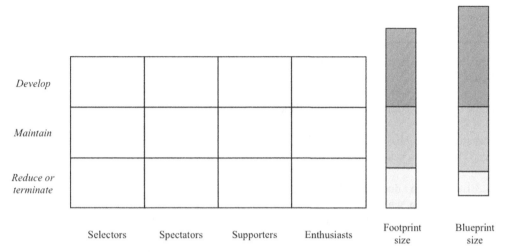

Figure 11.3   *Customer-strategy framework*

11.3   DEVELOPING REVENUE BLUEPRINTS

In order to develop actionable revenue blueprints, we need to combine factual, explicit knowledge about customers with subjective, tacit knowledge about customers. To do so, we use past revenue data and salespeople's judgements. Both inputs are readily available in any organization—as mentioned, relevant data are stored in a firm's ERP or CRM systems, while information on salespeople's judgements is available from the salespeople themselves.

In our experience, starting with data and then verifying the initial data-driven results with members of the sales force produces the best results because the data-analysis step is free from bias and offers a new interpretation of historical data. Nevertheless, important details that constitute tacit customer knowledge can only be found through interpersonal dialogue as opposed to mathematical analyses. Therefore, the blueprint-development process starts with calculations in step 1 and proceeds with salespeople-driven verification of those calculations in step 2. The process concludes in step 3 with implementation planning focused on assigning a strategy to customers to allow for realization of the potential revealed in the verified revenue blueprints from step 2.

We explain the development process for revenue blueprints using an anonymized and simplified example. The example illustrates the logic of and steps in revenue blueprinting. The

Table 11.1   Customers' footprint sizes by category (revenue per calendar year, in USD 1000)

Customer	Alpha	Beta	Gamma	Delta	Total
Total revenue	500	6900	3002	3200	*13602*
Revenue by category					
Frames	300	4100	2000	2000	*8400*
Wheels	100	1200	1000	400	*2700*
Chains	15	240	1	125	*381*
Pedals	85	1360	1	675	*2121*

case company is an industrial wholesaler of metal parts that serves the bicycle-manufacturing industry.

11.3.1   Step 1: Calculate Revenue Blueprint Using Revenue Data

This step is solely based on the supplier's explicit customer knowledge in the form of revenue data. The process is as follows.

11.3.1.1 Step 1A: document footprint size
In this initial step, we collect revenue data for all customers on the category level and feed that information into a spreadsheet, as illustrated in Table 11.1. In our case company—a wholesaler of bicycle parts—the categories are frames, wheels, chains, and pedals. As illustrated in Table 11.1, information on the revenue contributed by each of four customers is collected in such a way that each customer's data fills one column. This step captures the facts of the past and, as such, helps to document the supplier's current practices—including the supplier's best implemented practice, which is "hidden" behind the numbers. In other words, the spreadsheet serves as a representation of how capable the supplier has been in the past.

11.3.1.2 Step 1B: calculate footprint pattern
We calculate the footprint pattern (i.e., the characteristic distribution of revenue across categories) by dividing each category's revenue by the corresponding customer's total revenue (as illustrated in Table 11.2). The resulting numbers indicate the percentage of revenue that a customer allocates to a category. For instance, in our case study, 60 percent of the revenue derived from Alpha comes from sales of frames.

Typically, purchasing patterns are not the same for all customers across all categories. In our case study, Gamma does not purchase any significant number of chains or pedals. To calculate revenue blueprints, the footprint pattern must reflect the purchasing behavior of the best performing customers with regard to their purchases across all categories (i.e., where the supplier has implemented its best practice in selling across the product and service portfolio). Our work has revealed that a suitable threshold for indicating a customer's general interest in a category is 75 percent of the category's average across all customers. To calculate this threshold, we calculate the average purchasing percentage across all customers and define the threshold at 75 percent of that number (see "Average" and "Threshold" columns in Table 11.2). When we

Table 11.2   *Customers' footprint patterns and best implemented practice pattern*

Customer	Alpha	Beta	Gamma	Delta	Average	Threshold (75%)	Pattern for best implemented practice
Revenue by category							
Frames	0.60	0.59	0.67	0.63	0.62	0.47	0.60
Wheels	0.20	0.17	0.33	0.13	0.21	0.16	0.19
Chains	0.03	0.03	0.00	0.04	0.03	0.02	0.03
Pedals	0.17	0.20	0.00	0.21	0.14	0.11	0.18

apply this threshold, Gamma and Delta fail to meet certain thresholds—Gamma is below the thresholds for chains and pedals, while Delta is below the threshold for wheels. As such, the footprint pattern of the best implemented practice is determined by averaging Alpha and Beta (last row in Table 11.2), as the supplier has succeeded in substantially selling all categories to these customers. Thus, the company's best implemented practice in terms of selling the categories in relation to each other reflects the average revenue footprint pattern of the best performing customers buying across all categories.

11.3.1.3 Step 1C: calculate revenue blueprints

The best implemented practice pattern indicates the percentage of revenue derived from a customer that a category should ideally contribute. In addition to this percentage, current revenue is known for every category (as noted in a customer's footprint). Applying this percentage and a category's current revenue, we can calculate the expected total revenue for a customer by dividing the category's revenue by the category's percentage. For example, if a customer buys USD 1 million worth of goods and services in one category and that category should account for 20 percent of revenue (given the pattern for the best implemented practice), that customer should generate a total of USD 5 million. Thus, the expected total revenue is based on realized category revenue (footprint) and the best implemented practice pattern.

This calculation is performed for all categories, resulting in as many estimations of expected customer revenue as there are categories. From this list, the highest revenue is chosen as the best implemented practice (BIP) revenue. For this "BIP revenue," the distribution across categories is calculated using the best implemented practice pattern. This establishes the calculated revenue blueprint (i.e., the revenue that could be achieved in each category if the best practice is applied to a customer). The difference between the revenue footprint and the calculated revenue blueprint is the growth potential.

As illustrated in Table 11.3, we can calculate the expected total revenue based on each category. The highest score indicates the maximum expected revenue given the current revenue footprint. In our example, wheels produce the highest score for customer Alpha. Therefore, wheels are the category in which the supplier has the best implemented practice with customer Alpha. If the supplier could spread that practice across all categories, the categories would grow to the numbers indicated as the "calculated revenue blueprint," which gives rise to a future revenue estimate of USD 535,000 spread across categories with the best implemented practice footprint pattern. The last column lists the calculated growth potential for each cate-

Table 11.3   Calculated revenue blueprint and growth potential for Alpha (in USD 1000)

Customer Alpha				
Revenue by category	Revenue footprint	Revenue estimates	Calculated revenue blueprint	Calculated growth potential
Frames	300	502	319	19
Wheels	100	535	100	0
Chains	15	463	17	2
Pedals	85	463	98	13
	BIP revenue	*535*	535	35

Table 11.4   Calculated growth potential

Customer	Alpha	Beta	Gamma	Delta	Calculated growth potential
Revenue by category					
Frames	19	324	1194	304	1842
Wheels	0	185	0	321	507
Chains	2	0	172	0	175
Pedals	13	0	981	33	1027
Growth	35	509	2347	659	3550

gory, which is the difference between the footprint (achieved revenue) and the calculated blueprint. In our example, the revenue from Alpha would increase by USD 35,000 if all categories were sold to the customer to the same extent as wheels.

If we repeat this analysis for all four customers, we end up with a calculated growth potential of USD 3.55 million (Table 11.4), which corresponds to sales growth of 26 percent. This estimate is purely based on existing sales data and, thus, reflects a practice that is already implemented in the firm. It assumes that all customers will buy from all categories according to the best implemented practice pattern and that they will do so to the extent that corresponds to their current best category.

11.3.2   Step 2: Verify the Calculated Revenue Blueprint Using Customer Insights

The above calculations are based solely on historical revenue data. In order to improve the predictive power of blueprints, sales representatives need to verify the results of those calculations based on their tacit customer knowledge. Sales representatives typically reflect on such issues as:

- Will the customer buy items in all categories from the supplier? Some customers may have relevant internal capabilities (e.g., Gamma may produce chains and pedals). Others may have strong business relationships with other suppliers in certain categories and, therefore, be unwilling to change.
- Is the customer willing to allocate more business to the supplier so that the supplier can improve its share of wallet? The customers may have several suppliers, which creates an

Table 11.5   Growth potential based on verified revenue blueprints

Customer	Alpha	Beta	Gamma	Delta	Calculated growth potential
Revenue by category					
Frames	19	324	1194	304	1842
Wheels	0	185	0	321	507
Chains	2	0	0	0	2
Pedals	13	0	0	33	47
Growth	35	509	1194	659	2397

opportunity to increase the supplier's share of wallet. However, if a customer is part of an industrial conglomerate, then it might be obliged to source internally whenever possible. Sales representatives often have good insights into the current share of wallet, either because they know the volume typically ordered by a customer given its size and industry or because they have an idea about their share based on negotiations with the customer. While truly committed enthusiasts procure 100 percent from their preferred suppliers, other customers source from various suppliers. Many firms' procurement policies explicitly state the extent to which they can rely on a single supplier (e.g., a maximum of 80 percent or 40 percent). Thus, salespeople can provide current share of wallet estimates as well as estimates of how much those percentages could rise.

- Is the customer's business growing or declining? Imagine that some bicycle producers experience sales growth when their bicycles become popular, which leads to higher revenue. However, the opposite might also be true—a crisis may harm customers' businesses and demand may decrease as a result.
- Will price pressures lead to changes in revenue?
- Are there abnormalities in the pattern? In the wholesale example, one would assume that one frame, two wheels, one chain, and two pedals would be reasonable per unit. However, a customer that produces tricycles would need more wheels. Subsequently, the percentage of the wheel category would be higher.

It is typically difficult to isolate each and every argument, and allocate a precise number to every factor. Instead, salespeople observe all of the clues and issues, and they develop a tacit model of how all of those clues affect revenue.

In our example, the sales representatives know that Gamma sources chains and pedals from a sister company. Therefore, they do not expect any sales in these categories other than the occasional ad hoc purchase. The sales representatives also know that Delta buys wheels from a competitor and, based on Delta's purchases in other categories, they believe Delta could be convinced to consider purchasing wheels from the supplier. As such, the revenue blueprint and, consequently, growth potential can increase and decrease in this step. Table 11.5 illustrates the verified growth potential based on the verified blueprints for all four customers.

Although the verified growth potential drops by about one-third, additional revenue is still greater than USD 2 million, giving a growth rate of 15 percent. Figure 11.4 illustrates Gamma's footprint (grey), its calculated blueprint (white), and its verified blueprint (dotted line).

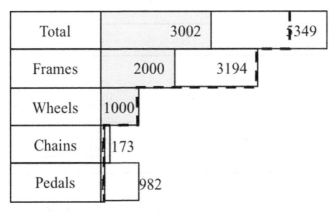

Figure 11.4   Revenue blueprint for customer Gamma

11.3.3   Step 3: Implement the Revenue Blueprints

Each customer needs to be allocated to a customer-relationship strategy. In other words, the supplier's intentions for a customer need to be clarified. For each customer, the revenue blueprint with its three elements (i.e., footprint, calculated blueprint, and verified blueprint) indicates an appropriate strategy for customer management and resource prioritization. All customers need be assigned to one of the categories, as illustrated for our example in Figure 11.5.

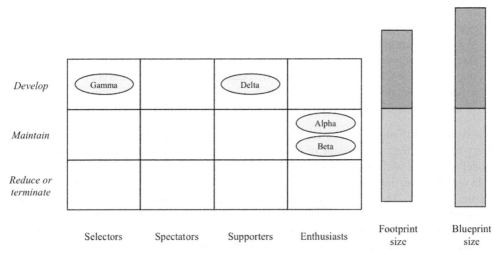

Figure 11.5   Implementation plan based on revenue blueprints

A specific customer strategy can be assigned to each customer depending on the revenue blueprint and customer insights, as the salespeople's judgements on how to sell to a customer are important. In this regard, operational sales excellence improves, as selling becomes targeted at harvesting explicitly identified revenue growth potential. Notably, our work indicates that moving customers by selling more categories from selectors to spectators to supporters to enthusiasts increases profitability by approximately 3 percentage points for each step. At the same time, revenue grows significantly. Furthermore, resources will be freed up from customers who are reduced and terminated as a result of the blueprinting process. These resources can be reallocated to further develop relationships with prioritized customers.

Figure 11.5 is derived from the revenue blueprint calculated using explicit revenue data in step 1, the verification process based on the salespeople's tacit customer insights in step 2, and the allocation of customers to specific customer strategies in step 3. It provides a unique basis for coaching salespeople, and for facilitating learning and knowledge sharing with regards to best implemented practice for realizing potential. Ongoing, direct interactions with customers based on this targeted approach will significantly add to the salespeople's tacit customer insight. Furthermore, the sharing of that knowledge through dialogues with colleagues will make best implemented practice accessible for all and, thereby, ensure accelerated and efficient realization of growth trajectories for individual customers, as presented in Table 11.5.

The customer insights used to verify the blueprints are also useful for enabling sales communications and, thereby, for securing a better conversion ratio. The process not only helps the firm understand what to sell to which customer but also how to do so. To further improve sales efforts, tacit customer knowledge can be transformed into explicit customer knowledge by developing customer segments that are stable, intuitively understandable, and effective with customers (Andersen & Ritter, 2008). This will further support revenue growth.

11.4 CONCLUSIONS

In this chapter, we propose a three-step process for revenue blueprinting as a way to utilize customer data and customer insights for revenue growth. This process is easy to implement, inexpensive, and data- and insight-driven. Moreover, it immediately produces results by shifting salespeople's attention towards best implemented practice and offers a high likelihood of success in harvesting revenue from competitors.

Based on our experience, the revenue-blueprinting process triggers immediate results, and leads to increased revenue and customer profitability. While this process typically reveals significant revenue growth potential, it is based on conservative rules. For instance, it only considers best *implemented* practice. In other words, it is based on the firm's revenue achievements. To further ensure the development of realistic revenue blueprints, the process includes salespeople's judgements based on their tacit customer insights. The revenue-blueprinting process is summarized in Figure 11.6.

The aim of this chapter is to illustrate the power of using data to develop businesses and the power of combining explicit customer knowledge with tacit customer knowledge. The approach to revenue blueprinting presented here can be extended to include more data about customers (e.g., profitability, strategic importance, cost to serve), the market (e.g., general market growth, regulation, technological trends), and selected competitors (e.g., competitive strategies, innovation pipelines). Although such extensions are possible, they will add complexity. Our suggestion is to start simply as described in this chapter, build up experience, and then enlarge the pool of inputs.

> 1. Calculate revenue blueprint using revenue data
>   *1A Document footprint size*
>   *1B Calculate footprint pattern*
>   *1C Calculate revenue blueprints*

> 2. Verify the calculated revenue blueprint using customer insights

> 3. Implement the revenue blueprint

Figure 11.6   The revenue-blueprinting process

We acknowledge that finding new customers and developing new offerings are relevant growth opportunities that suppliers should consider in their strategy-making processes (Ansoff, 1957). However, for the purposes of this chapter and the proposed data-driven growth analysis, we only consider a supplier's existing customers and offerings, as data on these factors are readily available.

Most of our work has been with industrial firms. However, the method presented here will also work in business-to-consumer settings, such as those found in the supermarket and online retail fashion sectors. Likewise, theme parks and packaged holiday travel are areas in which growth blueprinting may be readily applicable.

REFERENCES

Andersen, H., & Ritter, T. (2008). *Inside the Customer Universe: How to Build Unique Customer Insight for Profitable Growth and Market Leadership*. Chichester: Wiley & Sons.

Ansoff, I.H. (1957). Strategies for diversification. *Harvard Business Review*, 35(5), 113–24.

Bitner, M.J., Ostrom, A.L., & Morgan, N. (2008). Service blueprinting: a practical technique for service innovation. *California Management Review*, 50(3), 66–94.

Campbell, A.J. (2003). Creating customer knowledge competence: managing customer relationship management programs strategically. *Industrial Marketing Management*, 32(5), 375–83.

Cooil, B., Keiningham, T.L., Aksoy, L., & Hsu, M. (2007). A longitudinal analysis of customer satisfaction and share of wallet: investigating the moderating effect of customer characteristics. *Journal of Marketing*, 71(1), 67–83.

Cui, A.S., & Wu, F. (2016). Utilizing customer knowledge in innovation: antecedents and impact of customer involvement on new product performance. *Journal of the Academy of Marketing Science*, 44(4), 516–38.

Feldman, M.S., & Pentland, B.T. (2003). Reconceptualizing organizational routines as a source of flexibility and change. *Administrative Science Quarterly*, 48(1), 94–118.

Ganesan, S., Malter, A.J., & Rindfleisch, A. (2005). Does distance still matter? Geographic proximity and new product development. *Journal of Marketing*, 69(10), 44–60.

Jaworski, B.J., & Kohli, A.K. (1993). Market orientation: antecedents and consequences. *Journal of Marketing*, 57(3), 53–70.

Li, T., & Calantone, R.J. (1998). The impact of market knowledge competence on new product advantage: conceptualization and empirical examination. *Journal of Marketing*, 62(4), 13.

Nagji, B., & Tuff, G. (2012). Managing your innovation portfolio. *Harvard Business Review*, 90(5), 66–74.

Nonaka, I. (1994). A dynamic theory of organizational knowledge creation. *Organization Science*, 5(1), 14–37.

Ritter, T., & Geersbro, J. (2018). Multidexterity in customer relationship management. Managerial implications and a research agenda. *Industrial Marketing Management*, 69, 74–9.

Shostack, G.L. (1984). Designing services that deliver. *Harvard Business Review*, 62(1), 133–9.

Subramaniam, M., & Venkatraman, N. (2001). Determinants of transnational new product development capability: testing the influence of transferring and deploying tacit overseas knowledge. *Strategic Management Journal*, 22(4), 359–78.

Varadarajan, R. (2010). Strategic marketing and marketing strategy: domain, definition, fundamental issues and foundational premises. *Journal of the Academy of Marketing Science*, 38(2), 119–40.

PART IV

Transformations: getting there the right way

12. Transforming small and medium-sized enterprises (SMEs) to digitally enabled landscapes

Bård Tronvoll, Christian Kowalkowski and David Sörhammar

12.1 INTRODUCTION

Small and medium-sized enterprises (SMEs) are facing new challenges when novel technologies rearrange traditional business relationships and blurring market boundaries. These subsequent changes have fundamentally altered how organizations create value as well as how they collaborate and think about their businesses (Tronvoll et al. 2020). In seeking to exploit new technological and market opportunities, firms engage in digital servitization (Sklyar et al. 2019b). Digital servitization is defined as the transformation in processes, capabilities, and offerings within industrial firms and their associate ecosystems to progressively create, deliver, and capture increased service value arising from a broad range of enabling digital technologies (Sjödin et al. 2020). The main reason for SMEs to engage in digital servitization is to achieve a competitive advantage, and also better flexibility, costs and time savings, better product reliability, higher sales and profits, and an increase in customer satisfaction are essential factors (Kaňovská and Tomášková 2018).

SMEs have, for a long time, been engaged in servitization (Kowalkowski et al. 2013b); that is, transitioning from the sales of relatively uncomplicated goods and basic services to more complex, result-oriented solutions, where the product is ultimately substituted with a service. Traditionally, servitization is recognized as a multifaceted (Kowalkowski et al. 2012a), incremental, and emergent process (Palo et al. 2019). However, digitalization is dramatically changing how firms operate and create value in ways that are fast-paced and potentially disruptive (Nagy et al. 2016; Simmons et al. 2013). As a consequence, the disruption is fundamentally altering business models, challenging industry boundaries, and organizational identities (Ng and Wakenshaw 2017; Svahn et al. 2017; Tronvoll et al. 2020). The growth opportunities enabled by digital technologies challenge firms that are finding it problematic to shift "from selling equipment and aftersales service to selling digital solutions" (Parida et al. 2019, p. 14). The technological development drives digital servitization (Kohtamäki et al. 2019; Sklyar et al. 2019b) to support the firm's transformation from a product-centric to a (digital) service-centric business model (Ardolino et al. 2018; Coreynen et al. 2017; Vendrell-Herrero et al. 2017).

Most studies of servitization and digital servitization focus on large multinational firms (e.g. Gebauer and Kowalkowski 2012; Raddats and Easingwood 2010; Ulaga and Reinartz 2011), even though these challenges occur in all types of firms, including SMEs (Gebauer et al. 2012). In comparison with large multinational firms that work in strong networks, SMEs struggle on their way to digitalization. Their digital maturity is below average, and the firms are working on strategies to improve their competitive ability (Gierlich et al. 2019). An empirical investigation of European manufacturing firms even concludes that small and medium-sized suppliers are influenced as much as larger firms (Lay et al. 2010). With their limited size and resources (Greene and Storey 2010), SMEs need a different approach to transform into digital servitization as they are affected differently than larger firms (Gebauer et al. 2012). Despite a few studies of SMEs servitizing (e.g. Gebauer et al. 2012; Kowalkowski et al. 2013b; Malleret 2006), no explicit investigations consider how SMEs manage to transform in the digital landscape and become digitally servitized. As servitization research increasingly explores the opportunities afforded by digital technologies, focusing mainly on digitalization related to large firms (e.g. Kowalkowski et al. 2013a; Vendrell-Herrero et al. 2017), this research has sparked calls for more research on the digital aspects of servitization (Parida et al. 2019), especially related to challenges faced by SMEs. However, there is little available guidance on *how* SMEs can employ digital technologies to become servitized and develop new offerings and, thus, business models.

To better understand the abilities needed for successful digital servitization and transforming SMEs, it is essential to develop an understanding of the tasks facing these firms. It it useful to clarify the organizational transformation needed to exploit opportunities for digital service growth. Rather than focusing on new technologies and resources per se, this chapter focuses on how SMEs can successfully transform and employ strategies to gain competitive advantage. More specifically, it employs Tronvoll et al.'s (2020) investigation of organizational transformation to digital servitization as a starting point to provide valuable insights. This study considers three transformational shifts in understanding the challenges for SMEs when working with digital servitization: *dematerialization*, *identity*, and *collaboration*. SMEs' limited internal resources and comparatively weaker market positions already force them to engage in finding niches and create relationships with other actors in the service ecosystem. Specifically, we investigate how SMEs transform in the digital landscape to stay competitive and to enable service provision.

Overall, this chapter aims to illuminate the challenges SMEs are facing in transforming to digital servitization. First, we describe digital servitization. Second, we provide a thorough explanation of the transformational shifts that firms need to undergo to adapt to a digital landscape. Third, we clarify the characteristics and conditions of SMEs. Finally, we discuss the implication of the digital transformation on SMEs.

12.2   THEORETICAL BACKGROUND

Recent academic interest in how digital technologies drive the organizational transformation to service centricity reflects the emergence of major technological innovations (Sklyar et al. 2019a). Technological development has fueled the possibilities of novel ways of doing business, enabling servitization to embrace technology. Earlier studies of servitization have focused on *digitization*, which Ng and Wakenshaw (2017, p. 3) defined as "the conversion of analog information ... to a digital format so that the information can be processed, stored, and transmitted through digital circuits, devices, and networks." Digitization has facilitated servitization for decades, as in software systems for inventory handling and networks for condition monitoring (Anderson and Narus 1998; Macdonald et al. 2016; Neu and Brown 2005). However, successful digital servitization depends on *digitalization*, which refers to the use of new digital technologies to enable significant business improvements (Svahn et al. 2017) and includes socio-technical structures that go beyond technical processes (Lusch and Nambisan 2015). The core of digitalization—the transferability of any object as data—is both enabled and constrained by human actions (Hinings et al. 2018). The transferability of data distinguishes digitalization from other new technologies (Klötzer and Pflaum 2017), as the adoption process must permeate the whole organization.

Like digitalization, digital servitization is commonly seen to involve complex processes of organizational changes (Vendrell-Herrero et al. 2017). According to Coreynen et al. (2017), digital servitization can be viewed from two perspectives, where new technologies enhance either operational efficiency, resource allocation, and transparency or facilitate new types of customer interaction and closer integration. The integration of digital technologies affords opportunities for developing customized value propositions based on higher-quality services and relationships (Rust and Ming-Hui 2014). Firms can use digital data streams to provide integrated customer support, to increase the automation of support processes, facilitating a shift from a reactive break-and-fix approach to proactive service culture and ultimately enabling customers to solve their problems (Bilgeri et al. 2019; Sklyar et al. 2019a). Ulaga and Reinartz (2011) reported that service-related data processing and interpretation is a critical capability for pursuing servitization. However, the impact of the change will depend on the firm's service strategy and its capacity to exploit digital technology as an enabler of advanced service provision and a catalyst for servitization (Kowalkowski et al. 2013a). The integration of digital technologies supports deeper relationships with customers and more extensive and advanced services (Penttinen and Palmer 2007); the more advanced the service, the more critical it becomes to handle both perspectives. Despite this, digitalization requires that firms—small, medium-sized, and large—transform from being grounded in goods to become grounded in service and enabled by technology.

12.3   CHARACTERISTICS AND CONDITIONS OF SMES

The SME sector occupies an essential place in the economy as the driving force of business, growth, innovation, and competitiveness. It also plays a decisive role in job creation and generally is a factor of social stability and economic development. In the European Union, SMEs are the backbone of the economy, employing more than 87 million EU citizens. SMEs generate every second newly created job and produce nearly 60 percent of the GDP of the European Union (EC 2012). According to the European Union, SMEs are defined as enterprises that have at most 250 employees and an annual turnover not exceeding €50 million. Other sources define SMEs as businesses with fewer than 500 employees (Audretsch 1999) or even give different values for different sectors.

In the pursuit of digital service growth, various challenges or barriers hinder the businesses' success. Based on previous literature, there are five typical barriers for SMEs to succeed with digital servitization.

- *Technology issues*. Technology is core to digital servitization (Sklyar et al. 2019b), which most often is implemented in complex cyber-physical systems enabled by the internet of things, big data, cloud computing platforms, 3-D printing, mobile devices, mixed and augmented reality, advanced manufacturing solutions, and artificial intelligence. SMEs often face technological problems related to their offerings since the inclusion of digital technologies may necessitate a different design and business model.
- *Organizational issues*. Strategy and not technology should drive digital transformation. The strengths of digital technologies do not lie in the technology itself but rather on how firms integrate them to transform their business and exploit their strategic benefits (Kane et al. 2016). Digitization represents a radical change, although people have an inherent unwillingness to change, or are indifferent to the need to change. This is an essential cultural barrier to change and is often underestimated and not recognized by firms (von Leipzig et al. 2017). Servitization often implies significant cultural changes in SMEs (Peillona et al. 2018), and digitalization adds another level of complexity, thus reinforcing the depth of the needed cultural transformation.
- *Human resources issues*. Digitalization significantly increases the complexity, abstraction, and problem-solving skills needed by all employees which become a major barrier to the digitalization (Lerch and Gotsch 2015). Digital competence, as the ability to use digital technology effectively, is a prerequisite for the enhancement of digitalization. The recruitment of data scientists and other digital-literate employees is oftentimes a challenge for large manufacturing firms (Tronvoll et al. 2020) but given the limited resources of SMEs, they face an even greater challenge to build a diverse competence pool (Kowalkowski et al. 2013b).
- *Customer issues*. Customers' needs, ambiguity, hazy value propositions, and difficulty to convey benefits are among the major barriers for digital transformation (Klein et al. 2018). Customers fear the loss of control over information, privacy violations, security concerns, and security of access to corporate systems (Klein et al. 2018). Moreover, digital servitization needs customer insights in order to develop complex service offerings, which customers are often reluctant to provide (Raja et al. 2017).
- *Financial issues*. Financial strengths to acquire necessary technical and human resources as well as the strength to adopt digital technologies (Mittal et al. 2018) become vital. A stable and reliable infrastructure must support digital service offerings in order to be financially viable (Lerch and Gotsch 2015). As compared with large firms, SMEs generally lack the financial resources to make major investments, which makes them more dependent on other actors in their business networks (Kowalkowski et al. 2013b).

While SMEs are not able to exploit economies of scale at the same order of magnitude as big enterprises can (Audretsch 1999), they have the advantage of flat hierarchies and thus of being more flexible. A study by Kowalkowski (2013b) shows that this flexibility is a competitive advantage of SMEs when servitizing, as compared with larger competitors. Also, SMEs do not change their managers as often as large firms and, therefore, can concentrate on long-term strategies (Wang et al. 2007). SMEs often have high-specialized know-how in a specific area

Table 12.1   *Empirical studies of digital servitization in SMEs and large firms*

Authors	Findings
Hracs (2013)	Local firms adapt better than multinational, local operations during the technological disruption period.
Myrthianos et al. (2014)	The analysis indicates that multinational operations adapt better to disruptions than local firms ... music multinationals achieve, on average, a 7.43% greater ROA than SMEs.
Lerch and Gotsch (2015)	Large enterprises are more likely to have the resources and competencies needed to create and support digital components and digital services. SMEs often do not have IT service divisions and thus are not able to provide individualized digital solutions.
Peillona and Dubruc (2019)	SMEs that started to digitalize their offerings, face two main difficulties, internal and external. The first one is internal and organizational since they often struggle with the practical organization either of the tools they implement or of the digitalized services they offer. The second one is external and customer-related: their customers are often reluctant to give them access to their data, due to privacy and security concerns.
Paiola (2019)	The study shows that the position in the value chain and the sale model are critical variables for manufacturing SMEs in digital servitization. This has a profound impact on managerial considerations regarding the future shape of the business for every SME involved in the transformation, since the ability to govern the change instead of being disrupted by it will depend on how firms will use products, services, and data to influence (and even change) its own and other players' positions in the ecosystem.
European Commission (Consulted July 2020)	Digitalization and digital transformation are even more challenging for manufacturing SMEs, who need to follow large firms or risk being left out of digital supply chains.

that could be utilized in their service provision. In the SME sector, the role of management is always derived from the size of the organization and the position of the owner. The primary importance of the management function is created or at least affected by all management activities related to resources, competencies, and processes. The size of the organization, however, does not necessarily reduce the level of strategic management importance as a transformation to become digitally servitized. In large firms, responsibility for strategic management involves many employees and managers, but in SMEs, the primary strategic manager role is usually undertaken by the owner or managing director.

Compared with large firms, SMEs usually lack the necessary resources—staff, competences, facilities, and financial capabilities to provide all kinds of services that their customers require. SMEs often lack the resources to look at new avenues outside of their core competencies, and they have an in-built overall reliance on other firms in the network (Gebauer et al. 2012) and the resources needed to create and provide service (Fischer et al. 2010). Despite the differences, all firms, large or small, are embedded in networks of interconnected relationships that form a web of interactions constituting the service ecosystem. Within their service ecosystem, firms create value by configuring and integrating their resources into distinct, specific, and integrated structures (Corsaro et al. 2012; Möller and Rajala 2007). Such service ecosystems could serve an important purpose in enabling SMEs to provide service.

Few empirical studies have investigated the differences between SMEs and large firms and their digital servitization process, and these studies are somewhat mixed in their finding of who is best to accomplish a transformation to digital servitization (Table 12.1). Myrthianos et al. (2014), Lerch and Gotsch (2015), and the European Commission (Consulted July

2020) found that large firms are best in adapting to digital servitization, while Hracs (2013) found that SMEs do best. Peillona and Dubruc (2019) and Paiola (2019), on the other hand, found several obstacles for SMEs to succeed in digital transformation. While these hurdles to various degrees may apply also to larger firms, issues such as access to customer data is, *ceteris paribus*, more challenging for SMEs due to asymmetric power relationships with larger customers.

12.4 TRANSFORMATIONAL SHIFTS IN THE DIGITAL LANDSCAPE

The transformation to digital servitization is challenging for any organization since it demands a new way of thinking about identity, resources, and collaboration (Tronvoll et al. 2020). In their study, Tronvoll et al. (2020) identified three aggregated themes—dematerialization, identity, and collaboration—reflecting the transformational shifts a firm must make when pursuing digital servitization. The transformation highlights the dynamics of the change process. However, as the transformation to digital servitization is ultimately conditioned by dematerialization—disconnecting information from the physical—this shift is especially significant. By enabling the capture, use, and representation of data in myriad ways, dematerialization facilitates knowledge dispersal, affording novel opportunities for intra-firm and inter-firm innovation and collaboration. This emphasizes how digital servitization changes organizational identity and culture (Kohtamäki et al. 2019; Parida et al. 2019), driving the firm to a reactive-to-creative shift based on innovation, matching customer needs, and extensive cooperation among multiple internal and external partners. Rather than incremental, reactive change only, successful digital servitization depends on a systematic and coordinated change in the firm's service organization through dematerialization, identity, and collaboration.

12.4.1 Dematerialization

Recent changes have shown that economic value may evolve from material "stuff" to digital information; that is, software or data (Quah 1996). Thus, digitization has reduced material intensity in absolute terms. Berkhout and Hertin (2004, p. 916) remark that "the digital economy is embedded in the material and economic world and physical infrastructures, both it is own and those it coordinates and motivates."

Digitalization creates a separation between data and physical manifestations such as machines and interfaces through what Normann (2001) referred to as liquidization, which makes it possible to transfer and multiply representations of any digital object (Hinings et al. 2018). Normann (2001) emphasizes two dematerialization mechanisms—*liquification* and *unbundleability*. Liquification refers to dematerialization through the separation of information from the physical world, allowing it to be easily moved about. A case in point is the remote monitoring and control of equipment, which provides new service opportunities for companies. The liquidization of resources may take managers by surprise, as they find there are more data available than they could handle in any given situation. For SMEs, in particular, having the capability to automate data processing and analytics may be important due to the limited human resources. The dematerialization of resources creates a state of abundance, and data can no longer be regarded as a scarce and inimitable resource. This insight drives a fundamental shift from the perceived scarcity of resources to recognize them as abundance. Firms realize that a change of mindset is needed, rather than possession and protection, plentiful raw data invite sharing with trusted actors in the service ecosystem. As a growing number of managers and employees realize that there is plenty of data, a creative data-centered understanding is promoted. Importantly, the dematerialization fuels the possibilities in combining new digitally servitized resources and enables actors to begin to identify data-related opportunities. Only then might the organization start to migrate toward data centricity (e.g. Svahn et al. 2017). The dematerialization shift is marking a new departure for the firm, its partners, and all involved actors in the service ecosystem.

Dematerialization is the base where information is separated from the physical world (Normann 2001), and as a result, generates an abundance of data. This means that data mining and analytics capability becomes an essential resource for developing advanced algorithms and knowledge. The ability to manage this abundance of data—for example, as input to machine learning systems—is crucial for future competitiveness. The strength of digitalization is that information does not just become dematerialized, but instead, "the information can be moved about and remanifested in many different ways" (Normann 2001, p. 33). Unbundleability, on the other hand, refers to the separation of activities well defined and held together in time and place by the actor. The opportunity for a provider to remotely analyze product and process data and thereby provide fleet management services on behalf of the customer is one such example. The dematerialization through liquification and unbundleability promotes rebundle-ability, which allows the creation of new densities capable of being combined with customer resources to create a new configuration of values. This implies an active and co-creative role of customers and other market actors in the establishment of the service ecosystem (Michel et al. 2008). Normann (2001, p. 6) suggests, "today's value-creating context allows a much more 'dense' packaging together of various actors into different patterns of 'co-production' of value." These concepts can be used to explore the shaping and fluidity of markets through the reconfiguration of value-creating service ecosystems. A prerequisite for "reframing" the overall system is through means of which "prime movers" redefine their own and other actors' roles in the system (Normann 2001).

The digital landscape is changing the view on how interaction takes place not only between human actors but also mobile devices, enabled through the internet. Today, business-to-business (B2B) customers may never physically meet their service providers, but choose to engage with them digitally, as in the case of automatic software updates, remote monitoring, and order tracking. At the industrial level, the internet has already had a disruptive effect on business markets, sharply reducing the costs of sensors and data storage and processing, which permits the decoupling of machine software from hardware throughout the socio-technical system, using "unbundling, dematerialization, liquidity, and density."

12.4.2 Identity

The identity shift relates to the focal firm's identity; that is, "who we are as an organization" (Gioia et al. 2013, p. 123). A transformational shift drives cultural openness to digital technologies and redefines the firm as a digital technological organization. Rather than refining and exploiting existing resources to improve overall efficiency, the firm must focus on exploring novel ways of working facilitated by technology. The identity transformational shift also manifests in changing the employee mindset. Like other servitization processes, influential service culture, and customer focus (Story et al. 2017) are essential for the successful development and adoption of the digital service offerings. However, changing identity is oftentimes one of the most challenging aspects of the service transformation. As one manager of a company explained: "Deep down in our heart, we are a manufacturing company. We produce stuff. We move boxes. It's our DNA" (Kowalkowski and Ulaga 2017, p. 22). In line with the existing servitization literature (Fischer et al. 2010), the entrepreneurial and innovative mindset inside the firm helps to leverage radical change. However, the digital servitization process differs from a more traditional servitization journey in one crucial respect: the central importance of an agile mindset to cope with the fast-paced development life cycle of software and digital infrastructure. Employees' ability to adopt these novel ways of working is a crucial issue.

Identity is the essential concept to any member of a society or an organization to invoke, helping to make sense, and explain action (Gioia et al. 2013). The change of identity challenges the individual themself, the relationship between individuals in the organization, and the organization itself, both in terms of organizational culture and the relationship to other actors in the service ecosystem. Identity is defined as those features of an organization that, in the eyes of its members, are central to the organization's character or "self-image," making the organization distinctive from other similar organizations, and are viewed as having continuity over time (Albert and Whetten 1985). Features that are central for identity are manifested as fundamental values, labels, products, services, or practices, and so on and are deemed to be important characteristics of organizational self-definition of "who we are."

To understand identity as an essential issue of digital transformation, we agree with Gioia et al. (2013) who view identity as a social construction, holding that organizational identity is a self-referential concept defined by the members of an organization to articulate who they are as an organization to themselves as well as outsiders. This view focuses primarily on the labels and meanings that members use to describe themselves and their core attributes. Since identity is understood as central, enduring, and distinctive to an organization, this is of particular interest in the process of transforming the organization in the digital landscape. The stability of identity over time as an enduring identity proposition is contrasted by the position that sees identity as more changeable as a dynamic identity proposition (Gioia et al. 2013). Albert and Whetten (1985) discussed whether identity is actually enduring or having continuity and thus can change within relatively short periods. There is sizeable empirical evidence which affirms that identity often changes over relatively short time horizons, albeit perhaps in subtle ways. The acknowledgment is that inside members tend to perceive identity as stable, even when it is changing over time because they continue to use the same labels to describe their identity even as the meanings of those labels change without conscious awareness. In other words, the labels are stable, but their meanings are malleable—thus leading to the appearance of stability even as identity evolves (Gioia et al. 2000).

Organizational identity may also impact the way firms approach and interact in inter-firm arrangements as part of a service ecosystem (Nätti et al. 2014). Organizational identity may shape how an organization deals with the transformation to digital servitization, its partners, how the service ecosystem is governed, how consensus is reached, and how relationships are ended. Some studies demonstrate the importance of network behaviors on improving both relationships and performance (Kohtamäki et al. 2013; Walter et al. 2006) and the role of organizational identity as a central component in determining such behaviors in strategic networks through managerial perceptions (Clark et al. 2010).

12.4.3 Collaboration

Many large firms are traditionally organized in separate departments leading to siloes that reflect a reactive mentality based on hierarchy and authority. Change agents argue that this mindset is hindering attempts to harness the business potential of digitalization and, more worryingly, the creation of service-centric value propositions based on customers' actual needs. To support, facilitate, and act on specific data-related opportunities, firms need to break the silo mentality. This required multi-actor coupling (Raja et al. 2018) between front-end and back-end employees as well as general management. The traditional silo perspective on authority has the potential to hinder the development and adoption of digital servitization. A service champion who carries and personifies the transformation and has experience and credibility helps to drive such change and bring different stakeholders together.

The dematerialization of data brings firms closer both operationally and strategically to its partners and customers. The generation, collection, utilization, and analysis of the data make the partners knowledgeable about their customers. As a result, the creation of reciprocal value propositions based on data-related opportunities and customer needs among the service ecosystem partners is vital. Research findings show that accepting reciprocal value propositions aligns relevant stakeholders and improves coordination and collaboration (Kowalkowski et al. 2012b). Tronvoll et al. (2020) show that the success of transformational shifts depends on interdepartmental communication within the firm and open communication among network partners, including customers. Such multi-actor coupling helps to consolidate the reciprocal value proposition among different stakeholders (Nambisan et al. 2017). Novel reciprocal value propositions in the form of new digital services depend on collaboration among diverse actors in the service ecosystem. Harmful uses, for instance, by creating a value proposition based on the data toward the customer's competitors, could immediately ruin not only the business relationship but also the customer's competitive situation.

The shift to become digitally servitized drives collaboration among actors by moving the firm from a silo-based command hierarchy toward multi-actor collaboration underpinned by collective agreements, trust, and accountability. Closer dialogue and in-depth knowledge of customers' overarching needs play an important part in the collaboration, as the value proposition is aligned to the maturity of the individual customer. This entails a focus on teamwork within and across organizations in the service ecosystem and requires an open, trustful conversation about how to use technology to facilitate value co-creation among service ecosystem actors. By collaborating, the actors can scale digitalization projects to leverage complexity and save resources (Coreynen et al. 2017). The collaboration among service ecosystem actors enables us to set new resources free, leading to an enhanced network effect. Collaboration among network partners will overcome barriers of digitalization (Becker et al. 2018; Coreynen et al. 2017) and form strategic alliances with partners in the service ecosystems.

12.5   THE DIGITAL TRANSFORMATION IN SMEs

SMEs are facing different conditions and challenges when trying to transform into the digital landscape due to their level of digitalization, which is below the industry average (Bley et al. 2016; Bogner et al. 2016). Barriers to successful digitalization for SMEs are found in lack of innovative culture, limited time and human capital, financial constraints, and limited managerial resources (Bernaert et al. 2014). Despite all the challenges, it is vital to understand the transformational shifts that SMEs most likely have to undergo in pursuing digital servitization and how they can adapt to the emerging digital landscape. This chapter reflects upon the three transformational shifts identified by Tronvoll et al. (2020) and what the firms have to undergo as part of this process. The shifts illustrate how the firm can utilize digitalization to rethink value creation, collaboration, and servitization of the market offerings. We are aligned with Tronvoll et al. (2020) that transformations within these overarching strategic areas represent shifts in how the firm and its network partners foster dematerialization, identity, and collaboration. These three shifts seem to be the cornerstones of successful digital servitization, each demanding a change in focus and mindset to drive the change. During these shifts, SMEs are also facing other barriers compared with large firms, such as less resources; however, we argue that SMEs are better able to grasp the opportunities the transformation may offer.

The shift driving dematerialization requires, typically, an innovative culture that enables the organization to be creative in how service can arise, not only from the current narrow product focus but as a holistic view where data is in the center. The biggest challenge for SMEs, due to their less available resources compared with larger firms, is to manage the decoupling needed in the dematerialization process. Also, the decoupling entails a mind-shift on how to look upon the existing products and launch new solutions based on data and not on the physical appearance. The shift from a product focus to data focus underpins the shift in data scarcity to data abundance, which can be eased by transformative technologies such as artificial intelligence and predictive analytics. New datasets based on replicated and (re)distributed structures, at a marginal cost, enable innovative service to enhance competitive advantage. In most cases, SMEs are not "early adopters," mainly because of the fear of investing in the wrong technologies or adopting inapt practices. SMEs have to learn fast about emerging technologies and digital practices to compete (Fallera and Feldmüller 2015) with the large firms who have already begun their digital servitization journey.

Second is driving a new identity that is more entrepreneurial, accommodating both service-centricity and technological innovation—two facets that are often difficult to reconcile (e.g. Perks et al. 2017). The identity shift includes rethinking commercial advantage by recognizing the opportunities of digitalization, and challenging the firm to facilitate change by establishing innovative structures and cultural openness to novel uses of technology. SMEs can advance a clear, shared, and convincing digital vision for the organization and encourage the ecosystem partners to join in this effort. Even though SMEs have a smaller amount of resources to establish a digital vision, it is crucial that the leaders promote a new mindset. The greater openness and transparency enabled by digitalization arguably makes this more critical than in traditional organizations, and leaders must learn how to leverage the firm's inherent abilities and practices to shape the new mindset. In particular, it becomes crucial to build in an agile mindset, as digital services are primarily conditioned by fast-paced software development and digital infrastructure life cycles. To manage this, the firm often needs new or sometimes radically different knowledge and competences. Thus, the firm must often recruit new people to follow up and monitor the data collection and management to find digital market offerings. While competitive advantage may previously have been dependent on superior expertise in the firm's core business areas, the need in a digitally servitized environment is for business analytic competences. This will challenge SMEs even more than large firms, and their identity shift might be even harder.

The third shift drives changes in the collaboration; that is, firms need to rethink the way they collaborate. The SMEs should have an advantage in this shift given they are already specialized and used to collaborating with other firms. Furthermore, the shift to digital servitization may need even closer integration with other service ecosystem partners. The specialization seems to be even more critical and requires that the SME establishes closer alliances with several firms in the service ecosystem. Tighter integration also requires sharing data and information, challenging the collaboration in a new and different manner. Furthermore, data science capabilities (algorithm development, cloud computing, cybersecurity, and so on) are crucial yet scarce resources and are difficult and costly for most SMEs to develop in-house, which makes collaboration even more important as compared with "traditional" servitization. Existing literature points out that to start collaborating, partners must recognize a potential gain (Dodgson 1993). However, the firm's motivation for collaboration varyies from the avoidance of external threats to attaining legitimacy and sharing the risk (Oliver 1990). Independent of the reasons for collaboration, the advantages gained are vital because actors in the service ecosystem need to team up to achieve goals that are unreachable alone (Huxham 1993). While SMEs usually primarily depend heavily on other actors in the service ecosystem to achieve success, participation in new value constellations can enable them to obtain new capabilities and develop new services. Kowalkowski et al. (2013b) find that such collaboration can help SMEs to start charging for their services and the new value constellation. Besides, SMEs may also harness some of their advantages to spur service growth, as compared with larger firms, including a more entrepreneurial culture, a more flexible and agile organization, greater proximity to customers and network partners, and better inter-firm adaptability. This becomes very visible when it comes to digital servitization as the entire service ecosystem needs to transform as a collaborative unit (Tronvoll et al. 2020).

12.6   MANAGERIAL IMPLICATIONS

As these three transformational shifts address vastly different aspects of the firm, the managerial conditions will also be summarized in three different processes. During each transformational shift, different steps are suggested that can be taken to improve the firm's likelihood of success to accomplish digital servitization.

12.6.1   Dematerialization

- Step 1: Get things online by using wireless sensors that log real-time information about the firm's products. This gives the firm a quick and easy digital overview and notification that the product causes something out of the ordinary—for example, identify water leakage, unusual machine vibrations, and so on

- Step 2: Analyze the data by using business intelligence tools. After collecting data, the firm can gain insight into the customer's use of the products by studying and comparing the numbers. By comparing data over time and space, the firm can more easily see connections that can provide more appropriate routines or a better understanding of essential processes.
- Step 3: Integrate the different data streams into the business intelligence system even though the data is collected from different vendors.
- Step 4: Do advanced analysis and machine learning based on (big) data. This gives opportunities for more advanced offerings and a possibility for changing the firm's business model.

12.6.2 Organizational Identity

- Step 1: Collect data and get employees' interpretations of artifacts and their symbolic significance.
- Step 2: Analyze the organizational members and find patterns that point to specific values and norms. Every organizational culture is unique. By mapping, the organization will reveal the culture of power, personal culture, culture of tasks, and role culture as well as the customer or user cultures, depending on the contact the organization has with its surroundings.
- Step 3: Revealing patterns to more profound underlying beliefs, basic assumptions, and symbolic meaning helps to shift the organizational culture toward a digital servitization transformation. The manager can influence the organizational culture and identity in different ways; for example, by enforcing diverse rituals and ceremonies in the organization, through storytelling to bring to life the organization's values, using metaphors to simplify a complicated everyday life and establish organizational myths through a symbolic and value-based leadership.

12.6.3 Collaboration

- Step 1: Sharing information, experiences, and knowledge about the service offerings as well as knowledge of contextual matters to network partners. An essential motivation for collaboration is to strengthen the professional environment among engaged stakeholders.
- Step 2: Develop a common problem understanding and knowledge translation. Each network partner gives its reflection on future collaboration, so the network possesses the same situational picture.
- Step 3: Change in practice and behavior in the industry sector. Collaboration is often complex and resource-intensive, especially if there are many small businesses involved. The inter-organizational and digital collaboration will lead to changed practices in working methods, which in turn makes it important to focus on the organizational culture.
- Step 4: Development of common goals, strategies, and measures. To find common solutions and to prepare a set of activities will benefit the network and its partners better than if the individual firms had each prepared on their own. Among the collaborating partners, specific priorities or choices must be made.

- Step 5: Strategic anchoring. The various network partners must gain ownership of the agreed-upon strategies and tactics. They must be anchored across the management, and they must be able to translate the strategy into a specific and realizable action plan.

12.7   CONCLUSIONS

SMEs have the precondition to become digitally servitized and face the new digital landscape because of their general ability to change and find niches. In a smaller firm, the degree of bureaucracy is usually lower, meaning that decisions can be made faster, and the consequences of the choices may be more predictable and possible to foresee. SMEs have their most substantial possibilities to collaborate and coordinate activities together with other actors.

The biggest challenge for SMEs is to make the dematerialization shift because it usually requires a higher level of technical awareness and financial strength, and many SMEs are often missing either the technical facilities, technical competencies, or financial strength. In the process of dematerialization, systems are needed that can collect, store, and analyze big data and innovative culture to bring that data into commercial solutions for the customers. Also, shifting the identity might be hard for SMEs, even though they have fewer employees than the global firms typically studied. SMEs are often organizations with a clan culture (Cameron and Quinn 2011) and this influential organizational culture has been proven to be more resistant to change. However, the SMEs' strong point is that they are closer to the customer and thus have a better understanding of their customers' (and customers' customers) needs. Being more flexible and nimble, if needed, they might find a way to overcome the clan culture and focus more on a collaborative organizational culture together will their service ecosystem partners.

REFERENCES

Albert, Stuart and David A. Whetten (1985), "Organizational identity". *Research in Organizational Behavior, 7,* 263.

Anderson, James C. and James A. Narus (1998), "Business marketing: understand what customers value". *Harvard Business Review, 76*(6), 53–65.

Ardolino, Marco, Mario Rapaccini, Nicola Saccani, Paolo Gaiardelli, Giovanni Crespi and Carlo Ruggeri (2018), "The role of digital technologies for the service transformation of industrial companies". *International Journal of Production Research, 56*(6), 2116–32. doi: 10.1080/00207543.2017.1324224

Audretsch, David B. (1999). "Small firms and efficiency". In Z.J. Acs (ed.), *Are Small Firms Important? Their Role and Impact* (pp. 21–37). Boston, MA: Springer US.

Becker, Wolfgang, Oliver Schmid and Tim Botzkowski (2018), *Role of CDOs in the Digital Transformation of SMEs and LSEs: An Empirical Analysis.* Paper presented at the the 51st Hawaii International Conference on System Sciences, Hawaii.

Berkhout, Frans and Julia Hertin (2004), "De-materialising and re-materialising: digital technologies and the environment". *Futures, 36*(8), 903–20. doi: 10.1016/j.futures.2004.01.003

Bernaert, M., G. Poels, M. Snoeck and M. de. Backer (2014), "Enterprise architecture for small and medium-sized enterprises: a starting point for bringing EA to SMEs". In J. Devos, H. van Landeghem and D. Deschoolmeester (eds), *Information Systems for Small and Medium-sized Enterprises: State of Art of IS Research in SMEs.* Berlin, Heidelberg: Springer Berlin Heidelberg, pp. 67–96.

Bilgeri, Dominik, Elgar Fleisch, Heiko Gebauer and Felix Wortmann (2019), "Driving process innovation with IoT field data". *MIS Quarterly Executive, 18*(3), 191–207. doi: 10.17705/2msqe.00016

Bley, K., C. Leyh and T. Schäffer (2016), *Digitization of German Enterprises in the Production Sector: Do They Know How "Digitized" They Are?* Paper presented at the Americas Conference on Information Systems, San Diego.

Bogner, E., T. Voelklein, O. Schroedel and J. Franke (2016), *Study Based Analysis on the Current Digitalization Degree in the Manufacturing Industry in Germany.* Paper presented at the Procedia CIRP.

Cameron, Kim S. and Robert E. Quinn (2011), *Diagnosing and Changing Organizational Culture: Based on the Competing Values Framework.* San Francisco, CA: Jossey-Bass.

Clark, Shawn M., Dennis A. Gioia, Jr. Ketchen, David J. and James B. Thomas (2010), "Transitional identity as a facilitator of organizational identity change during a merger". *Administrative Science Quarterly, 55*, 397–438. doi: 10.2189/asqu.2010.55.3.397

Coreynen, Wim, Paul Matthyssens and Wouter Van Bockhaven (2017), "Boosting servitization through digitization: pathways and dynamic resource configurations for manufacturers". *Industrial Marketing Management, 60*, 42–53. doi: 10.1016/j.indmarman.2016.04.012

Corsaro, Daniela, Carla Ramos, Stephan C. Henneberg and Peter Naudé (2012), "The impact of network configurations on value constellations in business markets—the case of an innovation network". *Industrial Marketing Management, 41*(1), 54–67. doi: 10.1016/j.indmarman.2011.11.017

Dodgson, Mark (1993), "Learning, trust, and technological collaboration". *Human Relations, 46*(1), 77–95. doi: 10.1177/001872679304600106

EC (European Commission) (2012), *EU SMEs in 2012: At the Crossroads. Annual Report on Small and Medium-sized Enterprises in the EU*, Vol. 2011/12.

European Commission (Consulted July 2020), "Internal Market, Industry, Entrepreneurship and SMEs".

Fallera, Clemens and Dorothee Feldmüller (2015), *Industry 4.0 Learning Factory for Regional SMEs.* Paper presented at the The 5th Conference on Learning Factories.

Fischer, Thomas, Heiko Gebauer, Mike Gregory, Guangjie Ren and Elgar Fleisch (2010), "Exploitation or exploration in service business development?" *Journal of Service Management, 21*(5), 591–624. doi: 10.1108/09564231011079066

Gebauer, Heiko and Christian Kowalkowski (2012), "Customer-focused and service-focused orientation in organizational structures". *Journal of Business & Industrial Marketing, 27*(7), 527–37. doi: 10.1108/08858621211257293

Gebauer, Heiko, Marco Paiola and Bo Edvardsson (2012), "A capability perspective on service business development in small and medium-sized suppliers". *Scandinavian Journal of Management, 28*(4), 321–39. doi: 10.1016/j.scaman.2012.07.001

Gierlich, Maren, Ronny Schüritz, Thomas Hess and Malte Volkwein (2019). *SMEs' Approaches for Digitalization in Platform Ecosystems.* Paper presented at the Twenty-Third Pacific Asia Conference on Information Systems, China.

Gioia, Dennis A., Majken Schultz and Kevin G. Corley (2000), "Organizational identity, image, and adaptive instability". *Academy of Management Review, 25*(1), 63–81. doi: 10.5465/AMR.2000.2791603

Gioia, Dennis A., Shubha D. Patvardhan, Aimee L. Hamilton and Kevin G. Corley (2013), "Organizational identity formation and change". *Academy of Management Annals, 7*(1), 123–93. doi: 10.1080/19416520.2013.762225

Greene, Francis and David Storey (2010), "Enterprise policy and practice". *Small Enterprise Research, 17*(1), 4–6. doi: 10.5172/ser.17.1.4

Hinings, Bob, Thomas Gegenhuber and Royston Greenwood (2018), "Digital innovation and transformation: an institutional perspective". *Information & Organization, 28*(1), 52–61. doi: 10.1016/j.infoandorg.2018.02.004

Hracs, Brian J. (2013), "Cultural intermediaries in the digital age: the case of independent musiciansand managers in Toronto". *Regional Studies, 49*(3), 461–75. doi: 10.1080/00343404.2012.750425

Huxham, C. (1993), "Pursuing collaborative advantage". *Journal of the Operational Research Society, 44*(6), 599–611.

Kane, Gerald C., Doug Palmer, A.N.H. Nguyen Phillips, David Kiron and Natasha Buckley (2016), "Aligning the organization for its digital future". *MIT Sloan Management Review, 58*(1), 1–28.

Kaňovská, Lucie and Eva Tomášková (2018), "Drivers for smart servitization in manufacturing companies". *Agris On-Line Papers in Economics & Informatics, 10*(3), 57–68. doi: 10.7160/aol.2018.100305

Klein, Maximilian Michael, Sebastian Simon Biehl and Thomas Friedli (2018), "Barriers to smart services for manufacturing companies—an exploratory study in the capital goods industry". *Journal of Business & Industrial Marketing, 33*(6), 846–56. doi: 10.1108/JBIM-10-2015-0204

Klötzer, C. and A. Pflaum (2017), *Toward the Development of a Maturity Model for Digitalization within the Manufacturing Industry's Supply Chain.* Paper presented at the the 50th Hawaii international conference on system sciences, Honolulu.

Kohtamäki, Marko, Jukka Partanen, Vinit Parida and Joakim Wincent (2013), "Non-linear relationship between industrial service offering and sales growth: the moderating role of network capabilities". *Industrial Marketing Management, 42*(8), 1374–85. doi: 10.1016/j.indmarman.2013.07.018

Kohtamäki, Marko, Vinit Parida, Pejvak Oghazi, Heiko Gebauer and Tim Baines (2019), "Digital servitization business models in ecosystems: a theory of the firm". *Journal of Business Research, 104,* 380–92. doi: 10.1016/j.jbusres.2019.06.027

Kowalkowski, Christian and Wolfgang Ulaga (2017), *Service Strategy in Action: A Practical Guide for Growing Your B2B Service and Solution Business.* Scottsdale, AZ: Service Strategy Press

Kowalkowski, Christian, Daniel Kindström, Thomas Brashear Alejandro, Staffan Brege and Sergio Biggemann (2012a), "Service infusion as agile incrementalism in action". *Journal of Business Research, 65*(6), 765–72. doi: 10.1016/j.jbusres.2010.12.014

Kowalkowski, Christian, Oscar Persson Ridell, Jimmie G. Röndell and David Sörhammar (2012b), "The co-creative practice of forming a value proposition". *Journal of Marketing Management, 28*(13–14), 1553–70. doi: 10.1080/0267257X.2012.736875

Kowalkowski, Christian, Daniel Kindström and Heiko Gebauer (2013a), "ICT as a catalyst for service business orientation". *Journal of Business & Industrial Marketing, 28*(6), 506–13. doi: 10.1108/JBIM-04-2013-0096

Kowalkowski, Christian, Lars Witell and Anders Gustafsson (2013b), "Any way goes: identifying value constellations for service infusion in SMEs". *Industrial Marketing Management, 42*(1), 18–30. doi: 10.1016/j.indmarman.2012.11.004

Lay, Gunter, Giacomo Copani, Angela Jäger and Sabine Biege (2010), "The relevance of service in European manufacturing industries". *Journal of Service Management, 21*(5), 715–26. doi: 10.1108/09564231011092908

Lerch, Christian and Matthias Gotsch (2015), "Digitalized product-service systems in manufacturing firms". *Research Technology Management, 58*(5), 45–52. doi: 10.5437/08956308X5805357

Lusch, Robert F. and Satish Nambisan (2015), "Service Innovation: a service-dominant logic perspective". *MIS Quarterly, 39*(1), 155–76.

Macdonald, Emma K., Michael Kleinaltenkamp and Hugh N. Wilson (2016), "How business customers judge solutions: solution quality and value in use". *Journal of Marketing, 80*(3), 96–120. doi: 10.1509/jm.15.0109

Malleret, Véronique (2006), "Value creation through service offers". *European Management Journal, 24*(1), 106–16. doi: 10.1016/j.emj.2005.12.012

Michel, Stefan, Stephen L. Vargo and Robert F. Lusch (2008), "Reconfiguration of the conceptual landscape: a tribute to the service logic of Richard Normann". *Journal of the Academy of Marketing Science, 36*(1), 152–5. doi: 10.1007/s11747-007-0067-8

Mittal, Sameer, Muztoba Ahmad Khan, David Romero and Thorsten Wuest (2018), "A critical review of smart manufacturing & Industry 4.0 maturity models: implications for small and medium-sized enterprises (SMEs)". *Journal of Manufacturing Systems, 49,* 194–214. doi: 10.1016/j.jmsy.2018.10.005

Myrthianos, Vasileios, Ferran Vendrell-Herrero, Glenn Parry and Oscar F. Bustinza (2014), "Firm profitability during the servitization process in the music industry". *Strategic Change, 23*(5/6), 317–28. doi: 10.1002/jsc.1979

Möller, Kristian and Arto Rajala (2007), "Rise of strategic nets—new modes of value creation". *Industrial Marketing Management, 36*(7), 895–908. doi: 10.1016/j.indmarman.2007.05.016

Nagy, Delmer, Joseph Schuessler and Alan Dubinsky (2016), "Defining and identifying disruptive innovations". *Industrial Marketing Management, 57,* 119–26. doi: 10.1016/j.indmarman.2015.11.017

Nambisan, Satish, Kalle Lyytinen, Ann Majchrzak and Michael Song (2017), "Digital innovation management: reinventing innovation management research in a digital world". *MIS Quarterly, 41*(1), 223–38.

Neu, Wayne A. and Stephen W. Brown (2005), "Forming successful business-to-business services in goods-dominant firms". *Journal of Service Research, 8*(1), 3–17. doi: 10.1177/1094670505276619

Ng, Irene C.L. and Susan Y.L. Wakenshaw (2017), "The Internet-of-Things: review and research directions". *International Journal of Research in Marketing, 34*(1), 3–21. doi: 10.1016/j.ijresmar.2016.11.003

Normann, Richard (2001). *Reframing Business: When the Map Changes the Landscape.* Chichester: Wiley.

Nätti, Satu, Pia Hurmelinna-Laukkanen and Wesley J. Johnston (2014), "Absorptive capacity and network orchestration in innovation communities—promoting service innovation". *Journal of Business & Industrial Marketing, 29*(2), 173–84. doi: 10.1108/JBIM-08-2013-0167

Oliver, Christine (1990), "Determinants of interorganizational relationships: integration and future directions". *Academy of Management Review, 15*(2), 241–65. doi: 10.5465/AMR.1990.4308156

Paiola, Marco (2019), "Digitalization and servitization: opportunities and challenges for Italian SMES". *Sinergie (Verona), 107*, 11–22. doi: 10.7433/s107.2018.01

Palo, Teea, Maria Åkesson and Nina Löfberg (2019), "Servitization as business model contestation: a practice approach". *Journal of Business Research, 104*, 486–96. doi: 10.1016/j.jbusres.2018.10.037

Parida, Vinit, David R. Sjödin and Wiebke Reim (2019), "Reviewing literature on digitalization, business model innovation, and sustainable industry: past achievements and future promises". *Sustainability, 11*(2), 319. doi: https://doi.org/10.3390/su11020391

Peillona, Sophie and Nadine Dubruc (2019). *Barriers to Digital Servitization in French Manufacturing SMEs.* Paper presented at the 11th CIRP Conference on Industrial Product-Service Systems, Zhuhai and Hong Kong, China.

Peillona, Sophie, Nadine Dubruc and M. Mansour (2018), "Service and customer orientation of corporate culture in a French manufacturing SME". *Procedia CIRP, 73*, 91–5.

Penttinen, Esko and Jonathan Palmer (2007), "Improving firm positioning through enhanced offerings and buyer–seller relationships". *Industrial Marketing Management, 36*(5), 552–64. doi: 10.1016/j.indmarman.2006.02.005

Perks, Helen, Christian Kowalkowski, Lars Witell and Anders Gustafsson (2017), "Network orchestration for value platform development". *Industrial Marketing Management, 67*, 106–21. doi: 10.1016/j.indmarman.2017.08.002

Quah, Danny (1996), *The Invisible Hand and the Weightless Economy.* London: London School of Economics and Political Science.

Raddats, Chris and Chris Easingwood (2010), "Services growth options for B2B product-centric businesses". *Industrial Marketing Management, 39*(8), 1334–45. doi: 10.1016/j.indmarman.2010.03.002

Raja, Jawwad Z., Thomas Frandsen and Jan Mouritsen (2017), "Exploring the managerial dilemmas encountered by advanced analytical equipment providers in developing service-led growth strategies". *International Journal of Production Economics, 192*, 120–32. doi: 10.1016/j.ijpe.2016.12.034

Raja, Jawwad Z., Mehmet Chakkol, Mark Johnson and Ahmad Beltagui (2018), "Organizing for servitization: examining front- and back-end design configurations". *International Journal of Operations & Production Management, 38*(1), 249–71. doi: 10.1108/IJOPM-03-2016-0139

Rust, Roland T. and Huang Ming-Hui (2014), "The service revolution and the transformation of marketing science". *Marketing Science, 33*(2), 206–21. doi: 10.1287/mksc.2013.0836

Simmons, Geoff, Mark Palmer and Yann Truong (2013), "Inscribing value on business model innovations: insights from industrial projects commercializing disruptive digital innovations". *Industrial Marketing Management, 42*(5), 744–54. doi: 10.1016/j.indmarman.2013.05.010

Sjödin, David, Vinit Parida, Marko Kohtamäki and Joakim Wincent (2020), "An agile co-creation process for digital servitization: a micro-service innovation approach". *Journal of Business Research, 112*, 478–91. doi: 10.1016/j.jbusres.2020.01.009

Sklyar, Alexey, Christian Kowalkowski, David Sörhammar and Bård Tronvoll (2019a), "Resource integration through digitalisation: a service ecosystem perspective". *Journal of Marketing Management, 35*(11/12), 974–91. doi: 10.1080/0267257X.2019.1600572

Sklyar, Alexey, Christian Kowalkowski, Bård Tronvoll and David Sörhammar (2019b), "Organizing for digital servitization: a service ecosystem perspective". *Journal of Business Research, 104*, 450–60.

Story, Vicky M., Chris Raddats, Jamie Burton, Judy Zolkiewski and Tim Baines (2017), "Capabilities for advanced services: a multi-actor perspective". *Industrial Marketing Management, 60*, 54–68. doi: 10.1016/j.indmarman.2016.04.015

Svahn, Fredrik, Lars Mathiassen and Rikard Lindgren (2017), "Embracing digital innovation in incumbent firms: how Volvo cars managed competing concerns". *MIS Quarterly, 41*(1), 239–54.

Tronvoll, Bård, Alexey Sklyar, David Sörhammar and Christian Kowalkowski (2020), "Transformational shifts through digital servitization". *Industrial Marketing Management, 89*, 293–305. doi: https://doi.org/10.1016/j.indmarman.2020.02.005

Ulaga, Wolfgang and Werner J. Reinartz (2011), "Hybrid offerings: how manufacturing firms combine goods and services successfully". *Journal of Marketing, 75*(6), 5–23. doi: 10.1509/jm.09.0395

Vendrell-Herrero, Ferran, Oscar F. Bustinza, Glenn Parry and Nikos Georgantzis (2017), "Servitization, digitization and supply chain interdependency". *Industrial Marketing Management, 60*, 69–81. doi: 10.1016/j.indmarman.2016.06.013

von Leipzig, T., M. Gamp, D. Manz et al. (2017), "Initialising customer-orientated digital transformation in enterprises". *Procedia Manufacturing, 8*, 517–24. doi: https://doi.org/10.1016/j.promfg.2017.02.066

Walter, Achim, Michael Auer and Thomas Ritter (2006), "The impact of network capabilities and entrepreneurial orientation on university spin-off performance". *Journal of Business Venturing, 21*(4), 541–67. doi: 10.1016/j.jbusvent.2005.02.005

Wang, C., E.A. Walker and J.L. Redmond (2007), "Explaining the lack of strategic planning in SMEs: the importance of owner motivation". *International Journal of Organisational Behaviour, 12*(1), 1–16.

13. Facilitating big data transformation in Danish SMEs: insights for managers

Pernille Rydén and Helle Rootzén

> The journey of a thousand miles begins with one step.
> Lao Tzu

13.1 INTRODUCTION

The small and medium-sized enterprise (SME) sector in Europe is a vital innovation and job creation engine for sustaining growth. However, there is an urgent need for digital capabilities (i.e., the power and ability to generate a positive outcome from digitalization) if Danish SMEs are to take the leading position in the European Union (EU). For SMEs to take the step up and ensure a commercial advantage of big data, a knowledge gap in terms of big data analytics and affiliated management issues must be closed (Britzelmaier et al., 2020). To succeed, individual and organizational learning capabilities (i.e., the capacity to maintain or improve performance based on experience and assimilating and applying new information) must precede big data upgrading (Orlikowski, 2002). A vital part of that is to ensure that every employee knows about digitalization, understands concepts like big data, artificial intelligence, blockchain, and machine learning, and can make sense of the digital journey of their company, which requires a broad and varied range of learning approaches from very basic to highly advanced. A common language for people, companies, and science is also needed to be able to digitalize smarter and to bring the best from the past into the future and trigger new, better products and services. The reasoning behind giving SMEs a helping hand is that the first step to big data deployment is the hardest. Once started, it will be easier to realize strategic aims.

This chapter therefore presents a digital learning concept developed for SMEs by the Technical University of Denmark (DTU)[1] and the learning outcome of the digital transformation journeys of 12 Danish SMEs. With a big data technology competence boost, SMEs can better engage in – and take advantage of – the vast opportunities that data and analytics bring for creating new consumer insights, business intelligence, increasing decision-making power in the company, as well as triggering new ways of thinking and interacting with the market (Sen et al., 2016; Ringberg et al., 2019).

To contribute to scientific development through a deeper understanding of the context and by capturing experiences (Flyvbjerg & Budzier, 2011), we first outline the data potential in a Danish SME context and identify the unique potentials and barriers. Second, we introduce the purpose, principles, and process of the digital learning concept "KomDigital" and its methodological underpinnings. Third, we illustrate empirically the managerial dilemmas and concerns, as well as the drivers and triggers for digital learning and transformation of two

Danish SMEs. We then condense the learning experiences of the 12 companies into practical steps in a digital transformation learning process that SMEs can take to initiate the big data journey. Finally, we present the managerial implications for those ready to take the first steps towards data-driven growth.

13.2 WHAT IS BIG DATA?

Big data definitions have evolved rapidly, which has raised some confusion (Gandomi & Haider, 2014) and it remains a somehow diffuse and distant technology instead of being regarded as a tangible strategic business tool to use for either optimizing business processes, such as business planning, logistics, cost optimization, resource utilization, and other measurements, or as new revenue-generating business models. Though the impact of big data has caught many SMEs by surprise – many of which have not yet entered the learning curve – "big data" quickly disappeared from Gartner's hype curve in 2015, replaced by concepts such as "blockchain," "machine learning" (ML), and "artificial intelligence" (AI) (Rydén et al., 2017).

Big data can be defined as "high-volume, high-velocity and high-variety information assets that demand cost-effective, innovative forms of information processing for enhanced insight and decision making" (Gartner IT Glossary, n.d.)[2] whereas "big data analytics" is a method for creating value of the data generated by organizations, by users on social media or provided by Internet of Things (IoT) devices. Defining big data by three descriptive Vs only (Volume, Velocity, Variety) does not sufficiently capture the multiple data aspects to manage. We therefore aggregated the descriptive (what is) and normative (what should be) aspects of big data implementation into the 9V model (Rydén et al., 2017) depicted in Figure 13.1

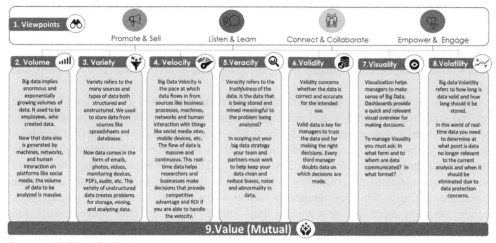

Source: Rydén et al. (2017).

Figure 13.1 The 9V model

"Viewpoint" (strategic mindset) is the central aspect of the 9V model as the strategic mindset determines the assessment of the remaining Vs. The model excludes a fifth mindset identified (Pry & Punish, p. 7) as this mindset is not deemed appropriate for building a sustainable business and hence we try to help the managers avoid ethical pitfalls of using big data. The definition of the big data building blocks gave the management teams an overview of the managerial facets and helped them gauge the readiness of the organization to gain full value from using big data. By carefully evaluating the importance and accessibility of each V, the managers could see how close the company was to achieving its big data goals and to benchmark the progress.

13.3   DANISH SMEs AND THEIR CONDITIONS FOR USING BIG DATA

The term "SME" is an umbrella term because it is used for segmenting a heterogeneous group of businesses across a wide range of industries which are operating in various markets. SME owners, managers, and employees therefore embody different types and levels of capabilities, capital, technological and digital sophistication, and growth orientation. Accounting for nearly 99 percent of the European businesses, the 15.8 million SMEs represent the backbone of the EU economy. From 2012 to 2017, SMEs created 85 percent of the new jobs, while representing two-thirds of the total workplaces of the private sector in the area. For those reasons the EU Commission has intensely prioritized the rollout of programs that stimulate business action in a SME context (European Commission, 2017[3]). But the geographical, cultural, and industrial diversity add to the complexity of gearing up SMEs at a more general level, which is calling for local action.

Zooming in on one of the most innovative and digitalized countries in the EU (DESI, 2019)[4] – Denmark ranks first in the parameter "SMEs selling online." With an excellent broadband infrastructure (99 percent 4G coverage), Denmark provides the best digital services for businesses in Europe.[5] This gives large enterprises and SMEs, which account for the majority of Danish companies, excellent conditions for using big data to drive productivity, growth, and innovation.[6]

Data now combine across organizational, sectoral, and industrial silos and are becoming free and available for the public and offering new opportunities for SMEs to harvest. With the rollout of 5G services, real-time connectivity will be even more pervasive in big data technologies disrupting business and society (Makridadis, 2017). Real-time is a big potential-releasing feature of big data (Rydén & El Sawy, 2019b, p. 22): "The ability to process huge amounts of data gives organizations the possibility to have data or results being present at the same time as data are coming in. This development is seen as a new potential for business management, because normally there will be a shift in time, where you collect data, process, work and decide, and implement. Now you can do it at the same time in concurrent cycles."

However, despite the fact that Denmark is among one of the most digitalized countries in Europe, the Danish SMEs are lagging behind when it comes to big data deployment.[7] Big data influence business environments and new capabilities are needed to stay competitive, especially among the Danish SMEs. Data are an important source of generating new business models to create customer value, and scale up businesses at a faster pace (Sen et al., 2016), but the SMEs enrolled in the KomDigital project find that redeeming the value that lies in data is an evolutionary process rather than a revolutionary process (Ringberg et al., 2019), in which the gradual understanding of the potential of big data and the routinization of processes play a crucial role (Janssen et al., 2017). This confirms that SMEs tend to be slow adopters of big data and data analytics and thus risk being left behind in the competitive race of Industry 5.0 personalization and mass-customization. Like the Fortune 500 companies, SMEs can save costs and increase revenues by using big data for optimizing value for their customers and other stakeholders, as well as creating societal growth and new jobs.

The Danish government has acknowledged that there is a clear need for digital and technical capabilities if Danish SMEs are to take the leading position in the EU. The ambition is that more SMEs invest in digital transformation and e-commerce so within 2021, 2000 SMEs will have strengthened their digital muscles by promoting a significant boost in competences within Industry 4.0 and the use of digital technologies, data analytics, connected devices, ML, and AI. To support and speed up this process, they are offering grants for counseling, participation in innovation courses, and the opportunity to strengthen the digital management capabilities. One of those initiatives is the *KomDigital project* that contributes to a better flow of qualified workforce with IT capabilities throughout Greater Copenhagen by developing new forms of virtual and face2face learning.[8] The project development phase SGC1 completed pilots with 12 companies and 150 employees in 2018 and 2019, and SGC2 expands to 50 companies in 2020 and 2021.[9]

According to the SMEs we worked with, the reasons for hesitating with big data are that they do not fit with the content and form of the existing market; it is hard to navigate in the vast ocean of questionable offers; they lack the basic knowledge of digitalization and are unsure about what digitalization capabilities and structures to invest in, and how to strengthen competitiveness through increased digitalization, Moreover, investment in education often gives a small return to SMEs, as the learning does not translate into actual capabilities in the company. KomDigital therefore helps SMEs answer the question of *how to transform the SME towards utilizing big data?*

13.4   DIGITAL TRANSFORMATION METHODOLOGY

KomDigital co-designs digital solutions and transformation of SMEs based on their unique business challenges through an "involving" type of learning for digital development. It differs from ordinary education by merging tech workshops, action learning, business development, expert consulting, and team-dynamics to ensure flexible, relevance, and practical processes. The team-learning activities take place at the company location as workshops supported by business developers, technology experts, and researchers can adapt instantly to the local context and combine knowledge transfer with coaching and practical work. It is mandatory that the team includes the head to ensure sufficient top management support and legitimacy, usually the Chief Executive Officer (CEO) of smaller enterprises, but for medium-sized enterprises it could be the Chief Information Officer (CIO), Chief Financial Officer (CFO) or head of research and development (R&D). The learning teams thereby develop a common language and a common frame of reference for the new knowledge.

13.4.1   The Theoretical Learning Principles of Big Data Digital Transformation

Experimentation is important when SMEs embark on a digital learning journey. Especially small experiments carried out in a short time period are efficient. They give the company the possibility to integrate user experience (UX) in its daily work making the development process more flexible and faster. This is based on an assumption that we learn most effectively when we are curious, when we collaborate with others, when we have fun and are in flow (Csikszentmihalyi, 2008) following the theoretical underpinnings of *social learning theory* (Bandura, 1977, 2001), *Action Learning theory* (Neil & Marsick, 2007), *socio-cognitive theory* (Rydén et al., 2015; Rydén et al., 2017), *absorptive capacity* (Cohen and Levinthal, 1990), *dynamic capabilities* (Teece 1988, 2007), and *flow theory* (Csikszentmihalyi, 2008; Rydén & El Sawy, 2019a, 2019b). For example, the team learning principle is vested social learning theory (Bandura, 1977). Here, learning is considered a social phenomenon, rather than just a mental phenomenon, that happens through mutual influence between the three elements: individual, environment, and behavior (Wood & Bandura, 1989). *Action Learning* (Neil & Marsick, 2007; Rootzén, 2015) stresses that we can gather knowledge by working in peer groups to find a solution to a problem or drawing scenarios. In doing so, we will be able to develop individual and collective capabilities and knowledge simultaneously.

Socio-cognitive learning theory (Bandura, 2001) underscores that the minds and experiences of team members are the basis for collective efficacy, which mandates our emphasis on mindsets to promote the learning processes. This approach contributes to making digital transformation meaningful for the management and for the employees by departing from the practical needs and current digital state of the individual SME. This is vital because there is empirical evidence that established firms often have difficulty adapting to radical technological change because learning is deeply rooted in the way managers model new technology and the problems it is expected to solve (Ringberg et al., 2019; Tripsas & Gavetti, 2000). Tripsas and Gavetti's (2000) story of how Polaroid shifted from analog to digital imaging clearly illustrates the relationship between managers' mindset and the accumulation of organizational capabilities. So does Rydén et al.'s (2015) study showing how the managers' shared mental models of business-customer interactions create different sensemaking of social media. These examples underscore the importance of managerial mindsets in directing search processes in a new learning environment, the evolutionary trajectory of individual and collective capabilities, and ultimately processes of organizational adaptation.

Thus, digital technologies, managerial mindsets, and capabilities must go hand-in-hand to be effective – investing in new technology alone is not enough. Besides handling the inertial forces associated with the local nature of learning processes, we must further ensure that learning is anchored in the corporate routines and practices while driven by customer and market orientation. To do so, we combine these approaches to digital transformation based on identifying dominant, yet tacit, managerial mindsets of the business-customer interaction leading to five inherently different big data strategies (Rydén et al., 2015; Rydén et al., 2017), as illustrated in Figure 13.2.

The framework is useful for identifying what mindsets are at play within the management team and the SME, and how their dominant mindset fits with the mindset of their customers and market. Since these tacit mindsets affect how companies deploy new big data technology, it is vital to ensure that they are based on the optimal strategic value foundation. However,

Big Data Dogma V9 model

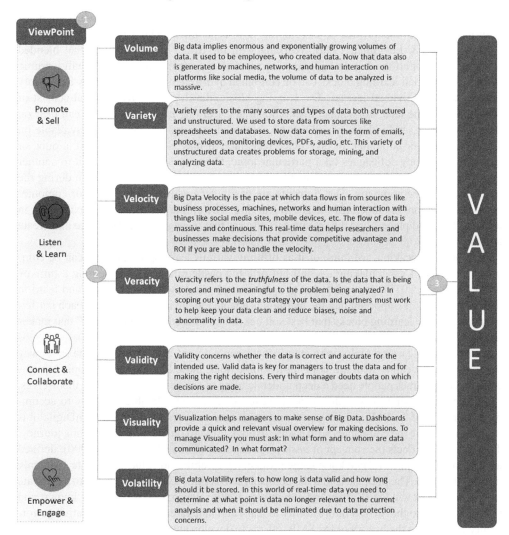

Figure 13.2　Big data mindsets

a disparity between strategic orientations among managers can be constructive for the learning process and introduce new ways of thinking. To find out, the management team did an online test[10] revealing their individual mindsets, the interpretations of their company strategy as well as their underlying expectations, assumptions, and preferred approaches to a digital transformation.

13.4.2   Why and How Small Steps Lead to a Bigger Journey

Organizational learning may be increased by building on existing capabilities, which involves improving current capabilities or developing new capabilities which involve a change in culture (Cohen & Levinthal, 1990). Working with the SMEs clearly showed that blended learning can support the big data journey, so we built a system consisting of small learning blocks. These small learning blocks can be combined in different ways and thereby be flexibly adapted to the individual learner. The learning blocks developed for KomDigital consist of on-site and online tech workshops, inspirational and learning podcasts that one can hear on the way to work, and videos, which can be combined in many different ways, available on the phone, iPad or computer, or take place face2face. It may also be a short text, a quiz, or a discussion among colleagues on a particular topic. Other options include a visit to another company in the same industry, participation in a workshop or a short presentation during the lunch break at the company. The elements are easily accessed by phone, iPad or computer combined with on-site meetings for group learning. The online part provides flexibility – in terms of time and place – and the on-site part ensures that managers and staff share and create together.

Figuratively speaking, we think of it as offering various learning blocks that can be combined in different ways making a small hut or a big castle rather than presenting a turnkey house (Rootzén, 2015). Assuming that people are motivated by different things and learn in different ways, it is important that the learning is adapted to the individual. Thus, each participant can pick the learning blocks that best suit her or him to customize the "house" that makes the most sense.

This modular learning philosophy entails that people do not have to learn in the same way though they are dealing with the same topic. Sometimes, basic knowledge of a topic is sufficient and other times people need a deep understanding to create new solutions by themselves.

The action learning philosophy is indented to make learning flexible and easy to accomplish. For most of the SMEs, this way of working is a new experience, but for KomDigital it is important to leave the companies with a way to move forward on their digital learning journey. This approach reflects the concept of *absorptive capacity* (Cohen & Levinthal, 1990), defined as the function of prior related knowledge influencing its ability to value, assimilate and apply new information. The premise is that the company needs prior related knowledge to assimilate and use new knowledge (Cohen and Levinthal, 1990). Hence, what is already known and mastered is key to the SME's future ability to learn and innovate. When the innovative performance depends on the history of the SME, efforts to develop absorptive capacity in one period will make it easier to accumulate it in the next one, which can drive the process forward. Zahra and George (2002) expand the concept to *realized absorptive capacity*, defined as the function of the transformation and exploitation capabilities, that is, the SME's capability to develop and refine the routines that facilitate combining existing knowledge and new knowledge to apply the newly acquired knowledge in products or services that it can financially benefit from. These concepts help us consider what are the right areas of expertise to invest in to ensure the future development of big data learning capabilities.

SMEs can avoid inertia, falling into competency traps, and letting old mindsets influence the direction of its big data transformation by changing routines and practices to adapt its capabilities to the changes needed for successful commercialization (Helfat et al., 2003). Absorptive capacity thus becomes *a dynamic capability* (Teece, 1988, 2007; Jacobides & Winter 2005) necessary for achieving sustainable competitive advantage in fast-developing and turbulent markets. It describes the company's ability to build and reconfigure competences to address changes in the business environment. Dynamic capabilities thus relate to the learning ability and the level of innovation that the company can accommodate (Teece, 1988).

13.4.3   The Process

The screening tool for company recruitment was developed based on the first pilot experiences to introduce the methodology and to measure the level of leadership, digital maturity, team reflection practices, and growth ambition. In conjunction with information from the companies' websites and initial telephone contacts prior to the first dialogue meeting, the screening results guide the facilitator in deciding which companies match the project criteria and to suggest learning design.

The companies pick a digital topic for the project (big data, blockchain, social media, ML, or AI) that taps into their overall strategy. See Figure 13.3 for a schematic picture of the process:

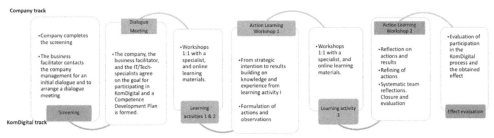

Source: Based on Kristensen and Poulsen (2018).

Figure 13.3   The constitutive part of the KomDigital process

The upper part of the figure presents the steps in the process seen from the company's point of view and the lower part depicts the process from KomDigital's point of view. Each step of the process is rather flexible and tailored to the individual company but during the pilot phase it turned out that the process as described in the figure seems to provide most value and fits into the needs of SMEs in general. When working with projects like this it is important to balance flexibility for the companies and the ability to upscale the number of SMEs involved while ensuring that the project is manageable for the stakeholders.

The main purpose is to move the SME from one step to the next. Defining the next most important step is maybe the biggest advantage for the company. This is done in the dialogue meeting step. To be able to do this in an optimal way requires knowledge about the company which is gained in the screening phase (screening plus telephone calls). When the problem is defined, the company enters a sequence of workshops and action learning events. Finally, it is completed by an evaluation. The four levels of the ladder are linked to the concepts of absorptive capacity (Cohen & Levinthal, 1990) and dynamic capability (Teece, 2007), that is, *Level*

1: increased absorptive capacity measured as more knowledge of the technologies and their applications; *Level 2*: increased absorptive capacity and development of capabilities in the use of specific technologies, such as design thinking or data science; *Level 3*: increased dynamic capability meaning that management actively works for – and invests resources in – building new capabilities; *Level 4*: increased dynamic capability and absorptive capacity measured by how the SME works with reflexive processes in its use of digital technologies (Kristensen & Poulsen, 2018). Here, the dialogues anchored the learning in the team and in the organization.

Two anonymized cases supply the general takeaways harvested from the project and illustrate more specifically the big data digital transformation journey. Our direct involvement enabled us to collect data through various sources such as internal documents, screenings and tests, written accounts and evaluations, as well as observations by the project managers and facilitators. Moreover, the opportunity to test, in situ, how to organize and facilitate such comprehensive transformation processes gave the KomDigital team better comprehension of the development tools that eventually boost big data sensemaking and capabilities, job satisfaction, and employability. This real-time action learning research approach and the case studies' research methodology (Yin, 1989) provide a deeper understanding of the factors influencing big data learning in organizations and is well suited for investigating organizational issues (Benbasat et al., 1987).

13.5   INTRODUCTION TO THE CASE COMPANIES

Operating in the business-to business (B2B) and business-to-company (B2C) sectors, the SMEs are offering their products and services to the Danish market and with fairly identical learning needs and wants. To boost their digital transformations through team-based action learning, we developed and facilitated workshops for top and middle managers at the company locations, supplemented with big data courses at DTU.

13.5.1   Company A

This well-renowned product and service provider was founded more than a hundred years ago. Run in a classical top-down manner, its board of directors contributes to the strategic development and financial growth but are not involved in the development of digital capabilities. Managers and employees experience the influx of new technologies in a very conservative industry and that has impacted their daily operation and workflows. As their customers went digital, their basic data structure has become obsolete, while being busy using existing data to support the continued sales of physical products. The company went online with some of their services around the turn of the millennium, but when a foreign investor acquired the company a few years ago, they called for a digital transformation. The management acknowledged that to work more intelligently with data, a "digital-first" approach to data processing and business processes was required. To succeed, they had to overcome the culture, structure, and processes challenges to integrate across business areas.

Company A enrolled in the project to overcome those challenges to create a common strategic platform for the use of data between Content, Technology, and Markets. These business areas have overlapping tasks but are difficult to integrate due to competition and interest conflicts. Earlier, they tried virtual teams and project-based collaboration, but the jobs to be done ended with the project manager. Though several of their administrative functions were automated and digitalized, such as enterprise resource planning (ERP), customer relation-ship management (CRM), purchase and inventory management, the financial gains of their investments were moderate, and they only experienced to some extent a better overview of the business processes. The data generated from these processes were primarily used in the day-to-day operation and decision-making and for incrementally innovating products, ser-vices, or processes. Central to this is that technology and learning investments must go hand in hand to have an effect.

The management team of representatives from the three business areas engages in strategic networks with industry collaborators and customers on a regular basis and are assumed to have sufficient capabilities to drive a digital transformation process. Their digital capabilities are stronger than those of the employees and this is an area of managerial attention. The employees work in independent teams and, according to the management, they face some issues regarding resistance to change and motivation and time to learn and reflect critically on their existing practices. Moreover, staff are not involved in the strategic and financial decision-making or innovation and development of products and services, but they have a say in the decision-making regarding digitalization.

13.5.2 Company B

Established 40 years ago, the company offers a range of services primarily for business clients and end-users. They have an egalitarian culture and agile structure of well-functioning high-trust management teams consisting of relatively young people in comparison with company A. The management considers themselves as relatively open for change, but time is a scarce resource with limited room for critical reflections and learning time-outs. In fact, more than one-third of the participants find that big data is not a priority and only half of the man-agement team find that their daily functions depend on new technologies like big data. Like company A, company B is experiencing how the digital era has affected their daily operation and workflows, and they have also automated many administrative functions as well as their internal core functions. Their expectations of these efforts were higher than the outcome as the savings on operational costs has also been moderate. They describe their IT integration and flow in the digital business ecosystem as "high," but they do not use the data generated suffi-ciently and would therefore like to utilize their customer data better and develop a more digi-talized business model and services. The focus is on improving sales, marketing and business development through data analytics. As opposed to company A, they find that their employees are better equipped to meet the digital challenges and are ready to transform though they are not involved in the strategic decision-making. Later, they had to revise that assumption. Table 13.1 summarizes the external and internal drivers of digital transformation with big data.

Initially, the KomDigital facilitators expected a Connect & Collaborate approach to the learning process and development of big data opportunities, but several of the companies came with an expectation of meeting experts who could show the way from the start and roll out solutions in a "Promote & Sell" manner. The management workshops held in the two companies sparked fruitful dialogues that brought a new view of the different mindsets and the underlying assumptions and values. The participants realized from the first workshop that big data transformation is driven by personal and cultural change rather than technology

Table 13.1   Drivers and triggers of digital business transformation with big data

Business goals	Company A	Company B
Financial growth	x	X
Become market leaders	x	
First-movers on digital transformation	x	
Increased profitability through digitalization	x	X
Investments in technology is above average	x	
Investments in training of staff is above average	x	
Drivers for change		
Changing customer preferences towards digital services	x	X
Increased competition due to new digital market players		X
Suppliers/business partners demand more digitalization	x	X
New digital business models emerge in the industry	x	X
New digital technologies enable new lines of businesses or niches	x	x
Legal, regulatory market standards demand digitalization	x	x
Changes in the value chain sparked by digitalization		x

deployment, which redirected the focus from technology to people. From the two cases we identify big data potentials for SMEs and share the managerial challenges that the companies faced. The competence boost was organized according to four learning domains: the market (customer needs), the technology (IT/Data needs), the business (innovation needs) and the process (management and employee development needs), illustrated in Figure 13.4.

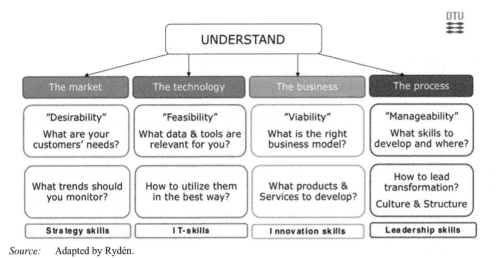

Source: Adapted by Rydén.

Figure 13.4   The building blocks of KomDigital

13.6   DISCOVERING THE BIG DATA POTENTIAL

The findings confirm an emerging general awareness of the analytical value of big data (and small data) parallel with the development of data-generating technologies such as Business Intelligence (BI) platforms and social media. The managers acknowledge that the big data concept is not just hype; it impacts the ordinary lives of ordinary people which also sparked a growing interest in big data for business. The majority of the SMEs across industries enrolled in KomDigital see big data opportunities to boost growth (Promote & Sell) and optimize processes for generating more customer value (Figure 13.2).

The management teams in companies A and B had a clear ambition of using big data to develop their business and become more cost efficient. They were all positive about the digital efforts but needed help connecting big data with their core tasks instead of becoming an add-on technology. Top management supported the big data project with an ambition of becoming digital first-movers. The goal was to develop their mindset and acquire digital knowledge to better understand the potentials and to define a transformation strategy founded in the application of Industry 4.0 technologies. They saw a number of benefits from adding big data analytics to existing business practices, but the mindset profile analysis revealed that big data was also considered one of the key drivers of the digital innovation (Sen et al., 2016; Ringberg et al., 2019). To realize this potential, it was necessary to expand their strategic horizon. Here, by testing different forms of "Connect & Collaborate" interaction with the market the team strengthened their market orientation towards a more customer-driven digitalized business. This strategic lens helped the companies discover the business ecosystem they were operating in. After expanding their definition of market as a "business network," they started searching for inspiration in other companies and industries on how to work with metadata and specific problem metrics such as focused Q&A search. The management discovered how they, with this mindset, can support a higher degree of user involvement in designing solutions towards need-driven information and knowledge segmentation, for example, observations to understand the customer's real needs as well as ongoing market feedback. But with this comes emerging technical and structural complexities to be managed.

13.7   MANAGERIAL CHALLENGES IN A SME CONTEXT

Though big data may indicate IT resource and capability challenges in particular, our project shows that usually other factors condition the poor adoption of big data and learning from data in order to make smarter business decisions. We present some of the current challenges organized around the learning interventions.

13.7.1   How Do We Convert a Product Focus into a Customer Focus?

Like the case examples, most SMEs, except from platform enterprises, collect data manually and store and utilize mainly structured data by recording and monitoring business transactions. So, when customers begin to demand services based on metadata instead of physical products it is a resource-demanding paradigm shift. Producing information valuable for customers requires infrastructure for gathering, processing, and managing large data volumes. Though large companies are better at taking advantage of the opportunities that big data afford, it is not necessarily the size of the company that presents the biggest barrier; the SME owners/ leaders are often not aware that they can do the same and/or because they are run by domain specialists having an entrepreneurial orientation. A crucial big data success criterion is to take a customer-focused approach to the big data process to ensure mutual value for customers and company – rather than simply optimizing internal processes. The lack of market orientation, strategic management capabilities and the narrow operation in highly specialized fields also prevent the SMEs from absorbing new IT developments and relevant market trends.

Another barrier identified is *knowledge over-confidence* (Fabricius & Büttgen, 2013). Often, their knowledge of their customer base is tacit, so though it is possible to crunch customer and payments data to surprise and attract customers in smart new ways, the value of such innovative efforts can be hard to realize. The owner and staff may be convinced that they know their customers by what they order, so no fancy data are needed to proactively advise their customers or boost sales or customer loyalty.

In the two companies, the first challenge was to take an outside-in approach to big data strategy. Given the experience of significant pressure from the outside world, the most critical issue appears to be transforming the core business to meet the increasing customer demand of convenient digitalized information and knowledge services. This was the case with company A operating in a very conservative industry. For many years, they had been offering physical products. As their customers went digital, their basic data structure has become obsolete, because they were busy using existing data to support the continued sales of physical products. Such a strategic turnaround basically involves the entire organization and a relatively high degree of senior management involvement to set the frame and define the time horizon. We therefore suggested that they consider involving their employees and relevant external stakeholders in the more strategic long-term decisions from an early stage, for instance, through active involvement of the content department.

By doing a stakeholder analysis based on customer segments and the variety of wants and needs, the teams discovered that talking of "our customers" as a homogeneous segment only confined the potential of big data to identify and target individual customers and outline a whole chain of activities in which various actors play a role. Moreover, the curiosity sparked by rethinking "who are our customers?" created the potential for discovering entirely new customer segments that could be reached and met through big data-driven services and an Industry 5.0 vision. This finding supports that learning orientation stimulates market orientation behavior and positively affects long-term relationships with strategic clients (Santos-Vijance et al., 2005).

After the first workshop with the two management teams, the task was clear to everyone: before we start building big data capabilities and educate our employees, we must introspect the mindsets of our managers and redefine our mission and vision. Then we must take an inside-out view and look more closely at our customers and their new needs and align these internal and external factors.

13.7.2   How to Get an Overview of Big Data for Decision-making?

A second challenge was tech infrastructure. The management teams acknowledged that to work more intelligently with data, it demanded a "digital-first" approach to data processing and business processes. Many business activities take place in the big data digital ecosystem, whether bookings, ordering supplies, or filing taxes, so big data is essential for the survival of many companies. Working with big data reduces – as well as adds – to the complexity of a company that, for example, can use descriptive analytics to summarize, condense, and aggregate data to make big and complex sales data more easily accessible for managerial understanding and decision-making. But to record, monitor, and control a sales process takes different data sources and formats coming at different rates of acquisition and granularity (Coleman et al., 2016). This means that management will have to cope not only with data complexity but structural complexity as well. Thus, the ability to analyze and forecast business and consumer behavior with big data is an organizational and cultural change challenge for many SMEs.

In both companies, some were uncertain whether the high data analytics set-up costs would yield the future returns due to lack of capabilities needed to develop a data analytics unit. Their databases were rapidly expanding, and data availability was increasing, but the big challenge was to present data and documents in a digital format to a content-focused staff. Though they focused on creating customer value, it was somehow detached from the big data initiatives initially suggested by the companies. Examples were using data to increase sales, but this Promote & Sell approach is only customer-focused if the customers want to buy more and find the transactional interaction with the company most valuable.

13.7.3 Big Data Transformation is Primarily a Managerial and Organizational Challenge

Figure 13.3 suggests that it requires more than big data technology deployment to create value for the company and customers; new innovative viewpoints (mindsets) on how to approach the market must support the strategic use of big data. The management acknowledged that identifying and developing existing mindsets was the focal aspect of big data transformation. Because this type of learning involved changing culture, norms, and values it was the root of the challenge of adopting new technology.

Whereas many start-ups are entrepreneurs in mind and mode, which provides an advantage in agile and adaptive learning, established SMEs are struggling with rigid structures and processes. Newly started businesses may see the advantage in using geolocation on mobile devices to track customers and provide them with content that corresponds to the geographic location without violating privacy rules or geo-demographical services and data that can provide detailed insight into customer profiles and devise new store locations. But some SMEs are old and proud family businesses, who have crafted their businesses and refined their business models for generations. Their prior history constrains future behavior in that learning tends to be premised on local processes of search (Levitt & March, 1988; Teece, 1988). Stable operation, rather than innovation, is regarded as the source of success and the attitude is often that consultants cannot help and if they could they would be unaffordable for many SMEs (Felber, 2011).

This is where collaboration with research institutions and universities can become particularly valuable as the "consultancy" collaboration is not transaction-based, but learning-based. According to Felber (2011), recruiting, retaining, and retraining people are typically the challenges that SMEs face. They need help to release their potential by facing the key issues of how to adapt to the market and build effective leadership and organization. In the two case companies, the managers and owners discovered that it becomes increasingly harder to operate and do "business as usual" in a business ecosystem that is going digital at a very fast pace. Here, it becomes central to work with the resistant attitude that prevents them from investing in digital education and big data and affects prioritizing issues too, since even small projects may seem too big to handle when busy.

To help other SMEs embark on their big data transformation journeys, we describe in four steps how the KomDigital pilot SMEs managed to overcome the challenges outlined above and how they managed the different learning aspects.

13.8   FOUR STEPS IN FACILITATING BIG DATA TRANSFORMATION IN DANISH SMEs

13.8.1   Step 1. The Learning Driver: Why Big Data?

The SMEs acknowledged how vital is was to get the strategic purposes in place first and gain better insight into their organization and what challenges their employees actually face to roll out big data successfully. To succeed, seeing the big why of big data was deemed essential for onboarding all the employees in the process and that involves more than understanding the technology; to understand the business, the market, and the processes is just as important. So, part of the task for the SMEs is to facilitate digital transformation based on the four building blocks of Figure 13.2. Thus, strategic use of big data cannot be done only by hiring data scientists to show the direction and devise solutions to strategic challenges. As part of the first step, the management should ensure the resources needed to accomplish the big data journey and prioritize efforts for operationalization and time, which is often the most critical resource to consider. A CEO explained how they underestimated how demanding and time-consuming it would be:

> Initially, I had expected to get more out of it, preferably something concrete, a finished product. But in the process, I could see that it was not possible because of the time pressure in our organization, and therefore it was better to call it an experiment.

It is nearly impossible to set realistic expectations when you move into unknown territory. Moving to more advanced big data technology use is all about getting started and dedicating time to it, so planning the time-outs is crucial to ensure that operation does not kill innovation. SMEs can use the resources available by identifying "volunteers" motivated to take the lead. Getting the strategic foundation in place first based on the type of business-customer interaction that big data should support helped the companies answer the big why. The mindset test triggered critical reflections about their existing business approaches and assumptions, which turned from tacit to shared knowledge for the management team. After the mindset exercises, the task was to expand the business horizon through an idea generation exercise driven by two central questions: *what type of business-stakeholder interaction can create what value to the business, the customers, and the society? What big data do we need to accomplish that?*

A mindset is experience in solving problems so the underlying assumptions about what it takes to succeed with big data may be flawed (Rydén et al., 2017). New mindsets can create value in new ways for frontline to back office and to customers. Thus, the companies discovered from the mindset exercise that when taking the Empower & Engage approach to big data, it offers opportunities to innovate with higher-order purposes of solving, for example, environmental challenges and sustainability (Mackey & Sisodia, 2014). It helped the SMEs to understand the value of redesigning their businesses as both effective and socially and environmentally responsible. This is fundamental to establishing a well-positioned presence in the market, but many SMEs do not have the resources to do strategic analyses and market research to develop strong competitive advantages. This makes learning exercises a valuable tool as it can reflect individual understandings and make them subject to critical relevance testing (Schön, 1983).

13.8.2   Step 2. The Learning Context: Who Has What Data?

Collaboration was crucial for building big data capabilities and developing processes for understanding the contextual meaning to use big data for decision-making (Janssen et al., 2017). People around the companies have access to – and use – different types of data, but it often turns out that they are not aware of who has access to what data. Understanding the context requires a good overview of data sources and how they can combine. By drafting a data map in collaboration with peers, they got a better overview of the aggregated company data and the people responsible for generating it. This exercise was a stepping-stone for combing the data across the organization and evaluating the quality of the data resources. It helped them figure out what others do with data and inspired the individual managers to expand their vision of what they can do with their data and what they can actually achieve by using multiple data in the company as well as from sources outside the company. The next step was to create an overview of the big data network, which requires that external data stakeholders collaborate closely with domain experts to understand the analysis and implications. By engaging in daily dialogues with customers, suppliers, and users about data needs and data use, SMEs can find out what data are available and learn what they need and decide whether they are willing and able to supply it. A daily time-out exercise that can ensure continuing learning is to ask peers: "What data do you have that could be interesting to combine with my data?"

13.8.3   Step 3. The Learning Content: How Do We Get To Know Big Data Better?

All learning processes involve acquiring new information and trying something new and often require stepping out of the comfort zone (Senge, 1990). Management can create a safe learning space for themselves and their staff by establishing "local labs" to dare to experiment with data and explore opportunities. Datasets are often unique, so people need to experiment to find good solutions locally that can be anchored in their core capabilities and practices where the learning takes place. Moreover, when the big data initiatives can be tied to their individual operational tasks it increases the sensemaking processes, well-being and attention, and people are more willing to change behavior (Weick, 1990). Though some data analytics frameworks and tools can be relatively easily deployed, many assume that data analytics take advanced capabilities. Curiosity and an open view are just as important in the beginning and exploration and experimentation must be mandated. This is because digital transformation is the corporate culture work of linking new mindsets and new technology (Ringberg et al., 2019). Experimentation will make the staff better able to deal with collecting and processing data and prepare them for the next step of integrating big data into existing processes. In another case company that we worked with, the small start-up business needed help with their social media strategy, so this became the starting point for their journey. When big data development involves strategic marketing and branding (Kumar et al., 2013) it demands people with a broad range of different capabilities (Figure 13.4) to assist the companies in those processes.

Generating customer insights and trends in a more purposeful manner does not always require complex software or a group of data scientists, but for small companies it will require considerable effort. A small step is to start with the website data and use it to acquire specific details and to adjust to changes in real-time and make changes concurrently. The next small step can be to supply the website information with social media data on their customers (Hennig-Thurau et al., 2013). Analyzing marketing data can be a good place to start, especially for smaller start-up businesses, as they can often see the effects of their action rather quickly. It can help them launch more effective campaigns and in customizing their offers and promotions, whereas customer reviews on social networks, communities, and forums help track insights on consumer behavior and sentiment (what the customer thinks and feels about the products or services).

13.8.4   Step 4. The Learning Process: How Do We Prepare the Company for Big Data?

It can be hard for SMEs to change their mindset while implementing digital strategies and to focus on specific collaborations for big data implementation. It will require the participation of many people and be resource demanding. A range of activities with more focused scopes is preferable, as this would fit more precisely to the core tasks and lead to a tangible outcome. One place to start big data prototyping is by analyzing who the customers are, where they are, and what they do and say. It enables SMEs to better allocate resources and avoid miscalculated budgets, which can be critical to SMEs and helps convince the rest of the organization of the positive effects of big data and may even motivate others to engage in similar projects.

Embedding big data at the operational level is difficult (Janssen et al., 2017), but in company A, which was bound by cultural procedures and principles, institutionalizing big data in a separate unit holding the decision-making power of what data to collect and analyze eased implementation. It can also attract people with big data capabilities such as data analysts instead of having to rely on the capabilities of the existing workforce. An internal challenge in both companies was that the people involved are positive about digital change and transformation and curious about big data. It is therefore important that participants are seen as positive ambassadors for change rather than as representatives of the whole. If not aware of such bias, it can be hard to involve the remaining members of the company.

The methods for querying and mining big data are very different from traditional statistical analysis on small samples and more challenging for SMEs as they need to be able to deal with noisy, dynamic, heterogeneous, untrustworthy data and data characterized by complex relations (Coleman et al., 2016). But affordable data science instruments and data management tools are available that can enhance the exactness and effectiveness of this process significantly, for example, by offering business intelligence visual data representations of various cost heads and allowing SMEs to trim down costs. Subscription-based Cloud storage options like Dropbox or Google doc give access to centralized data and files anywhere anytime. But to become truly customer demand-driven and acquire, store, filter, analyze, and visualize big data,[11] and generate the insights needed for future actions, new architectures and algorithms are often required. However, small data and qualitative approaches also provide a meaning-based understanding of customer behavior, which is integral to the revenue-generating process. Most importantly, people should remember to analyze the assumptions at each step of the data management process and their effects on the results.

13.9   CONCLUSIONS: BIG DATA TRANSFORMATION IS NOT A PREDICTABLE PATH OF LEARNING

The journeys of the 12 companies ended up differently from what the SMEs and KomDigital anticipated. Initially, the expectations from the project were high in some of the cases, and unrealistic, it turned out. The majority imagined that the focus would be on big data analytics, ML, or AI from the start and assumed that their learning would be much more technology-intensive than it actually was. The outcome of the learning process in the case companies is that they now know how to coordinate data, data learning initiatives, and can now follow-up on big data activities, demands and create cross-border collaborations internally. This turned out to be their biggest obstacle to big data success.

Discovering that the biggest challenges related to traditional management and organization issues came as a surprise to the SMEs. By taking this first step back to refocus their business strategy to release the big data potential, they were ready to take the next step forward. It was a positive experience to learn cross-collaboration from a big data perspective and setting realistic expectations about the strategic potential of big data, as stated by one of the managers:

> Aligning expectations gathered people and made us aware that we needed to learn first before we started educating the staff and that this now became the purpose of the project.

Some had preferred to end up with a ready-to-plug technology, but in the process, they discovered that it was not possible at the particular stage of their organization. The first exploration with the data specialists indicated that the big data solutions to their challenge may not exist today, which would require in-house innovation to develop the solutions. The capabilities for doing so were not there yet so the management decided to reframe it as a big data experiment. From the learning processes, the managers cleared their big data expectations, which strengthened the teams, but most important, they acknowledged that they had a lot to learn, and allocating more time and resources was a crucial factor for releasing the big data potential. The CEO in one company found the dialogues valuable:

> they moved us mentally and new views have emerged that move us in our understanding of ourselves and what we want. We were challenged and provoked, but it forced us to rethink ourselves and the whole process.

Persistent action learning creates a unique space where roles can be changed. Listening leaves more room for reflection and gives reluctant or introvert participants a voice. They specifically mentioned the action learning exercises as being crucial for expanding their mindset and to come up with new and better ways to work with digital transformation, for example, by involving customers and employees in the development at an earlier stage. When applying the methodology, one must be aware of the formal hierarchy of a group, where some are silent with the boss in the room. The reflection methodology was so effective and beneficial for developing Empower & Engage strategies that some of the SMEs decided to apply the methodology on other projects and use it as a tool for empowerment and employee involvement.

Our project shows that it is the combination of learning formats and action learning processes that creates the highest levels of learning integrated in change and digitization efforts. The SMEs began to uncover what they have and can do and have acknowledged the need to build up the Data and BI themselves and not just rely on what they get from other suppliers. To improve the quality and pace of managerial decision-making about big data, SMEs can search for trends, patterns, and interconnections by filtering large amounts of unstructured data with text mining. More accurate analysis and interpretation of big data makes it easier for managers to make decisions. IoT technology further enables the products to provide important contextual information and brings IT and product design together (Gandhi & Gervet, 2016).

To summarize, the challenges involved individual as well as organizational learning processes to change the focus from product-centric to customer-centric, take a strategic perspective on big data, and see big data transformation as a cultural transformation. To overcome these challenges, SMEs must therefore consider these aspects of learning:

- *The learning drivers (why)*: why should we change our mindset, behavior, and routines and learn about big data? Here, the learning process contains exercises that increase the participants' mindset awareness and help them zoom out and see the bigger perspective.
- *The learning content (what)*: what new knowledge do we need? There is a vast ocean of courses, approaches, and literature to consider, so by defining the strategic purpose of using big data it is easier to know what to look for and what to ask for. It also helps the SMEs define the learning criteria and the scope and depth of innovative knowledge that is needed.
- *The social learning context (who and where)*: who should we involve in the learning processes, where should the learning take place, and how to allocate sufficient resources in the right place? Considering people who are motivated and have existing knowledge and access to relevant data that more easily can be used for learning and experimentation will ease the process in the short run, but the biggest effect may actually come from "resistant" and skeptical employees, who have managed to convert their mindset and "see the light." This is usually very inspirational to other "nay-sayers."
- *The learning process (how)*: To operationalize a big data transformation the intentions must fit with the reality of the organization and importantly how the employees experience it. An important step for the management was to realize that learning and changing habits is a "small steps game" that takes time and is resource demanding. To ensure that the capabilities are developed and applied, goals and plans must be realistic and defined in collaboration with the employees.

13.10 MANAGERIAL IMPLICATIONS: ONE STEP BACK CAN BE THE FIRST STEP AHEAD

One of the most difficult things for the 12 SMEs was to take the first step. Many companies knew if they would do AI, ML, or blockchain, but in most of the cases the next step is not just to jump directly into programming an algorithm. This means that dialogues for setting the intention of the company's efforts are very important. SMEs who want to take small steps towards data-driven growth should start by taking one step back and scrutinizing their existing managerial mindset (Armstrong & Hardgrave, 2007). This should be a key priority for SMEs because their product focus and entrepreneurial orientation influence how the company implements and uses digital technologies such as big data. SME managers usually have experience with data, but not with big data, which means that no practical experience is developed by doing "business as usual." Could the first step be to look into already existing data, to make a small experiment trying to use user experience (UX), or to even look at a new business model? This also implies that working with digitalization is not a quick fix. It consists of many small steps and continuous learning. Relevance and timing increase the learning focus, so avoid "pseudo-projects" as this may inhibit the focus but work on experiments that can be implemented in the company.

To ensure that continual improvements are built into the big data processes, managers should train and raise the data awareness of all stakeholders in their value network, but for the same reason it is critical to clarify all processes related to the management of time and energy resources to succeed. Action learning fits well because SMEs have some special resource requirements that are taken into account. The overall assessment of the companies' evaluation indicates that KomDigital's methodology is meaningful and effective for SMEs. The effects of action learning processes, when and where they work, can lead to rapid anchoring and change in corporate practice, as one of the managers confirmed:

> Participation is easy as we are taken by the hand all the way. In fact, I think that is important, especially when you approach SMEs, because time is important and therefore not having to spend time figuring out where to go, having doubts about what to do, etc. is important.

Digital transformation moves in mysterious ways so managers should expect the unexpected. Though SMEs may not need technology consultants or big data experts to tell them what to do, they can benefit from sparring with learning facilitators and a holistic understanding of people, processes, and technology.

NOTES

1. KomDigital is funded by Regionale Erhvervsforskningsmidler and The European Regional Development Fund.
2. http://www.gartner.com/it-glossary/bigdata/
3. https://ec.europa.eu/info/index_en (accessed March 4, 2020).
4. According to the recent Digital Economy and Society Index: https://ec.europa.eu/digital-single -market/en/desi
5. With a score of 100 percent: https://investindk.com/insights/denmark-is-among-the-most-digital -countries-in-europe
6. SMEs are defined as legally independent companies with a relatively smaller number of employees. The EU and a large number of OECD countries set the upper limit of the number of employees in SMEs between 200 and 250, whereas Japan defines it as no more than 300 employees. In the US, the limit is 500 employees. See: https://ec.europa.eu/growth/smes/business-friendly-environment/ sme-definition_da
7. https://em.dk/media/13083/statusrapport_digitalt_topm%C3%A3-de_til_tilg%C3%A3 -ngelig_pdf_final-a_3131.pdf (accessed May 8, 2020).
8. https://smvdigital.dk/ https://wp.komdigital.dk/wp-content/uploads/White-Paper-red1_.pdf; https:// komdigital.dk/forloeb/nye-digital-teknologier-hvad-og-hvordan (accessed April 25, 2020).
9. https://komdigital.dk/om-kom-digital (accessed April 25, 2020).

10. http://surveys.efficiens.nu/s3/Your-Big-Data-mindset-2017 (accessed May 7, 2020).
11. Also known as text mining or natural language processing (NLP).

REFERENCES

Armstrong, Deborah J. and Hardgrave, Bill C. (2007), "Understanding mindshift learning: the transition to object-oriented development," *MIS Quarterly*, **31**(3), 453–74.

Bandura, Albert (1977), *Social Learning Theory.* Englewood Cliffs, NJ: Prentice Hall.

Bandura, Albert (2001), "Social cognitive theory of mass-communication," *Media Psychology*, **3**, 265–99.

Benbasat, Izak, Goldstein, David. K., and Mead, Melissa (1987), "The case research strategy in studies of information systems," *MIS Quarterly*, **11**(3), 369–86.

Britzelmaier, Bernd, Graue, Carolin, and Sterk, Matthias (2020), "Big data in SME – findings of an empirical study," *Global Business and Economics Review*, **22**(1/2), 115–34.

Cohen, Wesley M. and Levinthal, Daniel A. (1990), "Absorptive capacity: a new perspective on learning and innovation," *Administrative Science Quarterly*, **35**(1), 128–52.

Coleman, Shirley, Göb, Rainer, Manco, Guiseppe, Pievaltolo, Antonio, Tort-Martorell, Xavier, and Seabra, Marco (2016), "How can SMEs benefit from big data? Challenges and a path forward," *Quality and Reliability Engineering International*, **32**(6), 2151–64.

Csikszentmihalyi, Mihalyi (2008), *Flow – the Psychology of Optimal Experience.* New York: Harper Perennial.

Fabricius, Golo and Büttgen, Marion (2013), "The influence of knowledge on overconfidence: consequences for management and project planning," *International Journal of Business and Management*, **8**, 1–12.

Felber, Suzanne (2011), "SMEs vs the consulting industry, European CEO," accessed 26 April 2020 at http://www.europeanceo.com/business-and-management/smes-vs-the-consulting-industry/.

Flyvbjerg, Bent and Budzier, Alexander (2011), "Why your IT project may be riskier than you think," *Harvard Business Review*, **89**(9), 601–3.

Gandhi, Suketu and Gervet, Eric (2016), "Now that your products can talk, what will they tell you," *MIT Sloan Management Review*, **57**(3), 49–50.

Gandomi, Amir and Haider, Murtaza (2014), "Beyond the hype: big data concepts, methods, and analytics," *International Journal of Information Management*, **35**, 137–44.

Helfat, Constance E. and Margaret A. Peteraf (2003), "The dynamic resource-based view: capability lifecycles," *Strategic Management Journal*, **24**(10), 997–1010.

Hennig-Thurau, Thorsten, Hofacker, Charles. F. and Bloching, Björn (2013), "Marketing the pinball way: understanding how social media change the generation of value for consumers and companies," *Journal of Interactive Marketing*, **27**(4), 237–41.

Jacobides, Michael G. and Sidney G. Winter (2005), "The co-evolution of capabilities and transaction cost: explaining the institutional structure of production," *Strategic Management Journal*, **26**(5), 395–413.

Janssen, Marijn, van der Voort, Haiko and Wahyudi, Agung (2017). "Factors influencing big data decision-making quality," *Journal of Business Research*, **70**(C), 338–45.

Kristensen, Frank Skov and Poulsen, Camilla Gudrun (2018), *Teamlæring og innovation med industri 4.0.* White paper published as a part of the KomDigital project.

Kumar, V., Bhaskaran, Vikram, Mirchandani, Rohan and Shah, Milap (2013), "Creating a measurable social media marketing strategy: increasing the value and ROI of intangibles and tangibles for hokey pokey," *Marketing Science*, **32**(2), 194–212.

Levitt, Barbara and March, James G. (1988), "Organizational learning," *Annual Review of Sociology*, **14**, 319–40.

Mackey, John and Sisodia, Raj (2014), *Conscious Capitalism.* Cambridge, MA: Harvard Business Review Press.

Makridakis, Spyros (2017), "The forthcoming Artificial Intelligence (AI) revolution: its impact on society and firms," *Futures*, **90**, 46–60.

Neil, Judy, O. and Marsick, Victoria, J. (2007), *Understanding Action Learning*. New York: AMACOM (a division of American Management Association).

Orlikowski, Wanda J. (2002), "Knowing in practice: enacting a collective capability in distributed organizing," *Organization Science*, **13**, 249–73.

Pry & Punish, https://yourbigdatamindset.com/pry-punish-a-new-big-data-mindset-emerging-in-g2c/

Ringberg, Torsten, Reihlen, Markus,and Rydén, Pernille (2019), "The technology-mindset interactions: leading to incremental, radical or revolutionary innovations," *Industrial Marketing Management*, **79**, 102–13.

Rootzén, Helle (2015), "Individualized learning through non-linear use of learning objects – with examples from Math and Stat," in *Proceedings of the 14th European conference on e-learning – ECEL15*.

Rydén, Pernille and El Sawy, Omar (2019a), "How managers perceive real-time management: thinking fast & flow," *California Management Review*, **61**(2), 155–77.

Rydén, Pernille and El Sawy, Omar A. (2019b), "Real-time management in the digital economy," in T.K. Das (ed.), *Time Issues in Strategy and Organization*. Charlotte, NC: Information Age Publishing, pp. 59–92.

Rydén, Pernille, Ringberg, Torsten and Wilke, Ricky (2015), "How managers' shared mental models of business-customer interactions create different sensemaking of social Media," *Journal of Interactive Marketing*, **31**, 1–16.

Rydén, Pernille, Ringberg, Torsten and Jacobsen, Per Ø. (2017), *Disrupt Your Mindset to Transform Your Business with Big Data*. DK, CPH, Efficiens.

Santos-Vijande, María Leticia, Sanzo-Pérez, María José, Álvarez-González, Luis I., and Vázquez-Casielles, Rodolfo (2005), "Organizational learning and market orientation: interface and effects on performance," *Industrial Marketing Management*, **34**(3), 187–202.

Schön, Donald (1983), *The Reflective Practitioner: How Professionals Think in Action*. New York: Basic Books.

Sen, Doruk, Ozturk, Melike, and Vayvay, Özalp (2016), "An overview for Big Data for growth in SMEs," *Procedia – Social and Behavioral Sciences*, **235**, 159–67.

Senge, Peter M. (1990), *The Fifth Discipline: The Art and Practice of the Learning Organization*. New York: Random House.

Teece, David J. (1988), "Technological change and the nature of the firm," in G. Dosi, C. Freeman, R. Nelson, G. Silverberg and L. Soete (eds), *Technical Change and Economic Theory*. London: Pinter, pp. 256–81.

Teece, David J. (2007), "Explicating dynamic capabilities: the nature and microfoundations of (sustainable) enterprise performance," *Strategic Management Journal*, **28**, 1319–50.

Tripsas, Mary and Gavetti, Giovanni (2000), "Capabilities, cognition, and inertia: evidence from digital imaging," *Strategic Management Journal*, **21**, 1147–61.

Weick, Karl E. (1990), "Technology as equivoque: sensemaking in new technologies," in P.S. Goodman and L.S. Sproull (eds), *Technology and Organization*. San Francisco, CA: Jossey-Bass, pp. 1–44.

Wood, Robert and Bandura, Albert (1989), "Social cognitive theory of organizational management," *Academy of Management Review*, **14**(3), 361–84.

Yin, Robert K. (1989), *Case Study Research: Design and Methods*. Newbury Park, CA: Sage Publications.

Zahra, Shaker A. and George, Gerard (2002), "Absorptive capacity: a review, reconceptualization, and extension," *Academy of Management Review*, **27**(2), 185–203.

Index

Printed and bound by CPI Group (UK) Ltd, Croydon, CR0 4YY

16/04/2025

14658494-0001